CITIZENSHIP:
THE CIVIC IDEAL IN WORLD HISTORY, POLITICS
AND EDUCATION

Citizenship:
The Civic Ideal in World History, Politics and Education

DEREK HEATER

LONGMAN
LONDON AND NEW YORK

Longman Group UK Limited,
Longman House, Burnt Mill, Harlow,
Essex CM20 2JE, England
and Associated Companies throughout the world.

Published in the United States of America
by Longman Inc., New York

© Longman Group UK Limited 1990

First published 1990

British Library Cataloguing in Publication Data

Heater, Derek, *1931–*
Citizenship: the civic ideal in world history,
politics and education.
1. Citizenship
I. Title
323.6

ISBN 0-582-05582-2 CSD
ISBN 0-582-05583-0 PPR

Library of Congress Cataloging-in-Publication Data

Heater, Derek Benjamin.
Citizenship: the civic ideal in world history, politics, and
education/by Derek Heater.
p. cm.
Includes index.
ISBN 0-582-05582-2: £18.00 (est.). – ISBN 0-582-05583-0 (pbk.):
£9.95 (est.)
1. Citizenship. I. Title.
JF801.H43 1990   89-12126
323.6 – dc20   CIP

Set in Linotron 202 11/12pt Garamond Roman 3

Produced by Longman Singapore Publishers (Pte) Ltd.
Printed in Singapore

Contents

CONTENTS

Preface

'The nature of citizenship', Aristotle declared, '. . . is a question which is often disputed: there is no general agreement on a single definition,'[1] Yet the terms 'citizen' and 'citizenship' are in constant use throughout the world today: the concepts are central to everyday political discourse. Is it therefore good enough for 'citizenship' to be a 'Humpty-Dumpty' word, in danger of crashing into fragments while asserting that it means just what it chooses to mean? Surely not. Citizens should know what their status implies; and they should understand when politicians abuse the term by according the whole concept only a partial range of attributes. It is, moreover, important to understand the complexity of the role of citizen and to appreciate that much needs to be learned if civic rights are to be exercised, civic duties are to be performed and a life of civic virtue is to be pursued. The citizen, in short, must be educated; and no teacher can properly construct the necessary learning objectives if semantic confusion surrounds the very subject to be studied.

This is not to argue in a world of richly diverse political traditions that a detailed prescription of universal application is either possible or desirable. Rather to suggest that those who use the words 'citizenship', 'world citizenship' and 'education for citizenship' should be aware of the long history and great wealth of meaning which lie behind them. Furthermore, only confusion and harm can arise from loose employment of the term. If we can but reach an agreement on some definitional highest common factor, political discourse and social education can only benefit from the clarification. To this end the present work is offered as some contribution. One particular note concerning an issue where agreement is so difficult is necessary, relating to the gender of nouns and pronouns used in the book. I am, I hope, properly sensitive to the complaint of feminists that women are, on the whole, treated as second-class citizens. I have nevertheless persisted in using words such as 'mankind' and 'he' for two reasons. First, for much of historical time women were denied citizenship rights. And second, devices such as 's/he' merely draw attention inelegantly to the sensitivity of the matter. Let the reader draw the true meaning from the context.

The book attempts to synthesise a great deal of historical, political and educational material. And the task of moulding it into some comprehensible shape has not been easy. It would never have been accomplished without the support of my wife's optimistic encouragement, kindly criticism and indefatigable word-processing. With affection and thanks I dedicate the book to her.

Derek Heater
Rottingdean

REFERENCE

1.   Aristotle, *Politics* (ed. E. Barker, Clarendon Press, 1946) p.93.

PART ONE

History

CHAPTER ONE

The origins

1.1 POLIS AND COSMOPOLIS

. . . what we have in mind is education from childhood in *virtue*, a training which produces a keen desire to become a perfect citizen who knows how to rule and be ruled as justice demands. I suppose we should want to mark off this sort of training from others and reserve the title 'education' for it alone.

Plato[1]

The Greek city-state

Through the wide sweep of recorded world history the status of citizen is but rarely found. The personal bonds of tribesman to chief, of feudal vassal to lord, of subject to monarch were for millenia the ties which commonly held communities together. Loyalty to a person is easily understood and readily exacted. Even in a state as advanced as seventeenth-century France, Louis XIV strove with his characteristic dedication to the task of being the very personification of his country: *L'état, c'est moi*, he is reported to have asserted to the politically ambitious magistrates of the Paris *parlement*. Citizenship, on the other hand, requires the capacity for a certain abstraction and sophistication of thought. A citizen needs to understand that his role entails status, a sense of loyalty, the discharge of duties and the enjoyment of rights not primarily in relation to another human being, but in relation to an abstract concept, the state.

Little wonder, then, that the idea and practice of citizenship was first thoroughly explored by the Greeks. For they combined the essential facility for abstract thought with the conviction that participation in public life was crucial to the full and proper development of the human personality. Nor is the cultivation of the concept by the Greeks merely of European significance. For, except perhaps in Judaic and Babylonian history, there is little evidence of even a similar idea developing in antiquity in any other part of the world. In the words of Max Weber, 'the notion of citizens of the state is unknown to the world of Islam, and to India and China.'[2]

The earliest thorough discussion of citizenship we owe to that most distinguished of political scientists, Aristotle. In the *Politics* he expresses himself often in a most forthright way on the subject. The matter was, after all, in his view, of central significance since he held that man is a political animal, that is, he could reach the full potential of his life and personality only by participation in the affairs of a *polis* (city-state). He was consequently at pains to distinguish true citizens from those who cannot justly claim the title. The young, the old and workingmen ('mechanics') worried him. Immaturity and infirmity respectively should bar the first two categories even when the individuals belong to the citizen class (for the status was in practice very commonly inherited). Workingmen presented a different problem. Aristotle had reluctantly to agree that in practice in many states they were admitted to citizenship,[3] though by virtue of their occupations they have neither the aptitude nor leisure to display true excellence in citizenship qualities. Aristotle recognised that citizenship is indeed a relative term, depending upon the features of any given constitution. However, as a general rule a citizen is a man 'who enjoys the right of sharing in deliberative or judicial office [for any period, fixed or unfixed].' Citizens are '*all* who share in the civic life of ruling and being ruled in turn'.[4] A good citizen therefore 'must possess the knowledge and the capacity requisite for ruling as well as for being ruled, and the excellence of a citizen may be defined as consisting in 'a knowledge of rule over free men from both points of view'.[5]

Aristotle was quite dogmatic that in order to discharge their functions effectively citizens must inhabit a city-state that is exceedingly compact and close-knit. He severely took to task his mentor Plato for indicating in the *Laws* that a citizen-body of 5000 would be ideal. This number, he asserted, would require space of 'unlimited' extent, such as the sprawling land of Babylon. 'It will need all that', he judged, 'to support 5000 in idleness, especially when we reflect that they will be augmented by a crowd of women and attendants.'[6] Military command, public communication and judicial judgement would be impossible in such a large community. The quality of citizenship would be bound to suffer from the lack of necessary intimacy. For, Aristotle believed that,

Both in order to give decisions in matters of disputed rights, and to distribute the offices of government according to the merits of candidates, the citizens of the state must know one another's characters.[7]

Aristotle's vision of ideal citizenship was, of course, coloured by the social and political environment in which he lived. Yet even Athens in the fifth century BC – the most polished form of Greek political life – fell short of his standards of perfection. In size alone Aristotle must have considered it a monstrosity. If he denied that a community of 100,000 could be considered a proper state,[8] and if he ridiculed Plato's figure of 5000 citizens as an 'assumption which is plainly impossible'[9] – what must he have thought of Athens' quarter of a million population, 40,000 of whom were citizens? Furthermore, by no means all of those 40,000 were 'supported in idleness' so that they could concentrate on public affairs.

3

Even so, some Greek city-states and notably Athens at its political zenith, were by no means totally deficient of the qualities so admired by Aristotle. The practice of citizenship was the very core of life. Citizens really were involved in the judicial processes and really did participate in public debate as an essential preliminary to the formulation of policy and the making of political decisions. A larger proportion of the Athenian population was directly involved in civic affairs in the fifth-fourth centuries than in any other state for well over two millenia. All citizens had the right to attend the Assembly; a selection, chosen by lot, were members of the executive Council of 500, and composed the huge-sized juries. Athenian pride in their political maturity was the *leitmotif* of the oration Pericles delivered for the citizens who fell in one year of the Peloponnesian War. It includes the following passage:

Here each individual is interested not only in his own affairs but in the affairs of state as well: even those who are mostly occupied with their own business are extremely well-informed on general politics – this is a peculiarity of ours: we do not say that a man who takes no interest in politics is a man who minds his own business; we say he has no business here at all.[10]

The message reflects the feelings that conscientious Greeks had for those who neglected their civic duties and for whom they reserved a special word: 'idiot'.

But it is Aristotle's insistence on the personal knowledge citizens must have of each others' characters that provides an insight into the real heart of the Greek concept of citizenship. Citizenship was a bond forged by the intimacy of participation in public affairs. The bond was moreover a relationship which was guarded with some jealousy by those privileged to enjoy it. It was neither a right to be claimed by nor a status to be conferred on anybody outside the established ranks of the class, no matter how worthy such an outsider might be. Indeed, Greek citizenship depended not so much on rights which could be claimed as on responsibilities which had with pride to be shouldered. Pericles himself was responsible for tightening the exclusiveness of Athenian citizenship – and was hoist with his own petard. In 451 he introduced a law to restrict the status to persons who could show citizenship on both their father's and mother's side of the family. When his legal sons died of plague, he was forced to plead with the Assembly to waive this restriction in respect of the bastard offspring of his mistress who hailed from Miletus, a Greek city of Asia Minor.

Citizenship in the Greek city-state was a privilege. Generally speaking it was a status which was inherited. Not until the Hellenistic and Roman periods was it normally conferred in recognition of services. Resident foreigners, women, slaves and the peasantry of the rural environment of the city were all excluded. (Though one should note parenthetically that the idea of women in politics was abroad by the early fourth century. It was lampooned by Aristophanes in his *Women in Parliament*, and taken for granted by Plato in the *Republic* as a logical consequence of his categorisation of people by ability.) Only citizens were allowed to own freehold property. Thus, even where there were wide discrepancies in wealth between rich and poor citizens they

4

remained an order in society quite distinct from non-citizens. Indeed, the very existence of a diversity of interests among the citizen body was considered, especially by Aristotle, as essential to the practice of being a citizen. Good government derived from the virtuous balancing of these varying perspectives. And, of course, virtue was precisely the mark of the good citizen – the quality of moral goodness that was essential for selfless, co-operative civic life.

Greek civic education

Whether in ideal theory or confused practice, it is clear that the Greeks expected considerable skill from their citizens: they were required to fulfil the functions of politicians, administrators, judges, jurors and soldiers. How were the citizen class educated for these duties? We may distinguish two basic models. One encouraged individual political and forensic skill, notably rhetoric and judgement. The other emphasised the training, indoctrination even, of the youth to obedience to the laws, submission to the government and a readiness to defend the state by recourse to arms.

The first of these traditions (though not earlier chronologically) was epitomised by Athenian educational practice as it had evolved particularly by the fifth century BC. In some ways, in such a heavily political society, it was difficult for the youth not to absorb some understanding of civic standards and institutions. The very drama of the theatres often had a substantial political content – even the phallus-and-farce comedies of an Aristophanes. While in the schools and in public places the laws of Solon, the legendary author of the Athenian constitution, were constantly recited. However, in terms of formal educational provision only a small proportion of adolescents received any thorough political education, and this of a very practical style. At the age of about fifteen the privileged, wealthy youth of the city attended the law-courts and other public places to listen to the debates and witness for themselves the operation of the judicial and political systems. At the age of eighteen the young man could enrol as an *ephebus* for a year of national service. His oath of initiation bound him not just to defend the city, but also committed him to political responsibilities:

I will leave my country not less, but greater and better, than I found it. I will obey the magistrates and observe the existing laws, and those the people may hereafter make. If anyone tries to overthrow or disobey the ordinances, I will resist him in their defence.[11]

The original *ephebic* school was founded in Athens but the institution soon spread to scores of Greek cities from Marseilles to the Black Sea, being particularly popular in Asia Minor. Run as micro-political communities themselves, in their heyday these schools provided a judicious mixture of education in social graces, sport and civic affairs.

By the late fifth century there was a demand for training in more explicit political skills, notably the art of rhetoric. Teachers, often non-Athenians, set up schools to cater for this need. These were the Sophists, whose style of teaching the arts of citizenship is characterised by Protagoras as portrayed by Plato. Some of these schools were of evident benefit alike to their students and the city. The most distinguished of all these teachers was Isocrates, an Athenian who was a great adornment to his city, of which he was so proud. For he devoted much of his extraordinarily long life (a near-centenarian) to teaching his students the vital importance of using oratory not just as a political device but as a vehicle for conveying an encouragement of high moral standards. Unfortunately, however, many Sophists were guilty of that sleight of argument for which the term 'sophistry' was coined. This cynical manipulation of oratory was but one symptom of the decay of the Athenian political ideal, which can be discerned by the end of the fifth century and which was dramatically symbolised by the eventual subjugation of Athens by her Spartan rival at the conclusion of the Peloponnesian War in 404 BC.

Indeed, the political and educational writings of Plato and Aristotle may be interpreted as attempts to restore to their city some semblance of political health. Plato wrote with greater emotional intensity because the politically diseased Athenian state had condemned his friend, Socrates, to death. Given the central importance of politics in Greek life and given their urgent search for better programmes of socialisation, it is scarcely surprising that both Plato and his pupil Aristotle held politics and education in the closest of intimate relationships. For them education for citizenship is virtually synonymous with education *tout court*. Thus the *Republic* is a work simultaneously of political and educational philosophy. Aristotle located the bulk of his discussion of education as books VII and VIII of his *Politics*. In the *Laws* Plato stated the position quite bluntly in the passage quoted at the head of this chapter. But the curricula which each devised as a means of cultivating civic virtue were designed for a moral liberal education rather than a study of political science. What they sought was rather a frame of mind which will respond in a just, responsible and selfless manner to public issues. For this they considered the harmonious influences of literature, music and gymnastics to be most apposite. Any specific political studies were for the Guardian class in the *Republic* and reserved for adults, an opinion shared by Aristotle. Thus in the *Nicomachean Ethics* he declared:

. . . political science is not a proper study for the young. The young man is not versed in the practical business of life from which politics draws its premises and its data. He is, besides, swayed by his feelings, with the result that he will make no headway and derive no benefit from a study the end of which is not *knowing* but doing.[12]

Incidentally, Aristotle condemned the Sophists as useless teachers of politics precisely because of their lack of first-hand political experience.[13]

Those commentators like Plato and Aristotle, who surveyed the corruption and political instability of their age with dismay, argued for a more responsible and effective form of education for citizenship. To their mind the Athenian state had been far too casual in its neglect of this crucial area. By allowing families to educate their sons as they wished in civic duties, the state fatally failed to provide for itself the necessary underpinning of a citizenry conscientiously committed to Athenian civic values. And so, for all their differences in the detail of their political analyses, Plato and Aristotle were both utterly committed to the principle of the state provision of education. The *Republic*, of course, is a famous blueprint for a system with particular emphasis on the training of the ruling class. Moreover, in the *Laws* Plato laid down that the Guardian of the Laws shall also have control of education, with the power to select as teachers only those willing to teach about the laws and traditions of the state in the manner the Guardian determines. In both the *Ethics* and the *Politics* Aristotle made his view quite evident: 'education ought to be conducted by the state'.[14] As a student of comparative government Aristotle was very aware that the style of preparation for citizenship must fit the style of government: a powerful argument in itself for state regulation. Thus he asserted that,

The greatest . . . of all the means . . . for ensuring the stability of constitutions – but one which is nowadays neglected – is the education of citizens in the spirit of their constitution . . . the citizens [must be] attuned, by the force of habit and the influence of teaching, to the right constitutional temper.[15]

Both Plato and Aristotle believed that different styles of civic education should be used for different purposes. Plato emphasised training in self-sacrifice for rulers and obedience for the ruled; Aristotle emphasised the need to match the educational objectives to the form of government.

These pleas for education for citizenship directed by the state in the interests of political stability were not just theoretical musings. For the writers in fourth-century Athens there was a clear alternative practical model: victorious Sparta. Sparta has become notoriously identified with the grim and detrimental regimentation of its youth to total dedication to the state. This characteristic was established by the very founder of the Spartan state, Lycurgus, who, in the words of his biographer Plutarch, 'bred up his citizens in such a way that they neither would nor could live by themselves; they were to . . . be by their zeal and public spirit . . devoted wholly to their country.'[16] The constitution was unique in ancient Greece in requiring every youth of the citizen class to undergo the most rigorous, even brutal, training. From the age of seven, boys were subjected to a phased programme designed to mould them into obedient soldiers, who eventually in mature manhood could graduate to full citizenship. A liberal wielding of the whip and a judicious selection of patriotic songs assisted the process.

By the fourth century the contrast between the lax behaviour of Athenian youth and the discipline of the Spartan was strikingly evident. The most notable Athenian to be won over completely to their stern form of citizenship was Xenophon. Distinguished equally as a military commander and as a writer, he was exiled to Sparta, whose culture he gladly embraced, subjecting his own sons to his adopted city's rigorous educational process. He urged in his writings that Athens should introduce a state-controlled system of education with a view to stifling unsettling freedom of thought by civic regimentation. In his biography of King Cyrus of Persia, *Cyropaedia*, he reinforced his message by emphasising the Spartan-style excellence of Persian educational practices:

. . . the Persian laws, by anticipation, are careful to provide from the beginning, that their citizens shall not be such as to be inclined to any action that is bad and mean . . . The boys attending the public schools, pass their time in learning justice . . . Their presidents [i.e. tribal leaders and teachers] . . . teach the boys self-control . . . They teach them also to obey their officers.[17]

Although Plato and Aristotle were far too sophisticated as political thinkers to accept uncritically the excesses of Spartan discipline, they both none the less displayed some sneaking regard for the benefits of the system. The educational regime provided by Plato for his Guardians in the *Republic* clearly owed much to the Spartan example. And Aristotle in his *Ethics* wrote:

. . . we do not grumble at the law when it orders what is right. Yet Sparta . . . is the only state in which the law-giver seems to have been at pains to regulate the nurture and day-to-day life of the community.[18]

The cosmopolitan idea

If there were hesitations about the suitability of Sparta as an alternative model of citizenship to the degenerate Athenian, was it not possible that the fault lay with the very institution of the city-state itself? To the great Athenian philosophers from Socrates to Aristotle such a suggestion would have been almost literally unthinkable. Socrates drank the hemlock without hesitation. He had no doubt that it was his duty to obey the laws of his city, even if unjust and even to the point of ultimate sacrifice. His death was a true act of selfless citizenship. Even so, he felt able to embrace a parallel loyalty to mankind at large. Indeed, his generosity of spirit was often subsequently recalled by later writers in justification of their commitment to world citizenship as a valid concept and ideal. For example, the French essayist Montaigne wrote:

We are all confined and pent up within ourselves, and our sight has contracted to the length of our own noses. When someone asked of Socrates of what country he was, he did not reply, 'Of Athens', but 'of the world'. His was a fuller and wider imagination; he embraced the whole world as his city, and extended his acquaintance, his society, and his affections to all mankind; unlike us who look only under our feet.[19]

The cosmopolitan idea, either as an alternative to state citizenship or as a complement to it, has indeed had a long existence, episodically stirring into quite energetic life.

Nor has the idea been confined to western civilization. A century before Socrates, Confucius was trying to teach in China the concept of *ta t'ung*, the greater unity — the world commonwealth in which all men once strove for general welfare and harmony and which, he urged, should be restored. In India a similar view was more readily embraced; 'It is mean-minded,' it was said, 'to enquire whether a man is one of ourselves or an alien'.[20] In Europe the idea that the whole world could in some sense be conceived of as a cosmopolis or universal state seems to have emerged in the fifth century BC in Greece. A few philosophers, most notably Democritus, toyed with the idea; a number of Sophists spread the notion. Thus Plato has Hippias declare in the *Protagoras*, 'I count you all my kinsmen and family and fellow citizens — by nature not by convention.'[21] He was thus challenging as artificial the conventional restriction and allocation of citizenship by mere local, man-made laws. But this was a tentative position compared with the forthright teachings of Antiphon. It is he who can perhaps be first credited with the really significant propositions that a Universal Law exists above any local laws and whose existence therefore must undermine the deep-rooted conviction at the time of the fundamental distinction between Greek and barbarian. The idea of the cosmopolis was taken up by Diogenes. This citizen of the Black Sea Greek colony of Sinope has gained immortal fame by the dramatic way in which he symbolised his philosophy of Cynicism: he renounced with scorn the trappings of society by living in a tub. And part of the social junk he discarded was the current political notion of citizenship. The clues to the good life, he taught, were a return to a less artificial mode of life, and the pursuit of wisdom through the use of the human faculty of reason. The real community of men is that part of humanity which has cultivated its rational powers. Thus the only citizenship status that is worth worrying about is the citizenship of the community of the wise, that is, those who would consequently reject the corruption and evil of contemporary Greek society. This community knows no geographical limits, nor is it committed to any man-made laws or constitutions. It is the 'cosmopolis', the 'city of the universe'. At the same time (the early fourth century BC), the Cyrenaics, the forerunners of the Epicureans, were also teaching a renunciation of the city-state culture in favour of an amoral hedonistic cosmopolitanism. By the end of the fourth century BC the idea of world citizenship enjoyed a certain vogue. The ideal of Greek citizenship associated with the city-state was under question. At the same time, the city-state as an autonomous institution was itself being undermined in practice.

By one of the exquisite ironies of which History is so full, Aristotle, the classical exponent of citizenship as the very embodiment of civilized life, was employed by the royal house of Macedon, the destroyer of the Greek city-state system upon which that very concept of citizenship was built. In 342 BC Philip summoned Aristotle to become tutor to his son, Alexander, who succeeded his father six years later. Philip defeated the city-states militarily; Alexander absorbed them politically into his extensive empire. Alexander the Great conceived the ambition to expunge the distinction between Greek and barbarian and to gather all under his sway into a 'union of hearts' or '*Concord*'. What is more, he started in his brief life to put these revolutionary ideas into practice. In the words of his biographer, Plutarch,

He did not, as Aristotle advised him, treat the Greeks in the spirit of a leader and the barbarians in that of a master . . . rather he believed that he had a mission from God to be the reconciler of the world . . .

He wished to show that all things on earth were subject to one principle and included in one polity, and that all men were one people; and he demeaned himself accordingly. If the power that sent the world the soul of Alexander had not quickly recalled it, one law would have governed all men, and they would have turned their gaze to one system of justice as though to a common light.[22]

In vision, let alone in the policy which he had the power to implement, Alexander showed himself a more positive and creative cosmopolitan than Diogenes (who coincidentally died on the same day as the Hellenistic Emperor). He was, it is true, helped by the temper of the times. For, he lived at the opening of the era of a half-millenium or so from c.350 BC when the Mediterranean and Middle Eastern worlds were ripe to receive a more confident and dramatic philosophy than that of the Cynics. For one thing, the geo-political reality of the region during this period was the all-embracing empire; not just the brief Macedonian empire, but, of course, the later and much less temporary imperium of the Romans. Secondly, with the loss of the social intimacy of the Greek city-state it was no longer plausible to equate the good life with the political life. Similarly the republican traditions of the old city-state of Rome were submerged by the grossly distended geographical scope of its territories. The creation of the role of Emperor signalled both the impracticability and undesirability of retaining active personal citizen-involvement in a state of unprecedented magnitude. The political colouring of moral philosophy faded. Interest centred on the nature of the good life for the individual *qua* human being rather than political animal, or on the recognition that basically all human beings are really rather similar. The belief in the essential uniformity of mankind was reflected in the acceptance that all men are endowed with reason and all are subject to the same basic laws of nature. These humanistic considerations were reinforced by the monotheistic theologies of Judaism and especially its more hospitable offshoot, Christianity. One of the implications of their monotheism was that all humans are God's creatures and are moulded in His image.

In these circumstances it is scarcely surprising that the vague, romantic primitivism of the Cynics was soon superseded by the tougher, creative cosmopolitanism of the Stoics. In the same year that Aristotle was appointed as tutor to the adolescent Alexander, there was born of Phoenician parents at Citium in Cyprus a man called Zeno. He later settled in Athens, where he set up his own academy and founded the school of Stoicism, (so dubbed from the building's painted colonnade – *stoa poikile*). Its influence spread throughout the Mediterranean world. One of its important centres was Tarsus in Asia Minor, by which route it penetrated Christianity through the writings of that city's most famous son, St Paul. Of parallel significance was the impact Stoicism had on Roman and hence subsequent political thought as mediated through the writings of Cicero, Seneca and Marcus Aurelius. Although the essence of Stoic thought was its cosmopolitanism, the tradition of city-state politics in Zeno's time was still too powerful in both theory and practice for its vocabulary to be completely jettisoned. In retaining the terms

'city' and 'citizenship' the Stoics continued their almost metaphorical meanings in accordance with the figurative usage of the Sophists. Plutarch's exposition of the philosophy, some four centuries after Zeno, confirms this interpretation:

The much admired polity of Zeno, the founder of the Stoic School, is directed to this
one main point, that we should . . . regard all men as fellow-parishioners and
fellow-citizens; and there should be one way of life and one system of order, as it
were of one flock on a common pasture feeding together under a common law. Zeno
wrote this as one imagining a dream or mental picture of a system of law and polity
based on philosophy.[23]

Stoicism asserted that man and God (or the gods) are rational beings; and
that because all men are sons of God and because of this common attribute
of reason, all men, of whatever race or social status, slave or free, are equal.
(This egalitarianism of the Stoic philosophy was reflected in St Paul's conception of a universal Church 'Where there is neither Greek nor Jew,
circumcision or uncircumcision, Barbarian, Scythian, bond nor free'.[24]
Moreover, since, echoing Diogenes, the Stoics deemed the only qualification
necessary for citizenship to be wisdom, all men the world over and without
distinction are capable of attaining this status by developing their rational
faculties. Thus is the concept of citizenship opened up to universal application.
However, a good citizen must obey the law. That indeed is tautologous; but
what law is a citizen of the world to obey? The Stoic answer was 'the law of
nature', a code consisting of fundamental principles of justice emanating from
divine reason and discernible by man through the exercise of that same faculty.
And if local, man-made laws clash with the law of nature, so much the worse
for them; the law of the world-city must take precedence over the law of the
city-state. Two facets of the Stoic system were crucial and were to have far-
reaching, not to say permanent, influence. One was the religious concept of
the relationship of God and man. Thus Chrysippus, the prolific codifier of
Stoic thought, wrote that 'the universe is, as it were, a polis consisting of
gods and men, the gods holding sway, the men obeying'.[25] The other was
the conflation of law and nature, considered utterly distinct in pre-Stoic Greek
thought. The first of these features of Stoicism was obviously vital for its
absorption into Christian doctrine; the second became the basis for the notion
of natural law, which still underpins, for example, codes of human rights.

The idea of a universal law of nature was of great utility to the Romans
as their political sway expanded to embrace peoples of widely diverse customs.
It was Cicero in the first century BC who transmitted the basic Stoic ideas
of human equality and brotherhood beneath a universal law of nature.

There is in fact a true law – namely right reason [he wrote] – which is in accordance
with nature, applies to all men, and is unchangeable and eternal . . . To invalidate
this law by human legislation is never morally right.[26]

His influence was extraordinary. He had a voracious appetite for Greek
philosophy and popularised the ideas in such elegant style that his works be-

came both the basis of much Roman jurisprudence and the core of classical education while it lasted in our schools. Seneca, writing a century after Cicero, emphasised the Stoic idea of man's membership of a universal *moral* community. Seneca believed that the good life, pursued in the interests of humanity at large, had to be lived on a different plane from the more sordid life of the citizen of a state. In this sense his universalist ideas were of a spiritual or religious character, as of course they had been to the founders of Stoicism. He expressed his view most elegantly in the following passage;

Accordingly with a generosity of spirit we have not closeted ourselves within the confines of a single city, but have extended our sense of fellowship all over the globe, declaring that the universe is our native land with the intention that there be a larger arena for the practice of virtue.[27]

However, Seneca was living in a Roman Empire where these two-fold theoretical loyalties clashed in bloody reality in the persecution of the Christians. True, the Christians were taught by the Gospels to 'Render therefore unto Caesar the things which are Caesar's, and unto God the things that are God's'. Nevertheless, their allegiance to their 'heavenly kingdom' seemed threatening to the Emperors. If men, over and above their political identity, felt a loyalty not just to mankind as a whole but to a spiritual belief, how much true moral commitment could be expected of them to the Roman state? The conscience of the sensitive Marcus Aurelius, Emperor at the end of the first century, was cruelly torn on this dilemma. As a Stoic he knew it was his duty to be tolerant and humane to all mankind as brothers. He expounded the Stoic philosophy with characteristic lucidity;

If the capacity for intelligence is common to men, so too is the faculty of Reason . . . If that is so, then that part of reason . . . which tells us what to do and what not to do, is also common. If that be so, so too is law. If law is common, we are all fellow citizens; and if that be so, the universe is, as it were, one State or city.[28]

But he was also an emperor, and in that capacity he knew it was his duty to extirpate Christianity. If only the two duties could be made to coincide! He voiced this tantalising desire for all patriotically loyal world citizens down the ages;

. . . my nature is a rational and civic nature; my city and my country, so far as I am [Marcus Aurelius] Antoninus, is Rome; but so far as I am a man, it is the universe. Whatever therefore is to the advantage of these two cities, and that only, is good for me.[29]

In the fullness of time Marcus Aurelius' particular torment was eased as the Roman Empire embraced Christianity and Christianity embraced Roman Stoicism. And so it came about that the Stoic universal city of men and gods, the City of Zeus, was transmuted into the Christian City of God. But the fundamental dichotomy and tension remained, as St Augustine in the fifth century showed in his book *The City of God*, because the demands of temporal and spiritual authorities could well be at odds. Moreover, by emphasising this dichotomy, the Christian adaptation of the concept of a cosmopolis rendered the idea even more mystical and detached from earthly reality. The City of God is to be attained only in Heaven, or, possibly, on earth only with the Second Coming. The more mundane cosmopolitan views of the Cynics and early Stoics were consequently somewhat submerged while Christian theology dominated political thought in the Middle Ages.

As to the preparation of the young in the classical age for the status of world citizenship, there is little evidence that this was afforded any really deep consideration. Indeed, no determined effort was made to educate young people as embryonic world citizens until our own century. On the other hand, this is not to say that the task was totally ignored in the ancient world. After all, was not Zeno, the founder of Stoicism, a teacher? The young men who studied at his school, which remained in existence for centuries, would have imbibed his cosmopolitanism with the rest of his philosophy. Indeed, the cosmopolitan political ideas and practices of the age of Alexander the Great were so pervasive that it would be remarkable if they were *not* mirrored in education. In fact, scholarship and literature did become markedly internationalised, especially by the spread of Greek as a *lingua franca* throughout much of the Mediterranean and west Asia. And the new city of Alexandria in Egypt became, through its incomparable library collections, a truly international centre of learning.

Nor did the Middle Ages totally lose sight of the ideal of human unity on earth. Thus the fourteenth-century English Franciscan, William of Occam (interestingly echoing Plutarch's ovine metaphor), bewailed the fact that:

All human beings, however far apart from one another on this earth, could enter into relations so as to form one community, one sheepfold, one flock, one body, one city, one college, one people, one kingdom, were they not separated by ill-will.[30]

A generation earlier the Italian poet Dante had written the most forthright medieval argument for universal government in his *De Monarchia*, Dante argued the necessity for a global monarch as the ultimate fount of authority in a world confederation of states and cities. He drew this conclusion from two premises. One, adapted half a millenium later by Kant, was the belief that human reason must be given full rein to be exercised and that universal peace was an essential pre-condition for this to happen. Secondly, Dante believed in hierarchies, so that in government it followed that the very peak of a pyramidal political structure – a universal monarch – must be nearer to perfection than are the humbler strata. But if Dante dreamed of a world *government*, he did not dream of world *citizenship*. There was no room in his scheme for individual participation. In this, of course, he was in tune with his age. Citizenship in the Middle Ages, as we shall see below (pp. 20–23), was focussed on the small scale of the city.

At the opening of the modern era the voyages of discovery quickened interest in the nature of mankind as a whole and the Renaissance revived the humanist concerns of the classical world. The virtue of a universalist attitude of mind, revealed by Montaigne (p. 15), was also expounded across the Channel a quarter of a century later by Francis Bacon. In his essay, 'Of Goodness, and Goodness of Nature', he wrote:

The parts and signs of goodness are many. If a man be gracious and courteous to strangers, it shows he is a citizen of the world, and that his heart is no island cut off from other lands, but a continent that joins to them.[31]

(An interesting echo of Donne's famous geographical metaphor, 'No man is an island unto itself'.) A great deal of thought was given in the seventeenth century to the nature of international society and international law. But the great thinkers of the age were caught between the universalist, natural law and Christian assumptions of the Middle Ages on the one hand and, on the other, the modern consolidated authority of the sovereign state. For the theory of sovereignty as expounded by Jean Bodin (pp. 25–26) was slow to be transferred into international law. It is therefore not entirely surprising to detect in some of the writers of the age a certain hesitation in denying that individuals as opposed to states (or their princes) could act in an international context. While insisting that subjects must in most circumstances obey their prince, they recognised the primacy of a man's duty to universal moral law. The Spanish jurists Suarez and Victoria, the Frenchman Cruсé and the Italian Gentile, for example, all believed in the world as a quasi-cosmopolis, in which international law imposed duties on and provided protection for all. In the words of Francisco de Vitoria,

International law has not only the force of a pact and agreement among men, but also the force of a law; for the world as a whole, being in a way a single state, has the power to create laws that are just and fitting for all persons, as are the rules of international law. Consequently, it is clear that they who violate international rules, whether in peace or in war, commit a mortal sin.[32]

Meanwhile, in the sphere of education the belief was kept alive throughout the Middle Ages that scholars should not be circumscribed in their quest for knowledge and wisdom by the confines of their own countries. Scholars not only wandered, but arrived, from various lands, at universities of international repute – Europeans journeyed to Paris, Africans to Timbuktu, for instance. Nor was European learning an incestuous process; much Arab mathematical and medical understanding was also absorbed. And in Europe, of course, Latin provided a universal mode of communication until well into the modern era. Indeed, paradoxically, the age of the Renaissance, which witnessed the consolidation of the nation-state in much of Europe, renewed the Medieval ideal of international scholarship with a revivification of Classical learning. Erasmus, owning to no narrow civic loyalty, was a splendid personification of this cosmopolitan attitude to scholarship.

This long and powerful tradition related to scholars and the higher learning, not to pupils sitting at their school desks. None the less by c. 1600 the needs of children's education in this respect were coming to be recognised. Thus, to cite Montaigne again:

This great world . . . is the mirror into which we must look if we are to behold ourselves from the proper standpoint. In fact, I would have this be my pupil's book. So many dispositions, sects, judgements, opinions, laws, and customs teach us to judge sanely of our own, and teach our understanding how to recognise its imperfections and natural weaknesses; which is no trivial lesson. So many national revolutions and changes of public fortune teach us to consider our own no great miracle.[33]

Montaigne's comments are but the brief allusions of an essayist, not of a distinguished educationist. Such a title can however certainly be accorded to Comenius (the Latinised form of the name Komensky). He was what we would today term an education consultant and later became a Bishop of the Moravian church. Comenius wrote against the background of the horrifically vicious Thirty Years War, which was sparked by an incident in his native land when he was 26 and which forced him for some time to be a refugee. Perhaps indeed his own wretched experiences contributed to the evolution of his plans for a unified peaceful world. A significant element in his scheme was his belief in education. For, despite the horrors of seventeenth-century religious conflict, he retained a touching confidence in human perfectability, a confidence sustained by a deep religious faith and an appreciation of the progress of scientific discovery at the time. He foresaw the possibility of a 'world city', in which local loyalties and disparities of wealth were overlaid by the unifying power of religion, mass communication and education. Among his copious educational works he sketched out a scheme for a College of Light. He conceived this as a group of distinguished persons, committed to the pacific principles of Christ, 'the fount of light' and to leading mankind towards the light of international understanding, peace and justice. Comenius believed that to achieve these ideals the College should monitor the teaching in schools and the publication of books. In fact he listed ten major responsibilities of the College. Included in this list was attention:

(iii) To the schools, as the workshops of light;
(iv) To the heads of the schools, as the light-bearers;
 (v) To teaching methods, as the purifiers of light;
(vi) To books, as the vessels of light.[34]

Comenius' widespread fame as an educationist brought him invitations to visit Sweden, France and England to work in those countries for the improvement of their educational systems. He felt that England would be the most congenial country for the implementation of his ideas.

Ironically, as the concept of world citizenship was being revived in the seventeenth century, the European states system was being consolidated. The principle of sovereignty, the notion that each state is a self-sufficient entity, was accepted as the foundation of international law and behaviour by the Treaties of Westphalia, which finally brought the Thirty Years War to a close in 1648. The new secularised politics was being built in both theory and practice round a dominant feature utterly antithetical to the cosmopolitan ideal.

1.2 FROM ROME TO RENAISSANCE

Rome and Italy were respected as the centre of government. A national spirit was preserved by the ancient and insensibly imbibed by the adopted citizen.

Edward Gibbon[35]

The Roman citizen and his education

Citizenship in the Greek city-state was parochially practical but exclusive. Citizenship of the cosmopolis was generously ecumenical but hollow. It fell to the legally-minded and administratively adept Romans to develop a form of citizenship which was both pragmatic and extensible in application. Yet that very elasticity was the cause ultimately of the perishing of the ideal in its original noble form. Compared with the Greek mode of citizenship, Roman was more complex, flexible and legalistic. This difference was evident even before the end of the monarchy (c.500 BC) when Servius Tullius conferred citizenship upon the Plebs. These were the unprivileged aliens domiciled in Rome, traders and merchants – the kinds of people from whom Greek citizens held aloof and would not admit to their ranks. In practice, however, social discrimination persisted. Consequently, in the mid-fifth century BC, in response to plebeian protests, the Twelve Tables were produced. These were literally engraved tablets setting down in crisp propositions the rights of and relationships between citizens. They remained the basis of Roman civil law for centuries, despite the destruction of the originals by the Gauls soon after their fabrication. Full citizenship entailed six privileges. Four of these were public rights: service in the army, voting in the assembly, eligibility to public office and the legal right of action and appeal. The two others were the private rights of intermarriage and trade with other Roman citizens. The benefits could be considerable. Citizenship opened up the possibilities of careers for which a non-citizen would be ineligible.

In the fourth century the Romans introduced three historically very significant adaptions to the basic concept of citizenship. The context was the territorial expansion of the city to control the whole region of Latium. In 381 BC, fearing hostile action by the enclave city of Tusculum, Rome offered total incorporation by conferring full Roman citizenship on its free male inhabitants. The concept of dual 'Latin' and 'Roman' citizenship was also introduced so that a man could be simultaneously a citizen of his own city and of Rome. Half a century after the deal with Tusculum the inhabitants of other Latin towns were offered a kind of half-citizenship – *civitas sine suffragio* (citizenship without franchise). By this device the private but not the public privileges could be enjoyed. The concept of citizenship was now changed. The Romans annexed the loyalty as well as the territory of their defeated enemies, for the status of Roman citizenship became much prized. The calculated generosity of the Romans was certainly an extraordinary reversal of the widespread established practice of subjugating the losers in war to a condition of slavery. It was a policy that was inconceivable to the Greeks, who, until the decline of the city-state, even treated the citizens of neighbouring Greek

16

cities as foreigners. Indeed, when Rome hesitated to extend its rights of citizenship to all its Italian allies (*socii*), they rebelled in the fiercesome 'Social War' (90–87 BC). The war was brought to an end only by concession of the status.

By the first century BC Rome had extended its sway over the whole Mediterranean basin and Gaul by the dexterous combination of the whip of military skill and the carrot of citizenship enrolment. Neither race nor religion nor riches were determinants for acceptance; Roman citizenship provided complete equality before the law. Yet the Republican institutions were crumbling beneath the weight of this mighty empire. Cicero, whose absorption of the Stoic cosmopolitan ideal we have already had occasion to notice, strove in these difficult times to sustain the quality of the Roman concept of citizenship, a concept which, a century before, the Elder Cato had tried to raise by personal example and exhortation to impossibly puritanical standards of pride, patriotism, duty and devotion to the law. It is absolutely essential, Cicero believed, that a state be a moral community. By holding in the forefront of his consciousness the ethical and legal nexus of rights and obligations, the citizen must ensure that the state remains whole and wholesome. It was Cicero indeed who coined the famous assertion of pride: *Civis Romanus sum* (I am a Roman citizen).[36] For he saw no inconsistency in holding simultaneously to his belief in a universal law and his conviction that the citizen must love his country and do his duty by it. It is in the writings of the late republican and early imperial eras that the Roman ideal of citizenship qualities become particularly manifest – in Cicero and Livy, for example. The good Roman citizen, like the good Greek, must be possessed of virtue – the willingness to serve his state, though perhaps the stress on military compared with juridico-political service is greater in the Roman model. There is a difference, too, in the Roman belief that this quality is more likely to be found in the sturdy farmer than the city-dweller. This image of the perfect citizen came to be personified in the idealised story of Cincinnatus. This old man twice left his land to heed the desperate call for leadership in the wars of the early fifth century BC; but 'returned to his plough' after performing his duty. The episode also provides an interesting example of the Aristotelean concept of citizenship of ruling and being ruled in turn.

One of the most famous successful appeals for the protection of Roman citizenship was made by a citizen from Asia Minor a century after Cicero – St Paul. Although arrested in Jerusalem hundreds of miles away from his native city of Tarsus, he could still claim his rights, as the following exchange reveals:

As they bound him with thongs, Paul said unto the centurion that stood by, Is it lawful for you to scourge a man that is a Roman, and uncondemned? When the centurion heard that, he went and told the chief captain . . . Then the chief captain came, and said unto him, Tell me, art thou a Roman? He said, Yea.
. . . I was free born. Then straightway they departed from him which should have examined him; and the chief captain also was afraid, after he knew that he was a Roman, and because he had bound him.[37]

Paul successfully pressed his claim as a Roman citizen to be tried in Rome. The incident provides a convenient illustration of another significant facet of Roman citizenship. He declared himself a citizen of Tarsus; for the Romans recognised a duality in the status. A Roman could be simultaneously a citizen of his city and of the Empire.

Roman citizenship was borne with pride and enjoyed as a privilege. But pride wanes with the vulgarisation of privilege; and is extinguished by the overshadowing of rights by duties. It happened thus in the Roman Empire. The changes were wrought partly by gradual alterations of practice and partly by decree. By the first century BC, citizenship was being increasingly conferred, especially in the western provinces of the expanding empire. And important differences from the constitutional theory of citizenship emerged. Class status started to become more important than the rank of citizen. Landowners and the military were treated with more respect than poor citizens. Thus, by c.200 AD the kinds of privileges St Paul had successfully claimed might very well not be forthcoming to a citizen of modest social standing. It was the Emperor Claudius who first conceived a plan of utmost generosity for widespread conferment of Roman citizenship, a few years before the arrest of Paul. The scheme was lampooned by Seneca, who described an imaginary deathbed scene with the Fate Clotho waiting to cut Claudius' thread of life:

I had thought [she says] to give him a few more minutes so that he might bestow the citizenship on the handful of men who have not already received it (for he had determined to see all Greeks, Gauls, Spaniards, and Britons clad in the toga).[38]

Not for another century and a half was such a massive expansion of the citizenry in fact implemented — by the notorious Emperor Caracalla by means of the equally notorious *Constitutio Antoniniana*. At a stroke the status of citizenship was extended from the Italians and the provincial élites to virtually all men within the confines of the Empire, except slaves. We have already noticed that in practice class had replaced citizenship as a realistic badge of status. Caracalla's edict finally debased the coinage of citizenship to virtual worthlessness. For his motive was transparent: it was to gather more people into his fiscal net for indirect taxation as a means of coping with his severe financial crisis. And as the sense of honour declined so did the sense of civic responsibility. This code of public duty, upon which Rome had formerly been able to rely and her greatness was built, was decaying. Lacking these high standards of citizenship, Rome was but a sprawling empire bereft of any moral stamina or purpose.

It is likely, in any case, that, long before Caracalla's edict, the educational system had utterly failed to sustain the citizenship ideal. In the period of the Republic the characteristic Roman civic qualities had been instilled into boys by their fathers. For education was largely a function of the family rather than schools until the later years of the Republic. These qualities were a formidable list: firmness, courage, religious reverence, self-restraint, dignity, prudence and justice. In addition to this character-training, boys had a specifically civic education through the general practice of learning about the exploits of past heroes, singing suitably patriotic songs and learning by recitation the famous Twelve Tables. Since the pedagogical responsibility lay mainly with the family it was inevitable that the quality of education varied greatly from home to home. For example, a very specific political education for public life — 'a novitiate of the forum' — was undertaken only by the interested youth of the higher ranks of society. For a year these 16–17 year-olds were taken in hand by a suitably experienced friend of the family, who taught his charge the elements of law, government and oratory.

It was Rhetoric that came to dominate much of the curriculum from the end of the Republic to the final collapse of the Empire in the west. The purpose, at least initially in the model expositions of Cicero and Quintilian, was furthermore civic: to combine moral uplift with oratorical persuasiveness in the discussion of public affairs. Quintilian, who lived in the first century AD, interestingly personifies the dominance of oratory in the imperial educational system: he was simultaneously the most eminent of Roman educational theorists and one of the most notable authorities on public speaking. His *Institutio Oratoria* (Education of an Orator) was the standard manual on education in general and oratory in particular for centuries. In this book he emphasised the civic purpose of the style of education he advocated:

My aim, then, is the education of the perfect orator . . . The man who can really play his part as a citizen and is capable of meeting the demands of public and private business, the man who can guide a state by his counsels, give it a firm basis by his legislation and purge its vices by his decisions as a judge, is assuredly no other than an orator.[39]

Moreover, he asserted that no child, once he has acquired the fundamentals of speech, was too young to be started on this educational process.

To family education and oratory must be added a third form of Roman education for citizenship. This was the systematic use of schools to Romanise the conquered provinces. During the first and second centuries AD, the provincial citizenry came increasingly to welcome the Roman schools, the curricula of which were built round the vogue study of oratory. In the Western portion of the Empire young men's colleges were established, which, like the ephebic shcools in the Athens of Hellenistic times, practised their own self-government.

The Romans were a practical-minded people and this trait is reflected in the utilitarian approach to education. Philosophy and the arts, such conspicuous features of Greek education, were scorned. Given the high levels of civic and patriotic consciousness which prevailed at least until the first century AD, this scale of priorities allowed for considerable emphasis to be placed on preparation for citizenship in the broadest sense of the term. However, as the Empire declined the degeneration of citizenship standards was accompanied by a degeneration of educational standards. The core courses in oratory became feeble caricatures of the Ciceronic and Quintilian ideal as the emphasis came increasingly to be placed on mere technique and cheap effect. Whether a more vigorous educational system with sustained civic standards could have stayed the imperial collapse is impossible to conclude. It is unlikely, in view of the severity and complexity of the problems facing the governments from the third century onwards. In any event, clear objectives for a reformed citizenship education would have been difficult to shape. For, following Constantine's Milan Edict of 313 conceding religious and civic freedom to Christians, the Christian ethic had to be incorporated in the judgements and actions of the citizen. Henceforth, certainly until the age of the Reformation, the role of the Church as distinct from the state in commanding loyalty and setting moral standards dominated both politics and education.

The Medieval citizen

Following the collapse of the western portion of the Roman Empire in the wake of the infiltration and invasions of the various Germanic peoples, citizenship was temporarily almost lost as a political concept. The legal and ideological centralisation of power in the hands of the Emperor in the eastern rump of the Roman Empire produced the stern Byzantine autocracy; while the consolidating communities in the west were based on the personal fealty of the people to their leaders. Furthermore, as new political patterns and relationships evolved in the Middle Ages, the characteristic feature in both theory and practice in Western Europe was of a multi-faceted loyalty. Whereas the Graeco-Roman tradition of citizenship, underpinned by tradition, law and education, had required a concentration of loyalty on the state, the more complex Medieval pattern of relationships inhibited for centuries the development of a comparable civic concept. Both Church and Prince claimed allegiance. As a consequence, *qua* Christian, the individual behaved as the ecclesiastical authorities required; *qua* subject of a Prince, as the administrative and legal authorities required. Nor was this dichotomy either merely theoretical or confined to the highest levels of controversy as, for instance, between Holy Roman Emperor and Pope. The people of England certainly learned the realities of this dualism when, during the reign of John, the Pope imposed an interdict on the land: no religious rights, not even burials, therefore, could strictly, be conducted.

If a subject's loyalty could be diverted by the Church, in everyday terms it was demanded in practice by the local lord. Again, the interests of the lord and of the monarch might or might not coincide. In the modern world, of course, the citizen's loyalty is sharply focussed by the powerful concentrating forces of patriotism and nationalism. One of the interesting tensions in the Medieval and Early Modern eras is that between a regional sense of identity and the attractions of a burgeoning nation-state. Geographically and culturally coherent, nation states in some recognisably modern form were already struggling to emerge in parts of Europe in the Middle Ages — England and France most obviously, but also Poland, Hungary and Bohemia. As inhabitants of these lands came to identify themselves primarily as Englishmen, Frenchmen and so forth, so feelings of patriotism at the national level began to blossom. By the age of Shakespeare this was a most powerful sentiment. The dying

Gaunt may have emotionally exaggerated the splendid qualities of his land — 'This other Eden, demi-Paradise' — but there is little doubt that it struck at the time, and has many times since, an intensely sympathetic note in the hearts of English patriots. And yet side-by-side with this process of national integration, feelings of local or regional identity persisted to a powerful degree, sustained by memories of independent traditions and separate linguistic habits. The proud distinctiveness of the southern French of the Langue d'Oc, for example, remained for centuries; while in Spain the demand for Catalan autonomy in our own day is a reminder that the Hispanic unification of Ferdinand and Isabella half a millenium ago is still by no means complete. In England, the county was for generations, until the Industrial Revolution certainly, a very real focus of immediate commitment. As landowners, magistrates and MPs the local gentry *were* social and political authority, they *were* the county. And in so far as ordinary folk in their day-to-day lives felt any sense of identity beyond their families and villages, it was as 'men of Sussex' or 'Yorkshiremen'. Only in times of national crisis would a sense of national loyalty momentarily drown out the local by its insistent call.

The Medieval Frenchman was a *subject* of the Capetian monarch, not a *citizen* of France; likewise, the term 'citizen' was quite inappropriate to describe an Englishman's relationship with his county. In practice, the term was confined in the Middle Ages to the relationship of freely exercised rights and duties in a city or town. Indeed, etymologically the word 'citizen' reveals its urban origin. And not just in English and the Romance languages (French, *citoyen*; Spanish, *cuidadano*): German for 'citizenship', for instance is *Bürgertum*. In the words of Weber,

In the middle ages, the distinguishing characteristic [of a city] was the possession of its own law and court and an autonomous administration of whatever extent. The citizen of the middle ages was a citizen because and insofar as he came under this law and participated in the choice of administrative officials.[40]

This Medieval urban citizenship was founded on the twin principles of freedom and fraternity. Any bondman was free who escaped from his lord to a town for a year and a day; and this was such a common convention that the motto 'town air makes free' was a widely used expression. The principle of fraternity was institutionalised in a common commitment to military service and, typically, in the guild system.

The extent of citizenship status and of citizen involvement in the affairs of his town naturally varied a great deal. In England, the early establishment of a strong central monarchy and the early development of an effective national representative institution inhibited urban citizenship to all intents and purposes to autonomous tax bargaining with the crown. In Germany and Italy, in contrast, where the creation of a nation-state was distinctly retarded, the growth of significant urban corporate rights, autonomy even, had so much more scope. Indeed, if we are seeking exemplars of Medieval citizenship in its most sophisticated practice, we must look to the city-states of northern and central Italy. These small towns — for most were no more in population size – gradually emerged from the political confusion of the Dark Ages to make successful demands for independence from the local lord or bishop. By the twelfth century some two hundred or so of these municipalities had evolved, each with a citizenry as communally compact, legally defined, patriotically loyal and politically involved as any city-state of the ancient world, to which they were clearly so closely analogous. Qualification for citizenship, as might be imagined, varied greatly from city to city and over time. It was commonplace to grade citizens into major and minor classes; though some kind of property-ownership was usual as an intent of commitment to the community. For example, in Parma a 'stranger' would be admitted to citizenship if he built a house worth 100 *lira* and on condition that he was 'a true friend to Parma, not a usurer or murderer and not exiled or banned for any crime.'[41] A high proportion of the citizenry was engaged in political and administrative activities of various kinds, normally on a part-time basis. Assemblies and councils were often large, thus enabling a relatively high percentage of the citizens to be involved in debate and decision-making.

Not only was the lack of a powerful monarchy or consolidated nation-state an important factor in allowing these city-states to evolve; so too was the flickering continuity of Roman law and sense of Roman civic responsibility. This sustained respect for the ancient world therefore provided a hospitable context for the reception of Aristotelian ideas, the whole corpus of which was reintroduced into European consciousness through the talents and dedication of a three-man team of Dominican friars. Of these, the Neopolitan Thomas Aquinas was the most distinguished and the most significant for the revival of Aristotle's concept of citizenship. He expounded his version of Aristotelian politics in his *Commentary* on the *Politics* and his *Summa Theologica*. Although St Thomas, 'the angelic doctor', has become revered in the Roman Catholic Church as a consummate theologian, through his exposition of Aristotle he helped to loosen the grip of the Church on secular political life. For he reiterated Aristotle's key distinction; 'it is possible to be a good citizen without possessing the qualities of the good man.'[42] Aquinas rendered the idea as:

It sometimes happens that someone is a *good citizen* who has not the quality according to which someone is also a *good man*, from which follows that the quality according to whether someone is a good man or a good citizen is not the same.[43]

Aquinas has little advice about precise constitutional formulations and indeed had no visible immediate impact on political institutions and behaviour. Nevertheless, his resuscitation of Aristotle's concepts of the state and citizenship had a revolutionary impact on political theory. It was possible once again to conceive of a state as an abstract entity with which the individual *qua* citizen has a vital relationship in both senses of the word. It thus became possible in theory for the political man to be judged by criteria different from those used in judgement of the Christian soul; and for the active citizen of the state to supersede the passive subject of the prince.

It is hardly likely, however, that Thomas would have been canonised if he had expelled God totally from the political process. And indeed, in his view, the citizen, in enacting human laws, is, by the light of divine reason, reflecting God's universal natural law. It was left to Marsilius of Padua to sever this final spiritual connection — and to be damned by popes for his pains as heretical, pestiferous and a son of Belial. For Marsilius the state was a self-sufficient entity: in conducting their political affairs the citizens had no need of divine guidance nor in that capacity were subject to divine judgement. Marsilius' ideas were indeed remarkably modern in tone, even though he hesitated to allow the lower orders of society a full citizen role. He held that the constitution of a state should be determined by the citizenry and indeed that no government could be good or stable without the consent of the citizens; for 'when a law has been put before them and passed with their consent — then the ordinary citizen is willing to obey it and carry it out. . . because he can feel that he has laid it down for himself.'[44] He also advocated the device of representation to overcome the difficulties of direct participation by a large body of citizens; even the holders of executive and judicial offices should be elected.

This restoration of the concept of citizenship as a political role, consequent upon the renascence of Aristotle's political theory in the thirteenth and fourteenth centuries, was soon followed by a broadening of the concept through a quickening of studies in Roman law and history. The most notable names in each of these fields are Bartolus of Sassoferrato and Niccolo Machiavelli respectively. Bartolus, who lived in the first half of the fourteenth century, was a most distinguished professor of Roman Law at Perugia. No doubt influenced by the vitality of citizenship in the nothern Italian cities we have already noticed, he provided a firm underpinning of theory for this practice. The key to Bartolus' work was a synthesis of the ancient Roman status of citizen, the quasi-legal Roman principle of the sovereignty of the people and the Roman concept of customary law. He concluded that these Roman traditions justified the belief that the people as a whole should hold the ultimate, sovereign power and that only in a state where this held true were the people effectively free. Like Marsilius, Bartolus accepted the need for elected representatives. Since the citizen was such a central figure in his system, Bartolus felt it necessary to define a person's eligibility for this status. He thus distinguished between citizenship acquired by birth and that acquired by legal conferment. In defining the second category he even conceded the status (in a limited sense) to women by asserting that, upon marriage, a foreign woman becomes a citizen of her husband's state.

Renaissance civic consciousness

The intensification of Classical studies by the humanist scholars of the Renaissance might be thought to have brought about a heightening of civic consciousness in practice. At first, this did not happen because of the persistence of the tradition that scholarship was to be pursued in the tranquillity of the study, away from the hurly-burly of city life. However, by c,1400

Florence was showing the way quite remarkably in both theory and practice towards the recovery of the classical ideal of active citizenship. Almost alone in an age of burgeoning tyranny in Italian cities Florence retained a constitutional form of government. The rank of citizen was enjoyed by all men except members of the lesser guilds and labourers. Consciously echoing Pericles, Leonardo Bruni wrote his own *Funeral Oration* in 1428 as a paean in praise of the Florentine constitution. He provides at the same time a splendid definition of and case for citizenship:

Equal liberty exists for all . . ., the hope of winning public honours and ascending is the same for all, provided they possess industry and natural gifts and lead a serious-minded and respected way of life; for our commonwealth requires *virtus* and *probitas* in its citizens. Whoever has these qualifications is thought to be of sufficiently noble birth to participate in the government of the republic . . . This, then, is true liberty, this equality in a commonwealth: not to have to fear violence or wrong-doing from anybody, and to enjoy equality among citizens before the law and in the participation in public office . . . But now it is marvellous to see how powerful this access to public office, once it is offered to a free people, proves to be in awakening the talents of the citizens.[45]

Bruni was in fact a key figure in the revivication of citizenship. He helped in a signal way to accelerate the transition from the ideal of studious contemplation to an active civic life; from a belief in hierarchical society to an egalitarian polity; and from an acceptance of tradition to faith in the possibility of controlling in some measure one's own destiny. It must not, however, be thought that the men of the Renaissance were oblivious to the problems of citizen-participation. Far from it. They recognised, along with the Greeks, the tendency of all regimes to instability. This could be staved off if civic virtue remained uncorrupted by self-seeking.

The most distinguished of all Florentine writers to wrestle with these problems was, of course, Machiavelli, drawing more on Roman than on Greek history to supplement his practical experience. Like Bruni he too was a Florentine civil servant as well as a student of history and politics. Machiavelli's ideal of civic behaviour (as distinct from his cynical princely advice to Lorenzo the Magnificent) was founded on a reading of Livy. He expounded his views in the *Discourses on The First Decade of Titus Livius*. This incomparable Roman historian (who, like Marsilius, lived in Padua), has probably been more responsible than any other Latin author for our heroic view of ancient Roman character. Indeed, he frankly declared, 'I do honestly believe that no country has ever been greater or purer than ours or richer in good citizens and noble deeds'.[46] Taking his cue from this idealised picture of the Roman Republic, Machiavelli argued that the best form of government, though rare, is the republican. In such a polity a people endowed with a generous measure of virtue guides the fortunes of the state. A system like this is rare precisely because of the rarity of virtue. By 'virtue' in this context Machiavelli meant pimarily the manly and martial qualities necessary to defend the state against internal discord and external attack; but, in the case of the ideal ordinary citizen, it also embraced the essential qualities of public-mindeness, probity and patriotism. The citizen must vigilantly guard the state against its seizure by a tyrant. Indeed, Machiavelli, in line with other Renaissance political commentators like Bruni, was convinced that a citizen-army was the quintessence of proper citizenship. The argument worked in both directions. If the citizen is not ready to bear arms to defend his state, he must be so seriously lacking in civic virtue as barely to deserve the title of citizen at all. And if, in default of a citizen army, professional or mercenary troops are recruited, these cannot be relied upon to fight with the same commitment and courage as citizen-soldiers defending what they hold most dear. The decline in the morale and efficiency of the Roman legions and the collapse of the Empire was surely, they argued, a consequence of the decay of the republican military citizenship ideal. However, Machiavelli held out little hope that such a political utopia would come to pass in his own Italy. He brooded pessimistically on the fate of his land, which, slumped in corruption and strife, had neither preserved the vigour of medieval city-state citizenship nor progressed to a peninsular unity capable of giving life to a civic patriotism of nation-wide dimensions.

Concern to strengthen political authority against debilitating fratricidal strife also motivated Jean Bodin, the erudite French lawyer, who published his *Six Books of the Commonwealth* in 1576, in the middle of the generation-long French wars of religion. We must make a special note of this rambling work partly because he devoted two chapters specifically to the matter of citizenship, and partly because he treated the topic in some ways in a very modern fashion. His starting-point, however, strikes the modern reader as somewhat quaint. Bodin was obsessed with the vital importance of the family. Consequently, he viewed citizenship as the surrender by the *pater familias* of the unquestioned authority he exercised domestically in order to act as an equal with other heads of families for the conduct of public affairs. *Qua* citizen he is not a master but an associate of other heads of families and subject to the sovereign. Furthermore, it is this relationship between subject and sovereign that Bodin asserted to be the characterising feature of citizenship. He rejected definitions which emphasise eligibility for public office or the enjoyment of rights and privileges. What 'makes a man a citizen', he declared, was

the mutual obligation between subject and sovereign by which, in return for the faith and obedience rendered to him, the sovereign must do justice and give counsel, assistance, encouragement, and protection to the subject.[47]

This may seem little different from the feudal relationship. However, Bodin made the distinction that whereas a man can be the vassal of more than one lord, 'a citizen cannot be the subject of more than one sovereign'. Bodin was interested too in legal and social questions relating to citizenship status. Citizenship may be acquired, he stated, by birth, adoption or enfranchisement. On the other hand, he rejected any equalising function of the status, arguing that there never has been a state in which all citizens have been equal in rights and privileges.

What is particularly modern about Bodin's theory of citizenship is the cohesive function he provided for the role. Ever concerned to piece together the French state, Bodin used the concept of citizenship to repair the damage wrought by other sources of loyalty:

The whole body of the citizens . . . when subjected to a single sovereign power of one or more rulers, constitutes a commonwealth, even if there is a diversity of laws, language, customs, religion and race. [48]

This bold assertion accorded citizenship a significance in the evolution of the infant modern state comparable with the Aristotelian in the definition of the mature Greek city-state. Yet the potential of Bodin's idea for counteracting the fissiparous tendencies of other loyalties was not immediately realised, because his bulky, diffuse tome was too tedious to be widely read.

In the history of Medieval education there is little to parallel the practice of urban citizenship or the revived political and juridical theory. Machiavelli refers at one point to 'a corrupt city, where education has not been able to infuse any spirit of good into [men's] minds.'[49] But he was no doubt referring to what we would today call socialisation. It was the general educative process of living in a civically active environment that sustained Italian urban citizenship rather than any lessons taught in the schools. Indeed, schools remained almost universally in Europe under ecclesiastical control and were devoted to an education in the 'three Rs' and the liberal arts. Only in the universities, and again particularly in the Italian cities, was any kind of political education undertaken, and this in the form of the teaching of Roman Law.

The major, partial, exceptions to this scene of aridity with respect to education for citizenship in the Middle Ages may be found in the works of Vergerio, yet another son of Padua, and Vittorino of Feltre. Vergerio provides another example of the transmission of revived Roman ideas – in Vergerio's case, of Quintilian and a pseudo-Plutarch text on education. Responding to the Roman tradition and in contradiction of normal Medieval practice, Vergerio advocated a practical, civic purpose to the liberal studies undertaken by the Italian gentleman. His interest in education for citizenship is scarcely surprising in the light of his friendship with Bruni, the enthusiastic exponent of civic humanism. Moreover, he spent some years in Florence, where teaching for this purpose flourished in the early fifteenth century, nourished by the belief that a literary culture and political freedom are interdependent. He advocated the study of History and moral philosophy to instil a sense of civic virtue and warned that,

For the man who has surrendered himself absolutely to the attractions of Letters or of speculative thought follows, perhaps a self-regarding end and is useless as a citizen or as a prince. [50]

The most notable exponent of Vergerio's ideas was Vittorino, who studied and taught in Padua for many years and who strove to instil in his pupils a sense of their duties as citizens.

By the sixteenth century the need to promote national unity or to nurture a budding sense of national consciousness was reflected in considerations about education, especially in France and England. We have already seen how Bodin worried about the political disintegration that so marred the age in which he lived. Even before the outbreak of the first of the nine hideous French civil wars he was advocating a public system of education as a means to social and political cohesion. In 1559 he addressed a gathering in Toulouse in which he propounded this view. He denounced the unsocial nature of private education. The social bonds forged by the experience of being educated in childhood in 'comprehensive' schools he believed to be crucial for civic harmony. No laws, however sacred, he opined, could compete in bonding quality with education. After painting a picture of contemporary violence, he told his audience:

We saw not such a long time ago, waves of civil war endanger neighbouring kingdoms and peoples, who have still not restored peace completely and who will restore it only by introducing a comprehensive education [lit: identical education] regulated by an organic law, for the children of all citizens.[51]

Meanwhile, in England, Elizabeth had just ascended the throne. The gruesome religious conflicts of her sister's reign were, of course, still vivid memories. Elizabeth determined as a matter of extreme urgency to produce a religious settlement which would calm the dogmatic frenzy. Thus in the second year of her reign she issued a series of Royal Injunctions, which included the requirement 'that all teachers of children shall stir and move them to the love and due reverence of God's true religion now set forth by public authority.'[52] Note that the 'true' religion is specified. Later in her reign the author of a school textbook entitled *De Proeliis Anglorum* (On English Wars) commended his own work to the Queen's chief counsellor, Lord Burghley, Its patriotic tenor, he argued, would render it so much more educationally beneficial than Ovid's *Metamorphoses!* The Privy Council, feeling that it would meet this political need, ordered the bishops to have it read in the schools. Thus in the reign of Elizabeth was a sense of national cohesion fostered in the schools by means of religious orthodoxy and historical pride.

By the end of Elizabeth's reign the Renaissance concept of élite citizenship was coming to be associated with the civic roles performed by the gentry locally and nationally. Furthermore, the right of electing MPs to the House of Commons, now flexing its power, provided an embryonic form of citizenship in practice for those enjoying the franchise. By the following century these ordinary voters had attained some political significance.

1.3 THE THRESHOLD OF MODERN CITIZENSHIP

Who then are to be accounted citizens? Those who obey the laws, who maintain human society, who would rather undergo every hardship and every peril for the well-being of their fellow-countrymen, than, through cowardice, grow old in dishonourable ease.

George Buchanan[53]

Seventeenth-century political theory and practice

The seventeenth century was the pivotal age. Without the simultaneous pressures of mutually reinforcing developments and ideas of that time it is difficult to imagine the opening out of the modern egalitarian form of citizenship. We may discern some half-dozen factors operating in this crucial period. The first is the emergence, ratified by the Westphalia peace settlement, of the doctrine of state sovereignty. As we have already noted, citizenship needs the legal construct of a state to which the individual can relate. The consolidation of the concept of the state as an entity in international law consequently assisted this process. Secondly, the need was increasingly felt in the seventeenth century to define allegiance and rights. Thus legal distinctions between inhabitants and aliens and the principles of naturalisation were tightened in some countries.

In the third place, the unquestioned authority of the prince was beginning to be challenged in some quarters. The issue of the right to depose a monarch was a keenly debated problem in the late sixteenth century. The question generated heated passion because of the religious context in which it was raised, the ultimate claim of justified tyrannicide, and the need to appeal to popular sovereignty as the alternative legitimate source of power. The scene was set in France as the Huguenots desperately sought arguments in defence of their resistance to the crown in the agonising saga of the Wars of Religion. The issue also became pertinent to Scotland during the tormented reign of Mary. This crisis prompted Buchanan (the Queen's former Latin tutor) to argue in favour of her deposition and, in so doing, present a virtually democratic concept of citizenship, part of which is quoted at the head of this section. The idea that the people as a whole have the legal or, at the very least, the moral right to make the ultimate decisions concerning their laws and mode of government was given a new lease of life (as the fourth factor) particularly by the political crisis in England in the seventeenth century. These recent precedents were cited; as were the arguments of the Romans, for the doctrine of popular sovereignty has an ancient lineage. The religious passions released by the Reformation was the fifth element. Protestants and particularly Puritans appealed in some lands to the rights of the ordinary people to enjoy religious freedom contrary to the wishes and policies of a doctrinally hostile government. Finally, it must be emphasised, most of these significant developments found initially only a limited sympathetic response. Geographically they occurred in a small corner of the globe, in countries bordering on the North Atlantic, most notably England and Scotland and their American colonial offspring. Moreover, as some opportunities presented themselves actually to put the theory of active citizenship into practice, the prospect provoked considerable nervousness among the classes of substance and power. At the time, therefore, the effective implementation of a generous interpretation of citizenship was rare. And the educational implications of the new developments were only barely discerned. Nevertheless, the legal, political, social and educational implications of a fully developed citizenship at least could not now be totally ignored.

The crisis of the Stuart monarchy provided the stimulus for much of this rethinking and made England and Scotland the most influential centre of debate and experimentation. However, the Dutch Republic and the American colonies played important minor roles and a few words are therefore needed about their experiences. As early as the 1560s the Netherlanders rebelled against their Spanish king, Philip II, and appealed to the principle of popular sovereignty to justify their actions. This theory was supplemented by the healthy Medieval tradition of citizenship in the administration of the substantial towns like Amsterdam. Thus, when the Englishman, Sir William Temple, wrote his *Observations upon the United Provinces of the Netherlands* in the early 1670s, he provided a veritable Aristotelian picture of the practice of citizenship:

. . . in the Assemblies and Debates of their Senates, every man's Abilities are discovered, as their Dispositions are, in the conduct of their Lives and Domestick, among their fellow-citizens. The observation of these, either raises or suppresses the credit of particular men, both among the people and the Senates of their Towns; who . . . give much to the general opinion of the people in the choice of their Magistrates.[54]

On the other hand, even the Dutch Republic, which had a reputation for being advanced in its political feedom, could stake no claim to the description 'democratic'. In the seventeenth century the forces of oligarchy were so extremely powerful that a distinction was drawn between 'citizens' on the one hand and the 'populace' or 'rabble' on the other.

Medieval left-overs and hardening social divisions restrained a speedy development of a broad citizenship in practice in the United Provinces. The American colonies, however, were largely free of these inhibitions. True, the commercial interests which created some settlements and the link with the British crown and parliament, which bound them all, placed a number of constraints on self-government by the colonists. On the other hand, two other factors proved more powerful in the long run. These were the sense among the Puritan settlers of founding a totally new society *ab initio;* and the need to attract new immigrants and to define the status of these later arrivals to the New World. The most famous expression of the first of these factors was the Mayflower Compact. The Pilgrim Fathers drew up this document firm in the radical Puritan belief that any group of men who so wished could create both their own church and their own government. Their understanding of civic participation, rights and duties is clear in their declaration that:

We . . . covenant and combine ourselves together into a civil body Politick, for our better Ordering and Preservation, and Furtherance of the Ends aforesaid: And by Virtue hereof do enact, constitute, and frame, such just and equal Laws, Ordinances, Acts, Constitutions, and Officers, from time to time, as shall be thought most meet and convenient for the general Good of the Colony.[55]

The colonists took with them, naturally, the English habits of law and local government. And insofar as these provided fruitful contexts within which a characteristically English style of citizenship evolved, the American colonists in some measure shared these. In one important respect, however, their views on citizenship were already diverging in the seventeenth century. Ever since the Middle Ages the English law relating to membership of the community had been confused. What was the distinction, for example, between someone born an English subject, a naturalised subject and an alien? The Medieval approach to these questions inevitably focussed on the personal relationship of the individual to the king. In 1608 Sir Edward Coke gave a legal opinion which reinforced this position: he defined allegiance to and membership of the community in terms of a natural, perpetual and personal relationship with the king. The American colonists could not accept this. As more and more immigrants were encouraged to settle in order to boost the population, they had to be naturalised. It was evident that these people became members of their new communities by voluntary acts of migration on their part and of acceptance on the part of the host colonists. Clearly a contractual explanation of this community membership, or embryonic citizenship, reflected the reality more truly than the English law. Thus developed in the Thirteen Colonies the modern view of citizenship, based on voluntary allegiance to a community defined by territory, instead of the Medieval concept of a personal allegiance, involuntary because it was acquired by virtue of birth. Often, too, there was a high level of political consciousness even though participation in the assemblies was restricted by property franchises.

A similar awareness of public affairs beyond the narrow ranks of the enfranchised characterised seventeenth-century England also. The dramatic events of the middle of the century naturally concentrated popular interest in political matters to an artificial intensity. Nor should one underestimate the influence of the people at large in shaping those dramatic events. What in general practical terms did citizenship mean for the seventeenth-century Englishman? If an idea of citizenship was emerging, the pattern of loyalties, rights and duties was still very medieval in style. In particular, class distinctions remained sharp and the local scene was dominant. The gentry class controlled local government as justices. Only the men of property were full citizens in the sense of enjoying the right to vote, discharging the function of jurymen and suffering the duty to pay taxes. Even in the quasi-democratic atmosphere of the Commonwealth the government refused to extend the franchise for fear of a parliament antipathetic to its policies. Nevertheless, within its own limitations the electoral system before the Civil War was quite healthy – healthier certainly than it was to become in the following century. Perhaps as many as one in six male adults had the vote (say, a quarter of a million); and the distortions of patronage and corruption operated on a limited scale. Insofar as the common man had citizen status this took the parochial and county form of paying rates for the succour of the poor and serving in the militia for the defence of his country. On the other hand, we must not underplay the extent to which some men of modest means could be considered to have played quite active citizen roles on a national plane. The franchise in some boroughs was relatively unrestricted and although few outside the landed gentry class stood as parliamentary candidates even in the boroughs, the craftsmen and merchants were probably often sufficiently politically aware and articulate to force their concerns upon the attention of the MPs. And finally we must note that towards the end of the century legal reforms enhanced the rights of the ordinary citizen. From 1670 juries were protected from victimisation in the event of clashing with the judge's opinion on the case; the right of Habeas Corpus was strengthened by the act of 1679; and various laws were passed from 1676 to 1709 to safeguard the rights of English subjects, especially trading privileges, against the intrusion of aliens.

But the most widely accepted facet of citizenship was religion: 'the cement of society' in the current phrase. Since religion was reckoned the prime ingredient promoting civic cohesion, it followed that religious heterodoxy would raise serious doubts concerning an individual's claim to citizenship. This attitude was, moreover, reinforced by legislation. Attendance at Church of England services was mandatory until 1642, while during the Restoration a series of laws forced Catholics and some Dissenters into a category of second-class citizens. The Corporation Act and the Test Act deprived anyone who could not conform to the established Church the rights of local and public office and of the opportunity to teach. In the great flurry of pamphlets and books generated by the Civil War and 'Bloodless Revolution' this position was confirmed. Richard Baxter, the extraordinarily prolific Puritan cleric, was fierce in his denial of the right to full citizenship of the socially wicked and sinful, let alone the doctrinally heretical. Even that sceptical philosopher, Locke, would exclude atheists from civic rights. Although 'neither Pagan nor Mahometan, nor Jew, ought to be excluded from civil rights or the commonwealth because of his religion', those who deny the existence of God must be, because 'Promises, covenants and oaths, which are the bonds of human society, can have no hold upon an atheist.'[56]

Since there was a broad consensus that the status of citizenship must have a religious foundation, this matter occasioned little debate. What was constantly defined, redefined and argued over was the nature of popular sovereignty. It was this issue that particularly exercised the minds of the intellectuals and the emotions of the radicals. The supporters of monarchical authority, most notably Hobbes, did not advance the concept of citizenship very far. In the *Leviathan* Hobbes argued that, until the citizens consciously withdrew their support from the monarch, he must be deemed to act with their authority. In practice, therefore, the citizen's role is in normal circumstances the passive function of obedience. The other giant of seventeenth-century English political theory, Locke, placed much greater emphasis on the need for popular consent for the legitimation of government. But more than that, by projecting a powerful message concerning the rights of citizens, he revolutionised political thinking. If, as Locke maintained, the state exists to protect the lives and liberties of its citizens, then the needs and wishes of the citizens must clearly be given high priority as an absolute right.

Substantial quantities of ink flowed from the philosophers' quills in analysing the nature and implications of the contracts imagined as lying at the root of civil society and political authority. But in practical terms what interested the would-be reformers was the breadth of the franchise. If the people were

31

sovereign, who exactly were 'the people'? If, in everyday language, the exercise of that sovereignty meant the election of representatives to parliament, who should be allowed the vote? Was it 'the multitude' or a restricted stratum of 'the better sort'? Even Locke, whose political ideas were in so many ways almost subversive, was no democrat. Effective political power, he held, should be in the hands of a property-owning oligarchy. Indeed, there was probably slender support in the country for anything more advanced.

And yet such more advanced notions were brought to the surface of debate by the highly charged political atmosphere of the 1640s and 1650s, the period of bloody civil war and uncertain republican government. As early as 1645 the anonymous author of the tract *England's Miserie and Remedie* wrote of the sovereignty of the people in egalitarian terms. A decade later, Harrington, in his utopian vision, *Oceana,* would have all males over 30 other than servants enfranchised. However, the issue was engaged with the most famous and vigorous rhetorical force in the Putney Debates. This exchange of fundamental political principles was an episode in the struggle for power between Parliament and its own creation, the New Model Army. What is more, the rank-and-file in the army were particularly attracted by the radical political and economic ideas being expounded by the Leveller party. During the course of these debates, held in Putney Church in the autumn of 1647, the Leveller programme was adjusted from a demand for outright male adult suffrage to a householder franchise. But the dilemma remained – a basically democratic or oligarchic political citizenship – a dilemma epitomised in the clash between Colonel Rainsborough and General Ireton on the second day:

Rainsborough: . . . I think that the poorest he that is in England has a life as the greatest he; . . . and I do think that the poorest man in England is not at all bound in a strict sense to that government that he has not had a voice to put himself under . . .
Ireton: . . . that by a man's being born here he shall have a share in that power that shall dispose of the lands here, and of all things here, I do not think a sufficient ground.

But I am sure if we look upon . . . what was originally the constitution of this kingdom . . . and which if you take away, there is no man has any land, any goods, you take away civil interest, and that is this: that those that choose the representers for the making of laws by which this state and kingdom are to be governed are . . . the persons in whom all land lies, and those in corporations in whom all trading lies.[57]

The nature of citizenship in its political guise was to be fought out on the choice between these two irreconcilable positions for many subsequent generations.

Seventeenth-century civic education

Attitudes towards citizenship education would also, inevitably be affected by the antithesis between democracy and oligarchy, participation and obedience. And on this educational issue, too, quite naturally the Levellers and Hobbes were at odds. One of the most remarkable experiments undertaken during the Commonwealth was the creation of the communist digger community at Cobham in Surrey. After it collapsed its leader, Gerard Winstanley, wrote *The Law of Freedom* to expound his ideals in some detail. His views on education are contained in Chapter 5. They include the injunction that the youth 'read the laws of the Commonwealth [i.e. the state]', and for three reasons:

First, by being acquainted with the knowledge of the affairs of the world, by their traditional knowledge they may be the better able to govern themselves like rational men.

Secondly, they may become thereby good Commonwealth's men in supporting the government thereof, by being acquainted with the nature of government.

Thirdly, if England have occasion to send ambassadors to any other land, we may have such as are acquainted with their language. [58]

Not a bad succinct set of objectives for preparing citizens for participation, loyalty and internationalism.

Meanwhile, Hobbes produced his *Leviathan,* in which he argued that the Sovereign should ensure 'the instruction of the people in the Essentiall Rights . . . of Sovereignty' as a protection 'against the danger that may arrive to him-selfe in his naturall Person, from Rebellion.' His 'syllabus' for this civic instruction contained seven basic messages, supported by references to the Ten Commandments. First, was patriotic commitment to the status quo: 'they ought not to be in love with any forme of Government they see in their neighbour Nations, more than with their own, nor . . . to desire change.' Second, was resistance to demagogues: 'they ought not to be led with admira-tion of the vertue of any of their fellow Subjects, how high soever he stand, nor how conspicuously soever he shine in the Common-wealth.' Third, was respect for the established government: 'how great a fault it is, to speak evill of the Sovereign Representative . . . whereby he may be brought into Contempt with his People, and their Obedience . . . slackened.' Fourth, specific provision should be made for this civic education; 'seeing people cannot be taught this, nor when 'tis taught, remember it . . . without setting a part from their or-dinary labour, some certain times . . .; It is necessary that such times be determined, wherein they may assemble together, and . . . hear those their Duties told them, and the Positive Lawes, such as generally concern them all, read and expounded, and be put in mind of the Authority that maketh them Lawes.' The fifth principle concerns discipline inculcated in the home: 'be-cause the first instruction of Children, dependeth on the care of their Parents; it is necessary that they should be obedient to them.' Sixthly, the people should be taught about law and order: 'to abstain from violence to one anothers person, by private revenges; from violation of conjugall honour; and from forcible rapine, and fraudulent surreption [i.e. theft] of one anothers good.' Finally, right attitudes as well as right behaviour are to be fostered: 'that not only the unjust facts, but the designes and intentions to do them . . . are Injustice.' All this is, of course, a decidedly conservative prescription. And one of the implicit conservative features is that this instruction be ab-sorbed mainly by adults. He assumes that the majority of people will acquire this civic education 'chiefly from Divines in the Pulpit, and partly from such of their Neighbours, or familiar acquaintance, as . . . seem wiser and better learned in cases of Law, and Conscience, than themselves.' Hobbes looks to the universities to give an effective grounding to this educative élite.[59]

Insofar as there was any political socialisation in the western world in the seventeenth century, this was transmitted very largely from the pulpit. The schools did not consider it their function. Specific political education, it is true, was coming into vogue, but for the upper classes of society. Young gentlemen were taught Geography, History, Jurisprudence and Politics explicitly to fit them for public service. (Though not women, as the Frenchman Fénélon was at pains to emphasise in his *On the Education of Girls*, since these subjects could have no possible relevance for them.) In his *Some Thoughts Concerning Education*, Locke revealed himself a veritable martinet by the tough programme of study he laid down. His 'set books' included Cicero, Grotius and Pufendorf in a 'general Part of Civil-law and History, . . . which a Gentleman should not barely touch at, but constantly dwell upon, and never be done with'. In addition, he prescribed a course of reading in English Constitution, Government, Law and History.[60] The product of such a course would have been splendidly well endowed, at least intellectually, to provide the kind of neighbourly civic leadership Hobbes recommended. But what the modern state would eventually be seeking was the secular civic education of the whole of its citizenry. A hint of what was to come was given in the seventeenth century by Duke Ernest the Pious of Gotha. In an extraordinary programme of educational reform he initiated compulsory schooling for all the children of his Duchy with a curriculum which included Civics among its subjects.

In the seventeenth century citizenship and citizenship education, the one in a more advanced condition of maturity than the other, were like chrysalids waiting to burst forth from their casings. Citizenship but wanted the convulsions of the age of revolutions to liberate it; citizenship education was to be freed by the democratisation this process unleashed and the cohesive needs of the new creed of nationalism.

REFERENCES

1. Plato, *Laws* (trans, T. J. Saunders, Penguin, 1970), p. 73.
2. M. Weber, 'Citizenship' in *General Economic History* (1927, Transaction Books, 1981), p. 316.
3. Aristotle, *Politics* (ed. E. Barker, Clarendon Press, 1946), p. 108.
4. Ibid., pp. 95 & 134.
5. Ibid., p. 105.
6. Ibid., p. 57.
7. Ibid., p. 292.
8. Aristotle, *Nicomachean Ethics* (trans. J. A. K. Thomson, Penguin, 1953), p. 281.
9. See note 6.
10. Thucydides, *The Peloponnesian War* (trans. R. Warner, Penguin, 1954), pp. 118–19.

11. Quoted in W. Boyd, *The History of Western Education* (A. & C. Black, 3rd edn 1932), pp. 21-2.
12. Aristotle, *Nicomachean Ethics* p. 287.
13. Ibid., p. 314.
14. Aristotle, *Politics* p. 333.
15. Ibid., p 233.
16. Quoted in E. B. Castle, *Ancient Education and Today* (Penguin, 1961), p. 18.
17. Xenophon, *Cyropaedia,* vol. 1 (trans. W. Miller, Loeb ed., Heinemann, 1914), pp. 4-5.
18. Aristotle, *Nicomachean Ethics,* p. 312.
19. Montaigne, 'On the education of children', *Essays* (trans. J. M. Cohen, Penguin, 1958), p. 63.
20. Quoted in H. Hadow, *Citizenship* (Clarendon Press, 1923), p. 166.
21. Plato, *Protagoras* (trans. W. K. C. Guthrie, Penguin, 1956), p. 71.
22. Plutarch, *De Alexandri Fortuna aut Virtute* reprinted in E. Barker (trans.), *From Alexander to Constantine* (Clarendon Press, 1956), p. 8.
23. Ibid., pp. 7-8.
24. *Colossians*, 3, 1.
25. Quoted in T. A. Sinclair, *A History of Greek Political Thought* (Routledge & Kegan Paul, 2nd edn 1967), p. 257.
26. Cicero, *Republic*, quoted in G. H. Sabine, *A History of Political Theory* (Harrap, 3rd edn 1951), p. 148.
27. Quoted in Hadow, *Citizenship,* p. 169 (author's translation)
28. Marcus Aurelius, *Meditations,* reprinted in Barker, *From Alexander to Constantine,* pp. 319-20.
29. Ibid., p. 320.
30. Quoted in F. M. Stawell, *The Growth of International Thought* (Thorton Butterworth, 1929), p. 62.
31. Francis Bacon, *Essays;* 'XIII Of Goodness, and Goodness of Nature' (1597, Dent ed. 1906 (1975 imp.)), pp. 38-9.
32. Vitoria, *De Potestate Civile,* quoted in A. Linklater, *Men and Citizens in the Theory of International Relations* (Macmillan, 1982), p. 50.
33. Montaigne, *Essays,* pp. 63–4.
34. Reprinted in D. G. Scanlon (ed.), *International Education: A Documentary History* (Teachers College, Columbia University, N. Y., (1960), p. 40.
35. Edward Gibbon, *Decline and Fall of the Roman Empire,* vol. 1, quoted in Hadow, *Citizenship,* p. 18.
36. Cicero, *In Verrem,* See *Oxford Dictionary of Quotations*, p. 540.
37. *Acts*, 22, 25–9.
38. Seneca, *De Morte Claudii,* quoted in Hadow, *Citizenship,* p. 12.
39. Quintilian, *Institutio Oratoria,* quoted in Castle, op. cit., p. 136.
40. Weber, 'Citizenship', p. 318.
41. Quoted in D. Waley, *The Italian City-Republics* (Weidenfeld & Nicolson, 1969), pp. 105-6.
42. Aristotle, *Politics,* p. 102.
43. Aquinas, quoted in W. Ullmann, *A History of Political Thought: The Middle Ages* (Penguin, 1965), p. 176.
44. Marsilius, *Defensor Pacis,* quoted in Stawell, *International Thought*, pp. 58–9.
45. Bruni, *Funeral Oration*, quoted in H. Baron, *The Crisis of the Early Italian Renaissance* (Princeton University Press, rev. ed 1966), p. 419.

46. Quoted in Livy, *The Early History of Rome* (trans. A. de Sélincourt, Penguin, 1960), Introduction, p. 13.

47. Bodin, *Six Books of the Commonwealth* (trans. M. Tooley, Blackwell, 1967), p. 21.

48. Ibid., p. 20.

49. Machiavelli, *Discourses*, Book III, reprinted in M. B. Foster *et al.* (eds.), *Masters of Political Thought* (Harrap, 1947), vol. 1, p. 275.

50. Vergerio, *De Ingenuis Moribus,* quoted in J. Bowen, *A History of Western Education,* vol. 2 (Methuen, 1975), p. 217.

51. Bodin, *Discours au Sénat et au Peuple de Toulouse sur l'éducation á donner aux jeunes gens dans la république,* reprinted in P. Mesnard (ed.), *Oeuvres Philosophiques de Jean Bodin* (Presses Universitaires de France, 1951), p. 58 (author's translation).

52. Reprinted in D. W. Sylvester, *Educational Documents 800-1816* (Methuen, 1970), p. 125.

53. George Buchanan, *Of the Powers of the Crown in Scotland,* quoted in D. Wootton, *Divine Right and Democracy* (Penguin, 1986), p. 50.

54. William Temple, *Observations upon the United Provinces of the Netherlands* (ed. G. N. Clark, Clarendon Press, 1972), p. 69.

55. Reprinted in C. L. Ver Steeg & R. Hofstadter (eds.), *Great Issues in American History* (Vintage Books, 1969), pp. 73-4.

56. Locke, *A Letter Concerning Toleration,* reprinted in J. W. Gough (ed.), *The Second Treatise of Civil Government, etc.* (Blackwell, 1946), pp. 160 & 156.

57. Reprinted in Wootton, *Divine Right and Democracy,* pp. 286-8.

58. Gerard Winstanley, *The Law of Freedom in a Platform, or True Magistracy Restored* (ed. L. Hamilton, Cresset Press, 1944), pp. 173-4.

59. Hobbes, *Leviathan,* chap. XXX (Dent ed., 1914), pp. 180-3.

60. Locke, *Some Thoughts Concerning Education*, §§ 186 & 187, reprinted in J. L. Axtell (ed.), *The Educational Writings of John Locke* (Cambridge University Press, 1968), pp. 294-5.

CHAPTER TWO

Consolidation of the modern state

2.1 THE AGE OF REVOLUTION

We demand equality of rights, . . . that equality we claim is, to make the slave a man, the man a citizen and integral part of the state; to make him a joint sovereign, and not a subject.

Sheffield Constitutional Society[1]

Education and political theory in the late eighteenth century

By the late eighteenth century obsolescent social structures and political institutions lay like weakening geological faults beneath most of the states round the rim of the Atlantic Ocean. As the discontented strata of these societies shifted in rebellious mood, social and political tremors shook the whole region. In some countries, most notably France, the old régime crumbled in the convulsions; in others, notably England, the edifice remained seemingly firm though in truth undermined. The crisis passed and repairs and rebuilding were effected – with citizenship more firmly embedded in the fabric.

From Poland in the east to the American colonies in the west the spirit of the second half of the century was political. The need to disseminate and debate political ideas was satisfied by the remarkably rapid growth of political clubs and newspapers. Literary, constitutional and corresponding societies sprang up in the major towns of Germany, the Netherlands, France, Britain and America especially. Nor were their members short of pamphlet and newspaper literature to stimulate their meetings. To give just two examples. Within two years of publication, 200,000 copies of Part I of Paine's *Rights of Man* had been sold. Between 1789 and 1800 1350 new newspapers were launched in Paris. It is likely indeed that the term 'public opinion' was coined at about this time, so novel was this phenomenon of widespread political consciousness. One of the central issues in these discussions was the possibility, desirability and justice of consolidating and broadening the realities of citizenship. Demands for freedom from religious discrimination, for equality before the law, for freedom from arbitrary arrest, for the extension

37

of political rights to a wider spectrum of society were voiced through the length and breadth of this great geographical area. Though whether a basically aristocratic or democratic political settlement would emerge from the upheavals divided the revolutions in often bitter contention.

The epicentre of so much of the fundamental questioning of the status quo was France; and its force owed a great deal to the basic optimistic conviction that mankind was capable of improving his lot. This optimism in the possibility, even likelihood, of social progress was founded on the recognised power of the human mind to frame solutions to problems. It followed that, insofar as immense problems persisted, an insufficient number of properly trained minds had been focussed upon them. The way to progress lay along the path of educational reform. The matter was simply and categorically asserted by Helvétius: *l'éducation peut tout* (education is capable of everything).[2] Helvétius, a financier turned *philosophe* and a leading Freemason, was one of a number of influential writers who believed that because of the potential of education, it should be controlled by the state and serve a clear civic purpose. Three others writing in the 1750s to 1780s contributed their own characteristic recommendations to this burgeoning belief in civic education: La Chalotais, a passionate anti-Jesuit lawyer of the Parlement of Rennes; Turgot, the supremely efficient administrator, successively intendant of Limoges and a minister in the royal government; and Rousseau, the strange, wandering philosophical genius. A motley collection to have concentrated their minds on the same problem.

Helvétius published his *De l'ésprit* in 1758 and, despite its somewhat confused argument, it was widely read. He believed that government and education were in a symbiotic relationship: a good government produces good education and vice versa. He asserted that the public good should be defined by the government and that the general welfare of the state depended primarily on the education of children to this end. This education should contain overt instruction in civic and social science. And if the interests of the family were in conflict with the interests of the community at large, then the children should be reft from their families by the state for the public good. It comes as little surprise to learn that Helvétius held ancient Sparta in great admiration.

Five years later La Chalotais produced his *Essay on National Education*. His main motive was to attack the religious monopoly of education, and in particular the role of the Jesuits. The nation must control its own education for its own purposes. His views have been paraphrased in the following way:

The schools have to form good citizens, men capable of serving their country, therefore education should conform to the constitution and laws of the country. At the present time it is steeped in mysticism. What I say is, let it be made to train good citizens.[3]

On the other hand, La Chalotais was not too keen on the state wasting time educating the mass of the people, whose function was to work productively. Citizenship education was for the privileged. The idea that the state should wrest control of education from the Church ensured La Chalotais' *Essay* a sympathetic reception not just in France: state-directed reform, the style of the so-called enlightened absolutism, was marked by decidedly anti-clerical features, particularly in many of the German states.

A more liberal interpretation of the idea of a national civically-directed education is to be found in Turgot's utopian *Memoir on Municipalities*. In this work he projected a vision of a government operated through a pyramidal structure of assemblies from the villages upwards. Citizens would participate in a weighted-vote system, the less affluent enjoying less influence as 'fractional citizens'. Even so, all needed to be educated in the arts of citizenship. Turgot accordingly proposed a Council of Public Instruction. The duties of this body included making arrangements for the writing of school textbooks on citizenship and ensuring that civics featured prominently in the syllabuses of the institutions of higher education. With the touching optimism of the age Turgot declared that such a system could produce within a decade of its operation children as young as ten fully equipped to act as participative and patriotic citizens.

Turgot's plan is of interest for the advanced nature of his proposals rather than any influence they had. Rousseau, of course, had a far wider impact. And although in his *Emile* he recommended an education to shield the child from society, when he wrote of his political ideals, he assumed states purified of the corruptions that so offended him in the France of his own day. In those conditions education for citizenship, he argued, was of paramount importance. For only by harmonising the interests of the individual and the state could an ideal state be achieved. Young people should therefore be educated – indoctrinated some commentators aver – to conflating their personal interests and wishes with the general will, the interests of the community as a whole. Rousseau was much influenced by the classical models about which he learned at his father's knee: 'I was a Roman before I was twelve', he once declared.[4] One of the major conclusions he drew from this study was the danger of generalising from the Roman practice of relying on the family for civic education. As he wrote in the *Discourse on Political Economy*,

Rome was for five hundred years one continued miracle which the world cannot hope to see again. The virtue of the Romans . . . made all their houses so many schools of citizenship.[5]

An idealised Lacedemonian form of state-directed education he felt to be a much more practical proposition.

It is in this *Discourse*, in his article on *Political Economy* for the great *Encyclopedia* and in his *Considerations on the Government of Poland* that he expounded his ideas on civic education most fully. Children, he urged, should be taught from a very early age to appreciate the values and procedures which are so beneficial to society: equality, the rule of the General Will, patriotism. Teachers should be men of virtue and responsibility, who would,

transmit from age to age, to generations to come, the experience and talents of rulers, the courage and virtue of citizens, and common emulation in all to live and die for their country.[6]

Despite his adulation of the city-state as the best approximation to a perfect polity, Rousseau was one of the earliest theorists of the modern concept of nationalism. Moreover, he believed that education had a vital role to play in fostering a proper sense of nationality and national pride. Education will ensure that 'young citizens gather all their passions into a love of their country.'[7] And his pragmatic advice to the Poles was to inculcate a sense of national identity in order to avoid subjugation by the Russians. In this process the schools must ensure that the people become patriots 'by inclination, by passion, by necessity.'[8] For Rousseau, therefore, education in virtuous and patriotic citizenship was not just a dream for an ideal, stable, harmonious state; it was a grim and practical necessity in the hard, real world.

Rousseau's keen commitment to patriotism and nationalism naturally predisposed him to be hostile to world citizenship. He rejected the fashionable cosmopolitanism of his day (p. 56) as a dilution of vital civic cohesion. For, like Aristotle, he was convinced that life in a state, and preferably one of compact size, was essential for the moral maturity of the human being and the full realisation of his nature. Only by living as a citizen can a man develop a sense of justice and a moral and rational conscience. For the true citizen seeks the realisation of the General Will, the common good, not the satisfaction of his own selfish interests. Rousseau's ideal citizen has more than a little of the ancient Roman about him, endowed with the 'republican virtues' of moral integrity, strong personality, self-discipline and a deep patriotism. These qualities, he believed, would be cultivated by participation in decisions concerning the major matters requiring resolution.

This concept of a politically educative society was, at least at the time, plausible only if one assumed a city-state context. Despite his belief in nationalism, Rousseau retained a hankering after the cohesions of the small scale such as he had experienced in his own beloved Geneva. Only by direct involvement of the citizenry could the General Will be discerned and remain sovereign. This belief prompted Jeremy Bentham to sneer that Rousseau would not recognise the validity of any European law except perhaps that of the Republic of San Marino! Not that Rousseau was a democrat. 'If there were a nation of Gods,' he declared, 'it would govern itself democratically. A government so perfect is not suited to men.'[9] For Rousseau the citizen is a watchdog rather than a demi-god. His function is to monitor the government, be it monarchical or aristocratic, and every so often convene with his fellow-citizens to survey and, if necessary, amend the fundamental laws of the state. It is that ultimate legislative sovereign authority that belongs to the citizenry. Nor can it be delegated. He rejected the device of representation as a mockery and condemned the English system in a famous passage in the *Social Contract*:

The English people believes itself to be free; it is gravely mistaken; it is free only during the election of Members of Parliament; as soon as the Members are elected, the people is enslaved; it is nothing.[10]

Rousseau's famous Irish contemporary, Edmund Burke, held to the contrary view concerning representation. Elections, he believed, were opportunities for the enfranchised citizens to choose a wise élite to govern them. The function of the citizen is 'to deliver an opinion'; it is for the MP then to use his 'mature judgement' and 'enlightened conscience'.[11] Burke, moreover, reflected the widely held view that even this limited citizenship role should be exercised by only a small segment of the population:

. . . those of adult age, not declining in life, of tolerable leisure for such discussions, and of some information, more or less, and who are above menial dependence.[12]

Any lesser sort could not be trusted to act altruistically and responsibly. The view, which can be traced back as far as Aristotle, that ownership of property was a necessary condition for citizenship, held particular sway in the eighteenth century – and not just among the Whigs in England and America. Even Baron d'Holbach, the *philosophe* who had a vision of the future when princes had educated their people for the arts of citizenship, was similarly élitist. He distinguished between 'the stupid populace' and citizens, that is, men 'who can live respectably from the income of [their] property' or who own land.[13]

Radical politics and conformist education in England

Needless to say, in the unstable and heavily charged political atmosphere of the late eighteenth century there were many in Britain who sought to argue a case for a more democratic interpretation of the constitution. Not since the heady days of the mid-seventeenth century, to which some commentators indeed referred, was there such intense political consciousness abroad throughout the country. The expansion of a thriving middle class, especially in London; the burgeoning of the press; the creation of political clubs; the increasing resentment of discrimination against Dissenters; and the scandal of corrupt government combined to produce a public opinion eager to respond to radical ideas. A remarkable sequence of dramatic events ensured that the broadcasting of these thoughts, proposals and demands set up a sympathetic resonance among a substantial proportion of the population. These events included the extraordinary career of the squint-eyed rake, John Wilkes; the protests and uprising of the American colonists; and the sweeping reforms of the early years of the French Revolution.

From the 1760s to the 1790s demands were voiced for the democratisation of the parliamentary system and the abolition of the second-class citizen status of Dissenters, and even by a few bold spirits, of women. These demands became increasingly radical as opinion became influenced by events across the Channel after 1789. The reformers adduced various arguments to justify the widening of the franchise: the historical precedent of a putative freer and more egalitarian Anglo-Saxon age; the natural rights theory of Locke; and the utilitarian principle that political enfranchisement would lead to a more rational and just society. In terms of a practical programme, as early as 1780 the radical Duke of Richmond presented to the House of Lords a scheme then being canvassed by the Society for Constitutional Information (p. 44)

41

for annual elections, equal electoral districts, secret ballot, abolition of property qualifications for MPs, payment of MPs and manhood suffrage: the very six points of the People's Charter which were to seem so impossible of acceptance even in the 1830s and 1840s (p. 65).

The basic ideas of popular sovereignty and equality nevertheless still left open for discussion precisely which segments of society should be raised to the status of full citizenship and which should still remain excluded to provide exceptions to prove the rule. Many Protestant Dissenters became vociferous about the penalties they suffered by virtue of their conscientious inability to abide by all the Thirty-Nine Articles of the Established Church. And from their ranks emerged powerful advocates of reform like Richard Price and Joseph Priestley. Their demands for effective religious freedom centred on the objectionable Test and Corporation Acts (p. 31). For not even William III, who had wished to repeal these laws, had been able to break the determination of Anglican Toryism to defend them at all costs. Furthermore, the Dissenters started to argue their case not just on the grounds of religious tolerance but on the grounds of political freedom — on the rights due to citizens. Anna Barbauld, wife of a dissenting clergyman and combining a poetic spirit with spirited pamphleteering, declared in 1790:

We could wish to be considered as children of the State, though we are not so of the Church . . . We claim it as men, we claim it as citizens, we claim it as good subjects . . . we wish to bury every name of distinction in the common appellation of Citizen.[14]

It was unusual at the time for women to be at all politically active. Mary Wollstonecraft was, of course, the most famous exception. In her brief and rather sad life, she not only wrote *A Vindication of the Rights of Man*, a riposte to Burke's formidable *Reflections on the French Revolution*; two years later she also wrote *A Vindication of the Rights of Women*. One would nevertheless be hard put to it to find anyone seriously advocating equal political rights for women. Women were not considered by nature to be political animals. What Mary Wollstonecraft herself advocated was not so much political rights as emancipation from the drudgery, the social and economic inferiority, which was woman's lot. If that could be achieved they could contribute in their own ways more fully to society. She predicted commonsensically that:

Would man but generously snap our chains, and be content with rational fellowship instead of slavish obedience, they would find us more observant daughters, more affectionate sisters, more faithful wives, more reasonable mothers — in a word, better citizens.[15]

It was, in truth, a modest enough definition of citizenship.

Whether full citizenship rights should be extended to Dissenters and women were particular, and in some senses at the time peripheral, issues. What concerned the majority of people in the debates was the perennial question of how far down the social scale these rights, especially political rights, should descend. If men are equal and have rights, if the people are sovereign, how can the exclusion of any from the suffrage be justified? On the other hand, if women and children were excluded by virtue of their social, even intellectual dependence, should not male social dependants also be excluded? Many radical campaigners sought refuge from this dilemma by holding to the belief that the poorer folk would be wisely deferrent if given the vote; others continued to harbour doubts about universal manhood suffrage. The idea that whoever engages in productive work and supports a family is worthy of civic recognition was a powerful argument and was marshalled, for example by Tom Paine. But absolutely *all* men without exception? The agonies of hesitation were most economically exemplified by a Dissenter pamphleteer:

All men at the age of eighteen, who are not vagabonds or in the hands of justice, have a right to vote [wrote David Williams]; because they contribute by their industry to the support of the state. I have had doubts concerning menial servants; on account [of] their dependence on their masters: but the injustice of excluding them, would bring greater inconveniences, than the trouble of preventing the ill effects of that dependence.[16]

All this, of course, is theory, pleading and rhetoric. Did the working class in any way at this time of political ferment act as participative citizens? There is considerable evidence that they did. It is possible to make three particularly telling points. The first is that the number of newspapers sold doubled in the forty years from 1750 to 1790. It is fairly obvious that such a rapid expansion would have included an extension into the craftsman class. Secondly, the repeated cheeky confrontations of the Establishment by Wilkes inspired a remarkable popular response. True, some elements of the Wilkite Middlesex mobs may barely have understood the issues. On the other hand, very many citizens of London and the provincial cities clearly did; and, moreover, appreciated the importance for the political health of the country of the particular conflicts he engaged in. The matters of the freedom of the press in the *North Briton* affair; of the legality of (anonymous) general warrants in the *Essay on Women* scandal; and of the constitutional right of Parliament to debar a duly elected MP in the Middlesex elections crises: all these events were eagerly discussed. And, as a result, the populace of England probably became more politically conscious than ever before in its history.

Indeed, clubs for the discussion of political matters were already springing up in many towns. And these represent the third piece of evidence of political activity in the artisan class. True, a number of these clubs, devoted to parliamentary reform, were of an exclusive kind: membership fees were high and their objectives reflected the property-owning interests. In contrast, Thomas Hardy started the London Corresponding Society in 1791, charging an entrance fee of a shilling and a weekly subscription of a penny and pressing for the six-point radical reform of parliament which had been rejected by the House of Lords in division eleven years before. The Society's attitude towards citizenship is interestingly revealed in a series of resolutions adopted in 1792. These included the statement,

That it is no less the *right* than the *duty* of every Citizen to keep a watchful eye on the government of this country.[17]

Hardy was a cobbler; his close associate, Francis Place, was a maker of leather breeches. It was to such people they appealed (in both senses of the word). Similar bodies were set up in several provincial cities. For example, the Sheffield society quoted at the head of this section, boasted a membership of 2,000 tradesmen, artisans and workingmen. Another organisation of democratic intent was the Society for Constitutional Information. Although its membership was much more exclusive that Hardy's Society, it is of considerable interest because, as its name indicates, its function was educative – to disseminate information about and argument for parliamentary reform.

Through discussion of its message in the radical clubs Paine's *Rights of Man* became a best seller. Certainly conservatives deplored its influence. For example, Malthus warned in his *An Essay on Population*:

The circulation of Paine's Rights of Man, it is supposed, has done great mischief among the lower and middling classes of people in this country. [18]

Indeed, in the same work Malthus deplored the failure of education in England to provide the lower orders with 'important political truths' so that they might protect themselves from 'ambitious demagogues'. He was but expressing a widely held view that the behaviour of citizens of the lower sort should be one of piety, submission and respect. Twenty years earlier, for instance, Adam Smith had recommended education for the 'inferior ranks' because 'instructed and intelligent people are always more decent and orderly than a stupid one. They [are] . . . more likely to obtain the respect of their lawful superiors. They are . . . less apt to be misled into any wanton or unnecessary opposition to the measures of government'.[19] The radicals, Godwin and Priestley drew the opposite conclusion from this lack of educational provision: they warned against a national system of schools for fear that the government would use it to manipulate the minds of young citizens. Even so, Priestley hoped for an education that would turn the populace into patriots and citizens.

The institutions which from the late eighteenth century performed this socialising function of moulding a deferent populace were the Sunday Schools (but see p. 87). By c. 1800 they were educating an astonishingly high proportion of the children – a quarter of a million already in 1787. Thus in the great revolutionary age the political education of working-class children in England was totally at odds with the political education of those working-class men who were sufficiently interested to take advantage of the opportunities available to learn of current controversies.

The status and education of American citizens

Modern war, in which political principles are at stake, heightens political consciousness. This phenomenon was certainly evident on both sides of the Atlantic in the American War of Independence. In the mid-eighteenth century the colonies collectively revealed a remarkable variety of fissiparous tendencies: between the individual colonies; between the settled eastern communities and those on the frontier; between the rich and the poor; between slave-owners and slaves; between different ethnic and religious groups; and, as the quarrel with the mother-country developed, between loyalists and patriots. On the other hand, that very quarrel helped to nurture a sense of American national consciousness, which started to override these other separate identities. Interest in political issues was sustained, as in Britain, by the founding of clubs, like the Sons of Liberty and the Philadelphia Patriotic Society, and the publication of an increasing number of newspapers and pamphlets. Moreover, the specific issue of the ratification of the Constitution generated a substantial literature on that subject. This included most notably the learned collection of essays, *The Federalist*, written for the citizens of New York state. The totality of this output bespeaks a degree of political literacy relatively high for the age. Modern war also often heightens political consciousness among the combatants, especially if they are recruited as a citizen army. Washington's troops defended the colonists' rights to citizenship with their bayonets just as much as the drafters of the Declaration of Independence did with their pens. And their pride in and commitment to the task deeply impressed Lafayette, the youthful French defender of freedom and friend of Washington. In a famous comment concerning the appalling conditions under which the American armies fought, he declared, 'only citizens could support the nakedness, the hunger, the labours, and the absolute lack of pay which constitute the conditions of our soldiers.'[20]

The most significant opportunity for large numbers to act as citizens and to display their willingness so to do was provided by the process of framing the state constitutions. The Declaration of Independence rendered the colonial constitutions *ipso facto* invalid. Each of the thirteen states consequently needed to draft new documents. Who held such constituent authority? The theoretical answer to this question and the practical technique of drafting the constitutions varied from state to state. None the less there was a general feeling that the people as a whole should perform this basic political role. And so in six states the assemblies asked for confirmation from the voters (on the existing colonial franchise) to confirm their right to draft a new constitution. In a few states some attempt was even made to secure formal ratification of the constitutions by the citizens. The best example of the procedure was Massachusetts. Here a referendum was held, in which all male adults had the right to vote, to confirm the authority claimed by the two houses of the legislature to draw up the constitution. The document was duly produced in 1778. The voters refused to ratify it. Back to the drawing board. The second attempt was agreed two years later, again by the votes of free adult males. This process of citizenship participation could be considered, however, more remarkable for its enabling intent than its conscientious implementation: only 23 per cent of the electorate voted in 1780.

The feeling that the Revolution should be taken as an opportunity to extend democratic processes was popularised by a number of commentators and theorists. The two most significant were Paine and Jefferson. Paine, the staysmaker from Norfolk, had a profound effect on the American colonists' decision to claim independence. The argument he pursued to this end in his popular *Common Sense* seemed to many to be irrefutable. In that same work he hinted at a conception of citizenship which almost echoes Aristotle's 'ruling and being ruled in turn' (p. 3). Paine suggested that,

. . . prudence will point out the propriety of having elections often; because as the *elected* might by that means return and mix again with the general body of *electors* in a few months, their fidelity to the public will be secured . . . And as this frequent interchange will establish a common interest with every part of the community, they will mutually and naturally support each other.[21]

Jefferson, the Virginian polymath, possessed a romantic and optimistic view of the people's political common sense. He wrote copiously on matters touching upon the topic of citizenship. By listing his authorship of the Declaration of Independence and the Virginian Statute for religious freedom in his auto-epitaph he obviously wished to be remembered most particularly for these documents. The Declaration, of course, provides a classic pronouncement of the doctrine that government, in justice, must be based upon the consent of the people. That he wished to define 'people' in a generous way — for the conduct as well as the legitimation of government — became very evident over the years. Thus on the particular issue of religious freedom he wrote, in the Virginian Statute:

. . . the proscribing any citizen as unworthy the public confidence by laying upon him an incapacity of being called to offices of trust and emolument, unless he profess or renounce this or that religious opinion, is depriving him injuriously of those privileges and advantages to which in common with his fellow-citizens he has a natural right.[22]

In the period immediately after the War he persuaded a sufficient number of men that citizenship should be liberally interpreted for the term 'Jeffersonian democracy' to be coined to describe this ideal. Not that it was a foregone conclusion even after the introduction into force of the federal Constitution that the Jeffersonian interpretation would gain universal acceptance. There were plenty who held the contrary opinion that the mass of the people, in Alexander Hamilton's words, 'seldom judge or determine right'.[23]

The legacy of the Revolution for the development of the American practice of citizenship lay in the potential of the basic constitutional documents for a broad interpretation. It would depend on the political will of future generations whether and how fast that potential was to be realised. In terms of the franchise the constitution is supremely vague: 'The House of Representatives shall be composed of Members chosen every second year by the People of the several States'.[24] Defining 'the People' provided opportunities for endless debates and controversy. Citizenship in the sense of suffrage was not the issue that concerned the constitution-framers. What they wished to define were the matters relating to naturalisation and federation. We have already noticed how the question of naturalisation had divided the colonies and metropolitan England (p. 30). It was in addition raised specifically in the catalogue of complaints in the Declaration of Independence, in which George III is accused of 'obstructing the Law of Naturalization of Foreigners'. The Constitution gave

Congress the power to establish 'an uniform rule of naturalization' for the whole country' (Art. I, sect. 8).

But the really tricky problem related to the concept that an individual was both a citizen of his particular state and of the United States. A first attempt at squaring this circle was made in the Articles of Confederation. This document was drafted in 1777 in order to provide the thirteen rebellious states with some semblance of unity in their war against England. Article 4, the so-called 'comity clause', stated:

. . . the free inhabitants of each of these states, paupers, vagabonds and fugitives from Justice excepted, shall be entitled to all privileges and immunities of free citizens in the several states.[25]

Yet this did not settle the matter. As Madison pointed out in *The Federalist*, the use of the different terms 'free inhabitants' and 'free citizens' could have produced a ludicrous anomaly: a non-citizen inhabitant of one state could claim the privileges of citizenship in another state not his own! The Constitution dealt with the problem succinctly: 'The citizens of each State shall be entitled to all privileges and immunities of citizens in the several States.' (Art. IV sect. 2) Legalistic 'nit-picking'? Perhaps; but it has been worth dwelling on the issue as an early illustration of constitutional lawyers wrestling with the problem of multiple citizenship, an issue to which we shall have cause to return.

The term 'citizenship' was mainly confined to these issues of naturalisation and the relation of the individual to his state. Nevertheless, in so far as the status must be understood to embrace important civil rights the Bill of Rights, the first ten Amendments to the federal Constitution added in 1791, were historically of prime importance. Henceforth any gross injustice suffered by an individual was not merely unlawful but an infringement of citizenship rights by virtue of being unconstitutional.

It was all very well expounding the rights of citizens: could they be relied upon to support the institutions and ethos of the infant republic? Many of the political leaders at least entertained some doubts and saw that the matter was, at least in part, a question of education. However, while the parallel concern to educate future generations of leaders was soon to express itself in the creation of colleges and universities, facilities for widespread popular education were slower to develop. There was no lack of exhortation, even if the practical political will to mass civic education was ambivalent. Washington himself lent his authority to the issue. In his first annual address to Congress he declared:

Knowledge is in every country the surest basis of public happiness. In one in which the measures of government receive their impressions so immediately from the sense of the community as in ours it is proportionally essential. To the security of a free constitution it contributes in various ways.[26]

An especially interesting contribution to the discussion was provided by Noah Webster, who highlighted the central importance of educating women in the principles of republican mores. For, after all, as mothers they exert the powerful early influences on young citizens in the homes.

Should such preparation for citizenship be available to all children (leaving aside slaves, of course)? And should it take the form of overt political instruction? Characteristically Jefferson addressed his energetic mind to these questions. He firmly believed that the liberties of the citizen had constantly to be protected by the general citizenry against the tendency of government to erode them. Thus in a report to the Virginia Legislature in 1818 he included in the objectives of primary education:

To understand his [i.e. the citizen's] duties to his neighbours and country, and to discharge with competence the functions confided to him by either; . . .
To know his rights; to exercise with order and justice those he retains; to choose with discretion the fiduciary of those he delegates; and to notice their conduct with diligence, with candor, and judgement; . . .[27]

This is a formidably ambitious prospectus, especially when one considers the geographically scattered nature of much of the American population at the time. And yet for the instruction of 'the mass of our citizens in . . . their rights, interests and duties' he advocated little more than basic literacy and a little History. Indeed, forty years earlier he had proposed a hierarchical system of free education: a meagre three years for the mass of children and by successive testing sieves a further education for 'the best geniuses . . . raked from the rubbish'.[28] In truth, Jefferson probably had more faith in a free press than civics classes for the political education of American citizens.

The status and education of French citizens

By the time that the educational implications of the American Revolution were being thought through France was shuddering in its own much more traumatic upheaval. And it was in the French Revolution that the concept, status and title of citizen came into its own. What better way for the individual to experience the ideals of liberty, equality and fraternity than by bearing the name, rights and duties of 'citoyen'? For liberty was won, or so it was claimed, by exchanging life as a subject of an absolute monarch for that of a citizen of a polity with a duly framed constitution. Equality was achieved by the abolition of class distinctions and titles and the substitution of the uniform title of 'Citizen' and 'Citizeness'. Fraternity was nurtured by the sense of common purpose in forging a new state – and, of course, in defending it: 'Aux armes, Citoyens!' sang the Marseillais citizen-soldiers marching north to stiffen resistance to the German invaders.

In 1789 a Frenchman's status was defined either as a subject of Louis XVI or as a member of one of the three estates of the realm: clergy, nobility and the third estate. The idea that the unprivileged third estate, the bulk of the population, should be considered as an entity, effectively the nation, was expounded by the Abbé Sieyes in his extraordinarily influential pamphlet, *What is the Third Estate?* By giving the answer *'everything'* to his own question he discarded the first two estates from any political consideration and established the principle of national sovereignty. There followed logically the need to define who should be eligible for the status of citizen of the French nation and what rights might attach to the status.

A Constitution, prefaced by a Declaration of Rights and largely written in 1789, though not implemented for two years, set down the guidelines very clearly. The second part of the Constitution listed who were to be considered citizens or be eligible for citizenship, and in what conditions a citizen might be stripped of his status. The first list was of remarkably generous length. Besides the obvious category: 'Those who were born in France of a French father', there were many more. For example, a foreigner's son born in France; a foreigner, after five years' residence, who bought land, managed a factory or farm or married a French wife; even, in exceptional circumstances, any foreigner who wished to become a French citizen. The only proviso for foreigners was that they should swear the civic oath:

I swear to be faithful to the nation, to the law and to the king, and to maintain with all my power the constitution of the realm decreed by the National Constituent Assembly. . .

Apart from the obvious reasons for loss of citizenship, such as naturalisation in another country or some criminal guilt, the Constitution also revealed its sensitivity to the egalitarian and secular nature of citizenship. For it decreed that the status was forfeited

By joining any foreign order of knighthood or any foreign body which would require either proofs of nobility or distinctions of birth, or which would demand religious vows.[29]

The rights which French citizens might expect to enjoy were proclaimed in the famous and influential Declaration of the Rights of Man and of Citizens. These two sets of rights were not kept absolutely discrete in the Declaration. Some of the Articles which overtly referred to citizens' rights included the following:

The law is an expression of the will of the community. All citizens have a right to concur, either personally or by their representatives, in its formation.
. . . every citizen may speak, write, and publish freely, provided he is responsible for the abuse of this liberty . . .
Every citizen has a right, either by himself or his representatives to a free voice in determining the necessity of public contributions . . . and their amount . . .[30]

'Either by *himself* or his representative' was, of course, a hypocritical formula. Despite a strong federalist movement, there was no real chance in a nation of twenty-six millions that Rousseauesque direct democracy would be created. So how were these representatives to be elected and who were they to be? When faced with the possibility of the democratic logic of their high-sounding generalisations, the middle-class members of the Assembly faltered. They introduced a property-qualification for parliamentary candidates. Even more tellingly they prescribed that some citizens should be more equal than others. The canny Sieyes devised the formula of dividing Frenchmen into 'active' and 'passive' citizens. Only active citizens could vote. Passive citizens – for example, domestic servants or those who paid little or no tax – were denied the right. The exact figures for each of these categories have been variously computed. No matter; what is important is the very introduction of the concept of second-class citizenship when the egalitarian potential of the status seemed on the brink of realisation.

Even so, one should not underplay the opportunities the French Revolution provided for participative citizenship. Even the procedures for the summoning of the States-General (the event that proved to be the political catalyst of revolution) generated widespread political consciousness. The prospect of constitutional reform inspired a vast quantity of pamphleteering (including the work of Sieyes already mentioned). Moreover, grievance lists (*cahiers de doléances*) were drawn up for the representatives to take to Versialles. Once the Revolution was under way the popular press flourished, catering for a wide spectrum of tastes: the official newspaper *Le Moniteur*, Desmoulin's liberal *Le Vieux Cordelier*, Marat's radical *L'Ami du Peuple* and Hébert's scurrilous *Le Père Duchesne*. Literacy and the capacity to comprehend the issues involved varied, especially from rural to urban areas. The level among the Parisian artisans was probably quite high. In any case, there was no shortage of interested folk to expound the ideas and demands at street corners, in villages and in army barracks. Clubs too sprang up, again notably but by no means exclusively in Paris, for those who were specially politically conscious. The most famous, the Jacobins, probably had a national membership of about half a million by 1794.

Words and ideas were also transmuted into action. The Constitution of 1791, for all its compromises, enfranchised a larger proportion of men than was to be the case in England until Gladstone's Third Reform Bill. Futhermore, local government and judges were now subject to popular election. In Paris and other major towns 'sectional' assemblies were organised to help direct the revolutionary fervour of the artisan/shopkeeper *sans-culottes*. Moreover, many a Frenchman volunteered for service in the citizen militia, the National Guard, and, after the outbreak of war in 1792, the army. During the critical year 1793-94, when inflation, invasion and civil war seemed about to smash the whole republican edifice, eager citizens became informers and members of surveillance committees or of tribunals to seek out and destroy 'counter-revolutionaries' in the heroically gruesome episode known as the Terror.

The Terror indeed may be viewed, in one of its facets, as an awful warning against taking the concept of citizenship too seriously too quickly in a society insufficiently prepared for the idea. Robespierre personified the dilemma. This small, intense lawyer from Artois strove desperately to raise the Revolution above the squalid politicking of a society in violent transition to an ideal he had mapped out in his own mind from his absorption of Rousseau's theories. Following Jean-Jacques (and indeed the Romans) he believed that the new society should be a republic of virtue; and that the people, being fundamentally virtuous, would share this ideal. But, in the dreadful year of crisis the people very evidently could not be relied upon. Some were openly hostile to the Revolution; some muttered complaints; most were simply apathetic. The atmosphere of the time was remarkably captured a century later by Anatole France in his novel, *The Gods are Athirst*. He has the joiner, Citizen Dupont, say to the main character regarding a petition to expel the moderate Girondin deputies:

I knew you'd come and put your name to it, Citizen Gamelin. Made of the right stuff, you are. That's the trouble with this Section; there aren't enough like you. Lukewarm most of them. No moral backbone. I've put it to the Committee of Surveillance that all those who don't sign this petition don't get their certificate of citizenship.[31]

What were Robespierre and his colleagues of the Committee of Public Safety to do? If the people were not behaving with true citizen virtue because they were still infected by the corruption of society, should they not be forced to assist in the cleansing operation? The apathetic must be galvanised to enthusiastic effort; the hostile expunged. The method was to harness terror to virtue: 'virtue, without which terror is disastrous, and terror, without which virtue is powerless,' Robespierre declared.[32]

But the citizenry of France were not prepared to be forced to be free by such vigorous measures as Robespierre justified. In his hour of need the citizens of Paris refused to rise up to save him from the guillotine. And within five years the people of France gratefully returned to the apolitical security of a paternalist government – the dictatorship of Bonaparte. Even the appellation of 'citizen', which had become almost universal in the autumn of 1793 was shown to be a false fraternity and was quickly discarded.

The government, especially of the Committee of Public Safety, had by no means neglected propaganda and ceremony in attempts to instil an enthusiastic citizen commitment. However, these were for the adult population. Unlike revolutionary régimes of the twentieth century, the French revolutionaries neglected the civic education of the younger generation. In fact, the whole educational system was thrown into chaos as clergy and teachers who refused to take an oath of loyalty were dismissed from their teaching functions. A number of schemes were suggested for reviving and revising in a civic manner the education of the younger generation. The most significant was by Condorcet – that supreme optimist, who wrote his book arguing mankind's rapid progress to a perfect society while in prison awaiting his own final journey to the guillotine. He believed, as a true Enlightenment *philosophe,* in the need for education and in the social benefits that would accrue from a modernised curriculum. He was charged with the task of compiling a report for the comprehensive reorganisation and revitalisation of education. A number of its recommendations were germane to the matter of education for citizenship. Since this was one of the earliest proposals to give such a clear commitment to the question, it is worth quoting at some length.

Condorcet distinguished five levels of education. Even at the primary level, the pupil was to be taught 'what he needed . . . to enjoy his rights to the full'. Furthermore,

This education will be sufficient even for those who take advantage of the lessons intended to fit men for the simplest public functions, to which it is proper that every citizen should be called, such as juror or municipal officer.

Condorcet believed that a critical understanding of public matters, well grounded in school lessons and constantly revised in adult life, was essential to political freedom. And so,

Each Sunday, the teacher will start a public lecture, which will be attended by citizens of all ages . . . Here . . . that part of the national laws, ignorance of which would prevent a citizen from knowing and exercising his rights, will be expanded upon.

Thus, in these schools the first truths of social science will precede their application. Neither the French constitution, nor the Declaration of Rights, will be presented to any class of citizens, as tablets from heaven, which must be adored and believed.

He considered 'moral and political sciences as an essential part of public education', asserting that

A people will never enjoy an assured and permanent freedom, if education in political science is not general, if it is not independent of all social institutions, if the enthusiasm which you stir in the hearts of citizens is not directed by reason . . . [33]

The idea of education being an independent service was also shared by Robespierre at first. However, by the time Condorcet came to present his report, in April 1793, Robespierre and the Mountain group of deputies were in the ascendant and such liberalism was unacceptable. Condorcet's scheme was replaced by another drawn up by Lepeletier and accorded the imprimatur of Robespierre's personal support. In this plan, young citizens were to be socialised into a civic virtue by a Spartan boarding-education. It too remained a mere paper plan.

If the age of revolution failed to create practical programmes of citizenship education, it nevertheless fully consolidated the concept of citizenship, which had hitherto, as we have seen, had various, even ambiguous meanings. In the words of Professor R. R. Palmer, 'In the English language the word 'citizen' in its modern sense is an Americanism, dating from the American Revolution.'[34] The term may have been adopted from the transatlantic study of Rousseau; for the French, as early as Bodin and influenced more by classical ideas that the English, had used the word more readily. But the change of usage was not simply of linguistic habit: it was a renunciation of traditional political relationships. This truth was clearly understood by Paine, whose remarkable political career was rewarded by the conferment of honorary French citizenship. In his *Rights of Man* he wrote:

The romantic and barbarous distinction of man into King and subjects, though it may suit the condition of courtiers, cannot that of citizens; and is exploded by the principle upon which Governments are now founded. Every citizen is a member of the Sovereignty, and, as such, can acknowledge no subjection; and his obedience can be only to the laws.[35]

2.2   THE TRIUMPH OF NATIONALISM

But [universal human values] never are universal, for they always bring with them a clump of native soil from the national sphere, a sphere that no individual can completely leave behind.

Friedrich Meinecke [36]

World citizenship and the enlightenment

The revolutions of the late eighteenth century were but one facet − albeit the most dramatic − of a deep reaction against the values and practices of the age. In the sphere of the arts it expressed itself in Romanticism. Both the Romantic movement and the proponents of popular sovereignty rediscovered the latent sentiment of nationality. The mixture of these beliefs, ideals and emotions in the form of nationalism proved extraordinarily potent. Nationalism has certainly given a distinctive colouring over the past two centuries to the concept of citizenship and the practices of popular education. Moreover, in its great strength it almost totally submerged its antithesis, cosmopolitanism.

Indeed, the eruption of nationalism in the Europe of the late-eighteenth century may in one sense be interpreted as a revolt against the cosmopolitanism that was one of the characteristic features of the age of the Enlightenment. In their commitment to universal standards of behaviour, as in other aspects of their thought, the men of the Enlightenment are reminiscent of such Renaissance thinkers as Montaigne and Bacon. The thinkers of both periods were educated in the Classics and were more interested in what they considered to be the proven power of human reason than the dubious truths of revealed religion. Thus the delightful Diderot, editor of the great French *Encyclopédie,* voracious for knowledge and excitable in his enthusiasms, took Diogenes as his idol; Voltaire, the crusading sage and very embodiment of the Enlightenment concern for reason, justice and toleration, looked to Marcus Aurelius as his model; while many of the *Illuminati* sought to retranslate the medieval City of God into secular terms. Certain basic tenets led inevitably to a universalist frame of reference: an interest in human nature meant that national, racial or religious distinctions were fundamentally superficial; and state boundaries were utterly irrelevant to artistic and scientific endeavours. Furthermore, the interests of the state seemed from experience to lead inexorably to oppression and war rather then human freedom and peace. Voltaire drew the melancholy distinction between the priorities of the citizen and of the citizen of the world when he wrote:

It is sad that, to be a good patriot, one is often the enemy of the rest of humanity . . ..

So it is the human condition that to wish for the greatness of one's fatherland is to wish evil of one's neighbours. The citizen of the universe would be the man who wishes his country never to be either greater or smaller, richer or poorer. [37]

More famously, the cosmopolitan revolutionary Tom Paine emphasised his personal rejection of current eighteenth-century régimes in favour of the ideals of world citizenship: 'Independence is my happiness', he declared in *Rights of Man,* 'and I view things as they are, without regard to place or person; my country is the world and my religion is to do good'.[38] However, it was Schiller, the giant of German literature, who expressed the idea with the greatest force and conviction when he said, 'I write as a citizen of the world who serves no prince. At an early age, I lost my fatherland to trade it for the whole world.'[39]

Furthermore, not only did many of the men of the Enlightenment, like Paine and Schiller, genuinely feel themselves to be citizens of the world and freely use the term, some also considered it their duty to act in accordance with the ideal. For many years d'Holbach entertained a galaxy of international talent to dinner – for example, Franklin from America, Beccaria from Italy, Sterne and Priestley from England, besides distinguished French thinkers such as Diderot, and Condorcet, . . . it is there,' declared Diderot, 'that the true citizen of the world is to be found'.[40] The English writer, Oliver Goldsmith, proudly adopted the title in his *Letters from a Citizen of the World to his Friends in the East.* Of those who sought to give practical application to the concept, one may mention Franklin, who urged the recognition of the 'Common Rights of Mankind' a century and a half before the UN document was compiled; while a number of the anti-slavery campaigners used the argument to deny the moral validity of enslavement.

However, the *philosophes,* such as Voltaire, were not great, original philosophers. Their attachment to the cosmopolitan ideal was not presented as a closely argued thesis, but rather as a *desideratum* derived from their concern for free intellectual discourse, their interest in human nature and their objections to contemporary governments. The great philosophers of the age who were interested in international affairs were Rousseau and Kant, of whom Kant is particularly significant for our purposes. Both were anxious to seek an answer to the terrible scourge of war. But Rousseau's almost Aristotelian concept of citizenship, let alone his emphasis on the need for a sense of national cohesion, led him totally to reject any idea of world citizenship. Nor did that precise Prussian professor, Kant, formulate the concept in any systematic way. However, his notion of Cosmopolitan Law provides a context in which such an idea can be nourished. In his two important works, *Idea for a Universal History* and *Thoughts on Perpetual Peace,* he argued an essentially optimistic thesis. It is that, through the agonies of struggle and violence, man's rational nature will ultimately bring him to the drafting of and obedience to an overarching world or cosmopolitan law, which will ensure peace. Kant's concept of a cosmopolitan law, existing over and above state and international laws, has evident affinities to Stoic and Christian thought. For example, in defining lawful freedom as an inalienable right of mankind, he declared that it

is affirmed and ennobled by the principle of a lawful relation between man himself and higher beings, if indeed he believes in such beings. This is so, because he thinks of himself, in accordance with these very principles, as a citizen of a transcendental world as well as of the world of sense.[41]

However, Kant was realist enough to recognise both the moral and practical existence of states. No more than the Stoics was he arguing for the desirability or likelihood of a world government. He did, however, foresee the evolution of a loose confederation of states as the end-product of historical evolution. He thus conceived of the obligation of the citizen to obey the local laws of his state as but an historical milestone on the road to a union of moral states acting in obedience to the cosmopolitan law. Moreover, this progress can be enhanced by the pressures of citizens; for, Kant claimed, only those states with constitutions which allow policy to be shaped by the citizenry are likely to pursue this moral course. He accepted that the process would be slow, and consequently admitted the need for 'a long and intensive education . . . an education of the spirit of all citizens in every country'.[42] Nevertheless, ultimately the conflict between the individual's obligation *qua* citizen to obey the law of the state and his obligation *qua* man to obey the cosmopolitan law will cease as the member states of the universal confederation cease to contravene the cosmopolitan law. As a consequence, the moral responsibilities of citizen and man will coincide and citizenship become a universal status. In Kant's words, 'The individuals who compose the state' whose constitution is 'formed in accordance with cosmopolitan law . . . may be regarded as citizens of one world-state.'[43] Moreover, mankind's potential can only be realised by the achievement of such a world citizenship. '. . . the highest purpose of Nature', Kant declared, 'will be at last realised in the establishment of a universal Cosmo-political Institution, in the bosom of which all the original capacities and endowments of the human species will be unfolded and developed.'[44]

The terms 'world state' and 'Cosmo-political Institution' must not be misunderstood. As we have seen, Kant did not advocate world government. Indeed, resistance to the very idea of concentrating power in a form of world government was very intense among the writers of the turn of the eighteenth century. The mood was one of suspicion of all political power and of faith in the beneficence of individual human reason and wisdom. This attitude was formulated with considerable conviction by Jeremy Bentham, the English eccentric genius who coined the very word 'international'. Bentham, perhaps even more than Kant, had enormous faith in the efficacy of public opinion, or 'popular sanction' as he preferred to call it. In international affairs he held that the evils of the world which emanated from government policies could be exposed and expunged by the force of public opinion through the medium of a free press. As revealed by the title of his tract, *Plan for an Universal and Perpetual Peace,* Bentham's main concern was for the elimination of war. But he was also opposed to international treaties, colonies and trade barriers. Bentham was personally the complete cosmopolitan in his outlook, famed as the greatest expert on constitutional and penal law throughout Europe and the Americas. If international contacts on the personal plane could be so mutually advantageous, how much happier would the world be if these were increased at the expense of the abrasive relations between governments?

The basic Benthamite idea has persisted to this day that the ordinary citizen can have a vision of a more peaceful, just and happy world and has both the right and power to coerce his own government to policies consonant with this ideal. Throughout the nineteenth century the creation of peace societies was encouraged by the increased carnage of war, and the increased circulation of newspapers. The former revealed the need for mobilising opinion, the latter provided the opportunity. However, most exponents of popular peace movements were not as naive as Bentham in expecting the public to be naturally internationalist and pacific in temper: public opinion had to be educated. On the other hand, as we shall see below (pp. 77–80), school systems in the nineteenth century were either controlled by the nation-state or at any rate engulfed in the prevailing nationalist atmosphere.

Origins of the nationalist idea

The countervailing force of nationalism proved so overwhelmingly powerful that the cosmopolitanism which briefly flowered in the eighteenth century has had a desperate struggle to survive at all ever since. This triumph of nationalism over cosmopolitanism should occasion little surprise, for the universalist sentiments of the Enlightenment grew only shallow roots. Rousseau cantankerously questioned the sincerity of those who professed world citizenship. In the *Emile* he accused 'such a philosopher' of 'loving the Tartars, in order to avoid loving his neighbours.'[45] In the first version of the *Social Contract* he was even more forthright. He wrote of a world society as 'a veritable chimaera' and condemned,

those pretended cosmopolitans who, in justifying their love for the human race, make a boast of loving all the world in order to enjoy the privilege of loving no one.[46]

What is perhaps more to the point is that in practice these cosmopolites were an educated and privileged élite, immersed in a French culture which had staked a claim to universal application. In the words of the French scholar, Hazard, such people 'identified Paris with Cosmopolis'.[47] In a cultural if not a geographical sense they were as a nation, bound together by a common language and mode of life, and by those same expressions of identity living a life distinct from the poorer and less educated majority.

By the late eighteenth century, however, nationalism in its modern ideological sense was emerging, its protean nature rendering it more acceptable than any other as a surrogate religion – and as a stimulant rather than a narcotic creed. The idea was abroad in the late eighteenth century that a people enjoying the cultural homogeneity of common language and traditions should recognise an especial bond of emotion and loyalty among themselves and to the land they inhabit. We have already seen that, at the same time, the revolutionary movements were loudly proclaiming the principle of popular sovereignty. Now, as Archbishop William Temple pointed out, 'The abstract logic of democracy may tend towards cosmopolitanism'[48], for 'the people' have no theoretical interest in the boundaries of states which dynastic jealousies had caused to be so bloodily defended and extended over the centuries. However, 'the sovereign people' came to be identified with the nation. This was partly a conscious reaction (especially in England) against the cosmopolitan pretensions of the aristocracy. And partly the current spirit of nationalism made such an identification natural. Additionally, however, it was an exceedingly useful device for refocussing a people's loyalty away from the monarch. Divine-right monarchy was an elegantly simple device for evoking emotional attachment. An aggregate of sovereign citizens could hardly perform that function. But the nation, personified through symbols and rituals could. And did.

The French Revolutionaries showed the way with the tricolore and above all Marianne, the personification of the new France and whose very millinery – the cap of liberty – proclaimed the new régime. The old régime had been symbolically overcome with the fall of the Bastille, the anniversary of which was celebrated by festivals throughout the land. The *ci-devant* subjects, now citizens, assembled before altars of the fatherland to read the slogan there inscribed: 'The citizen is born, lives and dies for the fatherland'. There too they sang patriotiç songs and swore to defend national unity. Thus citizenship became defined by nationality as well as by legal, political and social rights.

The French Revolution politicised the cultural concept of nationality. Subsequently (and one might add, consequently), during much of the nineteenth century the association of nationalism with popular sovereignty encouraged the liberals of central and southern Europe to plot and agitate for the realisation of the ideal in their lands. National unification or liberation (depending on local circumstance) and government according to a duly framed constitution seemed but two sides of the same reformist political medal. The upheavals of 1848, whatever their deep economic causes, were manipulated by the intellectuals in attempts to implement the principle of national self-determination. With logical but fearful courage some demanded democratic constitutions and rights despite the horror many entertained of 'the vile multitude'. The need to balance the demands of nationalism, justice, democracy and stability is interestingly reflected, for example, in the declaration issued by the Pre-Parliament, which met in Frankfurt to prepare the way for a national German government. Its definition of the franchise was a masterly piece of imprecision. It stated that 'Every citizen who is of age and is independent, is to be entitled to vote and be elected'. 'Independent', meaning economically so, was interpreted in some states as to exclude even wage-earners. Yet the list of basic rights at the end of the document was very comprehensive, including:

Equality of political rights for all without distinction of religious confessions . . .
Equal eligibility of all citizens for communal and state offices.
General German state citizenship.[49]

Nationalism finds its most persuasive raison d'être and its most potent support where nations and states do not coincide. In nineteenth-century Europe most nationalist movements sought to attain their aim by the disintegration of multi-national empires (the Ottoman, Romanov and Habsburg) or the unification of ethnically homogeneous peoples dispersed among numerous states (as in Germany and Italy). In either case, commitment to the nationalist cause involved discarding the loyalty owed by the citizen to the established state. A citizen of the Habsburg imperial state must seek to become a citizen of, for instance, the Hungarian nation-state; a citizen of the Grand Duchy of Baden must become a citizen of the German nation-state. In so far as citizenship can be said to have existed in any meaningful sense in these lands before the revolutionary constitutions of 1848, then nationalism required the individual to betray one citizenship for another. What is more, failure to behave in this treacherous way might itself be construed as treason against one's nation. The Hungarian declaration of separation from the Habsburgs was certainly crystal clear on this issue:

We . . . hereby proclaim . . . that all authorities, communes, towns, and the civil officers both in the countries and cities, are completely set free and released from all the obligations under which they stood, by oath or otherwise, to the said House of Hapsburg-Lorraine, and that any individual daring to contravene this decree . . . shall be treated and punished as guilty of high treason.[50]

However, a distinction is often drawn between the style of nationalist thinking derived from the French Revolution and that derived from German Romanticism. Where the former emphasised the political citizenship role of the members of the French nation, the Germans were at pains to underline the sense of belonging to the *Volk* derived from common blood and soil. For the German theorists like Herder nationalism was a spiritual rather than a political concept. And yet, whatever the starting-point, it became increasingly evident that an individual could not comfortably enjoy the status of citizen in a nation-state without being and feeling part of the nation, whether that be defined linguistically, racially or by any other test. Throughout Europe from c.1790 to c.1920 the most common test was language. Apart from the cultural identity this provides it is quite evident that full civic participation is extraordinarily difficult without firm command of the official language. Indeed, as early as the French Revolution all official documents and pronouncements were issued in French as part of a deliberate policy of Gallicising citizens who spoke other tongues such as Breton, Provençal, German or Italian. Two generations later, John Stuart Mill expressed the matter succinctly:

Free institutions are next to impossible in a country made up of different nationalities. Among a people without fellow-feeling, especially if they read and speak different languages, the united public opinion, necessary to the working of representative government, cannot exist.[51]

Nineteenth-century nationalism and citizen identity

No state has undertaken a more complex task of national assimilation than the USA:

Here is not merely a nation but
A teeming Nation of nations,

wrote the nineteenth-century poet Walt Whitman. For although the predominant culture has been, and certainly was in the nineteenth century, WASP (White Anglo-Saxon Protestant), constant waves of immigrants brought people from West Africa, East Asia, Latin America and most parts of Europe. Even as late as 1920 seventeen states had more than 15 per cent foreign-born, four, more than 25 per cent. In seeking security and social identity many immigrants experienced contrary national attractions: to retreat into their own comfortable ethnic sub-group or to pursue complete assimilation as 'hundred per cent Americans'. Most, especially those of the second generation, hankered after full Americanisation. If, therefore, a crucial facet of the modern concept of citizenship is nationality, then the American 'melting-pot' experience throws into sharp relief the distinction between the legal process of naturalisation and the socio-psychological process of assimilation.

The idea that citizenship may be acquired by a voluntary contract of naturalisation persisted from colonial times (p. 30). After the lapse of a decent period of time (usually a minimum of five years), the immigrant was eligible to be initiated into U.S. citizenship and recognised as an American national. Besides the formal oath of allegiance the novitiate citizen was required to learn in elementary form the principles which lay at the heart of American nationality in the political sense: the basics of the Declaration of Independence, the Constitution, the Gettysburg Address. But this was merely the visible surface of the subtle process of transmutation that changed an Italian or Chinese or Mexican into an American. Social pressures, especially among children and adolescents, to conform in styles of speech, dress and manners, were frequently irresistible. For the same age-groups the state provided a system of schooling which, as we shall see (p. 78), strove to inculcate the knowledge and attitudes of which, it was thought, hundred per cent Americans were made.

It is a rare nation-state that can boast a totally homogeneous and assimilated citizenry. Yet the very essence of nationalism requires ethnic homogeneity. What then is the status of minorities who cannot or will not be culturally and/or politically digested into the majority? In what sense can they be said to be citizens of the state in which they happen to live? The anomaly of minorities in a nationalist age could be handled broadly in one of six ways: toleration, conversion, discrimination, persecution, expulsion and annihilation.

Throughout Europe in the nineteenth century toleration was attempted honestly in only a few states, notably Austria. Programmes of cultural conversion became much more common, largely through the enforcement of the majority language, especially as a medium of instruction in schools. How could the legitimacy of the new German state, for instance, be based on nationality when Poles lived in Posen, Danes in Schleswig, French in Alsace-Lorraine? A very deliberate policy of Germanisation was undertaken in the 1880s and 90s. But the clearest example was Hungary. This large state which achieved 'home rule' within the Habsburg Empire in 1867, was a veritable babel of Magyars, Poles, Romanians, Serbs and Germans by linguistic identity. In 1868 there was issued the Hungarian Law of Nationalities, which in effect proclaimed the incompatibility of the principles of equal citizenship and 'pure' nationality in such a multi-ethnic state. For although it confirmed that 'all citizens of Hungary . . . form a single nation . . . to which all citizens of the country irrespective of their nationality belong, and enjoy equal rights', in the next breath the drafters of the law withdrew that equality in favour of linguistic conformity: 'Considering that, in view of its political unity, the language of the State is Magyar . . . The official language of the Government in all Government services is and will remain Magyar.'[52] Hard on the heels of this law came other provisions requiring government courts and universities to use Magyar. Non-Magyar speakers were clearly disadvantaged – yet in total they comprised just over half the population. The incentive to become Magyarised – or to secede – was powerful.

It is rare indeed for a national minority not to feel discriminated against. In the United Kingdom in the nineteenth century, although there were no anti-Irish discriminatory laws, in terms of economic independence and development, most Irish were justified in feeling a national minority and consequently second-class citizens. The term 'second-class' citizens aptly describes the status of minorities in the nationalist Europe of the nineteenth century. It is, however, an anachronism, having been coined in the 1940s to describe US blacks. Indeed, although the problem of minorities became a vital issue in the 1919 peace settlements (pp. 94–96), none were, in fact, denied citizenship rights with such vicious thoroughness as those who could be classified as 'racially' distinct, namely American negroes and European, particularly Russian and Polish, Jews.

Nationalism has been responsible for a marked intensification of discord in both intra-state and inter-state relations in the twentieth century. Such outcomes would have shocked two of the most distinguished theorists of the concept. For Fichte in his early writings and Mazzini were deeply committed to the cosmopolitan ideal. The theories of the Saxon philosopher and the Genoese revolutionary had important similarities. Both had a mystical belief in the progress of humanity to some form of unity and both believed in the historic responsiblility of their own nations to play the vital leading role in this process. Fichte believed that mind is more real than matter and that the individual mind is but part of the universal. But even in prosaic, political terms he believed that for security and the protection of rights, 'a commonwealth . . . must contain the possibility of uniting the whole of mankind.'[53] Even when, in the face of the French invasion and teaching in the Prussian atmosphere of Berlin, he delivered his *Addresses to the German Nation* he justified his nationalism in terms of the benefit to humanity at large. The Germans, he claimed from the evidence of the superiority of their language, are alone capable of pure nationalist commitment and are in consequence 'the elect of the universal divine plan.'[54] But that divine plan, Fichte came to believe in spite of himself, involved the absorption of the individual mind not in the universal but in the mind of the nation. Therein lay the duty of the citizen.

Mazzini dedicated himself to his ideal, in freedom and in prison, in Italy and in exile, with such zeal that he became something of the patron-saint of nationalism. Yet for him nationalism was anything but an exclusive ideology.

His vision was rather a synthesis of three of the most potent political ideas that influenced intellectuals at the time, namely popular sovereignty and schemes for abolishing war in Europe as well as the principle of nationality. He believed in a divinely ordained historical progress to a human society bonded together by brotherly love and respect exuded by contented, democratically governed nation-states. Only by achieving national freedom and unity can a people contribute to this design devised by God. 'Nationalism', he wrote, gives a people 'the freedom of the city of mankind.'[55] The realisation of unity, therefore, is but a means to an end: 'A people destined to achieve great things for the welfare of humanity must one day or other be constituted a nation'[56]; for 'Nationality should be to humanity only what the division of labour is in the workshop.'[57] Nevertheless, the process requires leadership and he justified his devotion to the cause of Italian unity by his belief that this was Italy's destiny and responsibility:

. . . the parent thought of my every design, [he wrote in 1864] was a presentiment that regenerated Italy was destined to arise the *initiatrix* of a new life, and a new and powerful Unity to all the nations of Europe.[58]

However, none of this could be achieved, so Mazzini argued, without the responsible participation of a civically conscious populace. Despairing of the older generation set in their apathetic ways he put his whole-hearted, some would say, naive faith in the youth properly educated and alert to their duties and opportunities: hence his secret societies (and their may imitations), Young Italy and Young Europe. He furthermore insisted that government in nation-states should be substantially decentralised so that the citizens could administer the affairs of their own communes and by the political experience thus gained, wisely judge the activities of their national government and foster the brotherhood of nations.

In the event, the centralising power of the modern bureaucratised state underpinned by the theory of Hegel ensured that Mazzini's open-hearted nationalism was almost totally overwhelmed by a variant which demanded the utter commitment of the citizen to his state and the total absorption of his interests by this superior organism. In his *Lectures on the Philosophy of History*, which he delivered at the University of Berlin some two decades after Fichte's Addresses, Hegel proclaimed that 'The State is the Divine Idea as it exists on Earth' and that 'all the worth which the human being possesses – all spiritual reality, he possesses only through the State.'[59] The corollary of Hegel's virtual deification of the state was that it is the sole fount of morality. The individual can in consequence lead a properly fulfilled moral life only by obedience to the laws of his state. Commitment to the two lower levels of social activity (namely the family and the economic life of 'civil society') had to be consigned to decidedly subordinate places. Hegel was indeed at pains to distinguish between economic man (the bourgeois) and political man (the citizen). Furthermore, any Mazzinian notion of fraternal relations between nations was quite out of the question. There was no valid supranational morality: the interest and strength of the individual state was the only criterion of political behaviour. Hegel's system thus raised the political relationship of the individual citizen to the state to a naturally ordained priority akin to the Aristotelian belief in man as a political animal. The marriage of Hegel's 'statism' with the current nationalism gave birth to the conviction that the individual has identity and meaning only *qua* citizen of a nation-state. An individual who lacks recognised legal citizenship or who is an ethnic misfit in his state is thus in danger of being cast into the limbo of the incomplete human. Furthermore, anyone who dares pretend a loyalty to a moral code embracing mankind as a whole is guilty of a blasphemy against the multiplicity of ethnic systems shaped by the divine purpose through the historical experiences of the separate states into which the human race is properly divided. Citizenship and nationality are one.

In the gradual process of transition from the status and concept of subject to citizen, the nationalist idea was historically significant. By consolidating the principle of popular sovereignty and weakening monarchical authority it considerably accelerated the pace of change. In a symbiotic relationship the patriotic and xenophobic citizen demanded more overtly nationalist policies of his government, while the government demanded an increasing concentration of loyalty to the state. Other foci of social identity, such as the region and the church, were demagnetised of their former powerful attractions. In practical terms the citizen could be required to display his national commitment through speech and action. As in so many other ways the French Revolution set the scene. Thus Barère declared, 'It is treason to the fatherland to leave the citizens in ignorance of the national language.'[60] While the *levée en masse* introduced the idea that the army was not a professional, even mercenary body, but the citizens in arms. Whether citizens enjoyed new privileges to compensate for the loss of old pluralities and the enforcement of new duties depended on the political and social reforms forthcoming from the nation-state.

2.3 NINETEENTH-CENTURY LIBERALISM AND SOCIALISM

We who were reformers from the beginning always said that the enfranchisement of the people was an end in itself. We said, and we were much derided for saying so, that only citizenship makes the moral man; and only citizenship gives that self respect which is the true basis of respect for others, and without which there is no lasting social order or real morality.

T. H. Green[61]

The extension of citizenship

Not since the days of Athens at the apogee of its political and intellectual sophistication had citizenship been considered of such import as in the urbanised societies of the nineteenth century. We may identify five influences from the late eighteenth century which led to this concentration of interest. As we have seen (pp. 41–44), the radical movement in England strengthened the national tradition of political freedom and set the scene for a modernisation of the parliamentary form of government. With the tide of emigration particularly to Canada, Australia and New Zealand these political principles flowed to other continents. Secondly, the Industrial Revolution contributed its own particular force to the shaping of citizenship. By concentrating the proletariat in unpleasant and degrading conditions it provided them with both the opportunity and motive for a growth of political consciousness which expressed itself characteristically in the formation of co-operative movements, friendly societies and trade unions. Furthermore, insofar as at least a basic education is a necessary condition for the intelligent and responsible exercise of the civic role, industrialisation assisted here also. For the state felt impelled to provide elementary schooling for the sake of an efficient work-force. In the third place, the French Revolution provided a glimpse of what might be. Despite the horrors of the Terror, the freezing (to use Saint-Just's word) of civic initiative and the retrogression of Bonapartism and the 1815 Restoration, the French ideals of citizenship and of constitutional government provided a pattern upon which European liberals of the early nineteenth century modelled their demand. Thus, when revolutions broke out in Portugal, Spain and Naples in 1820, it was the restoration of the French-drafted constitutions of 1812 that provided the centre-piece of the demands for reform.

However, the failure of the French Revolution to effect very much in the way of social welfare reform, combined with the intensification of such need by the Industrial Revolution, generated powerful socialist doctrines and movements – the fourth influence. The relationship of this thread in the history of popular mobilisation to the particular issue of citizenship is ambivalent. On the one hand, through the creation of working-class and socialist organisations and parties, it provided opportunities for non-violent participation and the exertion of political leverage, which the working class would not otherwise have had. On the other hand, socialism in its Marxist form as we shall see below, was suspicious of the citizen-state relationship as contrary to the class interests of the proletariat.

Finally, the theory of citizenship was attended to more explicitly in the nineteenth century than at any time before or since, with the exception of the pioneering work of Aristotle. The Idealist German philosophers, notably Kant and Hegel, by so emphasising the ethical basis of duty and the prime significance of the state, forced on to the agenda of discussion the political and moral relationship of the individual to that institution.

Meanwhile, across the Atlantic the USA, following its own revolutionary severance from colonial control, was forced to wrestle with the issue of citizenship in hydra-headed form. The constitution, based on the theory of popular sovereignty, had of course to be operated in practice. This required both political institutions like parties and the political education of the populace. These needs were perhaps more intensely felt than in the Old World precisely because of the opportunity to create a state almost *de novo*. But added to this were the three major problems of the federal relationship, of slavery and of massive foreign immigration.

All these influences produced a case for the illogicality and injustice of confining the status and rights of citizenship to an élite portion of the populace. Even if 'hedgers and ditchers' strove to defend a contrary argument, the case was fundamentally unarguable. For, if a segment of society was given full citizenship rights in the name of popular sovereignty, in neither reason nor justice could it be denied to the whole circle of the populace. Even so, opposition to a democratic interpretation of citizenship was mounted from a number of quarters. The conservatives, by virtue of their fear of popular ignorance and extremism, entertained the most sombre doubts. In the context of the 1832 Reform Bill in Britain the Duke of Wellington pronounced the unreformed system beyond improvement; while Lord John Russell earned the soubriquet 'Finality Jack' by declaring the 1832 measure, which increased the small electorate by less than 50 per cent, as the farthest he was prepared to go. In France ten years later Guizot condemned the demand for universal male suffrage as an 'itch for political rights' that would be harmful to liberty and public order.[62] But even the liberals were ambivalent in their support for democratisation. The European middle classes, while wanting increased political influence for themselves, were in no hurry to endanger their economic interests by plunging into the uncertainties of mass enfranchisement.

Nor was conservative recalcitrance in the face of the broadening of citizenship confined to parliamentary opposition to extensions of the franchise. Highly successful opposition was also mounted to a whole variety of means by which a wider spectrum of the population could attain an effective civic status. For example, the legalisation of trade unions and the provision of effective education for citizenship in the schools were delayed (pp. 71 & 80–86). Perhaps even more fundamentally obstacles were placed against reasonable opportunities to express critical political opinion. Radical journalists throughout Europe had to struggle most vigorously against taxation and censorship of the press. In Britain, the last newspaper duty was not abolished until 1861; and not until twenty years later did France introduce a law guaranteeing the press against government interference. In some other states, most notably Russia, censorship continued unrelaxed.

Nevertheless, by c. 1920 citizenship existed as a reality for a larger proportion of the European population than a century previously. In that sense demands for and concessions of reform were successful. But what were the motives of those demanding and those conceding? Clearly reforms were extracted from those on the right of the political spectrum out of fear – fear of the violent consequences of continued resistance. Memories of 1789 were vivid, and were in any case refreshed by 1848. Some intellectual politicians, like Lamartine in France, were persuaded that a broader spread of political involvement would be beneficial to the state because of the corruption and injustices of élitism. Many other politicians jockeyed for the support of the populace. In surveying the political history of Europe in the nineteenth century cynicism is quite in order. The views of an English radical journalist writing at the time of the 'Great' Reform Bill could be translated to wider application:

The promoters of the Reform Bill projected it . . . to consolidate [our aristocratic institutions] by a reinforcement of sub-aristocracy from the middle classes . . . The only difference between the Whigs and Tories is this – the Whigs would give the shadow to preserve the substance; the Tories would not give the shadow, because stupid as they are, the millions will not stop at shadows but proceed onwards to realities.[63]

Nor were the motives of those who campaigned for citizenship rights necessarily any more altruistic. Participation in political processes was demanded not just out of any sense of civic virtue but also as a means to economic improvement. There was no need to accept the whole panoply of Marxist theory to believe that those who controlled the political institutions looked after the material interests of their own kind. And so, as the Rev. J. R. Stephens, one of the Chartist leaders explained, that movement was more a knife-and-fork question than a question of the ballot-box. Political enfranchisement was seen throughout Europe as a means to the end of economic improvement. Leaders might proclaim the political justice of enfranchising the producers of wealth; but insofar as that working class rallied to meeting-halls, banners or barricades they wanted political justice to take on a tangible form.

An obvious, simple demand was indeed for the suffrage – a clear if rather crude indicator of citizenship. By this test there were precious few full citizens in Europe at the beginning of the nineteenth century. The widest franchises c. 1830 were to be found in the small states of south and south-west Germany – Baden, Bavaria, Hesse-Darmstadt, Nassau and Würtemberg. Baden, for example, had an electorate of about one million. France, with a population of some 30 million and for all its revolutionary democratic pretensions, boasted a *pays légal* (electorate) of a mere 90,000. In England, with two-thirds the population of France, a little over 400,000 had the franchise. In a number of countries, most notably Russia, of course, there was no parliament at all.

Where a parliamentary system did exist in 1830 the main restriction on the franchise was the need for wealth, normally in the form of property, especially land. For instance, the qualification in France was the payment of 300 francs in direct taxation, which in practice, given the widespread ownership of and investment in land, meant a landowner electorate. The same was true, though to a slightly lesser extent, of the bizarre English 'system', despite its confusion of potwalloper and scot and lot borough franchises. Religion too could disenfranchise a man, particularly if he were a Catholic in a Protestant state or a Jew. Religious toleration gradually opened up the rights of citizenship in Britain. Local government was liberalised in this way by the Repeal of the Test and Corporation Acts (p. 31) in 1828. The Catholic Emancipation Act followed in the next year. The Jews had to wait until 1858. On the continent anti-Semitism became so rife in France, Germany, Austria-Hungary and Russia towards the end of the century that Jews could scarcely count themselves citizens on a par with their Gentile co-nationals, whatever their legal rights.

Popular pressure ensured the gradual extension of the franchise throughout the century. In this regard Britain was unusual. There was little violence, apart from the notorious Peterloo Massacre. A French witness to the melting away of the drenched and bedraggled Chartist supporters at Kennington Common in 1848 commented that there would never be a revolution in England because of the climate! Or perhaps the governing and capitalist classes were too canny. The electorate was steadily expanded and electoral corruption gradually expunged by a constant trickle of legislative enactments. On the continent, in contrast, the revolutionary outbursts of 1848, although temporarily extracting enfranchisement concessions, provoked a powerful conservative backlash with substantial reductions in voting rights.

The whole process of translating the doctrine of popular sovereignty into universal adult suffrage was erratic and was by no means completed until well into the twentieth century. Even among the states which had fully experienced the stimuli of the political and economic revolutions of the eighteenth and nineteenth centuries, few could claim to be truly democratic before 1914 – only Australia, New Zealand and Norway had introduced a reasonably universal suffrage by that date. Italy did not even abolish its literacy test until 1911. But the exercise of voting rights is only an indirect way of participating in government. If citizenship is to have its fullest meaning it must include the right, as Aristotle argued (p. 3), of direct engagement in the process of ruling. Generally speaking the restrictions on candidature for European assemblies in the nineteenth century were tighter than for merely casting a vote. For instance, in France under the Orleanist July Monarchy (even with its 'Citizen King') electors had to be 25 and pay 200 francs a year in direct taxes, whereas candidates for the Assembly had to be 30 and pay 300 francs in taxation. In Britain, although the ownership of property ceased to be a qualification for an MP in 1859, because MPs received no payment until 1911 no one without private means could afford to enter parliament. And so the gradual lowering of restrictions on the suffrage came in advance of any lowering of restrictions on parliamentary candidature.

In countries where the traditional hold of the bourgeoisie and squirearchy on local government was loosened, more opportunities for involvement in public affairs was available at the community than the national level. The early bold attempts of the French Revolutionaries and, following their example, of Stein in Prussia, were soon reversed – by Napoleonic centralisation in the one case and Junker reaction in the other. It was left therefore to England to undertake the earliest permanent opening up of local government to more democratic modes of operation. By requiring towns to have duly elected corporations, the Municipal Corporations Act of 1835 overwhelmed the corrupt lethargy of centuries. The new urban régimes were able to encourage that civic participation and pride which became such a positive feature of English citizenship for some one and a half centuries. The French had to wait until 1884 before they could benefit from a similar reform. But even then the two systems were still marked by their historical differences. In England, while the mayor was the honorific leading citizen, decked in a decorative chain of office, the French mayor had real authority as the elected representative of his municipality and link with the national government, as symbolised by his tricolore sash. In Germany, the position was different again. The long-established tradition of urban citizenship (p. 21) was by no means overlaid by a uniform national citizenship after 1871. For example, the status of citizen of Hamburg could still at the end of the century be attained only by the payment of a substantial fee (p. 171). Before leaving Europe, a brief word must be said about Switzerland, where, after the civil war of 1847, extremely democratic systems were introduced at both cantonal and federal levels, albeit with more enthusiasm by some cantons than others. The communal assemblies of all adult males provided a unique example of direct democracy à la grecque in an age of large complex nation-states.

The complexity of the USA

Because of the complexity and importance of the American situation it is convenient to deal with the USA separately. Nowhere since the theoretical propositions of Aristotle had the nature of citizenship been given so much consideration as in the USA in the quarter century c. 1850–75. The revolutionary democratic ideal was easier to sustain in America than in France. Washington had shrunk from any temptation to become a Napoleon; nor had there been, of course, a monarchical restoration. For a while, none the less, there was quite widespread suspicion of the masses. Then the potential of ordinary folk to play the active role of citizens was dramatically proclaimed by the election of Andrew Jackson to the presidency in 1828. In a bitterly fought campaign in which characters were trailed in the mud, the colourful short-tempered 'Old Hickory' secured a triumphant majority. Born into a family of abject poverty, Jackson made his way by sheer perseverance on the frontier in Tennessee. Through this experience he came to have a healthy respect for the commonsense and abilities of the ordinary man. His policy of encouraging those qualities has consequently been termed 'Jacksonian democracy'. Founded on the sturdy, armed, agrarian frontiersmen, Jackson's optimism concerning their qualities was more than a little reminiscent of Machiavellian civic virtue. 'The duties of public office,' he declared, 'are, or at least admit of being readily made, so plain and simple that men of intelligence may readily qualify for public office.'[64]

The first half of the nineteenth century and especially the 1830s and 1840s indeed witnessed a rapid democratisation of American political life – a process which Jackson symbolised as much as he personally promoted. The only real parallel at the time was the tiny, also federal, state of Switzerland. The civic consciousness and involvement in local community affairs of so many Americans struck the shrewd French observer Alexis de Tocqueville very forcibly. 'In no country in the world has the principle of association been more successfully used, or applied to a greater multitude of objects, than in

America.'[65] In constitutional terms the original thirteen seaboard states individually abolished their property qualifications for the franchise between 1778 and 1856. And although some introduced a replacement tax qualification, the rise in prosperity was so rapid that by the middle of the century most adult white males met that requirement. In addition, the religious and property qualifications for public office were gradually abolished. In the meantime, too, as the frontier was pushed westward and new states were admitted to the Union, their constitutions were from their foundation of a democratic style. They could hardly be other if they were to operate in harmony with the qualities of self-reliance and freedom which characterised frontier life.

The lowering of the barriers of wealth to voting rights in the USA were simple matters of political will and rising prosperity. The issue of citizenship was, however, very much more complicated than that, entangled as it was in the constitutional-legal problems of the federal-state relationship and the institution of slavery. How was an individual's state citizenship related to his status as a citizen of the USA? Which had priority? If the people were collectively sovereign, was the relevant collectivity the state or the nation? Was a slave a citizen? And if not, why not? These were exceptionally difficult and vital questions, yet the Founding Fathers ducked them. Indeed, except in Article IV section 2 (p. 47), the Constitution did not use the term 'citizen' at all; and that article was so brief as to invite confusingly different interpretations during the first half of the nineteenth century.

In 1857 the two issues of state versus national citizenship and the status of slaves coincided and were apparently resolved by a Supreme Court ruling in the Dred Scott case. As new territories were settled in the west the question of whether slavery should be allowed there was inevitably raised. In 1820 Congress accepted the Missouri Compromise. This prohibited slavery north of parallel 36°30'. Now, Dred Scott was a slave who had been taken by his master into this free territory. Several years later, abetted by a new master who was opposed to slavery, he claimed his freedom by virtue of this move. After a decade a ponderous litigation, reaching the Supreme Court, the Chief Justice issued judgement. First he declared that the case was void because Scott could not sue since he was not a citizen. Negroes, he declared, were 'not included' as citizens in the Constitution. Nor was it in the power of a single state to make a Negro 'a citizen of the United States, and endue him with the full rights of citizenship in every other State without their consent.'[66] Secondly, he declared, people who are citizens have their property rights protected by the Fifth Amendment. Slaves are property. Consequently the Missouri Compromise was unconstitutional if it allowed slaves freedom in the event of being taken across the line.

For those in the North the judgement was a bombshell. It simultaneously denied the status of citizenship to any Black and it asserted the priority of the state over the federal government. By implication, citizenship in the USA meant primarily the relationship of the individual to his state and only secondarily to his nation. Moreover, only the white man was eligible for this status in any case. It took a bloody civil war to reverse this twin definition of

American citizenship. In the aftermath of that war a series of enactments sought to clarify the whole issue. In 1865 the Thirteenth Amendment abolished slavery, thus destroying any basic distinction between black and white. In the following year the Civil Rights Act was passed, pronouncing that

all persons born in the United States . . . are hereby declared to be citizens of the United States; and such citizens, of every race and color . . . . shall have the same right[s], in every State and Territory in the United States . . . [as are] enjoyed by white citizens, and shall be subject to like punishments, pains, and penalties . . .[67]

In order to reinforce the principle it was written into the Constitution as the Fourteenth Amendment:

All persons born or naturalized in the United States, and subject to the jurisdiction thereof, are citizens of the United States and of the States wherein they reside. No State shall make or enforce any law which shall abridge the privileges or immunities of citizens of the United States.

The legal status of citizenship was clear: it belonged by right of birth or naturalisation and it adhered primarily to the American Union. The military decision made by the Federal armies was now legitimised by law in the years of the antebellum peace. But the Fourteenth Amendment made no mention of the suffrage. The Fifteenth Amendment was consequently necessary in order to confirm that

The right of citizens of the United States to vote shall not be denied or abridged by the United States or by any State on account of race, color or previous condition of servitude.

In the brief liberal glow of the Reconstruction period some Blacks, ill-equipped in education and experience as they were, seized their new opportunities. A few were even elected to state legislatures in the South, forming a majority in the lower house of South Carolina for half-a-dozen years. But the backlash was not long in coming. As early as 1873 a Supreme Court judgement cast considerable doubt on the right of the federal government under the Fourteenth Amendment to intervene to protect citizens' rights against the actions of state authorities. Nor was this of mere academic interest. For, by intimidation to the point of Ku Klux Klan lynching and by the imposition of blatantly unfair enfranchisement tests for Blacks, the southern states succeeded very rapidly in nullifying any equality of citizenship status which it had been the intention of Congress to confer. The struggle to achieve that equality had to be continued into the second half of our own century.

Women's rights

By highlighting the contribution which the ordinary citizen could make to his community, state and nation the mood of Jacksonian Democracy could hardly fail to provoke the womenfolk to demand equality of rights with the privileged males. In no other country perhaps had women displayed such political consciousness as the Americans had during the Revolution. At a meeting at Seneca Falls in 1848 a feminist movement was launched. They made their point beautifully by issuing a Declaration of Sentiments, consciously echoing the Decaration of Independence. 'We hold these truths to be self-evident,' they proclaimed: 'that all men and women are created equal.' They went on to demand 'immediate admission to all the rights and privileges which belong to them as citizens of the United States' and to affirm that 'it is the duty of the women of this country to secure to themselves their sacred right to the elective franchise.'[68] Attention was soon diverted by the slavery issue and civil war. Thereafter, steady progress was made at local and state level until the Nineteenth Amendment conceded female suffrage on a par with men in 1920.

The intensity of the prejudice against the involvement of women in public affairs in the nineteenth century is hard now to imagine. When Napoleon codified French civil law he explicitly excluded from such legal rights minors, criminals, the mentally deficient and women! Mary Wollstonecraft had insults heaped upon her head and subsequently upon her memory as a 'hyena in petticoats' and as a pitiful sufferer from penis envy. Sixty-four years after her death John Stuart Mill expressed his opinion in his *Considerations on Representative Government* that difference of sex was 'as entirely irrelevant to political rights as difference in height or in the colour of the hair.'[69] However, when he opened the debate in the House of Commons on a bill for female suffrage a few years later, he was too naïve in expecting its success. The measure was soundly defeated. Indeed, one MP, was even shocked that two wives of members had so far disgraced themselves as to have spoken in public on the issue! And yet some women had successfully exercised the right to vote in English parliamentary elections in the Middle Ages and down to the seventeenth century – as a result of the confused state of electoral law. For example, during the reign of Elizabeth I there were two occasions when women who owned boroughs returned the MP; while in the seventeenth century judges pronounced women freeholders eligible to vote. In 1644 Sir Edward Coke made it clear that such practices were unacceptable.

Despite these disabilities and prejudices, from the 1870s Englishwomen gradually infiltrated public life, in school and poor law administration. In 1888 the County Councils Act allowed some women to vote and be candidates in county elections. The campaign for parliamentary suffrage had however to be bitterly fought during the years before the First World War. The Liberal government was willing to perpetrate the barbarism of force-feeding and the 'Cat and Mouse Act' against suffragettes arrested for crimes of public disorder rather than concede the principle. Britain was in fact one of eight nations to grant women voting rights because of their unarguably vital role in the First World War. Their sisters in Belgium, France, Italy and Japan had to wait for the Second World War to have the same effect in their countries. But the greatest patience of all had to be exercised by the women of, of all countries, Switzerland. That otherwise advanced democratic state denied half the population the vote in federal elections until 1971.

The origins of social citizenship

The extension and consolidation of legal and political recognition and rights took the practice of citizenship a considerable way in most western countries in the nineteenth century. Yet all the while privileges of rank and wealth maintained the wide gulf between the working classes and their 'superiors' in the social hierarchy, the status of citizenship seemed to many unfulfilled if not a downright sham. Citizenship must be a two-way process. In the nineteenth century the great majority of citizens gave their loyalty to the state, their muscles and skills to the economy and, in the event of war, even their conscripted lives for their country. The meagre protection of the law and the slow and grudging concession of the vote hardly balanced in the scales. The state, it was increasingly argued, owed its citizens a measure of protection against poverty. Citizenship must incorporate social welfare. Throughout the western countries during this period working-class men engaged in various activities in attempts to exact from the state what they thought was their due. Some of these activities were demonstrative – mass gatherings, petitions, strikes and riots. Others were organisational – pressure groups, trade unions and working-class or Socialist political parties. Even movements which ostensibly sought working-class involvement in the political process for its own sake (e.g. demands for the franchise, political parties) wanted these changes in some measure as a means to social reform.

Although by the time of the First World War the social concept of citizenship had in many respects been conceded by a number of governments, the process had been extremely hesitant. Even the French Revolutionaries, by the Le Chapelier law of 1791, forbade trade unions. The British parliament followed suit with the Combination Laws at the turn of the decade. In Europe and the USA alike the fortunes of trade unionism fluctuated with economic conditions. In many European states they were strong enough in the 1870s and 1880s finally to extract legal recognition: Austria, 1870; Britain, 1871; Spain, 1881; France, 1884; Germany, 1890. In the USA, although trade unions were active, even violently so in some strikes, the situation was complicated by the ideological reluctance of the government to intervene in labour-employer relations. Thus it was possible, for instance, for the steel industry to outlaw unions until the 1930s following the breaking of the great Homestead strike in 1892 by the Carnegie Company. Similarly, in a number of European states, even where constitutions and laws allowed freedom of association as a right of citizenship, in practice many working-class movements were forced because of legislative restrictions or police harassment to operate underground.

The USA was different from many European states too in the failure of any of the attempts to establish a Workers' or Socialist party. Efforts to persuade the government to enact welfare legislation had therefore to be arranged by candidates sympathetic to the cause running for election in the major parties. This was also the pattern in Britain before the emergence of the Labour Party, particularly after the founding of the Labour Representation League in 1870 'to secure the return to Parliament of qualified working men – persons who, by character and ability, command the confidence of their class.'[70] On the continent the progress of Socialist parties was impeded by the division between Marxist revolutionaries and the Social Democrats, who were to work through the parliamentary system. However, by the end of the century most European states had Socialist parties. The immense potential support for the German Social Democrats was revealed by the extreme rapidity with which they won seats in the Reichstag, despite the severe restrictions imposed upon their activities by Bismarck. By the time of his dismissal from office in 1890 they were the largest parliamentary party. By 1914 the Social Democratic parties in France, Austria, Italy, the Scandinavian states and the Low Countries all had substantial parliamentary representation.

Yet in very few countries did these movements, devoted to the principle of social rights, achieve very much in the way of reformist legislation. By 1914 only Germany, Sweden and Britain had the effective beginnings of a welfare state. The case of Germany, which set the pace in this field, is, however, instructive. It was the Prussian aristocracy, not working-class deputies, who were responsible for the insurance schemes. By a series of enactments in the 1880s and 1890s Bismarck, Caprivi and Posadowski spiked the Socialists' guns and rendered the mass of German citizenry pacified and passive. As Bismarck cynically commented, 'Whoever has a pension for his old age is far more content and far easier to handle than one who has no such prospect.'[71]

Citizenship in nineteenth-century political theory

The halting and laboured march of political and social citizenry through the nineteenth century to the ultimate goals of full realisation was accompanied by a motley band of theorists. Utilitarians, Liberals, Social Democrats, Revolutionary Socialists and Idealists each contributed their characteristic modulations.

In Britain Jeremy Bentham and James Mill believed that the utilitarian principle of the greatest happiness of the greatest number could best be achieved politically by a democratic franchise. They believed that citizens in the mass would vote for representatives who would pursue policies beneficial to the community as a whole. But could the mass of people really be trusted to act responsibly? Would a majority abuse their freedom to constrict the freedom of a minority? It was questions like these that worried Benjamin Constant, Alexis de Tocqueville and John Stuart Mill – political thinkers who struggled to accommodate the growing idea of democratic citizenship to the prime political value of liberty. Constant compared the Classical world with his own, early nineteenth-century Europe. Tocqueville wrote brilliant studies of the French *ancien régime* and the USA in the 1830s. Mill drew his material mainly from mid-century England. They all recognised a range of problems. One was that people in general are motivated by self-interest: that they tend to give primacy to living their private lives and accumulating private property. These thinkers also recognised that democratic governments could well

72

lower the quality of life. And thirdly, they feared that, in their concern to defend their private, economic freedom, the citizenry as a whole, lacking any properly developed sense of communal, civic responsibility, would allow freedom in a public sense to be eroded.

Tocqueville recognised that the networks of status, rights and responsibilities of the old régime had been demolished in the revolutionary events of the late eighteenth century. A new sense of community had urgently to be constructed to defend freedom against an incipient despotism which would otherwise engulf western society. He declared that:

. . . only freedom can deliver the members of a community from that isolation which is the lot of the individual left to his own devices and, compelling them to get in touch with each other, promote an active sense of fellowship. In a community of free citizens every man is daily reminded of the need of meeting his fellow men, of hearing what they have to say, of exchanging ideas, and coming to an agreement as to the conduct of their common interests. Freedom alone is capable of lifting men's minds above mere mammon worship . . ., and of making them aware at every moment that they belong each and all to a vaster entity, above and around them – their native land.[72]

The 'great transformation', in tearing down the traditional European social and political patterns, opened up the possibilities of equality and material welfare. The pursuit of these new social goals, Tocqueville believed, had made people 'mean-spirited as citizens'[73] and had therefore to be restrained by a new concept of citizenship, based upon the primacy of freedom.

Mill too combined deeply-held beliefs in the importance of liberty and the moral value of a political consciousness with a nagging worry about the low level of civic virtue that could be expected from the mass of people – at least until they had become accustomed to democratic ways. The people as a whole had to be free for two reasons: to participate in the government of their country and the management of their workplace; and to guard against bureaucratic autocracy. Only by political participation, he argued, can the citizen develop the intellectual qualities of reason and judgement; and only by behaving politically can the individual attain moral maturity. For when an individual undertakes a public action he feels 'that not only the common weal is his weal, but that it partly depends on his exertions.'[74] But the consciousness of being a member of a community will not come about if individuals are politically excluded by being denied the vote. On the other hand, absolute equality in the exercise of the suffrage would, he feared, lead to the smothering of the wise and educated minority by the rude masses of the populace. He therefore supported various devices, 'fancy franchises' as they were dubbed at the time, for enhancing the influence of the 'superior' middle-class citizens.

Mill in addition shared with Socialist thinkers of the century, from the Owenites to the Syndicalists, the belief that a more just apportionment in the ownership of property and worker participation in factory management were also essential. The relevance of such views to citizenship is two-fold. One is that the industrious should in justice be recompensed for their contribution to the well-being of society not merely by incorporation in the political citizen body but also by economic benefits. The second is that if an essential element of citizenship is the act of participation, then assistance in running a factory or workshop is just as much a training in the responsible exercise of that function as similar involvement in a political context; both require judgements to be made and actions to be taken for the common good.

Marx, however, approached the question of citizenship, in his essay *On the Jewish Question*, in a very particular way. Like Hegel, he distinguished between civil society and the political state, though reversed Hegel's interpretation of their relative significance. As a member of a civil society the individual pursues his own selfish, economic interests, within the context of the prevailing economic system, i.e. in the nineteenth century, bourgeois. It is this civil society that has the greater reality. The individual's role in the state, *qua* citizen, is therefore rather theoretical in comparison. Marx argued that,

Man in the reality that is nearest to him, civil society, is a profane being . . . . In the state, on the other hand, . . . he is an imaginary participant in an imaginary sovereignty, he is robbed of his real life and filled with an unreal universality.

Marx, it is true, was ready to concede that the extension of citizenship rights by the bourgeois state had been a worthwhile achievement:

Political emancipation is of course a great progress. Although it is not the final form of human emancipation in general, it is nevertheless the final form of human emancipation inside the present world order.

Nevertheless, only when man has tamed his selfish, bourgeois nature by acting truly as a social and not individualistic being will the limitations of 'the present world order' be transcended. 'The actual individual man,' he wrote, 'must take the abstract citizen back into himself.'[75] Though in the long run, if the state is to 'wither away', the status of citizen will have no meaning, since the individual will have no political institution with which to relate, from which to glean rights, to which to owe responsibilities.

If Marx took Hegel's ideas and totally inverted his concept of the primacy of the state, there were other philosophers in England in the nineteenth century willing to accept and adapt Hegel's philosophy. The English Idealists started from Hegel's propositions that ideas or reason have greater reality than the seemingly concrete world; that Christianity can provide the basis for a social morality; and that positive freedom can be attained only through the institution of the state. Central to the Hegelian system of ideas (pp. 61–62) was the concept of citizenship:

It is false to maintain [he wrote] that the foundation of the state is something at the option of all its members. It is nearer the truth to say that it is absolutely necessary for every individual to be a citizen.[76]

The English Idealists undertook something of a crusade to draw out and render dynamic the creative form of citizenship which lay latent in the potential of the state and the consciousness of individuals. The key figure in this movement was T. H. Green. Although he died, in 1882, at the sadly young age of 46, through his teaching at Oxford and the posthumous publication of his lectures and writings, he exerted a considerable influence. A number of other Professors of Philosophy, including Bernard Bosanquet, Henry Jones and Edward Caird helped to develop this school of thought. Furthermore, in the construction of this ethical and political theory, as the quotation at the head of this section reveals, the idea of citizenship was the key-stone. Progress could be achieved once the state and the citizen recognized and acted upon their mutual responsibilities. 'The power of the good state empowers the citizen,' Henry Jones declared, 'and the power of the good citizen empowers the state.'[77]

The state in this relationship is not the laissez-faire institution of classical Liberalism. Apart from providing the focus for citizen loyalty and obligations, it has, in the Idealist view, a range of positive functions: to promote the good life for all irrespective of social class; to foster the moral nature of man; and to provide a basic minimum of social welfare. The appropriate verbs are those like 'promote' and 'provide'; there was no room in the philosophy of the English Idealists for a coercive state. Three particular features of this conception of citizenship are worthy of specific mention. One concerns the nature of freedom. This was interpreted as the positive ability of the individual to develop his God-given self, to reach self-fulfilment in a social context. This concept raises the second issue, namely the problem of poverty and the role of the state in its alleviation. It was clear to Green and his followers that no one could be a free citizen in this creative sense if all his efforts had to be devoted to subsistence. Indeed, following Hegel, they believed poverty to be corrosive of the social links which make citizenship a cohesive force. The state must therefore ensure a minimum level of welfare for all its citizens — but not to intervene so forcefully as to weaken the capitalist and property systems, nor to enfeeble the individual's self-reliant pursuit of his freedom. But inequalities of wealth were not, in the Idealist philosophy, any impediment to a universal citizenship. For the impetus to a civic responsibility lay in the acceptance and actualization of a Christian faith. If citizenship was the key-stone to Green's political edifice, it was cemented into place by religion. In a letter to one of his former students, Canon Scott Holland, he wrote, 'True citizenship "as unto the Lord" . . . I reckon higher than saintliness in the technical sense.'[78]

All successful political theories have an influence on political practice, if only in the intangible sense of creating a general attitude of mind. The impact of the English Idealists was probably more direct than that. Some of the politicians who piloted the early welfare state legislation through parliament, notably Lloyd George and Churchill, justified their work in such terms. Furthermore, the prime minister, Asquith, had been taught by Green at Balliol (and whose *Prolegomena to Ethics* he was reading in July 1914 as war approached). And a key figure was taken from his Oxford Idealist milieu by Churchill to advise on the problem of poverty. This was William Beveridge, a generation later to mastermind the British welfare state programme of the late 1940s.

Nevertheless even Beveridge as a young man in his late twenties could state quite categorically that the unemployed 'must become the acknowledged dependants of the state . . . but with complete and permanent loss of all citizen rights – including not only the franchise but civil freedom and fatherhood.'[79] The ferocity of this comment from someone closely associated with the Idealists and whose name was later to become almost synonymous with compassion is a vivid reflection of the deeply held élitist views of the age. Influential constitutional lawyers of the calibre of Sir Henry Maine and A. V. Dicey, besides numerous politicians, argued the inadvisability of spreading the full status of citizenship too thinly. Dicey argued that citizenship was a privilege not a right and should be restricted to those capable of responsible judgement. This category excluded anyone who was financially dependent on the community by virtue of unemployment or pauperism. The equation of citizenship with independence, which is a persistent theme throughout history, was thus reasserted to counteract the progress towards universal manhood suffrage.

Despite such rearguard actions, whether by the force of philosophical argument or by the pressure of hard economic, social and political facts, the reality of citizenship was expanded in the nineteenth century. It was extended to embrace in real terms an increasingly large proportion of the population; it was deepened in the level of rights and responsibilities that status entailed. But could the uneducated mass of the people fill such a sophisticated role? Could they extract their rights from reluctant governments? Could they be trusted with the responsibilities? Or was a properly devised and universally available civic education an essential concomitant of a universal concept of citizenship?

2.4   THE IMPACT OF POLITICAL DOCTRINES ON EDUCATION

Of all political questions this is perhaps the most important. There will be no stability in the state until there is a body of teachers with fixed principles. Till children are taught whether they ought to be Republicans or Monarchists, Catholics or Unbelievers, and so on, there may indeed be a state, but it cannot be a nation.

Napoleon[80]

Nationalist and state education

The great revolutionary eruptions of the late eighteenth century showered the western world with vital political ideas and doctrines – nationalism, liberal democracy and socialism. These doctrines taught such crucial notions about the relationship of the individual to state and society that they could hardly have failed to rouse major interest in the ways young citizens might most effectively be prepared for these roles. However, the pursuit of these political ideals did not always appear to be in the interests of the state as perceived by some governments. In most of North America and Europe therefore the state intervened to ensure that the transmission of these political values through the school system, was 'prudently' undertaken. Nationalism required a citizenry schooled to display enthusiastic loyalty; liberal democracy required a citizenry to cast its vote with understanding (i.e. with due deference to their betters!). Socialism was another matter in the nineteenth century, potentially particularly destabilizing to middle-class and capitalist establishments if its ideals percolated through to the young.

Any of these new political ideas could indeed bring the established order into question. They were also more readily embraced by members of the liberal professions than many other sectors of society. And this category included teachers. Consequently nervous governments acted to prevent such politically conscious and active people from purveying their views in the schools. The conservative reaction after the 1848 revolutions affected schools in this way. For example, Louis Napoleon, both as President and later as Emperor, strengthened the hold of the Church over education as a means of controlling an undesirable political atmosphere in the schools, especially of a Socialist nature. He even had teachers dismissed if they were known to have been involved in the uprising (as a result of which he had come to power!). In Prussia, which had developed a widely admired liberal system of education, the reaction had a traumatic effect. In 1851 Froebel's schools, which had pioneered Kindergarten education, were closed on the grounds that they formed 'part of a Froebelian socialistic system which is calculated to train the youth of the country to atheism.'[81] There followed a Regulation in 1854, which forbade the teaching in elementary schools of any subjects except religion and the three Rs. Furthermore, habits of discipline and acceptance of authority were inculcated by rigid classroom methods and adherence to prescribed textbooks.

From the point of view of educational theorists, the political and social pressures should have been powerful enough in the nineteenth century in the USA and western and central Europe to prompt them to a major consideration of the issue of citizenship education. Education for national identity, the state control of schools, the extension of the franchise to an ill-educated working class and the mobilization of that working class to demand improvements in welfare – all these practical developments should have provided splendid grist. In fact, the philosophers' mills were too busy grinding away at the tasks of freeing young minds from the burdens of inert knowledge (to use the term anachronistically) and of devising means of ensuring the fullest personal and moral development of the individual. Considerations about political and citizenship education were in consequence surprisingly scrappy.

To consider nationalism first: it was, in any case, scarcely an idea to call forth fundamental philosophical analysis, either political or pedagogical. What it required was the practical mobilisation of the whole population to a mass consciousness of national identity. To this end governments made widespread use of flags, patriotic songs and the celebration of national anniversaries. These techniques quickly spread from France where they had been systematically developed during the Revolution. Yet the need to engage the schools in this process was appreciated in many states to ensure a truly effective result. Indeed, the defeat of the French at Sedan in 1870 was described as 'the triumph of the Prussian schoolmaster'. Expressing the same idea negatively, it has been suggested that the relative lack of a sense of national commitment during the First World War in Italy and particularly Russia can be explained by the low levels of education in those countries. Throughout the nineteenth century the state came increasingly to take an interest in and control of the schools. Where the cultivation of national identity was at a premium because of the recent achievement of national independence or unity or because of difficulties of multi-ethnicity, there state education inevitably took on a particularly nationalist style.

Few educational theorists even managed to shake themselves free from the presuppositions of nationalist ideology. Two names are exceptions. One was the Frenchman, Marc-Antoine Jullien, sometimes known as 'the father of comparative education'. He proposed in 1817 a veritable Comenian scheme (p. 15). This was for an international bureau of education, a kind of secularised College of Light, the purpose of which was to promote mutual understanding among educators as a means of enhancing peace. During the nineteenth century a few international educational meetings were held. But it was not until the 1880s that the Dutchman Molkenboer tried to create a permanent network of teachers for promoting peace. Molkenboer's motivating principle was that young people should learn the desirability of disarmament so that in adulthood they would exert pressure upon their governments to that end. Simultaneously, it is interesting to record, the Baha'i faith was being founded in the Middle East, a religion which urges the teaching of 'the concept of world citizenship as part of the standard education of every child.'[82]

A varied programme was available to educators to shape the knowledge, attitudes and behaviour of young people into a nationalist mould. In addition to the ceremonies and symbols to which adults came to respond, schools adopted overt teaching strategies particularly in History and language for the same purpose. Just as the academic study of national History (as opposed to the study of the Classical world) was stimulated by nationalism, so the schools became the purveyors of a watered down and biased form of the same subject. Children were taught about the heroes, glories and traditions of their own nation, largely to the exclusion of any consideration of other nations and certainly of their merits. Language teaching was, of course, crucial in a polyglot state. In a particularly mixed community, notably of course the USA, the school performed the vital socialising function of homogenisation as no other institution could. In a book published in 1912 Mary Antin, who emigrated with her family from Russia to the USA, wrote most pertinently of this experience:

The apex of my civic pride and personal contentment was reached on the bright September morning when I entered the public school . . . On our second day . . . A little girl from across the alley came and offered to conduct us to school . . . we five between us had a few words of English by this time . . . This child, who had never seen us till yesterday, who could not pronounce our names . . . was able to offer us the freedom of the schools of Boston![83]

The state control and manipulation of the educational system was achieved only gradually and against considerable opposition. The fiercest struggles were with the Churches, traditional purveyors of education. In England, France, Belgium, Austria-Hungary and Germany the battle was engaged, most notoriously in Bismarckian Germany in the *Kulturkampf*. Once education became available to the mass of children, the nation-state could not countenance the loyalty of their young citizens being torn by competing demands. The desire of national minorities, where they existed, to hold on to their identity by the retention of their own languages also created tensions. These two sources of resistance may be vividly exemplified together by reference to events in the Polish regions of Germany at the beginning of the present century. In 1902 Polish children were flogged for refusing to say the Lord's Prayer in German. Four years later 40,000 school children went on strike to protest against religious education lessons being conducted in German.

A number of educational theorists from La Chalotais and his contemporaries onwards (p. 38) argued and justified the case for the 'nationalisation' of education. So also did a number of leading political theorists. The Germans, perhaps displaying their national character, were particularly thorough in expounding the idea. The military defeat at the Battle of Jena hurt Prussian pride most sorely. Fichte's nationalist rallying cry in his *Addresses* resonated sympathetically with popular feeling. This famed philosopher delivered his course of lectures in the winter of 1807–8 in the great hall of the Berlin Academy of Sciences to an audience of Prussian intellectuals (as well as members of the French occupying army!). Fichte urged the use of education as a means to the moral and patriotic resuscitation of the defeated Prussian state and German nation. He believed this could only be achieved by a system of universal education. Moreover, such were the corrupting influences of society that children had to be physically withdrawn and inculcated with the habits of patriotism and service to society in schools isolated from the rest of the community. This was clearly impracticable. Nevertheless, the civic purpose of Prussian education was boldly emphasised in a document published in 1819:

It is declared that . . . to work toward that condition when every school will be a nursery of blameless patriotism, is made the most sacred duty of all schoolmasters and mistresses.[84]

In the light of Hegel's conception of the relationship between the individual and the state, one would expect him to emphasise the civic function of education. Hegel indeed believed that the state has the duty in its own self-interest to provide a schooling system for the purpose of nurturing the development of the individual as an embryonic citizen. Since it is only through citizenship that the individual can achieve moral freedom, the very essence of education must be to assist the moral evolution of the individual from selfishness to civic responsibility. A generation later Treitschke asserted that the prime duty of the state was the educative function of infusing into its people a common language and culture.

Education and the development of democracy

The desire of the nation-state to develop an education system as a means of bonding its citizens more tightly as a community assumed of course that schools could be efficacious for such a purpose. The assumption seemed reasonable. If for centuries the clerically-controlled schools had produced Christians, even devout Christians, why should not state-controlled schools produce national citizens, even nationalists? There were few doubts in the nineteenth century about the general political potential of education. For example, in Britain in the second decade of the century, Robert Owen and James Mill expressed similar thoughts about the power of what we would today call political socialization. Owen wrote that,

Any general character . . . may be given to a community, even to the world at large, by the application of proper means; which means are to a great extent at the command and under the control of those who have influence in the affairs of men.[85]

While Mill declared that,

The Political Education is like the key-stone of the [educational] arch . . . . The play . . . of the political machine acts immediately upon the mind, and with extraordinary power; but this is not all; it also acts upon almost every thing else by which the character of the mind is apt to be formed.[86]

However, although English radicals like Godwin and Priestley (p. 44) warned that a national system of education would give the government dangerous power, few went on the offensive to argue that schools should teach the mass of pupils about political issues and encourage a sense of political efficacy. And yet with the opening up of government increasingly to democratic control, this facet of education for citizenship was becoming urgent. All that the Utilitarian thinkers in England such as Bentham and James Mill could suggest was a general need for educational provision. John Stuart Mill was even more convinced that the advance of democracy depended crucially on the general spread of schooling. But even his recommendations for specific political education were confined to the educative value of adult participation. He believed that by the very process of involvement working men could be brought to a level of political efficacy – a kind of self-generating and self-improving process of citizen-education. Following Rousseau's belief in the virtue to be derived from participative democracy, J. S. Mill argued that involvement in public affairs was essential for counterbalancing man's selfishness. But he also recognised that this heuristic learning could not, at least initially, take place on the national plane. Involvement in community affairs and the running of the workplace are his realistic suggestions:

We do not learn to read or write, to ride or swim, by being merely told how to do it, but by doing it, so it is only by practising popular government on a limited scale, that the people learn how to exercise it on a larger.[87]

This passage sounds a remarkably faithful echo of Tocqueville's views as expressed in his *Democracy in America*, a work Mill much admired. Tocqueville affirmed that he was:

far from thinking, as so many people do think in Europe, that men can be instantaneously made citizens by teaching them to read and write. True information is derived from experience, and if the Americans had not been gradually accustomed to governing themselves, their book-learning would not assist them much at the present day.[88]

Thus neither of these perceptive writers of the age of developing democracy felt that the schools could contribute much, if anything, to citizenship education. Perhaps this is a comment on the general state of schooling as much as a conviction in the efficacy of adult 'learning-by-doing'. For although Tocqueville judged the mass of Americans better educated than any other people, the European yardsticks for the judgement marked extraordinarily low standards; moreover, within Europe, as the great Whig politician, Lord Brougham, remarked, England was the worst educated.

Nevertheless, two writers who were primarily concerned with the role of education for the personal and moral education of the individual did write pertinently, albeit briefly, on education for citizenship. In Germany during the early years of the century Herbert taught that the child acquires both knowledge interests and ethical interests and that part of the latter is an interest in civic and national life. For Herbert all components are necessary for a rounded education. This was not the view of Herbert Spencer, who, in his influential little book, *Education — Intellectual, Moral and Physical* (published in the 1850s), relegated education for 'the functions of the citizen' to the fourth level of priority. This may well have been because of his extremely low opinion of what was in practice being undertaken. He complained that,

Of the knowledge commonly imparted in educational courses, very little is of service in guiding a man in his conduct as a citizen. Only a small part of the history he reads is of practical value; and of this small part he is not prepared to make proper use.[89]

What should be taught, he asserted, was 'descriptive sociology' informed by an understanding of biology and psychology: citizenship requires a knowledge of how human beings function.

Educational writing in Victorian England could not, of course, ignore the country's class divisions. No one did more in the field of education than Thomas Arnold to consolidate this hierarchical social structure and thus retard the emerging concept of an egalitarian citizenship. He believed that there should be three different kinds of schools for the three social classes. And the upper class should be trained for their élite citizenship by the 'tone' of their 'public' school and by extrapolating the lessons to be drawn from classical literature and ancient history. T. H. Green, whose crucial contribution to the idea of an egalitarian form of citizenship we have already noticed (p. 74–75), found such attitudes utterly objectionable and a major barrier to true citizenship. He wanted education to undermine not underpin class barriers and snobbery, looking forward to a comprehensive system of schools, which would unite 'both classes by the freemasonary of a common education.'[90]

It is in fact to Green and his fellow Idealist philosophers we must turn for a convinced commitment in England to the goal of a properly educated citizenry. Furthermore, their views had some influence, especially in the field of adult education, from c. 1870 to c. 1920. One of their number, Sir Henry Jones, even proposed a degree in citizenship. Green, together with fellow-spirits like Acland, Bosanquet, Bryce, MacCunn, taught that a moral life could not be lived without participating in society as a good citizen. But this quality of citizenship could be developed only through education and participation: it required both the education of the intellect and character and practical involvement in local affairs and in the workplace. John MacCunn, who became Professor of Philosophy at Liverpool, defined the position in a book, *The Making of Character*, which, though published in 1900, was a major influence in teacher-training courses for a generation. He wrote that

. . . the preparation of the citizen for his duties is a necessity. In part this is a preparation in knowledge, some knowledge at least of his country's history and laws, its political institutions and economic system. And the need for this will be intensified should these days come — as the socialists assure us they are coming — when self-government in industry and commerce will be added to self-government in politics.[91]

So much then for the theory of education for citizenship in the context of liberal democracy. How far in practice were young people being prepared for civic duties? The picture across the nations of Europe and North America is extraordinarily diverse. A few generalisations are none the less possible. In the first place, most states started to provide a basic education in literacy for their children. By the end of the century, therefore, a large proportion of Europeans and Americans could read and had experienced the socialising effects of school attendance. Furthermore, in many states, as we have already seen (pp. 77–80), the government consciously used the schools for nationalistic purposes. And as loyalty to the state came to be increasingly emphasised, so other loyalties were weakened. The most dramatic example of this process was the confrontation between anti-clerical educational policies and the traditional influence of the Roman Catholic church.

It was in France that the most systematic attempt was made to provide a coherent and thorough programme of citizenship education (*instruction civique*). By the centralisation of administrative and curriculum control, the state, from the time of Napoleon, was in a position to provide such direction; the opportunity was surely grasped during the Third Republic. As early as the Revolution a civic education of the most extraordinarily stilted kind was tried: the attempted enforced rote learning of the Declaration of the Rights of Man and the Citizen! Napoleon certainly was alert to the political potential of education. His military mind dreamt of a cadre of teachers akin in discipline and influence to the Jesuits. His strict control of the teaching profession was an overt political act (p. 76). However, it was not until the 1880s that France, stung by the humiliating defeat of the Franco-Prussian war, introduced curricula framed to a civic purpose for all pupils. This was the work of the energetic and determined Jules Ferry, Minister of Public Instruction for much of the period, 1879–85. His aim was no less than the education of each generation of school children as loyal French democrats. For example, his law on primary schools defined the teacher's function as 'to prepare a generation of good citizens for our country.' And his outline syllabus for 11–13 year olds included the following section:

The fatherland: what a man owes to his country: obedience to law, military service, discipline, devotion, fidelity to the flag. Taxes (condemnation of fraud towards the State). The ballot: a moral obligation, which should be free, conscientious, disinterested, enlightened. Rights which correspond to these duties: personal freedom, liberty of conscience, freedom of contract and the right to work, right to organize. Guarantee of the security of life and property to all. National sovereignty. Explanation of the motto of the Republic: Liberty, Equality and Fraternity.[92]

The document contains much of interest. In the first place was its status as a centrally imposed requirement on the schools. Secondly, the inclusion of the right to work and organise shows a revealing socialist influence. Thirdly, the concepts seem excessively difficult for this age range, however concrete the teaching might have been in practice.

Where France displayed a clear-cut policy decision implemented with bureaucratic efficiency, the Austro-Hungarian state pursued a policy of having no policy at all for the education of its young citizens. As a result, the constituent ethnic communities filled this void by using the schools to consolidate their national identities and consequently contributed to the total disintegration of the empire at the end of the First World War.

In the federal system of the USA in contrast, state autonomy was harmonised with an overarching national civic purpose. Moreover, the civic purpose of education was accepted there in practice earlier than in any other country; at least, in the opinion of Tocqueville: 'In the United States,' he wrote in 1835, 'politics are the end and aim of education. In Europe its principal object is to fit men for private life.'[93] This fundamental idea was developed by Horace Mann soon after Tocqueville made his observation. Mann gave up his career as a lawyer to become 'the father of American education'. In his capacity as Secretary to the Massachusetts Board of Education he was able both to implement his ideas and by that example influence other states. Mann believed that the suspicions entertained by many of the wisdom of Jacksonian democracy could be allayed by effective education of young people to responsible citizenship – indeed, if such an education were lacking, then fears of mob-led anarchy would be only too vividly realised. His panacea for political health was an elixir concocted from the socialising force of all pupils taught in 'common schools' and the knowledge of the fundamental principles of American republicanism. No adulteration of this mixture by an awareness of controversial and therefore divisive political issues was to be permitted.

The first curricular vehicle for civic education in the USA was American History. States gradually came to require its teaching by law – Vermont leading the way as early as 1827. Rapidly on the heels of American History came school courses in Government, Civics and Political Economy, introduced in a number of states in the 1830s and 1840s, far earlier than in Europe. The Civil War and the great influx of immigrants each in its way threatened the sense of cohesion of the United States. As a consequence school teaching during the last third of the century emphasised both patriotism and the excellence of the Constitution. By the turn of the century most states of the American Union were requiring explicit civic education by force of law. The following excerpt from a law enacted by the state of New York in 1917 is typical:

In order to promote a spirit of patriotic and civic service and obligations and to foster in children of the state moral and intellectual qualities which are essential in preparing to meet the obligations of citizenship in peace or in war, the regents of the state of New York shall prescribe courses of instruction in patriotism and citizenship, to be maintained and followed in all of the schools of the state.[94]

A rather more detailed survey of the situation in England reveals much more hesitation and muddle. For one thing, despite England's reputation since the seventeenth century for constitutional government and political freedom, there remained in the nineteenth century a formidable array of barriers to effective citizen education. First, the general quality of educational provision, certainly until the impact of Forster's 1870 act, was decidedly modest. Secondly, if we take the evidence of *Culture and Anarchy*, written in the late 1860s by Forster's brother-in-law and school inspector, Matthew Arnold, then the desire on the part of the bulk of the populace for any education in civic responsibility may be seriously questioned. In any case, and thirdly, the divisive school system, reinforced by Matthew Arnold's father, Thomas, precluded the evolution of a citizenship education of any egalitarian kind. But, most seriously, significant segments of the governmental and industrial establishment were convinced of the prime necessity of keeping the bulk of the populace politically ignorant and passive. This view was expressed most forcibly in 1807 in an education debate in the House of Commons by an MP speaking against parochial schools:

. . . instead of teaching them subordination, it would render them fractious and refractory . . .; it would enable them to read seditious pamphlets . . . .[95]

As we have already noticed (p. 44), the Sunday school system was designed to confirm the lower social classes in their stations in life. In fact, however, the effects of these classes were anything but antipathetic to the development of an active concept of citizenship. The radical Lancashire weaver, Samuel Bamford, describing their unintended influence from the perspective of 1817, wrote:

. . . the Sunday schools of the preceding thirty years had produced many working men of sufficient talent to become readers, writers and speakers in village meetings for Parliamentary reform.[96]

It was not until the passage of the 1867 Reform Act that serious attention was focussed in England on the need for schools to educate young people for the duties and responsibilities of citizenship. The depth of ignorance at this time was epitomized by T. H. Huxley, who judged that:

The child learns absolutely nothing of the history or political organization of his own country. His general impression is that everything of much importance happened a very long while ago; and that the Queen and the gentlefolks govern the country much after the fashion of King David and the elders and nobles of Israel, his sole models.[97]

The enfranchisement of the artisan classes by the Second Reform Act led a number of prominent figures to urge that a more effective civic preparation be undertaken by the schools. The extension of the suffrage provoked the MP Robert Lowe, a stern opponent of the measure, to the famous despairing remark, popularised as, 'Now we must educate our masters'. The need for effective elementary education was, he argued, 'a question of self-preservation . . . a question of existence, even of the existence of our Constitution'.[98] The same consideration was expressed, though in more measured language, by W. E. Forster when he introduced his Education Bill three years later to create elementary schools to 'fill the gaps' in the voluntary systems: 'On this speedy provision,' he declared, 'depends . . . the good, the safe working of our constitutional system.'[99] And yet, there were few men in public life to advocate the direct teaching of political matters. Basic literacy and a 'Whig' version of English (and certainly not *British*) history was the most frequently prescribed remedy. Perhaps the most distinguished voice to argue the insufficiency of such a curriculum was Sir John Seeley, Regius Professor of History at Cambridge. On different occasions in the 1870s and 80s he described the lack of any 'systematic study of politics' as 'perverse' and 'ominous'. 'In schools,' he observed, 'the subject is avoided, for fear of giving bias, though it is precisely on this subject that, in after life, we have to decide and vote.'[100]

Progress of sorts had been made by the turn of the century. In 1897 was founded the Moral Instruction League, which later added 'Civic' to its name. Under its influence the Codes issued episodically by the Board of Education came to incorporate with increasing precision a civic purpose in their objectives. Thus in 1904 children were to be taught by parents and schools to become 'upright and useful members of the community in which they live, and worthy sons and daughters of the country to which they belong.' By 1906 this had become 'lessons on citizenship may be given with advantage in the higher classes.'[101] Four years later with even greater firmness, the Code stated that 'the high function of the teacher is to prepare the child for the life of the good citizen.'[102]) It continued with a provision for thirty-five lessons in citizenship in the History syllabus. Nevertheless, the general expectation was still very much that of a passive citizenry. Schools were to inculcate habits of temperance and loyalty. The widely used textbook, H. O. Arnold Foster's *Citizen Reader*, which sold a quarter of a million copies from 1885 to 1916, was scarcely designed to provide an unbiassed picture. The radical journal *Justice* carried an article in 1894 bewailing the fact that working-class children were being taught basically to 'honour the Queen, obey your superiors.'[103] Nor was the civic education of the privileged classes much more positive. The

High Master of Manchester Grammar School had occasion in 1914 to complain
of the ignorance and cynicism of the schoolboy about civic affairs. He wrote:

The only governing law he recognizes in politics is the great law of swing-swang. As
for his political thinking, that is done for him by what Plato would have called the
arch-sophist of our modern society, the half-penny press.[104]

Even youth organisations like the YMCA (founded in 1844), the Boys'
Brigade (1883) and Scouts (1907) emphasised conservative religious, social
and political values. Preparation for an active mode of citizenship, insofar as
such provision was available in England, was more readily provided outside
the school and youth systems, in adult education services. From the 1790s to
the 1840s a variety of political and working-class organisations flourished –
Corresponding Societies, Hampden Clubs, Co-operative Societies, Chartist
groups. All of these encouraged reading and discussion about political issues
and broadened an understanding of what active, participate citizenship might
mean. And when the London Working Men's College was created in the middle of the century, its creed was clear: that no education for workers was good
which 'did not aim directly at the object of qualifying them to perform their
duties as citizens.'[105] By the 1870s lectures on Politics, Economics and History were widely available. To give just one example: A. H. D. Acland (a
member of T. H. Green's circle and a few years later to be an Education minister in Gladstone's and Rosebery's cabinets) delivered a series of lectures to
the North-West Section of the Co-operative Union. These were published in
pamphlet form in 1883 under the title *The Education of Citizens*. The lectures
served as an introduction to a full course of study, the syllabus for which
Acland outlined:

You will set to work during some winters to consider seriously, leaving, as far as
possible, all class prejudice and political party spirit aside for the time, subjects such
as these:- The labour and capital questions, health, education, the poor law, what our
English Government (central and local) is as a machine, what the machine does, and
in what directions we think it ought to work. You will spend other winters in
systematically studying the works and lives of our great English men and women of
bygone days. . . . You will study the 'History of our own Times' . . . .[106]

A comprehensive, not to say formidable, programme for tired workers! Yet
the demand by no means slackened. In 1903 the Worker's Educational Association was founded to co-ordinate these disparate activities.

Education and nineteenth-century socialism

Moreover, most workingmen were interested in politics not for its own sake
but as a means to counterbalancing the control of the political system by the
privileged classes of society. Education for an understanding of and participation
in political structures would provide the citizen with a basic preparation. But
for the working class and Socialists of various hues such an education offered
an induction into only the superficialities of citizenship. If citizenship was to
be construed in terms of welfare and working conditions in addition to legal

and political rights, then an awareness of left-wing theories and objectives had to complement political education. The early Socialists like Owen and Fourier stressed the virtues of co-operative behaviour in their school organisation, both in theory and in the utopian communities set up by their followers in the USA. Marx and Engels had little to say about education, except to note how schools like other social institutions reflect the control exercised by the dominant bourgeoisie. The *Communist Manifesto* declared:

The Communists have not invented the intervention of society in education; they do but seek to alter the character of that intervention, and to rescue education from the influence of the ruling class.[107]

Engels from his vantage-point in industrial Manchester in the 1840s was very impressed by the efforts the English working class were making to educate themselves and their children to an appreciation of the need for social reform. Many working-class organisations were impressively active in the educational field in the 1840s. Referring to the proliferation of schools and reading rooms, Engels noted that,

Every Socialist, and almost every Chartist institution, has such a place, and so too have many trades. Here the children receive a purely proletarian education, free from all the influences of the bourgeoisie.[108]

Socialist Sunday schools also flourished at this time.

Lectures on Socialist themes and the provision of reading matter of a similar nature for adults were even more readily available. For instance, 'Halls of Science' were built in the major cities for this purpose in the late 1830s and early 1840s. It was a tradition upon which the revived interest in adult education in England in the 1870s we have already noted (p. 86) could firmly build. It was to the Co-operative movement that Arnold Toynbee, yet another member of T. H. Green's Idealist group, looked for a revivification of education in citizenship. His study of the Industrial Revolution convinced him that industrialisation had shattered traditional bonds of citizenship and community. The restoration of a sense of civic responsibility, he argued in a lecture entitled *Education for Co-operators*, required a threefold citizenship programme of political, industrial and sanitary education.

If, however, we are to search for widespread Socialist influence in schools it is to be sought in the political persuasions of the teachers. We have already seen how the conservative and clerical reaction in continental Europe after 1848 targeted the feared intrusion of such ideas by teachers sympathetic to the doctrine (p. 77). It was in France that teachers displayed their left-wing sympathies most manifestly by creating the Fraternal Association of Socialist Teachers in 1849. By the end of the century Socialist ideas were much more pervasive; and indeed had been given institutional expression in many western countries in political parties and trade unions. Moreover, as the provision of elementary education rapidly expanded, so an increasing proportion of teachers were drawn from strata of society below the privileged. A fair proportion could in consequence be reckoned to favour political and social ideals to the left of the spectrum. The reactions of the governments of France and Germany in the 1880s to this development provide fascinating contrasts. In France the government's desire to purge the schools of clerical influence led to the veritable indoctrination of teachers-in-training to a radical and socialist frame of mind. By contrast, when Wilhelm II became German Emperor, he felt impelled to issue a decree instructing teachers that their foremost duty was to combat Socialist and Communist ideas. 'The school', he asserted, 'has to strive to convince the young generation that the doctrines of the Social Democrats not only contradict the divine order and Christian morality, but are also impracticable.'[109] A little later in Britain in 1903 the Conservative government shelved a proposal to reorganise the administration of education in London because of the feared increase in influence the proposal would have afforded to teachers. The radical sympathies of the profession were sufficient to worry the government.

Patterns of educational provision

In the late eighteenth century, say c. 1780, the conscious education of young people for citizenship barely existed. Four generations later, on the eve of the First World War educational practices in this regard had developed but at very different speeds. This variegated response by the state and the teaching profession to the increasing consciousness and significance of citizenship may be explained by the extremely varied historical experiences of the states of the western world in the nineteenth century.

In some European countries, notably Russia and the states of the three southern peninsulas, the literacy rate remained abysmally low and the influence of the Roman Catholic and Orthodox Churches remained (with the partial exception of post-unification Italy) paramount in what schooling was available. In Austria-Hungary, as we have noticed, the tangled nationalities problem equally inhibited any citizenship education in the schools. In the Scandinavian countries and England civic education was largely the function of religious and moral teaching together with some History. However, the position in England was complicated by the rigid social distinctions. These divisions separated the classes not just institutionally but by the overt and hidden curricula by which their civic attitudes were shaped. Moreover, the lack of any real central control over English schools meant that the state, even if individual ministers had so wished, could not impose a thorough programme of citizenship education.

Of the major western states France, Germany and the USA developed the most deliberate policies for citizenship education, though each with clear individual style. In France, unlike her southern Latin neighbours, the tussle with the Church was won by the state. As a result, the most highly centralised system was created, with a heavy emphasis on producing patriotic citizens. This objective was achieved largely by the teaching of blinkered national History and detailed instructions for teachers. For instance, a catechistic book used before 1914 required the following exchange:

Question: Can we love our neighbours, the Germans?
Answer: One cannot love the oppressors of Alsace-Lorraine.[110]

In Germany, still a federal system after unification, the policy of Prussia was the most determined. Founded on the traditions of Fichtean and Hegelian philosophy and Hohenzollern military discipline, schoolchildren were taught the morality of unswerving obedience to that mystical and majestic organism, the state. In the USA, whose federal structure makes generalisation difficult, the overall pattern is none the less evident. It is the introduction of national History and later Government courses by state fiat for the twin purposes of democratic efficiency and national cohesiveness.

Even so, hardly had the educational systems come to grips with the demands of nationalism and liberal democracy (and to a much lesser extent Socialism) than new, more vigorous ideologies burst upon Europe. In the aftermath of the First World War, Communism, Fascism and Nazism generated their own modes of citizenship education. What is more, the democracies were consequently forced to look to their much blander beliefs in education of the citizen to individual responsibility and international understanding. These were educational ideals that stood in stark contrast to the totalitarian and aggressive ideologies into which millions of young people were being inducted by the 1930s.

REFERENCES

1. Resolution passed in April 1794, quoted in H. T. Dickinson, *Liberty and Property* (Methuen, 1977), p. 262.
2. Helvétius, *De l'Homme, de ses Facultés intellectuelles, et de son Education*, quoted in F. A. Cavanagh (ed.), *James and John Stuart Mill on Education* (Cambridge University Press, 1931), p. vii.
3. P. Hazard, *European Thought in the 18th Century* (trans. J. Lewis May, Hollis & Carter, 1954), p. 198.
4. Quoted in M. Cranston (trans. & intro.), Rousseau, *The Social Contract* (Penguin, 1968), p. 10.
5. Rousseau, *Discourse on Political Economy*, reprinted in A. Arblaster & S. Lukes (eds), *The Good Society* (Methuen, 1971), p. 30.
6. Ibid.
7. Rousseau, *Discourse on Political Economy*, quoted in A. Cobban, *Rousseau and the Modern State* (Allen & Unwin, 2nd edn, 1964), p. 112 (author's translation).
8. Rousseau, *Considerations on the Government of Poland*, quoted in A. Goodwin (ed.), *The New Cambridge Modern History*, vol. VIII (Cambridge University Press, 1965), p. 165 (author's translation).
9. Rousseau, *The Social Contract* (ed. Cranston), p. 114.
10. Ibid., p. 141.
11. Burke, *Speech to the Electors of Bristol*, reprinted in B. W. Hill (ed.), *Edmund Burke on Government, Politics and Society* (Collins, 1975), p. 157.
12. Burke, *First Letter on a Regicide Peace*, quoted in D. Pickles, *Democracy* (Methuen, 1971), p. 46.

13. D'Holbach, *Système social*, quoted in G. H. Sabine, *A History of Political Theory* (Harrap, 3rd edn, 1951), p. 481.

14. Anna Barbauld, *An Address to the Opposers of the Repeal of the Corporation and Test Acts*, reprinted in A. Cobban (ed.), *The Debate on the French Revolution* (Nicholas Kaye, 1950), pp. 420–1.

15. Mary Wollstonecraft, *A Vindication of the Rights of Women*, quoted in Dickinson, *Liberty and Property*, p. 252.

16. David Williams, *Letters on Political Liberty*, quoted ibid., p. 228.

17. *Resolutions of the London Corresponding Society*, 2 April 1792, reprinted in M. Williams, *Revolutions 1775–1830* (Penguin, 1971), p. 124.

18. T. Malthus, *An Essay on Population*, quoted in H. Collins (ed.), Paine, *Rights of Man* (Penguin, 1969), p. 45.

19. Adam Smith, *The Wealth of Nations*, quoted in H. C. Barnard , *A Short History of English Education*, 1760–1944 (University of London Press, 1947), p. 53.

20. Quoted in J. M. Thompson, *Leaders of the French Revolution* (Blackwell, 1929), p. 45.

21. T. Paine, *Common Sense* (Penguin edn, 1976), p. 67.

22. *Virginia Statute of Religious Liberty, January 1786*, reprinted in Williams, *Revolutions*, p. 169.

23. Quoted in R. H. S. Crossman, *Government and the Governed* (Christophers, 1939), p. 97.

24. Article I, section 2.

25. *The Articles of Confederation, 1977*, reprinted in Williams, *Revolutions*, pp. 55–6.

26. Quoted in C. A. & M. R. Beard, *A Basic History of the United States* (Doubleday, Doran & Co., 1944), p. 154.

27. T. Jefferson, 'The Rockfish Gap Report, August 1818' reprinted in Williams, op. cit., p. 193.

28. Jefferson, *Notes on the State of Virginia* quoted in J. Spring, *American Education: An Introduction to Social and Political Aspects* (Longman Inc., 1970), p. 6.

29. Title II, *On the division of the realm and the status of citizens*.

30. Articles VI, XI & XIV, as printed in Paine, *Rights of Man*, pp. 133–4.

31. A. France, *Les Dieux ont soif* (trans. F. Davies as *The Gods Will Have Blood*, Penguin, 1979), p. 28.

32. Quoted in Thompson, op. cit., pp. 231–2.

33. Condorcet, *Une Education pour la démocratie* (ed. B. Baczko, Editions Garnier Frères, 1982), pp. 184, 185, 194, 195 (author's translation).

34. R. R. Palmer, *The Age of the Democratic Revolution*, vol. 1 (Princeton University Press, 1959), p. 224.

35. Paine, *Rights of Man*, p. 165.

36. F. Meinecke, *Cosmopolitanism and the National State* (1907, Princeton University Press edn, 1970), p. 20.

37. Voltaire, *Philosophical Dictionary* (trans. T. Besterman, Penguin, 1971), p. 329.

38. Paine, *Rights of Man*, p.250.

39. Quoted in G. A. Craig, *The Germans* (Penguin, 1982), p. 30.

40. Quoted in T. J. Schlereth, *The Cosmopolitan Ideal in Enlightenment Thought* (University of Notre Dame Press, 1977), p. 13.

41. Kant, *Perpetual Peace*, reprinted in P. Mayer (ed.), *The Pacifist Conscience* (Penguin, 1966), p. 75.

42. Quoted in Stawell, *International Thought*, p. 201.

43. Kant, *Perpetual Peace*, reprinted in Mayer, *Pacifist Conscience*, p. 75.

44. Kant, *Idea for a Universal History*, quoted in Linklater, *Men and Citizens*, p. 115.
45. Quoted in Cobban, *Rousseau*, p. 106.
46. Quoted in Royal Institute of International Affairs, *Nationalism* (Oxford University Press, 1939), p. 28.
47. Hazard, *European Thought*, p. 445.
48. Quoted in E. H. Carr, *Conditions of Peace*, Macmillan, 1942), p. 37.
49. Reprinted in Open University, *The Revolutions of 1848: Unit 3 – Document Collection* (OU Press, 1976), pp. 73–4.
50. Ibid., p. 91.
51. J. S. Mill, *Utilitarianism, On Liberty, and Considerations on Representative Government* (Dent edn, 1910), p. 361.
52. Quoted in C. A. Macartney, *National States and National Minorities* (Oxford University Press, 1934), pp. 119–20.
53. Fichte, *The Science of Rights*, quoted in Linklater, *Men and Citizens*, p. 54.
54. Quoted in N. Hampson, *The Enlightenment* (Penguin, 1968), p. 281.
55. Quoted in J. Droz, *Europe between Revolutions 1815–1848*, (Collins, 1967), p. 165.
56. Reprinted in H. Kohn, *Nationalism* (Van Nostrand, 1955), p. 119.
57. Quoted in F. H. Hinsley, *Power and the Pursuit of Peace* (Cambridge University Press, 1963), p. 113.
58. Reprinted in D. Mack Smith (ed.), *The Making of Italy 1796–1870* (Harper & Row, 1968), p. 48.
59. Hegel, *Lectures on the Philosophy of History*, reprinted in Kohn, *Nationalism*, pp. 110–11.
60. *Le Moniteur*, 28 January 1794, quoted in Macartney, *National States and Minorities*, p. 111.
61. Quoted in A. Vincent & R. Plant, *Philosophy, Politics and Citizenship* (Blackwell, 1984), p. 1.
62. Quoted in F. Ponteil, *La Monarchie Parlementaire 1815–1848* (Colin, 1949), p. 186 (author's translation).
63. *Poor Man's Guardian*, 25 October 1832, quoted in A. Briggs, *The Age of Improvement* (Longmans, 1959), p. 258.
64. Quoted in R. B. Nye & J. E. Morpurgo, *A History of the United States* (Penguin, 1955), p. 370.
65. Quoted in C. A. & M. R. Beard, *Basic History of the USA*, p. 227.
66. Quoted in W. R. Brock, *Conflict and Transformation* (Penguin, 1973), p. 154.
67. Quoted in J. A. Kettner, *The Development of American Citizenship* 1608–1870 (University of North Carolina Press, 1978), p. 341.
68. Quoted in C. A. & M. R. Beard, *Basic History of the USA*, p. 217.
69. J. S. Mill, *Representative Government*, p. 290.
70. Quoted in D. Thomson, *England in the Nineteenth Century* (Penguin, 1950), p. 147.
71. Quoted in D. Thomson, *Europe Since Napoleon* (Longmans, 1957), p. 370.
72. Tocqueville, *The Old Régime and the French Revolution* (trans. S. Gilbert, Doubleday, 1955), p. xiv.
73. Ibid., p. 118.
74. Quoted in C. Pateman, *Participation and Democratic Theory* (Cambridge University Press, 1970), p. 33.
75. Marx, *On the Jewish Question*, reprinted in D. McLellan (ed.), *Karl Marx: Selected Writings* (Oxford University Press, 1977), pp. 46, 47 & 57.
76. Quoted in Vincent & Plant, *Philosophy, Politics and Citizenship*, p. 162.

77. H. Jones, *The Principles of Citizenship*, quoted in ibid., p. 26

78. Quoted in M. Richter, *The Politics of Conscience* (Weidenfeld and Nicholson, 1964), p. 132.

79. Quoted in R. Barker, *Political Ideas in Modern Britain* (Methuen, 1978), p. 110.

80. Napoleon, Note outlining an Order of Teachers, quoted in J. M. Thompson, *Napoleon Bonaparte: His Rise and Fall* (Blackwell, 1953), p. 206.

81. Quoted in Bowen, *History of Western Education*, vol. 3 (1981), p. 341.

82. *The Promise of World Peace* (Bahá'i World Centre, n.d., but 1985?), p. 15.

83. M. Antin, *The Promised Land*, part quoted in A. Nevins & H. S. Commager, *America: The Story of a Free People* (Clarendon Press, 1942), p. 336; and part reprinted in J. Chandler (ed.), *Life, Liberty and the Pursuit of Happiness* (Oxford University Press, 1971), pp. 190–1.

84. 'Sketch of a General Education Law for Prussia', quoted in E. H. Wilds & K. V. Lottich, *The Foundations of Modern Education* (Holt, Rinehart & Winston, 3rd ed 1970), p. 326.

85. Owen, *A New View of Society* (Penguin edn, 1970), p. 99.

86. J. Mill, 'On Education', *Encyclopedia Britannica*, reprinted in Cavanagh, *The Mills on Education*, p. 72.

87. J. S. Mill, quoted in Pateman, *Participation*, p. 31.

88. Tocqueville, *Democracy in America*, reprinted in J. Stone & S. Mannell (eds.), Alexis de Tocqueville, *On Democracy, Revolution and Society* (University of Chicago Press, 1980), pp. 97–8.

89. Spencer, *Education – Intellectual, Moral, and Physical* (Warts edn, 1929), pp. 34–5.

90. Quoted in P. Gordon & J. White, *Philosophers as Educational Reformers* (Routledge & Kegan Paul, 1979), p. 80.

91. Quoted ibid., p. 183.

92. Quoted in D. Thomson, *Democracy in France* (Oxford University Press, 3rd edn, 1958), p. 146.

93. Tocqueville, *Democracy in America*, p. 98.

94. Quoted in Wilds & Lottich, *Foundations of Modern Education*, p. 338.

95. Davies Giddy, MP, quoted in B. Simon, *The Two Nations and the Educational Structure* 1780–1870. (Lawrence & Wishart, 1974), p. 132.

96. S. Bamford, *Passages in the Life of a Radical*, quoted in ibid., p. 183.

97. Quoted in G. Whale, *A Fragment on Political Education* (Ridgway, 1882), p. 9.

98. Quoted in Simon, *Two Nations and Educational Structure*, p. 355.

99. Quoted in T. Brennan, *Political Education and Democracy* (Cambridge University Press, 1981), p. 33.

100. Quoted in Whale, *Fragment on Political Education*, p. 9; A. H. D. Acland, *The Education of Citizens* (Central Co-operative Board, Manchester, 1883), p. 27.

101. Quoted in P. Gordon & D. Lawton, *Curriculum Change in the Nineteenth and Twentieth Centuries* (Hodder & Stoughton, 1978), pp. 103 & 116.

102. Quoted in Brennan, *Political Education and Democracy*, p. 34.

103. Quoted in D. Lawson & B. Dufour, *The New Social Studies* (Heinemann, 2nd edn 1976), p. 34. For Arnold-Foster's book, see B. Crick, 'The National Curriculum and Civic Education', *History Today*, May 1988.

104. J. L. Paton, 'The School in Relation to Civic Progress', *The Political Quarterly*, February 1914.

105. Quoted in Simon, *Two Nations and Educational Structure*, p. 358.

106. Acland, *Education of Citizens*, pp. 12–13.

107. Marx and Engels, *The Communist Manifesto*, (Ed. H. J. Laski, Allen and Unwin, 1948), p. 141.
108. Engels, *Condition of the Working Class in England in 1844*, quoted in Simon, *Two Nations and Educational Structure*, p. 256.
109. Quoted in D. Schmidt-Sinns, 'Political Education: A Reflection of Society' in D. Heater & J. A. Gillespie (eds), *Political Education in Flux* (Sage, 1981), p. 116.
110. Quoted in J. Carduner, 'The Making of French Citizens' in E. B. Gumbert (ed.). *In The Nation's Image* (Georgia State University, 1987), p. 102.

CHAPTER THREE

The Twentieth Century

3.1 STATES WITH A LIBERAL TRADITION

A clear vision of the aims and content of education is all the more desirable as there
is a tendency in democracies to discuss problems of organisation rather than ideas,
techniques rather than aims. There is no doubt that Democracy has lost a clear
conception of the type of citizen it wants to create.

Karl Mannheim[1]

Our own century presents us with a fascinating paradox. Never before has
the idea of citizenship been so widely accepted and the need of education for
that status and function so widely appreciated. And yet, at the same time,
we may observe a greater diversity of interpretations than ever before of
precisely what the role of citizen should entail. For, as the political ideas
which displayed such vigour in the nineteenth century were shaped and
reshaped by the powerful forces of the twentieth, so citizenship and citizenship
education have had to be adapted to fit the new patterns of political life. The
steadiest evolution took place in those states of Europe and America where
the tradition was well embedded and the political atmosphere most conducive
to natural growth. Even so, the issue in these societies has not by any means
been devoid of dispute and changes of emphasis.

National self-determination in Europe

The doctrines of democracy, sovereignty and nationalism were each in their
own ways replete with opportunities for very diverse interpretations. Yet by
blending them together, the US President Woodrow Wilson announced, like
some frontier-town quack, that he had concocted a panacea for Europe's if
not the world's, political ills. This political scientist turned politician had a
touching Rousseauesque faith in the essential goodness of people. He consequently came to believe that if this goodness could be allowed natural freedom
through the operation of national self-determination, then the world would
be a much more peaceable place. The basic idea, developing from Mazzini
(pp. 60–61), was that groups of peoples, identified by cultural national-

94

ity, should form states in the geographical sense, determine their own governments in the political sense, and be recognised as sovereign entities in the international sense. By 1918 it became urgent that he publicise the idea in order to gain its acceptance as the underlying principle for the post-war peace settlement. Therefore, in speeches he canvassed

. . . the principle of justice to all peoples and nationalities and their right to live on equal terms of liberty and safety with one another . . .[2]

And declared that

National aspirations must be respected; peoples may now be dominated and governed by their own consent. Self-determination is not a mere phrase, it is an imperative principle of action.[3]

In terms of citizenship Wilson had made an unwarranted assumption and established an impracticable principle. The assumption was that, if people had a free choice, they would opt for nationality as the test of political identity. This was not necessarily true. Insofar as demands were made at the time and subsequently for the implementation of national self-determination, explanations other than the spontaneous desires of the mass of the citizenry may be equally, if not more, plausible. For instance, there were probably fewer than a thousand active Slovak nationalists in 1918–19. It has often in fact been a vocal educated élite who have urged the primacy of nationality. Moreover, the very advocacy of the principle by Woodrow Wilson, and the conviction with which he initially argued his case, generated optimistic expectations, which otherwise people would not have dared harbour.

The force of the hopes which he thus unleashed seriously worried the American President. He, moreover, confessed that he had been ignorant of the complexity of the intermingling of nationalities in central and eastern Europe. Even after the radical redrawing of frontiers following the First World War a number of 'nation-states' perforce contained pockets of ethnic minorities. Attempts were made to cater for their interests by Minorities Treaties. These treaties were promises entered into by governments of states with substantial minorities and guaranteed by the League of Nations. Thus, the Polish treaty declared:

All Polish nationals shall be equal before the law and shall enjoy the same civil and political rights without distinction as to race, language or religion.[4]

During and immediately after the War the Turks chose a different solution. They tackled the problem of the Armenians in the north-east and the Greeks in the west of Asia Minor by a frenzy of nationalist passion which shocked the world. By massacre, expulsion and negotiated deportation, though the figures for the Armenians particularly are disputed, the Turks mercilessly rid themselves of perhaps as many as three and a half million people.

The problem of minorities none the less persisted throughout the inter-war period both as a source of domestic trouble and as a major irritant to harmonious international relations. For example, the Poles were quite blatant in their disregard for their treaty commitments, especially in their treatment of the Ukrainian minority. Indeed, the deprivation of citizenship rights, real or fabricated, of the German minorities in the Sudetenland and the Polish 'corridor' provided Hitler with a quasi-moral excuse for his intervention in Czechoslovakia and Poland respectively in 1938–39. The issue was solved in the aftermath of the Second World War by the brutal simplicity of mass flight and expulsions from many of the countries of east and central Europe. Consequently, apart from the continuing discrepancy of Germans being fragmented into the three states of East and West Germany and Austria, citizenship and ethnic-linguistic nationality now much more neatly coincide in most states of Europe outside the Soviet Union.

Participative citizenship

As the USA (pp. 58–59) and the states of Europe strove to simplify citizenship as nationality by the expedient of enforcing ethnic and cultural homogeneity, at the same time citizenship as political enfranchisement also evolved to a homogenous pattern from the hesitant compications of nineteenth-century suffrage restrictions. First, all adult males; then, over an incredibly wide time-span as we have seen (p. 69–70), all adult females; and finally, the lowering of the age of majority to 18. A number of US states led the way in introducing this last change, starting with Georgia in 1943. However, most western democracies effected the alteration c. 1970. The measure was more significant than merely allowing a person to vote three years younger than hitherto. It also afforded the full legal and social status of citizenship to people of that age. If every young man of 18 had the duty, in an age of military conscription, to fight and die as a soldier for his country, how could he be denied, on the grounds of age alone, the concomitant rights of a citizen to have a say in public affairs, including the issue of war and peace? The anomaly became untenable. So also, in consequence, was the argument that school leavers, of 16, 17 or 18, were too immature to be given any education for citizenship. The phenomenon of soon-to-be-enfranchised or actually enfranchised school pupils put paid to that argument (p. 220).

During the course of this century it has generally been held to be a mark of good citizenship for the citizen to use his or her vote. Yet the turnout has often been quite low. For instance, in the USA, despite the historically heavy emphasis on citizen rights, only 51 per cent of the electorate voted in the Presidential elections and 48 per cent in the Congressional elections in 1948. A few liberal countries – Australia is an example – have so felt the need to strengthen the credibility of their electoral systems that they have introduced a legal obligation on citizens to cast their ballots. Such legislation is a statement that citizenship is a duty as much as a right.

However, duty or right, the occasional visit to the polling-booth has seemed to many a pathetically inadequate definition of citizenship even in the narrow political sense. The essential requirement of opportunities for meaningful participation, expressed classically by Rousseau and Mill, has been taken up with some vigour in the twentieth century. True, there have been forceful arguments in praise of citizen apathy and passivity, most particularly in the light of Fascist and Nazi manipulative techniques; and a brief summary of the most influential of those arguments will be convenient here (see also pp. 214–216). They may be characterised by reference to one of the most widely read works of American political scientists, namely Joseph Schumpeter's *Capitalism, Socialism and Democracy* (first published in 1943). Schumpeter believed that the only valid function for the citizen is to elect leaders. He argued that the classical theory of democracy, based upon the requirement of more active citizen-participation, was humbug and dangerous humbug at that. The mass of citizenry are politically torpid, ignorant and eminently manipulable. Any meddling in the function of government by the ordinary citizens would therefore divert the properly elected leaders from the efficient discharge of their duties with unhappy consequences. Political apathy, it therefore come to be argued, might well be a symptom of health rather than sickness in a society. Citizens who are satisfied with their lot and remain undisturbed by self-seeking demagogues should live naturally in a state of political quiescence.

While this paternalist view of citizenship has satisfied many, it has equally worried others who are not so confident as Schumpeter that the political élite always exercises its authority with benevolence or sagacity. Citizen alertness cannot perhaps be surrendered so serenely. The problem is that through the expansion of population, the centralisation of administration and the intrusion, for both benign and malign reasons, into the lives of its citizens, the state has become a potential threat to free social life. Size renders bureaucracies remote and two-way communication difficult. Intrusiveness renders especially imperative the need of the citizen to help direct this intrusion. Harold Laski warned in 1928:

The scale of modern civilisation has of itself done much to deprive the citizen of his freedom . . . . We shall not make citizenship a reality until we make the demand of the average man both organised and coherent.[5]

But, how to achieve it? Citizenship in the western liberal tradition presupposes that the citizen and the state are mutually respectful and supportive. Now since direct participation in central government is impossible for the mass of the citizenry, alternative functional participative institutions are necessary. But if these are damaging of the balanced citizen-state relationship, then they cannot be said to enhance the kind of free citizenship the western tradition entails. Two attempts in the twentieth century fail this test. One was syndicalism, especially as espoused by Georges Sorel in its anarchist form. The idea, originating in the nineteenth century, was for the running of industry by the workers. But since Sorel argued that the end purpose of the arrangement was the violent overthrow of the state, anarcho-syndicalism, as developed in France and Spain, can scarcely be said to enhance citizenship. The other idea was Mussolini's adaptation of Sorelian philosophy in creating the corporatist state. Workers were encouraged to participate in trade union activities, but so that they might be more effectively controlled through these

97

organisations by a manipulative police state. The status of citizenship continued to be emphasised; however, the delicate balance was lost all the same.

What has been needed in the twentieth century to foster the adaptation and development of citizenship is the willingness and opportunity of a large proportion of citizens to participate in the running of their social lives through membership of a variety of associations, interest groups and pressure groups. These bodies must be so devised as to temper the potentially overbearing power of the state without at the same time undermining its essential functions and the loyalty owed to it by the citizens. Two very distinct sets of doctrines have sought to achieve this nice balance: Roman Catholicism and Guild Socialism.

It was natural for the Papacy to argue that a society which lacked any intermediary bodies between the individual and the state was unhealthy. Moreover, as the strengthening of the state at the expense of the Church accelerated in the nineteenth century, it became prudent to reiterate this basic tenet. In 1891 Leo XIII issued the Encyclical *Rerum Novarum*; and his successor, Pius XI, reminded the world of its message forty years later in *Quadragesimo Anno*. Drawing partly on the authority of Aquinas, they argued that the formation of groupings by individuals with common interests is an absolutely natural right:

if a state forbids its citizens to form associations, it contradicts the very principle of its own existence; for both they and it exist in virtue of the like principle, namely the natural tendency of man to dwell in society.[6]

Pius added his deep regret at the decay of such organically linked associations as had flourished hitherto. But not only should the state allow townships and trade or professional groups to exist, they should have 'powers of self-government'. The state 'should leave to smaller groups the settlement of business of minor importance, which otherwise would greatly distract it'.[7] In the early 1960s John XXIII echoed the message of the critical importance of 'a whole variety of intermediate associations' in both *Mater et Magistra* and *Pacem in Terris*. 'Such groups' he wrote in the latter encyclical, 'are essential for maintaining the dignity and freedom of the human person and fostering his sense of responsibility.' Through them also 'the public authorities will be brought into closer contact with the ordinary citizens and will be better able to discern the common good.'[8] (See also pp. 322)

The secular vision of Guild Socialism, as set down in some detail by the Oxford scholar, G. D. H. Cole, had interesting affinities with papal political thought. It harked back to a medieval era when men identified more readily than in modern times with social and economic groupings. It attempted to rein in the power of the state by the relative increase in the authority of local and industrial associations. And the pattern of both community and trade and professional bodies is similar in both visions. Cole, whose impact was most pronounced in the 1920s, was much influenced by Rousseau. He also reflected Mill's beliefs in the educative function of participation and the central importance of industry as the most apt context for participatory involvement.

Cole held that the full development of the human being and in particular the growth of a responsible, democratic attitude of mind were possible only through self-government in the workplace. He argued that the lowly status of the worker negated the theoretical freedom of political enfranchisement. 'A servile system in industry inevitably reflects itself in political servility.'[9]

Workers' Councils have existed in a brave experiment in Yugoslavia since the 1950s, but have been hampered by the country's poverty. An innovative scheme of industrial democracy was proposed for Britain by the Bullock Report of 1977, only to be rapidly shelved as being too radical. At the time of writing it is uncertain how far proposals for effective worker-participation in the Single-Market Europe after 1992 will in practice be adopted. And yet since the 1960s and in the 1960s especially there has been a widespread need, felt and expressed, throughout the western democracies for more practical means of self-government. The state had come to seem unresponsive to the wishes of decent citizens. The western democratic state has heaped up nuclear stockpiles; engaged in murderous colonial wars, of which Algeria and Viet-nam were merely the most obscene; and has polluted and plundered our life-sustaining planet. In the face of such evidence, what is the concerned and responsible citizen to do? Some in recent years, like the opponents of war, conventional or nuclear, have demonstrated; others, like the ecologically con-scious, have produced evidence – all for the persuasion of governments. Disillusion with the established system and demand for greater participation reached dramatic explosive-point in 1968. Students were in the forefront, though in France for a time they attempted common cause with industrial workers. One group declared: 'We believe that our struggles are milestones on the road to a society that will be run by the workers themselves'.[10]

However, the revolutionary ardour which carried away the emotions and coloured the pronouncements of the young generation of 1968 was hardly likely to produce a renovated citizenship. Again, the delicate balance of the state-citizen relationship was under threat. What the steadier citizens wanted was regional devolution of power, the opportunity for more functional neigh-bourhood, community involvement and an intelligent say in their place of work. These styles of participation have to some extent been gradually evolv-ing. In Britain, neighbourhood and tenants' associations, community relations groups and conservation societies have grown considerably since the 1960s.

The egalitarian principle and second-class citizenship

A constant refrain of commentators and researchers since the 1920s has been the low rate of participation, whatever the opportunities, by the poorly edu-cated and lower classes of society. And yet if all citizens are equal, they should have equal opportunities and motivation for participatory activity. Citizenship is distorted by the presence of gross inequalities of education and economic means. When certain segments of society are disadvantaged in these ways, so it may be argued, the state should take on the responsibility of introducing compensatory measures. We have already seen how this welfare-state dimension of citizenship was promulgated by the English Idealists in the late nineteenth century (pp. 74–76). Connecting links into the twentieth century were provided in the most distinguished forms of R. H. Tawney and William Beveridge. Tawney shared with T. H. Green both a deep Christian faith and a hatred of the English class structure, which he displayed to powerful effect in his lectures published in 1931 under the title, *Equality*. He was convinced that the concession of political equality through the suffrage without more social and economic equality was not only unjust and unchristian – it was dangerous. He argued for a levelling up of the disadvantaged classes by means of better education, in which he placed great hopes. It was he, in 1924, who coined the phrase 'secondary education for all', which became a Labour Party slogan and was given legislative reality by the Conservative minister R. A. Butler in 1944.

This Education Act was part of the welfare-state legislation, much of which was inspired by Beveridge. The Idealist citizenship purpose of these measures is crystal clear from his report, in which he wrote:

The aim of the Plan for Social Security is to abolish want by ensuring that every citizen willing to serve according to his powers has at all times an income sufficient to meet his responsibilities.[11]

A commitment to the levelling up of social and educational standards was a general feature of the domestic policies of most European governments following the Second World War. By the mid-1960s the states of Western Europe and Scandinavia were spending between 11 and 17 per cent of GNP on social services.

The relationship of such welfare provision to the status of citizenship in England was analysed by the Cambridge sociologist, T. H. Marshall, in a seminal series of lectures and published in 1950 under the title of *Citizenship and Social Class*. In this and subsequent works he focussed on the tension between civil and political citizenship on the one hand and social citizenship on the other. He portrayed England as a society in which the civil rights and legal status of citizenship were consolidated in the eighteenth century (from, roughly, the Habeas Corpus Act to Catholic Emancipation); political rights, mainly the franchise, were extended in the nineteenth; and the social rights of the welfare state and education were demanded and conceded in the twentieth. He viewed the extension of citizenship into the social sphere as a recovery on the national plane of the social rights which had been enjoyed in local communities before the depredations of the Industrial Revolution and the Poor Law Amendment Act. In the process of restoration he believed that the spread of education has played a major role:

Fundamentally it should be regarded, not as a right of the child to go to school, but as the right of the adult citizen to have been educated . . . the growth of public elementary education during the nineteenth century was the first decisive step on the road to the re-establishment of the social rights of citizenship in the twentieth.[12]

However, the egalitarian thrust of social citizenship raised a more serious challenge to the status quo than the earlier extensions of civil and political rights. Where the expansion of legal-political citizenship had been very much in the interests of the capitalist class, the expansion of social citizenship was very much not. It was a direct challenge to the hierarchical class structure of English society. Hence Marshall's somewhat startling core message: 'it is clear that, in the twentieth century, citizenship and the capitalist system have been at war.'[13] Citizenship is predicated upon the principle of equality, capitalism on inequality. A collision between the two was inevitable. But the problem, he came to see, was rather more complex than that. For as between the rival demands of welfare and profit the state has had to make a judgment: its taxation and expenditure policies have been shaped by the relative support accorded to each. However, the state has not resolved the tension. Consequently the extension of citizenship, because of these complicating forces, has led not to the proper outcome of a more cohesive society, but to a 'hyphenated society', which is inherently unstable.

The American philosopher John Rawls has attempted a form of reconciliation. He accepts the dual positions held by the individual: 'that of equal citizenship and that defined by his place in the distribution of income and wealth.'[14] In a good society, however, the tension will be resolved by adherence to the principles of liberty and justice. In particular, he argues that social and economic inequalities are acceptable if they are so arranged as to improve the position of the least advantaged. That would be fair; and it is a sense of unfairness that rankles.

Now, although Rawls' work has received the plaudits of academic philosophers, there is little evidence that his message has been digested by governments. On the other hand, the teachings of F. A. Hayek very evidently have. Liberty, he has taught, is of the utmost preciousness. If the state interferes with individual liberty and in particular with the free operation of the capitalist market, the results can only be pernicious. State planning, welfare schemes and taxation are detrimental to freedom. Such policies, as the evidence of the totalitarian states of the 1930s and 1940s proved, can only destroy individualism and lead us down the dark *Road to Serfdom*, as he called his influential 1944 book.

Hayek's work provided an intellectual undergirding to New Right policies of Thatcherite Britain and Reaganite America in the 1980s. The concept of social citizenship was rejected. Indeed, Mrs Thatcher attacked the very notion of social responsibility by asserting in 1987 that 'there is no such thing as society' (see p. 252). The welfare state and all that socialism stands for has led to an enfeeblement of moral fibre, a habit of reliance upon the 'nanny' state at the expense of self-help and self-respect. In the USA the reduction in federal budget provision for welfare programmes by the Reagan administration was brutally sudden. For example, the Budget for Fiscal Year 1982 slashed by 20 per cent and 17 per cent respectively the funds available for Food Stamps and AFDC (Aids for Families with Dependent Children). These were precisely the programmes upon which 80–90 per cent of poor had been dependent. For the New Right, citizenship is a splendid concept in so far as it brings out the virtues of good, law-abiding behaviour and enthusiastic national loyalty.

Liberty and fraternity are fine, up to a point, though one must be careful how one interprets fraternity. But equality is dangerous. If citizenship requires an egalitarian levelling of social differences, so much the worse for citizenship. Better there be different grades of the status. And, at the same time it would be prudent to damp down the enthusiasm for too much political participation (pp. 214–216).

Gradations of citizenship, certainly on grounds of race, have been noticeably persistent in the USA. The issue of racial discrimination has also raised awkward questions regarding the nature of citizenship in several European states since the 1960s, particularly Britain. For a life-span, c. 1875–1945), few people in the United States, not even the Blacks themselves, challenged the reality of Negro second-class citizenship. They could not trust the police, certainly in the southern states, to provide them with the protection of the law against victimisation. In politics, apart from the various unfair barriers to enfranchisement (p. 69), those who were eligible were hesitant to register themselves on the electoral roll. There were, after all, fearful disincentives, even as late as the 1960s. As the Black Muslim leader, Malcolm X, challenged:

Come down and try to register. You may lose your job, you may even lose your house. You may be beaten. . . but join us, come on down and register to vote.[15]

And in social terms there was prejudice, discrimination and segregation. The myth of separate but equal provision and 'Jim Crow' laws made it legal from 1896 to 1954 to require Blacks to attend different schools, ride in different parts of buses, eat in different areas of restaurants.

The Second World War changed the atmosphere. Was not one of the goals to destroy Nazism – a régime based on the proposition of racial distinctiveness? Wendell Wilkie was to popularise a phrase by writing in the *New York Times* in 1944, 'The Constitution does not provide for first and second-class citizens.' Subsequently by both government intervention and Black pressure the condition of second-class citizenship was gradually eased. In 1954 the Supreme Court ruled that 'in the field of public education the doctrine of "separate but equal" has no place.' (p. 111) After many dramatic events and demonstrations desegregation was achieved in many social contexts. Black people raised the consciousness of their own kind to the legality and justice of claiming their rights as citizens – through campaigns for civil rights and voter-registration. However, the leeway that had to be made up represented a daunting gap. The continuing efforts of Rosa Parks provides a personal exemplification of the need for dogged persistence. In February 1955 this black seamstress took a seat on a bus in Montgomery, Alabama. She refused to surrender it to a white man as custom demanded. Her courage was a catalyst for a black boycott of buses, which in turn became a massive Civil Rights movement. Thirty-three years later she commented, 'I think it's sort of sad to know that we have to persuade people to register after the long struggle we had in the South to become registered voters and to be able to vote freely.'[16] She was at the time involved in a campaign to persuade hundreds of thousands of Blacks and Hispanics in New York state to enter the electoral register. For as late as the 1980s both Blacks and the rising numbers of Spanish-speaking Americans were US citizens in only a marginal, strictly legal sense. Certainly in terms of the welfare test of citizenship, as well as in the sense of making use of the franchise, millions were cast into a second-class category. A report published in 1987 revealed that 27.3 per cent of Hispanics and 31.1 per cent of Blacks (compared with 11 percent of 'Whites') were living in a condition officially designated as poverty.

In the USA and Western Europe from the 1960s to the 1980s ease of transport and the magnet of employment possibilities attracted large numbers of people from ethnically different countries. This phenomenon became pertinent to the issue of citizenship in three ways. One concerned the status of migrant workers. For example, hundreds of thousands of Mexicans, Turks and Algerians were attracted to the USA, West Germany and France respectively. And yet, although many stayed for some years and became in a sense integrated in their host communities, they were denied any rights of citizenship. Legally they have had no cause for complaint: many have accepted temporary work permits; others are illegal immigrants. They present an anomalous worry none the less. The second problem concerns discrimination against coloured people, even though they are legally full citizens of the states in which they reside. This problem has been particularly evident in France and Britain. In both countries substantial numbers of coloured immigrants have settled perfectly legitimately from various parts of these nations' former extensive empires. Yet in both countries public opinion, the activities of neo-Nazi movements and the questionable tactics of the police have all helped to deny coloured inhabitants their full rights as citizens. By the late 1980s the one million French citizens of North African origin and the half-million of West Indian origin were subject to quite routine police harassment. In Britain a number of urban black communities, already depressed by poor housing and high unemployment, erupted in dangerous riots in the early 1980s in large measure because of resentment at methods used in policing these districts.

As a means of stemming further coloured immigration in the face of these communal tensions, governments of both states sought to redraft their laws on citizenship. The British story is by far the more convoluted. There are multiple reasons for this. It is partly the continuing British preference for defining citizens rather as subjects of the monarch (p. 293), itself in some way the result of having no consolidated written constitution. Partly it is the vagueness of the constitutional law which bound the components of the Empire to the metropolitan country. And partly it is the ambivalence of successive governments, caught between the fear of being dubbed racist if coloured immigrants were treated with too transparent a difference from white, and the fear of too violent a white reaction if large numbers of culturally distinctive immigrants were allowed to settle. A feeble attempt at definition was first made in the Imperial Act of 1914. By this measure all inhabitants of the Dominions and Colonies were deemed to owe allegiance to the Crown and were therefore British subjects. In the usual British way of handling such matters, little importance was attached to the need for precise definitions until Indian independence in 1947, involving, of course, very large numbers of coloured people.

In 1948 came the first of a series of attempts to clarify the law regarding British citizenship: the British Nationality Act. This made a distinction between a 'citizen of the United Kingdom and Colonies' on the one hand and a 'Commonwealth citizen' on the other. A Commonwealth citizen was a member of a self-governing state, for example, Canada or India. Since such people were most relevantly citizens of their own countries, the status of 'Commonwealth citizen' was really thought initially to be little more than a formal gesture. However, as an increasing number of colonies gained independence, so an increasing number of people entered this category and one issue became significant and contentious, namely, whether Commonwealth citizens had the right of unrestricted immigration into Britain. Fears of communal tension were heightened as the number of such immigrants increased in the 1960s. As a consequence this right of entry came to be more and more urgently questioned. Particularly difficult problems occurred with the attainment of independence of the East African colonies. The inhabitants were given the option of British or local national citizenship. Many of the Asian minorities opted for British citizenship. There then arose the subsidiary question of whether someone opting for, say, Ugandan citizenship could revoke that decision and subsequently apply for Britain citizenship. The issue became acute in Uganda in the 1960s when Idi Amin's manic tribalism and racism verged on the genocidal.

The legislative attempts to stem the flow of coloured immigrants into Britain culminated in the British Nationality Act of 1981. This was a baroque legislative edifice ornamented by a profusion of six categories of citizenship. The first category, the one which accords full rights, is confined to those born in Britain of British parents or a parent 'settled' in Britain, or those born overseas of at least one British parent or grandparent. Significantly, the act revoked the right of *ius soli* (p. 249), that is the right of citizenship according to place of birth irrespective of parentage. The other categories are: Citizens of British Dependent Territories, British Overseas Citizens, British Protected Persons, Commonwealth Citizens and British Subjects.

The main purpose of the act was to preclude people in these five categories from any automatic right of entry and domicile in Britain. Yet rarely, if ever, in the history of citizenship can attempts at legal definition have led to such contortions. It is scarcely surprising that the act did not prevent claims to citizen rights by many people who, wittingly or unwittingly, fall outside all categories. In the words of the Home Office minister responsible for immigration in 1987: 'Last year some 1,500 women and children arrived here claiming to be British citizens but with no supporting evidence.'[17]

Modern educational theory and citizenship

Many a commentator has remarked upon the critical role of education for ironing out the anomaly of second-class citizenship – whether this disadvantage derives from economic, social or racial causes. Education, it is felt, can raise the status of those discriminated against and lower the prejudice of the discriminators. However, insofar as major educational thinkers of the century have addressed the issue of education for citizenship, they have been concerned in the main with the relative importance of education for individual development compared with education for social purpose and the educational needs of a democratic polity.

Ever since the publication of Rousseau's *Emile* (1762) the concept of education as a 'leading out' (*educere*) of the individual personality has vied with the belief that its prime function is a preparation or moulding for life in society. With the coming of liberal democracy these two purposes were no longer quite so antagonistic. If the political system was based upon the primacy of liberty of opinion, choice and action, then its objectives must surely be in harmony with the free expression methods of child-centred education. The most influential educational thinker at the turn of the century was the American philosopher, John Dewey. His advocacy of heuristic activity methods, which he wrote about theoretically and confirmed pragmatically in his Laboratory School in Chicago, has had an impact well beyond the USA. He expounded the specific pertinence of his work for citizen education in *Democracy and Education* (1916).

At the heart of Dewey's education of the democratic citizen lay the implicit rejection of authority and tradition as the source of learning. The whole point of the Dewey technique is problem-solving. The child learns by finding out for himself. It is just such a questioning frame of mind that is required of the active and responsible citizen. But what he was just as much at pains to emphasise was his conviction that a democratic polity requires a socially generous attitude of mind, which it is the responsibility of the schools to foster. Modern democratic societies are characterised by change, and they can comfortably accommodate change only if their citizens are possessed of the essential qualities of understanding and empathy.

Such a society [he wrote] must have a type of education which gives individuals a personal interest in social relationships and control, and the habits of mind which secure social changes without introducing disorder.

Moreover, he defines this 'civic efficiency or good citizenship' as 'neither more nor less than capacity to share in a give or take experience'.[18] He believed that this quality was not just a matter of a co-operative atmosphere at the micro-level of the classroom, but the sharing of a common culture through the macro-level of a common national system of schooling. For Dewey the mode of learning was more important than the content. Indeed, he felt that good citizenship was more likely to be nourished through art and recreation than any formal political training. Insofar as Dewey's work encouraged citizenship education through subject teaching, it was to promote among his Progressivist followers the inquiring form of Social Studies in American High Schools as an alternative to rote-learned History.

Dewey had little to say about the desirable society which his style of education might be expected to promote. The influential interpenetration of educational and socio-political cultures did, in contrast, interest the two major thinkers who came from the European background of Sociology: Emile Durkheim and Karl Mannheim. Although better known for his general sociological work, Durkheim's chair at the Sorbonne was in Education. He was particularly conscious of the way each society shapes and needs to shape its educational institutions for the sake of homogeneity and stability. He thus came to define the purpose of education as

. . . to arouse and develop in the child a certain number of physical, intellectual and moral states, which are demanded of him by both political society as a whole and the social milieu for which he is specifically destined.[19]

Durkheim, however, lived in an age of comparative political consensus (he died in 1917). He could therefore write with confidence about 'homogeneity' and 'collective consciousness'. Mannheim, on the contrary, lived through the bitter ideological hatreds of the Hungarian Communist revolution of 1918–19 and the Nazi seizure of power in Germany, from whence he fled to England in 1933. As the quotation on p. 94 reveals, Mannheim was concerned to strengthen democracy. He believed that a good society could be developed, innocent of the evils of either laissez-faire capitalism or totalitarian regimentation. This could be achieved by detailed planning. He was obsessed with planning. And crucial to such a programme was education. Like Dewey he believed that schools should prepare young people for a society in constant flux and nurture in them a type of tolerant personality suited to the democratic polity he advocated. Indeed, he understood the interdependence of these two considerations. '. . . the democratic personality,' he wrote in his posthumous *Freedom, Power and Democratic Planning,* 'welcomes disagreement because it has the courage to expose itself to change.'[20]

The awareness that societal forces shape education has been a particularly potent idea during the second half of the twentieth century. However, most commentators have stressed, *pace* Durkheim, the heterogeneity, even divisiveness, of these forces. They have consequently argued that it is the dominant force in society that will effectively determine the attitudes imbibed by pupils in school. Both the overt and hidden curricula will be determined in this way and the youth will in effect be indoctrinated into acceptance of these values. The case fits especially neatly, of course, into a Marxist interpretation. Marx asserted quite plainly that the intellectual climate of a society is determined by its ruling class. A bourgeois society will teach bourgeois values. Many an educationist, consciously guided by Marxist principles or not, has become alert to societal pressures on schools. Not only can the selective co-existence of different kinds of schools be interpreted as sustaining privilege, but so also can the structuring of different curricula: Latin for the élite; craft for the *hoi polloi*.

The French Marxist Althusser has stretched the idea to its ultimate point. He has claimed, in his contorted prose, that the use of the educational system for indoctrinating purposes by the dominant class is the sole significant method of establishing its control. He wrote:

I believe that the ideological state apparatus which has been installed in the *dominant* position in mature capitalist social formations as a result of a violent political and ideological class struggle against the dominant ideological state apparatus, is the *educational ideological apparatus.*[21]

More temperate and more influential are the arguments of the older Italian Marxist trade unionist, Antonio Gramsci, as expressed in his famous *Prison Notebooks*. His central concept was hegemony. By this he meant the exercise of non-violent control by the dominant class over an acquiescent subordinate class or classes. A variety of social institutions, including schools, he argued, are responsible for instilling this quiet acceptance of the status quo. He did not, however, believe that the revolutionary substitution of a proletarian hegemony could be accomplished by changing school curricula. He believed rather in the political education of adults in the context of their work places, a process which would 'spread an awareness of the rights and duties of comrades and workers.'[22] However, rights and duties perceived through the refracting prism of class consciousness are not synonymous with the rights and duties of citizens. Or rather they are not, unless one accepts the case that an egalitarian citizenship existing in parallel with and beyond class distinctions is a mirage. Whether one holds that such a notion is a mental mirage or a concept of substance has inevitably a critical effect on one's view of education for the role of citizenship. Indeed, the objectivity of the so-called Social Sciences, the very intellectual tools for the shaping of citizens, is thrown into question by this argument. If there is a bourgeois Social Science and a Marxist Social Science, each denying the objectivity of the other, what chance has the student of achieving a clinical understanding of his role as an intelligent and responsible citizen? This was one of the central issues which the rebellious students debated on their campuses in 1968.

Variations in citizenship education

Much twentieth-century educational thinking in its variegated forms has been distinguished by its perceptive concerns for citizenship education, but examples of practical impact are somewhat scanty. One could expect to find such evidence in the USA, if anywhere. Dewey was respected and his ideas were purveyed in teacher-training courses; education for citizenship, as we have seen (p. 84), was firmly established as a social and political necessity by the end of the last century; and Social Studies came to be a significant slot on the time-table from Kindergarten to High School grade 12 as a means of conducting such education. Even so, little has been built on the early endeavours. One distinguished American academic could write in 1981 that

. . . the dominant pattern of the social studies . . . has persisted without substantial change for more than fifty years, despite phenomenal technological, economic and other social changes that have transpired during that period.[23]

By the start of the twentieth century the schools of the western nations were transmitting a certain amount of information and some kinds of attitudes to help form certain styles of citizenship. But there is little common pattern. What the schools have undertaken has been in response to varying intensities of governmental pressure and haphazard reactions to fluctuating academic enthusiasms.

Useful comparative evidence is available from two studies carried out half a century apart. The first, written in the late 1920s under the supervision of the American political scientist Charles Merriam, analysed nine countries. Summarising his colleagues' findings, he revealed that the USA was in advance of all the other countries in such curricular provision and made the following generalisation:

The German, French, Swiss, and American systems are similar in many ways. They represent types of civic education in which deliberate planning is emphasized, and a conscious effort is made to inculcate political interest and loyalty . . . an interest in orderly and systematic development of civic mores . . . is notably absent in England or at least until relatively recent times . . .. The Austro-Hungarian system is unique in its neglect of ordinary methods employed for the encouragement of civic interest and enthusiasm.[24]

The second survey (of ten countries) was commissioned by the International Association for the Evaluation of Educational Achievement and was published in 1975. The team reported civic education for 14-year olds, in the narrow sense of political syllabuses,

. . . in the Federal Republic of Germany, Iran, Israel, the Netherlands and in about half the United States and Finnish Schools; it is not taught in Italy or New Zealand.[25]

However, if History and Social Studies are included, an average of about 90 per cent of 14-year olds pursued such courses.

Not only have there been differences of provision between countries within this extremely general attitude of accepting that 'something should be done'. In addition there have on occasions been specific influences which have encouraged or forced schools to adapt. Obviously, traumatic political changes are bound to bring in their train drastic alterations to the work of schools in this sphere. The most dramatic examples relate to the establishment of dictatorial régimes and their subsequent democratisation. The oscillation of Germany from Imperial to Weimar to Nazi to Bonn régimes provides the most fascinating illustration of this process. However, this facet of the subject will be dealt with in the next section of the present chapter. Less intense pressures have also had their effects. A few examples may serve to illustrate this. During the inter-war period and more especially in the 1960s the Swedish government attempted to instil a greater appreciation of the country's industrial expansion by injecting a study of Economics into courses. In the USA the dreadful experience of the Depression occasioned a host of projects, including practical community work, to heighten the consciousness of young people to the social problems of the age. In England at this time the greatest concern was the threat to the democratic way of life posed by the rise of totalitarianism. The Association for Education in Citizenship was founded in 1934 to strengthen commitment to the English polity. In France the experiences of shame and division of the Second World War and the shock of the 1968 uprising shattered the very principles of national pride and cohesion upon which the *instruction civique* of the 1880s had been founded. More psychologically manageable was the lowering of the age of majority (p. 96). It nevertheless brought into sharp focus the inadequacy of the civic education received by many young citizens. The following expression of panic in a circular letter by the Belgian Senior Minister for National Education is very revealing:

You will be aware that Parliament has decided to set the voting age at 18. This presupposes that our young people have sufficient knowledge of our institutions, of political life and of government.
Currently it is evident that most adolescents are badly informed in this regard. . . .
. . . . as municipal elections are imminent, I felt it necessary to take exceptional measures.[26]

He instituted an immediate strengthening of History teaching in the first two years of secondary education.

The centralised direction of education for citizenship has varied from state to state. The best example of tight control has remained France. All schools have been required to devote full attention to national History. Until the 1970s this was chronological, political and nationalist in style. Then, the influence of the Annales school of historiography led to the complete rewriting of syllabuses and textbooks to reflect the new emphasis on analytical social History. However, popular opposition to this form of civic education led to further government intervention and, by the mid-1980s, the restoration of political chronology. Sweden has also had considerable governmental direction in both the time-allocation for and subject-content of civic education. Government has constantly tinkered with the pattern by various directives in 1919, 1946, 1962, 1969 and 1980. The USA provides the best example of diversity within a loose overall framework. A pattern was already emerging by the turn of the century. This was consolidated by a report published in 1916 by the federal government for the National Education Association Committee on the Social Studies. It provided for a syllabus-amalgam of History, Geography and Government, mainly American, though with some matter of wider scope. Syllabuses and textbooks soon fell into this conforming pattern. The spread of popular discontent and disorder in the 1960s prompted the federal government to provide funds for Social Studies and teacher training in Civics. Further again towards the pole of laxity of control may be found in Australia. Here, although educational institutions are formally free of government direction, some guidelines have been made clear. Primary schools have been expected to induct young children into a national consciousness, while

The Secretary of State has constantly required that teachers should avoid in their teaching all commentary on political questions or religious questions of controversial content.[27]

For the gentlest of central direction one must look to the case of England. The virtually unique arrangement whereby local authorities have administered schools and the schools themselves determined their own curricula allowed central government very little opportunity to influence the content or style of education. The Ministry of Education (under its various names) has issued handbooks and pamphlets and commissioned reports, and HMI (schools inspectorate) has provided advice on standards. Official encouragement for education for citizenship has been weak and intermittent. The phase of 'educating our masters' (p. 85) lasted into the early years of the present century. The prevailing attitude for decades then became the belief that political matters were beyond the comprehension of school children. Even when the· Association for Education in Citizenship tried to stimulate positive support for threatened democratic values in the schools in the late 1930s, they met stolid bureaucratic resistance at the Board of Education. Not until the 1970s did ministers display much real interest. And then because the lowering of the age of franchise and the influence in some schools of neo-Nazi groups rendered neglect of the matter respectively illogical and perilous. A key document was issued by two HMIs in 1977, in which they declared that

The school curriculum would be wise . . . to increase the likelihood of *responsible* participation by supporting it with knowledge and an informed understanding of the potential, and the limitations, of the contribution of individuals to their own government.[28]

Even so, they emphasised that this was a personal, not an official document. And nine years later a suspicious government made it illegal to promote 'partisan political views in the teaching of any subject in the school' and required 'a balanced presentation of opposing views.'[29]

Education and national cohesion

Insofar as governments have fostered civic education, their most common motive has been to sustain national pride. Even in Britain state schools interrupted their normal programmes once a year in celebration of Empire Day. Australian primary school teachers have been required to teach their young pupils about the monarchy and the Empire/Commonwealth. For much of the century France remained the epitome of this policy as school History lessons glorified 'La patrie'.

For most states History has been the staple of citizenship education. Partly this was the result of professional organisation. The American Historical Association (founded 1884) and the Historical Association, founded in Britain in 1906, were powerful influences. In any case, the subject, given its academic condition during the first half of this century, lent itself very readily to this use. Military prowess was remembered with pride through the exploits of commanders such as Napoleon; political achievements, through the analysis of documents like the American Constitution. In Sweden religion has played a significant partner role in 'God and my country' teaching; while in Switzerland cantonal history has featured alongside 'national' history. How many teachers realised before, say, c.1960, just how biassed their teaching was? In their great comic book, *1066 And All That*, Seller and Yeatman lampooned

110

the history of 'the Great British People without whose self-sacrificing determination to become top Nation there would have been no (memorable) history.'[30] A similar book could have been written in any western country — provided, of course, the people had the capacity to laugh at themselves and their civic traditions. Until comparatively recently, few states had multi-disciplinary Social Studies with a stress on contemporary affairs comparable with History syllabuses. This form of citizenship education was pioneered in the USA. Specifically political components in these programmes took root earlier than in most other western countries too. As a result, by the early 1960s nearly a fifth of High School students in the top four grades were taking government or civics courses, including the two-thirds of all twelfth-graders enrolled for courses in advanced civics and problems of democracy[31].

Symbolism and ceremony have continued as potent influences in both schools and youth movements. Cadet forces and civilian uniformed organisations, notably the Scouts, have reinforced the patriotic message in several nations. Referring to these bodies, Charles Merriam wrote in 1931:

These groups pursue the familiar methods of the Scout organization now well standardized throughout the Western world. Precept, symbolism, play, excursions, are relied upon to produce a responsible type of citizen in the broader sense of the term and a political citizen in the more restricted sense. There are in America roughly 1,000,000 members of these various organizations.[32]

The civic message of belonging has been muted for many Blacks in US schools for much of the century and in English and French schools in recent decades. Until c. 1960 'race relations, racism . . . ethnic group inequities in education and economic opportunity . . . were "closed areas" and discreetly sidestepped by social studies teachers in the USA.'[33] Not indeed until 1954 was segregation by race declared unconstitutional. In that year the Supreme Court made its famous ruling in the Brown v. Board of Education of Topeka case. This judgment declared that education

. . . is the very foundation of good citizenship. . . .[and] is a right which must be made available to all on equal terms . . . .. We conclude that in the field of public education the doctrine of 'separate but equal' has no place . . . .. Therefore, we hold that the plaintiffs . . . are deprived of the equal protection of the laws guaranteed by the Fourteenth Amendment.[34]

In England, the needs of the schools to respond to the increasingly multicultural character of the nation could no longer be ignored by the 1970s. As was the wont of English governments in such circumstances, a committee of enquiry was established. Its report, issued over the signature of its chairman, Lord Swann, was published in 1985. In addition to the obvious requirement to furnish minority groups with basic literacy skills in the host language, the report emphasised the central importance of civic consciousness and competence for all:

Learning how some long-established practices were originally developed to cater for a relatively homogeneous population should lead youngsters by extension to consider whether such practices are still appropriate to the changed and changing nature of

British society today. . . . In thus learning how racism can operate, youngsters from both the minority and majority communities may be better able to understand and challenge its influence and to consider positive and constructive changes to reflect the values of a pluralist democracy.[35]

School democracy

For some teachers, educating for active democracy by means of disciplining children passively to read books about the constitution, is at best a counter-productive contradiction and at worst an insult to the pupils. During the inter-war period particularly some educationists started to argue that the only honest and effective preparation for a democracy is to allow schools to function as democracies. An influential pioneer was the American Homer Lane, who, during the First World War, ran a school for slum delinquents in London. By expecting responsible behaviour of his charges they became responsible citizens of this Little Commonwealth. Lane's work was much admired by A. S. Neill, whose own school, Summerhill, became the famous model of pupil self-government. He expounded his credo on many occasions. At the end of his long life he wrote,

The Little Commonwealth was as near to a democracy as could be. . . .
. . . . at Summerhill self-government works. Each child has a vote and a voice, irrespective of age. . . . The children are learning to live with others by interacting with their peers, being judged by their equals and not by their fathers and mothers and teachers.[36]

Few state schools could risk this dismantling of the authority structure. Some introduced school councils with strictly limited powers. Then in the upsurge of participatory demands in the 1960s there was renewed interest in these ideas. Furthermore, a new dimension was added, namely, the belief that children have distinctive natural rights. This idea was internationally codified by the UN Declaration of the Rights of Children in 1959. Perhaps these rights are infringed by autocratic school management? For example, in 1982 the European Court of Human Rights defined corporal punishment as a violation of human rights. Certainly by the 1980s few schools in Western nations were as authoritarian as they had been a generation earlier. On the other hand, critics interpreted the changes as a tendency to the anarchy of pupil power rather than the democracy of mature citizenship.

A confused scene

Indeed, for all the attempts by the school systems of the Western world to respond to the task of citizenship preparation, there is little satisfaction in what has been achieved. The pessimism is expressed in various shades of gloom. Some commentators stress the resistance of government or the establishment to a form of teaching which can just as likely sponsor a critical questioning of as conformity with the status quo. Such considerations have led the Dutchman Langeveld to conclude, 'Possibilities for political education are probably marginal everywhere.'[37] Hostility to civic education has also derived from concern at the overcrowding of the curriculum. In particular, complaints have been voiced about the diversion of pupils' attention from the foundation skills of literacy and numeracy. In the USA and Britain the demand has been formulated as 'back to basics'; in France, as 'school exists in order to teach.' A Swedish committee reported in 1981 that 'the space allotted to social studies on the timetable has decreased sharply . . . since the end of the 1940s.'[38]

But even when there is agreement that citizenship education is desirable, there has been perplexing confusion about the precise objectives and content of such teaching. Part of this uncertainty has derived from the rapidity of social and political changes, especially since 1945. If there is no civic stability, a great strain is placed upon the schools to alter their teaching in response. One of the most interesting examples of this problem has been France. The clear, self-confident programme of the *instruction civique* of the Third Republic has been shown to be irrelevant under the Fifth. Mona Ozouf has commented that,

The past fifteen or twenty years have been characterized by the discovery of differences: social, ethnic, sexual, generational. They did not facilitate a type of instruction geared toward abstract and identical individuals: citizens.[39]

There has been deep professional disagreement among teachers and educationists, too, and not all derived from obvious socio-political factors. Even in the USA, where so much attention has been afforded the matter, John Patrick could make the following caustic comment the state of civic education in 1970:

Disparate topics such as consumer economics, life adjustment, occupations, health, personal grooming, and descriptions of government agencies are thrown together to form the content of instruction. Bland descriptions, superficial moralizing, and distortions of reality blight standard instructional materials.[40]

Nor have teachers always displayed the widespread and urgent commitment to improve matters which the specialists in the field have pleaded as necessary. Thus, in Australia Dr Dufty wrote in 1970 that 'too few educationalists had heeded' the words of Professor Connell, who had stated that 'the development of an effective and coherent programme of social studies' was 'the single most important reform needed in Australian primary and secondary curricula.'[41] A decade later Dr Stradling judged that in England 'comparatively few schools offer political education courses for students below the age of 16.'[42]

By the 1980s the modern concept of citizenship in the Western world was two centuries old and the practice of mass education had been established for a century. Yet the problem of working out the interconnections between these two developments had by no means been satisfactorily solved by the liberal democracies. In the meantime, however, an utterly different approach to the matter was adopted by totalitarian régimes.

3.2 TOTALITARIANISM

All over Oceania this morning there were irrepressible spontaneous demonstrations when workers marched out of factories and offices and paraded through the streets with banners voicing their gratitude to Big Brother for the new, happy life which his wise leadership has bestowed upon us.

George Orwell,[43]

The mobilization of citizens

As ideology and as a style of government totalitarianism has been shot through with ambiguities. Régimes to which we may justifiably affix this label are autocratic, yet founded on theories of government by the will of the populace; are terroristic, yet depend on the fervent expression of mass support; and are socially divisive in their policies, yet appeal to the cohering principle of citizenship. Theoretically there should have been little or no room for citizenship in either Communism or Nazism. According to Marxist analysis the individual's socio-political consciousness and identity are determined by his class, not by his relationship to the state; and, in any case, the state is a bourgeois construct, which is due to wither away. The theoretically orthodox Lenin, therefore, banished the terms 'state' and 'citizen' from the vocabulary of his 1924 constitution: Soviet people were identified as 'proletarians', 'peasants' or 'soldiers'. Nor did the Nazi creed hold much store by abstract principles like citizen-state relationships. What was real for them was identity with the *Volk* and personal allegiance to the Führer.

Nevertheless, in the Soviet Union Stalin felt the need to restore both the state and the citizen as constitutional concepts. Trumpeted as 'the most democratic in the world', the Stalin Constitution is a splendid monument to the desire of totalitarians to present a façade of impeccable constitutionality. It provided for the participation of all citizens over eighteen through voting in elections for the Supreme Soviet. There was, also, an impressive list of citizens' rights, including freedom of conscience, speech and assembly and inviolability of the person and his home. The list owed more to the bourgeois ideals of the French Revolution than the realities of life in Stalin's police state. More honest than the catalogue of rights was the list of the citizens' duties. These included: 'observing the law, maintaining labour discipline, honestly performing public duties, respecting the rules of the Socialist community, safeguarding and strengthening public, Socialist property, and defending the Socialist fatherland.'[44]

The first constitution of the Chinese People's Republic, promulgated in 1954, was analogous to Stalin's. All eighteen year-olds were given the right to vote in elections for a legislative National People's Congress, defined as 'the highest organ of state power' – in practice, subordinated to the parallel Party structure. The detailed pronouncement of civil and social rights did, in truth unlike the Stalin document, carry a codicil of honesty; for the government reserved the right to 'reform traitors and counterreactionaries'. Indeed, there

114

is a touching ingenuousness, or perhaps oriental subtlety, in the way Maoist China in contrast to Stalinist Russia attempted to square a Marxist 'people's dictatorship' with the bourgeois concept of citizenship enshrined in their constitutional laws. An outside observer may particularly relish the listing of the constitutional right to strike – on condition that the protest does not disrupt production!

The Nazis had no need to manufacture an artificial fig-leaf of liberal constitutionalism. They inherited the Weimar constitution, which was exceedingly democratic. In practice, of course, the power of Hitler's government became so distended that these constitutional safeguards shrank in proportion to no more than a legalistic fig-leaf. And they were just as useless for protecting the essentials from determined assault. In terms of law the Nazis were much more interested, not surprisingly, to define citizenship in terms of race. Laws were framed initially in July 1933 'on the revocation of naturalization and on the revocation of German citizenship'. These can now be seen as laying the foundations for the notorious Nuremberg Laws. In September 1935 Hitler summoned the *Reichstag* to a special session in that city. On the fifteenth a group of particularly determined anti-semites met in a beer-hall and sketched out on menus the two laws which were unanimously approved later that day. The first of these, the Reich Citizen Law, read as follows:

ARTICLE 1. (1) A subject of the State is one who belongs to the protective union of the German Reich, and who, therefore, has specific obligations to the Reich . . .
ARTICLE 2. (2) A citizen of the Reich may be only that subject who is of German or kindred blood, and who, through his behaviour, shows that he is both desirous and personally fit to serve loyally the German people and the Reich.

The second enactment, the Law for the Protection of German Blood and Honour, forbade Jews even from declaring their German nationality symbolically:

ARTICLE 4. (1) Jews are prohibited from displaying the Reich and national flag and from showing the national colours.[45]

Racial classification has also, of course, been central to the definition of citizenship in the quasi-totalitarian South Africa. Within the confines of the apartheid system a variety of devices has been conceived to offer the majority black 'Bantu' population some very partial concessions. For example, from 1936 to 1959 they had the right to elect a tiny handful of white representatives to the Senate. This system was summarily removed by the Promotion of Bantu Self-Government Act in the latter year. The objective of the gradual concession of so-called national independence to the ten Bantustan Homelands was that black citizenship should relate only to these scattered territories. The Minister of Bantu Administration and Development explained this in 1978:

If our policy is taken to its logical conclusion as far as the black people are concerned, there will not be one black man with South African citizenship . . . Every black man in South Africa will eventually be accommodated in some independent new state in this honourable way and there will no longer be a moral obligation to accommodate these people politically.[46]

In a determined effort to put the policy into practice over eight million were removed to the Homelands in the period 1976–1981, many very much against their wills. In effect this meant not just physical deportation, but wholesale deprivation of South African nationality for these people. By the mid-1980s, however, the practical difficulties of such a purist interpretation of apartheid (not to mention its likely breach of international law) caused the government to have second thoughts.

The status of citizen in totalitarian states can be imagined as stretching over a wide spectrum. True, democratic states have often relegated women and religious and ethnic minorities to a second-class grade. But under totalitarianism the categories of different grades of citizen have covered a much broader range. Millions of the inhabitants of Nazi Germany, Stalinist Russia and Maoist China were completely stripped of their rights of citizenship. The reasons were either their unacceptability to the prevailing ideology or their opposition to the régime, real or imagined. Jews could not be allowed the status of German citizen for reasons of race; nor Kulaks in Russia nor landlords in China by reasons of class. Since such people existed in dangerously large numbers, drastic measures had to be adopted to exclude them from the body politic. Mere disenfranchisement would not remove the threat they were said to pose to the racially pure/classless society being created. Accordingly they were exterminated or hidden away in concentration or labour camps. The idea of citizenship in such régimes places greater emphasis on the need for a positive commitment by the individual than in democracies. Consequently the retention of the status, once conferred, cannot be automatically taken for granted. The formal and legal stripping of an individual of his or her citizenship, so rare in democracies, is a common occurrence in totalitarian states. For example, the Soviet authorities, stung by Solzhenitsyn's revelations about the police-state system and particularly by the overseas publication of *Gulag Archipelago*, proceeded against this famous author in 1974. The Presidium of the Supreme Soviet deprived him of his citizenship 'for the systematic commission of acts incompatible with Soviet citizenship and damaging to the Union of Soviet Socialist Republics'[47] and deported him from the country.

The Chinese, on the other hand, have held great store by the possibility of salvation through 're-education'. The purpose of this system was to convince people of the benefits of socially productive and responsible life-styles. Physical, especially agricultural, work was considered the key to the process. Hard cases were sent to camps, some for many years, to achieve 'reform through labour'. Intellectuals, especially during the course of the Cultural Revolution, were required to soil their hands. Admonition and argument were constant as revolutionary cadres struggled to convince peasants, workers and soldiers, let alone members of the former privileged classes, of the virtue of positive commitment to the new Communist society. The assumption behind the campaign was that the bulk of people were potentially 'good' and by constant reminders would readily adapt. These expectations embraced not only acceptance of the ideology but socially thoughtful and responsible conduct in everyday life. Policemen, guards on trains, anyone in authority, would public-ly lecture individuals whose behaviour fell short of the required standards. For some, re-education was relatively painless, though for the unfortunately recalcitrant the experience was no doubt similar to the conversion by Shaw's zealous and muscular Christian, Ferrovius, of the young Roman whose hair turned snow-white during the course of the night's spiritual struggle.

Totalitarian régimes have thus sought to raise, by their own lights, the overall level of citizenship standards – by the elimination or re-education of those whose attitudes or actions are considered to dilute those standards. Nevertheless, they do recognise that the highest reaches of good civic be-haviour are attainable by only the dedicated minority of the population. The kind of zeal required is perhaps most famously expressed in Liu Shao-ch'i's *How to be a Good Communist*. The model citizens are the élite capable of ad-mission to the ranks of the Party. The history of the Communist Party of the Soviet Union (CPSU) is an interesting, and at times grim, tale of attempts by the leadership to maintain ideological conformity and earnest commitment in this élite. Membership rose from about half a million in 1923 to nineteen million sixty-five years later. Yet there have been numerous purges, most notably in 1933–38, when nearly two millions lost their membership (as well as, in many cases, their lives). Yet in the midst of this pruning, the Stalin Constitution declared that

The most active and politically-conscious citizens in the ranks of the working class unite in the Communist Party of the Soviet Union (Bolshevik).[48]

Totalitarian states are in fact torn between conflicting needs. On the one hand they strive with every conceivable device and exaggeration to present to the people at large their vision of perfection. The emigré Polish writer, Czes-law Milosz has explained the function of the arts in this respect:

'Socialist realism' . . . presents model citizens, i.e. Communists, and class enemies. Between these two categories come the men who vacillate. Eventually, they must – according to which tendencies are stronger in them – land in one camp or the other. When literature is not dealing with prefabricated figures of friends or foes, it studies the process of metamorphosis by which men arrive at total salvation or absolute damnation in Party terms.[49]

On the other hand, standards for admission to the Party have to be lowered from the ideal if the membership is to be large enough to take on all the roles of civic leadership and exemplary citizenship. Thus, from the mid-1960s annual recruitment to the CPSU exceeded proportionately the increase in population. But when Gorbachev came to power in 1985 he was shocked to discover how low the standards of civic morality were in the Party.

The Nazis had their street leaders; the Soviets, their party workers on the state farms; the Chinese, their cadres in the communes. What were the or-dinary citizens expected to learn from these exemplars and their like? The totalitarian state has expected the performance of some half-dozen duties by its citizens. As in liberal states, voting is the basic function, though the purpose is quite different. In totalitarian states the object, in elections and plebiscites, is to mobilise the expected and required popular expression of support for the Party candidates and government policies. By the combined use of the manipulated news media and imaginative mathematics the régimes have been able simultaneously to announce support from, say, 99.7 per cent of the citizenry and to admonish and encourage the remaining 0.3 per cent to examine their civic consciences. Polling booths are, however, unemotional places – except perhaps for the fear engendered by the police presence. The citizenry can best express the ecstasy of fervent support by means of mass demonstrations and psychedelic rallies, however contrived. And, of course, it goes without saying that unswerving patriotism is demanded of all – children, women and men alike. Mobilisation and manipulation were undertaken with astonishing thoroughness in Maoist China during the occasions of the various 'mass campaigns' such as Aid Korea and the Great Leap Forward. The presence of a great ocean of people in Peking in episodic support of the Great Helmsman Mao during the Cultural Revolution produced truly amazing spectacles.

The citizen is also expected to support the state, as embodied in the party or the father/motherland, in very material ways. Contributions to Nazi Party funds or dedicated hard work as undertaken by the celebrated Soviet miner, Stakhanov, became normal expectations. This demand for such complete identification with the régime is aptly revealed in the comment in 1938 of Robert Ley, the Nazi leader responsible for labour mobilisation, that the private citizen no longer existed: only sleep remained a private matter. Nor are women exempt from performing civic duties in their own ways, particularly by the production of children – a feature alike of the Soviet Union in the 1920s and Iran in the 1980s. Soviet women have been encouraged in this task by the institution of the Order of Motherhood Glory for those prolific enough to bear ten or more offspring. However, it was the Nazis who took the duty of motherhood especially seriously. Women's functions were twofold: to produce manpower to strengthen the German state and to nourish the man-child's militaristic nature in his tender years. At a great gathering in the Berlin sports stadium in 1930 a Nazi speaker explained quite succinctly what was expected of German womanhood: 'Every German mother should pray to see the glint of fight when first she looks into her new-born baby's bright blue eyes.'[50] Not quite what Machiavelli had in mind when writing of the civic virtue of the soldier-citizen!

Totalitarian political education

The child-citizens thus generated and nurtured have an allegiance to the party/state that takes precedence over any loyalty to their families. For just as adult citizens are expected to denounce 'anti-social' attitudes or behaviour in their neighbours, so children are encouraged to inform even against their parents. All these little spies in the family are epitomised by the story of Pavlik Morozov. As a Young Pioneer (junior Communist) he helped the secret police in their enforcement of Stalin's collectivisation of farms. In 1932, aged 14, he denounced his parents for criticising the policy and hoarding grain. They disappeared. He was killed in retribution by local peasants. Pavlik was soon made into a martyr-hero for good Soviet children to emulate, his portrait hung in countless classrooms and Young Pioneer centres.

The training of children in these sinister ways was but part of a comprehensive policy which totalitarians have called 'political education'. This euphemism for systematic indoctrination naturally embraced the whole populace. After all, the establishment of a totalitarian régime in the twentieth-century state requires total re-education into a new style of citizenship to match the structures and expectations of the new order. In an industrialised and educated society like Germany all the media of mass communication were available to a skilful propagandist like Goebbels. In a peasant society with low levels of literacy like China, village meetings conducted by reliable party cadres performed this work. The task of explaining, persuading and exhorting the adult population has to be a permanent feature of a totalitarian régime for a number of reasons. In all such states there is the need to keep up an artificially high level of political fervour. Then there is the desire to stimulate aggression against the 'enemies of the people' — the racial outcasts or counter-revolutionaries. A third motive is to sustain the momentum of progress towards the desired goal, most vividly witnessed in the Chinese Cultural Revolution. But how much easier for those in power to achieve this control if they can lay down a firm foundation of doctrinally correct political consciousness in the young.

Since totalitarianism involves the politicisation of the whole of life, it is hardly likely that schools and youth movements would be exempted. Indeed, recognition of the malleability of young minds has rendered such institutions prime targets for 'reform'. During the most fanatical periods of totalitarian rule the traditional functions of the school to provide basic training in skills and cultivation of the intellect have been blatantly subordinated to the shaping of pupils' attitudes and behaviour to the ideological mould. Thus the Nazi theorist Rosenberg declared that,

German education will not be formal and aesthetic, it will not strive for an abstract training of reason, but it will be in the first instance an education of character . . . . This cleansing of spirit and instinct . . . is perhaps the greatest task which the National Socialist movement now has before it.[51]

The most extreme example of this policy occurred during the Cultural Revolution in China when ideologically cleansing physical labour, political lectures and the recitation of the Thoughts of Chairman Mao often took precedence over even the teaching of literacy. As a result of imbibing a sense of these priorities a fourteen-year-old could declare to a German journalist in correct parrot fashion,

. . . in China thanks to the teaching of Chairman Mao and his comrade-in-arms Lin Piao, politics rather than academic learning will always be in command.[52]

Even when schools have been organised with a greater sense of balance, as for most of the educational history of the Soviet Union, their principal objective has been the inculcation of the moral, social and political principles of the ruling ideology.

This objective has naturally been utterly dependent on the ideological reliability of the teaching profession and youth leadership service. Schirach, 'Youth Leader of the German Nation', expressed the point most trenchantly:

The youth leader and educator of the future will be a priest of the National Socialist creed and an officer in the National Socialist service.[53]

The totalitarian régime must therefore expend a great deal of effort to ensure the political trustworthiness of the teachers and to help them present the political 'truth' in their classes. Teacher-training courses have contained obligatory elements in political education, while the governmental control of curricula and textbooks has hampered any deviant intentions that might be harboured by individuals whose own indocrination was incomplete. Social pressures on the teachers to conform politically have also been considerable. For example, party membership carried such clear professional advantages in Germany that one estimate has suggested that nearly 30 per cent of Nazi Party members were from the profession, mainly from the elementary schools. This felt need for political orthodoxy led to the vicious persecution of Chinese teachers by the young Red Guards during the most intense phase of the Cultural Revolution. Teachers who dared reveal in their work that they considered academic standards might take precedence over political zealotry were insulted, denounced and dispatched to work as agricultural labourers.

With an enthusiastic or at least compliant teaching staff the whole ethos of the school could become one of political consciousness. Portraits, posters, flags and adulation of the leader provided symbols. The wearing of a uniform integrated school with youth movements. The organisation of manual work for the pupils stressed the civic importance of useful labour. Let us draw our examples on this facet from the Soviet Union. Pictures and busts of Lenin adorn the schools, some even have rooms specially devoted to the founder of the Soviet state; and from very tender years children sing songs in his praise. The interrelated aims of political and moral education have been consistent features of school programmes since the formulation of the Soviet educational system, even though emphases have fluctuated. Absorption of Marxist doctrine has indeed often been less in evidence than adherence to collectivist mentality, productive labour, patriotic loyalty and civic duty. Every opportunity has been taken to instil these four fundamental messages. From kindergarten learning situations are devised to emphasise the cardinal importance of collective, that is co-operative, endeavour. As the individual learns progressively to subordinate his own wishes and interests to the group's, the group's to those of the class, those of the class to the school's, so he or she comes to discern that the ultimate collective, requiring ultimate submission, is the state. And what the state requires of the individual above all is useful work, which is essential to the individual for self-fulfilment in any case. Nor is this consideration only utilitarian; it has the imprimatur of Marx himself, who wrote that all young people should 'combine productive labour with instruction and physical culture'.[54] The state as motherland also must be defended. This was the lesson of both the Stalinist theory of 'Socialism in One Country' and the terrible experience of the 'Great Patriotic War'. As recently as 1974 a Soviet educational journal declared:

The school carries a great responsibility before society in the educating and training of brave and courageous citizens and patriots of our country.[55]

The war with Nazi Germany made the Soviet authorities very conscious of the need to stiffen the loyalty and discipline of Soviet youth. Hence the codification of twenty 'Rules for Pupils', which were issued in August 1943. These related mainly to standards of behaviour in the school; however, the first rule proclaimed it the duty of every pupil:

To acquire knowledge persistently in order to become an educated and cultured citizen and to be of the greatest possible service to his country.[56]

When we examine the content of classroom lessons we notice that the totalitarian school provides political education in three major ways. The most direct have been lessons on the constitution and the régime's ideology. Young people are expected to struggle with at least the main tenets of Fascism, Nazism or whichever brand of Marxism provides the official creed. But perhaps more important is the use of History as a vehicle for indocrination. This is inevitable in Communist states since, after all, Marxism is itself a philosophy of History. Thus in the USSR the historic role of the working class and, since the 1940s, the heroism of the Great Patriotic War have been constant features. Fluctuations in the official interpretation of the significance of individuals, notably Stalin, have necessitated the occasional pulping of textbooks, it is true. But such theoretical disputes have not displaced the subject from its central place in the curriculum. Italian education, as in so much of its political symbolism, placed great emphasis on Roman history in support of the myth that the Fascist state was the reincarnation of Rome. And the ideological purity of the subject was ensured by the reduction of the 317 textbooks available in 1926 to a single official text ten years later. Nazi History was blatantly teleological. Standard textbooks were entitled *The Eternal Road* and the *The Road to the Reich*. The past was interpreted to reveal the struggle of the heroic Teutonic/Aryan *Volk* to the zenith of glory achieved under Hitler's leadership. From the study of such matter young Germans were to achieve a heightened sense of national pride and racial identity.

Other subjects were also redesigned to perform political functions, often most inventively. The Nazi directive on elementary education of 1940 was quite explicit about the curriculum:

It is not the task of the elementary school to impart a multiplicity of knowledge for the personal use of the individual. It has to develop and harness all physical and mental powers of youth for the service of the people and the state. Therefore, the only subject that has any place in the school curriculum is that which is necessary to attain this aim.[57]

Reading primers were compiled and literature selected so as to reflect the political purpose of education. In Germany, Biology, not to mention the new pseudo-discipline of Race Science, was made to serve the spurious genetics of the Master Race. Even Mathematics was bent to the same purpose. In one notorious arithmetical problem the pupil was invited to compute how much the care of lunatics cost the state and how such a sum could be better expended!

Despite the great efforts to reconstruct the educational systems to their political ends, the results were not perhaps entirely to the totalitarians' satisfaction. There were practical hindrances. In Germany the Education Minister was a mentally unstable alcoholic; in Italy the Church remained influential; in Russia basic literacy was more pressing; in China the Cultural Revolution merely produced anarchy. In all these states it is likely that the young people were pressed more effectively into the required civic configuration by the youth movements. By attendance at ritualised meetings, rallies and camps, membership in these junior branches of the political parties ensured that the boys and girls became immersed in the myths and militarism of the movements, whether Fascist, Nazi or Communist. Although in China the age bracket for membership of the Youth League is quite high (15–25 since 1957), other totalitarian states have encouraged much younger children to be involved. In the USSR Octobrists are recruited at seven; and in Fascist Italy a boy of four could become a black-shirted son of the she-wolf! In most cases membership of such organisations has been voluntary, though social pressure has often forced many a young sceptic to join for appearance' sake. Only in Nazi Germany was membership of such an organisation – the Hitler Youth – made compulsory. A decree was issued to this effect in 1936 for all 10–18 year olds. The emphasis on good civic behaviour in these bodies may be illustrated by reference to the promise and rules of the Soviet Pioneers (10–15 year-olds). A candidate for membership promises:

I, a Young Pioneer of the Soviet Union, in the presence of my comrades solemnly promise to love my Soviet Motherland passionately, and to live, learn, and struggle as the great Lenin bade us and as the Communist Party teaches us.

The eleven-point list of rules includes the following political and moral precepts:

1. A Pioneer loves his Motherland and the Communist Party of the Soviet Union. . . .
3. A Pioneer honours the memory of those who gave their lives in the struggle for freedom and for the prosperity of the Soviet Motherland. . . .
4. A Pioneer is polite and well disciplined. . . .
10. A Pioneer is honourable and values the honour of his detachment. . . .[58]

However, not all Pioneers progress to the *Komsomols* (for 15–17 year-olds), membership of which is selective. Standards of enthusiasm and work requirements are kept deliberately high to ensure the success of the organisation as a training for the party élite. We have already had occasion to remark on the function of Party members in totalitarian states to behave as model citizens

(p. 117) It has therefore been felt by a number of such régimes that a selected few merit and need a special political education. Within the course of its brief existence the Nazi state developed its systems with considerable thoroughness and variety. Over thirty National Political Education Institutes were set up as boarding schools for (mainly) boys between the ages of 10 and 18. They received military training as well as ideological indoctrination. Parallel to these were the Adolf Hitler Schools specifically for the training of party officials. At the pinnacle of the system were the Order Castles for the cream of the Nazi youth.

The process of liberalisation

Totalitarianism is a tendency and an objective rather than an established political condition. There is therefore little to be gained in asking whether, for instance, Mussolini's Italy was or was not totalitarian. One can only profitably ask how far along the road to that ideal the Fascist régime was able to travel. Similarly, states which warrant the label may be reckoned as more or less totalitarian at various phases in their history. Even more interesting for us is evidence of the replacement of a totalitarian by a liberal system. Reactions to the excesses of Stalin and Mao after their deaths in 1953 and 1976 respectively have led to the dismantling of many of the features of the Soviet and Chinese states which had rendered citizenship a form of mass puppetry. Reforms in both countries seek, though more reluctantly and haltingly in China, to transform the citizen into a political animal not too dissimilar to the species found in liberal democracies. This involves the encouragement of realistic opportunities for creative participation and a reduction in crude indoctrination. The new mood in China in the years immediately following Mao's death provides some straightforward illustrations. In 1979–80 the radical Revolutionary Committees established during the Cultural Revolution were replaced by regional and local institutions as part of the constitutional government structure. Elections were held on a universal suffrage with some limited choice of candidates. And already in 1978 the leader Deng Xiaoping told an education conference:

There is no doubt that schools should always attach primary importance to a firm and correct political orientation. This, however, does not mean devoting many classrooms to ideological and political education.[59]

More famously have been Gorbachev's campaigns of *glasnost* (openness) and *perestroika* (restructuring) in the Soviet Union. On the other hand, one should not exaggerate the novelty of his efforts. In context they may be viewed as a determined acceleration of the muddled process of de-Stalinisation which can be traced back at least to 1956. What Gorbachev has seen more lucidly than his predecessors is that the drive for greater economic efficiency requires as a precondition of its success the democratisation of institutions; that the harnessing of the initiative and enthusiasm of the ordinary citizen is essential. But the framework had already been set in place before his appointment as

General Secretary by the promulgation of a new Constitution in 1977. Although the balance of citizens' rights and duties which appeared in the Stalin Constitution is retained, this feature is extended and given greater emphasis. Socio-economic rights, civil liberties and participatory rights and their corresponding duties are clearly delineated. The arbitrary infringements of the citizen's civil rights, which had been such a nauseous characteristic of Stalinism, had been substantially reduced by Khrushchev. The Constitution codified this improvement. However, dissidents, the root-and-branch opponents of the system, could gain no solace from this 'bill of rights', for civil rights are denied to those who abuse them to undermine 'the national interest'.

Gorbachev has concentrated on an attempt to stir the ordinary citizens in their millions to more energetic participation. By no means an easy task. Generations of autocratic repression conditioned the Russian to a lethargy which became such an acquired characteristic that no amount of artificial stimulation by Stalin's party cadres could trigger any real political mutation. At the 27th Congress of the CPSU Gorbachev set the agenda for such an alteration by the liberal device of increased responsibility. A whole section of his speech was entitled 'Further democratisation of society and promotion of the people's socialist self-government.' His reforming programme was based upon the blunt proposition that,

. . . the acceleration of society's development is inconceivable and impossible without a further development of all aspects and manifestations of socialist democracy.

He went on to assert that,

. . . even if its executives are masterminds, no apparatus will ever get what it wants unless it relies on the working people's motivated support and participation in government.

The problem, he urged, must be attacked on a broad front, using trade unions, *Komsomols* and collectives as the means. What he was pleading for was grass-roots democracy:

We must make better use of such reliable channels for the development of direct democracy as citizen's meetings, constituents' mandates, letters from people, the press, radio, TV and all other means of eliciting public opinion and of quickly and sensitively responding to the people's needs and mood.[60]

One would not have expected more from a Victorian liberal.

Even in the South Africa of the 1980s, in the midst of repressive police measures, the matter of citizenship has been gingerly thrown open for debate. In 1986 President Botha, in contradiction of recently stated policy (p. 115), declared:

We accept an undivided South Africa. All regions and communities within its boundaries form part of the South African state, with the right to participate in institutions to be negotiated collectively.
We accept one citizenship for all South Africans, implying equal treatment and opportunities.[61]

Caught between the anvil of extremist right-wing resistance to change and the hammer of growing demands for the demolition of apartheid, Botha clearly felt at that time that the issue of citizenship could not be ignored.

Communist régimes are in the process of democratisation by Fabian gradualness; and even some Afrikaners are entertaining the painful thought of ultimate reform. In contrast, other totalitarian states have had democracy abruptly thrust upon them — namely, the defeated Axis powers after 1945. Although Japan was not totalitarian in the ideological sense as Germany was, there are interesting parallels in the histories of the two nations. The modern Japanese and German states date from much the same time (1868 and 1871 respectively) and were based upon autocratic, nationalistic, racialistic principles. Both experienced liberal interludes, from 1918 to 1933 in Germany and, much more tentatively in Japan from 1918 to 1931. Both established parliamentary democratic constitutions after military defeat and underwent a process of political re-education under the watchful eye of the Allied occupying powers. Both settled down to a more stable political life and a less indoctrinatory educational system than hitherto. Both enjoyed 'economic miracles', in some measure facilitated by the commitment of the citizenry to the rehabilitation of their countries.

The new Japanese constitution asserted the sovereignty of the people and toppled the Emperor from his status as deity. The Fundamental Law of Education of 1947 aimed to make the school system congruent with this new style of government and politics. It sought to rear people

. . . who shall love truth and justice, esteem individual value, respect labour, and have a deep sense of responsibility, and be imbued with an independent spirit, as builders of a peaceful state and society.[62]

Great store was also placed on the education of adults to adapt to the new demands of active citizenship. Citizens' public halls were created as social and educational centres. Their purpose too was, in the words of the US commander, General MacArthur, to provide 'opportunities for the practice of democratic procedures on the part of the townspeople.'[63] This process of re-education has not, however, been lacking in problems. The Americans tried to slant the teaching in an anti-Communist direction; while indigenous right-wing elements have attempted to whitewash some of the dingier episodes of their country's past as portrayed in school History books.

The post-war reform of education in West Germany has been smoother. In guiding the new state along the democratic path the German politicians and the Allied advisers were inevitably very conscious of the melancholy Weimar experiment. How far did the failure of that short-lived republic suggest that constitutional and curricular innovations are unable to create from a people denied political experience a citizenry capable of sustaining a stable democracy (pp. 176–177)? Meanwhile, in the schools, nationalist and militaristic History teaching provided a strong bridge of such values from the Wildelmine to Hitlerite régimes.

The Second World War had barely started when some politically alert if at the time rather optimistic minds among the Allies turned their attention to the post-war political reform of Germany. Their purpose was to plan the expunging of Nazi ideology while avoiding the weaknesses of Weimar. A central feature of the plans being evolved in both Britain and the USA in the early 1940s for de-Nazification was 're-education'. This basic principle eventually became crystallised as Allied policy in the Potsdam Protocol in 1945, which included the following clause:

German education shall be so controlled as completely to eliminate Nazi militaristic doctrines and to make possible the successful development of democratic ideas.[64]

Responsibility for implementing this policy lay initially with the four occupying powers and then the two successor German states. The authorities were faced with three basic tasks: to replace teachers tainted with a Nazi past; to draw up new, academically respectable syllabuses and curricula; and to produce replacement textbooks. Let us briefly examine how far these goals were attained in the Western zones and the Federal Republic. The task of replacing teachers proved to be exceedingly difficult: there were too many with Nazi associations (p. 120) and too few qualified potential substitutes in the early post-war years. The other two tasks were tackled perhaps more successfully though with less eager rapidity than some would have wished. Even so, the remarkable stability of the West German democratic regime may be presented as evidence of the efficacy of the re-education process. The issue is in fact not quite as simple as that. Several other weighty factors like the Cold War and the 'economic miracle' have been substantial influences. Furthermore, education authorities gave little serious thought in 1945 to the kind of political education suitable for German school children, though they did subsequently, and with considerable resultant changes of focus.

Until the late 1950s, indeed, the task of political education was pursued with but tepid enthusiasm by both Education Ministries and the teaching profession. History syllabuses pusillanimously stopped short before the Nazi era, and what passed for direct political education consisted of depoliticised moral and social instruction and stark institutional descriptions. (Not of course that Germany was much different from other Western nations in this respect.) Insofar as political values impinged upon young people in the classroom, the message was anti-Communist. An educationist recalls her own experiences as a schoolgirl at the time:

The practical side of anticommunist teaching was the sending of parcels, mainly containing coffee and chocolate, to our poor 'brothers and sisters in the east'. The actual collection of foods and the wrapping and sending of the parcels, as well as the heart-moving letters of thanks made a lasting impression on me. The 'horror' of communism was instilled by the fact that it was a state which would not allow its old ladies to eat chocolate and drink coffee.[65]

The complacency of the German authorities was shaken by a worrying outburst of symbolic Nazi acts in the late 1950s – swastikas daubed on public buildings and synagogues vandalised. Frightened politicians blamed the teachers and demanded more effective political education in democratic attitudes. In response, the ten state Ministers of Education issued co-ordinated directives requiring schools to teach about the Third Reich and to teach about the fallacies and evils of Nazism. Textbooks for this purpose became available; and those which fell short of the standards of objectivity, as judged by the International Textbook Institute in Brunswick, were withdrawn from schools by the Ministries of Education. What is more, in common with the experiences of other western countries, dissatisfaction arose in the 1960s and 1970s over the limitations of courses in political and social studies, with the result that the study of political controversies and values was introduced to render the teaching more interesting, realistic and effective.

In the long history of citizenship, totalitarianism has been perhaps but a brief interlude. By examining the nature of citizenship in such Spartan regimes and the processes of conversion to less dynamic and repressive forms, the experience can throw a helpful light on the alternative Athenian liberal tradition. The history of totalitarianism displays its many offensive characteristics, not least the indoctrination of young minds. Yet it raises at least one positive question, namely, whether liberal states have developed too casual an attitude towards citizenship, such as to drain the term of all effective meaning. 'Citizen' has become so nearly synonymous with 'inhabitant' that the classical sense of status has been all but lost. In the words of Hitler in the 1920s,

The whole procedure of acquiring State citizenship is not very different from that of becoming a member of an automobile club for instance.[66]

Were the Nuremberg Laws the only conclusion to be drawn from this premise?

3.3 NEW NATIONS

In Bombay, I found . . . Abdus Samad Mukadam who was such a super-citizen that he was almost too good to be true. Mukadam was absolutely dedicated to the unity of India. He believed in small families. He thought all Indians had a duty to educate themselves, and he had put himself through many evening courses. He had been named Best Worker at his dock. In his village, he claimed proudly, people of all faiths lived together in harmony.

Salman Rushdie[67]

Imperial régimes

'Captive Greece captured her rough captor and introduced the arts to uncultured Latium.'[68] With such an inferiority complex the Roman Empire can hardly be interpreted as a conscious expansion of a superior Latin culture. Nor were the Romans any more self-confident about the validity of their religion. The poet Horace, who wrote this famous epigram, like other educated Romans, accepted the deification of Julius Caesar as a political device, but certainly not as a theological truth. Moreover, the Olympian deities were

127

looked upon as rather comic myths. The foreign cults of Mithras and Christ were eagerly embraced as substitutes. But if the Roman Empire involved neither a secular nor a religious cultural hegemony, the classical experience stands in sharp contrast to the imperialism of the European powers in the modern era. The colonists in the Americas, Asia and Africa knew without the slightest hint of dubiety that they were transmitting a superior secular culture to savages and the revealed word of the Christian God to heathens. The idea of conferring the status of full citizenship of the metropolitan motherland on people of such 'backward' races had therefore to overcome a kind of arrogant superiority which had not inhibited the Romans.

The imposition of European culture on populations of the colonial territories induced two kinds of political tensions which help to explain the evolution of citizenship as these peoples achieved their independence. In the first place, the imperial powers found it necessary to educate a certain number of the indigenous inhabitants in a European style. This policy was not just the pursuit of the civilising mission; it also had the very practical purpose of training personnel to assist in the administration of the colonies. But, of course, access to a European literary education could and did lead so easily to access to the modern European political traditions, with exciting ideas like democracy and national self-determination. Why should a highly intelligent clerk, teacher or lawyer in Algeria or India confine his reading to bureaucratic handbooks when Rousseau and Mill were available? Thus, efficient control of the colonies involved the schooling of an educated élite, whose consequent political consciousness undermined that very control they were meant to serve.

The second tension related to cultural and political identity. Nehru, for example, has described how, having been educated at Harrow and Cambridge, he was never quite sure whether he was Indian or English and consequently never completely comfortable as either. The process of European education produced 'wogs' – the culturally mongrel 'westernised oriental gentlemen'. Translated into political terms this meant an uncertainty about whether fully to embrace European ideals and institutions or to reassert ethnic traditions. However, since citizenship was essentially of European origin (p. 2), the concept and status was likely to flower in the Afro-Asian world only if European-style political systems were installed. Not, of course, that the indigenous inhabitants of the colonies had complete freedom to determine their political destinies. Both the process of imperial administration and the institutional preparations for independence bequeathed to the new nation-states European political styles.

The British Empire and Commonwealth dealt with these matters in a haphazard way. For many years, both metropolitan and colonial leaders displayed confused attitudes as to the desirable goals to which changes should be directed. We have already had occasion to outline the various legislative enactments in the present century with particular reference to the issue of United Kingdom immigration and citizenship status (pp. 103–104). It is necessary to examine the matter now mainly from the perspective of the development of political consciousness and progress to independence within the colonial territories. Even in the nineteenth century a substantial body of opinion held that the function of the British Empire was to guide these 'backward' peoples to ultimate self-government. This policy was most famously expounded in 1938 by the Colonial Secretary in a speech in which he said,

It may take generations, or even centuries, for the peoples in some parts of the Colonial Empire to achieve self-government. But it is a major part of our policy, even among the most backward peoples of Africa, to teach them and encourage them always to be able to stand a little more on their own feet.[69]

Not all British politicians, it is true, shared this liberal vision. Churchill in particular was adamant in his defence of the imperial edifice. In 1941 he refused to concede that the Atlantic Charter's commitment to political freedom was applicable to that context. Even in the imperial lands there was for many, until after the Second World War, a wish to devise a formula that could somehow combine imperial and local citizenship statuses. Thus at the Second Round Table Conference on Indian autonomy in 1931 Gandhi stated:

I . . . still hope to be a citizen not of an empire but of a community within perhaps an indissoluble association, although not imposed by one nation on another.[70]

In the meantime, confusing anomalies persisted in the various rights of citizenship that existed throughout the Empire. The 'white' Dominions were able to develop their own local institutions and their people came to be Canadian or Australian citizens, for example, by virtue of a growing sense of identity and involvement in their own political structures. Yet these developments were held back from Nigerians or Malayans, for instance. At the Paris Peace conference in 1919, where the principle of national self-determination was elevated to the prime test of political justice, the Indians were allowed their own delegation. At the same time General Dyer's troops in Amritsar shot and killed 379 Indians who were peacefully demonstrating for the implementation of that very principle. Strangest of all, the equality of status of British subjects throughout the Empire theoretically allowed colonials civic rights in the mother-country which they were denied in their own. In the 1890s two Indians took advantage of this constitutional oddity by securing election as MPs to the Westminster parliament. They could never have attained any analogous position if they had remained in India.

While the British were floundering in their confused liberalism, the French were impaling themselves on the logic of their constitutionalism. Since the Republic was 'one and indivisible' it was inconceivable to arrange any devolution of effective political authority such as the British provided for in their Dominions. Yet, at the same time, the civic assimilation of 'barbarian natives' was out of the question, since they were utterly devoid of the cultural standards which the status of French citizenship took for granted. The principle of the indivisibility of the Republic and hence of the integration of the colonies into France was first propounded during the Revolution, in 1790. A year later the sons of free parents (most French colonies were in the slave economies of the West Indies) were, temporarily, given the vote. The Third Republic reiterated the principle and allocated ten seats for the colonies in the Chamber of Deputies (Algeria being treated *sui generis* as departments of metropolitan France). Full citizenship rights were, however, severely restricted to those who came to be termed *évolués*. These were the indigenous élite who managed to acquire the necessary trappings of French civilisation. For example, in 1885 ten seats were allotted in the Chamber of Deputies for such colonial first-class citizens. The most famous and politically successful of all the *évolués* was Houphouet-Boigny of the Ivory Coast, who was even a cabinet minister for three years (1956–59).

Out of gratitude for their involvement in the fighting and concern to cement their loyalty, French governments during and immediately after the two World Wars extended civic rights in their colonial dependencies. The process was accelerated by the rise of nationalist demands. But the problem remained of relating the colonies to the metropolis. The Constitution of the Fourth Republic came up with the device of the French Union, declaring that,

All nationals of the overseas territories have the status of citizens, on the same basis as French nationals of Metropolitan France or the overseas territories. (Article 80)

However, the status proved to mean little enough in practice. And so, with the Fifth Republic, Union was replaced by Community (a scheme which Houphouet helped to construct). The overseas territories were to enjoy administrative autonomy. On the definition of citizenship Article 77 stated, 'There is only one Community citizenship.' But by this time the extended French Republic was only too evidently divisible. The Union, merely papering over the fissures, swiftly fragmented.

The Belgians and Portuguese had policies of assimilation into European culture superficially similar to the French: the Belgians had their *évolués* and the Portuguese, their *assimilados*. In fact, only a tiny handful reached that status, and even then the so-called rights of citizenship they enjoyed were virtually invisible. In 1950 only about one in two thousand of the inhabitants of the Portuguese African colonies were *assimilados*. And when, in 1961, the title of citizen was conceded to all, the English weekly *New Statesman* revealed the transparent dishonesty of the statute:

Can Africans who are full citizens of Portugal still be subject to forced labour? If so, what is the value of citizenship? If not, the present system of labour in Angola will collapse.[71]

The truth of the matter is that no modern imperial power solved the riddle of citizenship. There were two possible approaches: a unified imperial citizenship or local citizenship specific to individual colonies. In the first case, there were three insuperable problems. The status presupposes some sense of community and common loyalty. Yet cultural heterogeneity rendered this extremely difficult for the great bulk of Asians and Africans, especially in an age when the mother countries were culturally homogeneous. Secondly, citizenship as the right to a certain minimum of social welfare was impossible of extension to, say, the poverty-stricken millions of the Indian sub-continent. And thirdly, citizenship as equal political participation was impossibly dangerous for the imperial power to conceive, since the overseas electorate would in total submerge the domestic. In the words of the Frenchman Gonidec, the white vote would be

. . . overwhelmed and drowned by a superstitious mass whose votes could easily be manipulated by clever leaders and who would not realize the consequences of voting without a due sense of responsibility.[72]

If Disraeli thought the 1867 British Reform Bill was 'a leap in the dark', what a somersault into pitch blackness total imperial enfranchisement would have been. Imperial civic egalitarianism was never a serious possibility.

The alternative strategy, which was pursued with rather greater honesty and success, at least by the British and French, was the introduction of political rights at the local level. Nevertheless, there were still problems of educating the people to understand their responsibilities and to relate involvement in the European-established structures with their traditional village or tribal institutions and loyalties. What is more, if, for example, Ceylonese or Senegalese citizenship in this sense was to have a true meaning, its relationship to the doctrine of popular sovereignty would soon be raised. The effect of that, of course, was national independence for the colonies, not the retention of the imperial connection through a network of citizenships.

Problems in establishing citizenship

The achievement of independence did not automatically bring to birth citizenship in mature form. Even the publication of a declaration of rights in proper 1789 style, which so often happened, could not ensure that. And no wonder. The European concept and practice, as we have seen, took centuries to evolve. True, the Afro-Asian states had this experience to draw upon. But they still had to learn the difficult practical arts and attitudes that citizenship entails, not to mention the problems of reconciling them with their own, valuable social customs. In adapting the Western concept of citizenship the leaders of the newly independent states set themselves four tasks: to use the status to build a sense of national cohesion; to create a stable political system; to infuse a sense of political morality; and to develop programmes of political education as a precondition for the achievement of these three goals.

The ideas of nationalism and the nation-state have not transferred with any comfort to the Asian and African continents. The ethnic and cultural homogeneity which the term 'nation' denotes barely exists. The imperially delineated boundaries were determined by diplomatic and military means unrelated to any sense of identity the inhabitants might have felt. Many post-independence political leaders have consequently been faced with the hard task of welding into a nation peoples diverse in language, ethnicity and religion. Where this overarching nationhood has been rejected by minorities with their own powerful sense of community, the result has often been a bloody struggle. Ibos attempted secession; Bangladeshis succeeded; Eritreans and Kurds continue the fight. These peoples have wished to deny their status as Nigerian, Pakistani, Ethiopian and Iraqi citizens respectively.

The problem of creating an integrated nation-state from ethnically diverse peoples assumed a particular form in East Africa where Asians have existed as racially distinctive communities. When Kenya, Tanganyika and Uganda became independent the question was raised whether these people should be granted citizenship. The Africanisation of the public service had been eagerly awaited. But supposing Whites and Asians were allowed citizen status and still retained coveted posts after independence? In Tanganyika, Nyerere, that most sensitive and attractive of first-generation African leaders, had to fight hard to save his non-racist Citizenship Bill in 1961. Eleven years later he defended the institution of citizenship and denounced the persecution of Asian citizens by General Amin in neighbouring Uganda. He declared that,

Citizenship must be respected without discrimination, or it will be met with disrespect without discrimination . . . What does it mean, to say to a large group of people, 'From today – or tomorrow, or next week – you citizens are no longer citizens?' It means that they are people in the world who have no state, nor country, no place where they have a right to live.[73]

In some other new states problems arise on grounds of religion. By what right does a state enact secular laws based upon a religious code to which some of its citizens do not subscribe? Is national cohesion a sufficient justification? For instance, in Ireland, newly independent in 1921, the laws relating to divorce and birth control are governed by the teachings of the Catholic church; yet not all Irish citizens are Roman Catholic. In constitutionally Islamic states punishments are meted out according to Koranic law; yet by no means are all the citizens of Pakistan or Sudan, for example, Muslims. When convicted Christian southern Sudanese thieves had their right hands severed in the early 1980s, were they being treated in a manner appropriate to citizens?

In India discrimination contrary to the principles of egalitarian national citizenship results from the persistence of the caste system. Gandhi set the tone of Indian social ethical rethinking about the untouchables. He deplored the custom whereby they were shunned by the rest of society and condemned to begging and the performance of the most offensive tasks. In an effort to restore to them some human dignity he dubbed them *harijan* or 'people of the Lord'. When the founding-fathers of the Indian Republic committed themselves to a democratic constitution they were at great pains to guarantee basic equality of citizenship rights irrespective of religion, race, caste, sex or place of birth. Article 17 specifically outlawed discrimination against untouchables. The subsequent First Amendment to the Constitution went further. It empowered Parliament to legislate for positive discrimination in public appointments for any underprivileged class of citizen. It was, however, naïvely optimistic to expect that the dead hand of traditional social inertia could be swiftly raised by mere government fiat. True, a token untouchable would be appointed to government office. But the practice of discrimination for a hundred million so-called citizens remained, it must be said, virtually untouched. In 1964, in *An Area of Darkness*, the perceptive Indian writer V. S. Naipaul provided a vivid picture of their condition:

[Sweepers] are not required to *clean*. That is a subsidiary part of their function, which is to be sweepers, degraded beings, to go through the motions of degradation . . . In Jamma City you will see them collecting filth from the streets with their bare hands . . . They are dirt; they wish to appear as dirt.[74]

Alongside the obstacles to a cohesive sense of national identity have been other hindrances to the development of citizenship as participative support for the democratic systems of government. Conviction that citizenship in this sense is of inestimable benefit to new nations was expressed most cogently by Nkrumah in a broadcast to the Ghanaian people. The occasion was a plebiscite on the new Republican constitution. He said,

The Convention People's Party and the Government believe that the authority to govern a state should spring from the people and that the people's right to exercise these powers is based on the principle of one man, one vote . . . We realise that only when this principle . . . is adopted throughout the length and breadth of the continent of Africa, can the misery of oppression, which prevails in many parts of this continent, come to an end.[75]

But, of course, it has not been nearly as simple as that. The sheer problem of communication in technically and educationally underdeveloped countries has presented challenging difficulties. Messages have had to be simplified; pictorial representation widely used. In campaigning for independence the *Union Démocratique Nigérienne* in French West Africa typically adopted the camel as its symbol and the motto, 'Vote for the camel and you will be as free as he is.'[76]

In any case, for a host of economic, social and political reasons, few new states have enjoyed the political stability necessary for the full discharge of citizen responsibilities. Stability is to citizenship, in truth, as the chicken is to the egg. Instability has prompted the response of military government. Already in the nineteenth century the overwhelming difficulties facing the liberated states of Latin America brought into existence the *Caudillismo* style of government by military dictator. A century and a half later that tradition had not been outlived. Writing in 1980, the appallingly persecuted Argentine journalist, Jacobo Timerman, recalled the comment of Jorge Luis Borges a generation earlier that 'the Argentine is not a citizen but an inhabitant'. The failure to create such a civic consciousness led the country into its fearful history of 'political incapacity' yet 'capacity for violence'.[77] A similar judgement could be made of so many unfortunate Third World states.

One of the complications has been the deftness of craftsmanship that has been necessary to splice in the traditional codes of social ethics with the European idea of citizenship. In Africa Nyerere made a courageous attempt in his version of African socialism founded on the principles of *Ujamaa* or 'Familyhood'. In a pamphlet he wrote:

One of the most socialistic achievements of our society was the sense of security it gave to its members, and the universal hospitality on which it could rely. But it is too often forgotten, nowadays, that the basis of this great socialistic achievement was this: that it was taken for granted that every member of society . . . contributed his fair share of effort towards the production of its wealth.[78]

133

It is easy to see how readily this ethic of 'sense of security' and 'fair share of effort' could relate to citizenship.

The deepest thought was given to this matter of marrying indigenous and western practices by Mahatma Gandhi. The startling ambivalence of his own life made of him a living commentary upon the problem. For did he not exchange pin-stripe trousers for loin-cloth, law-books for spinning-wheel and amalgamate in his own philosophy the tender teachings of both Christianity and Hinduism? Gandhi recognised the potential of all states for oppression and violence, none more so than the modern highly bureaucratised state. His ideal political system was one bereft of as much centralised power as possible; and he declared that he would 'make use of the indigenous institutions and serve them by curing them of their proved defects'.[79] However, given the ubiquity of the modern European-style state, in reality, how was the citizen to behave towards it? Gandhi's theory of citizenship was based upon three fundamental tenets of his philosophy. One was *satya:* truth and sincerity. Another was *ahimsa:* nonviolence, in thought and deed. The third was *dharma:* moral law and duty. He taught that all states tend to violate *satya* and *ahimsa*. The citizen has the right, the duty even, to judge the state and its laws by the standards of *dharma*, which embraces the crucial virtues of *satya* and *ahimsa*. Since the state is a 'soulless machine' and the individual citizen is endowed with *dharma*, the latter has the moral authority to challenge, even disobey, the state. The duty of the citizen to undertake such moral monitoring is paramount. For, 'every citizen renders himself responsible for every act of his government.' And 'loyalty to a [capricious and corrupt] State is a sin, disloyalty a virtue.'[80]

Corruption is a problem that through the ages has worried political philosophers who have given consideration to the role of citizenship. Among the Greeks, the men of the Renaissance and Enlightenment one may find numerous writers who believed that citizenship held the key to political virtue and consequently stability. By nurturing in the citizenry both a compatibility with the prevailing style of government and a sensitive civic conscience, these philosophers sought to demonstrate the possibility of staving off corruption. The word itself has had a variety of meanings – from the general decay of social and unselfish behaviour to the specifically fraudulent use of political power to extract personal gain. The problem has been endemic to many Third World countries, in both the imperial and post-imperial ages. At the point of transition in the Gold Coast (later Ghana), the nationalist leader, Nkrumah declared,

Bribery and corruption, both moral and factual, have eaten into the whole fabric of our society . . . Our election to the Assembly shows that the public has confidence in the integrity of the Party, and that we will not stoop low to contaminate ourselves with bribery and corruption at the expense of the people.[81]

The persistence of such dubious practices is often explained and even excused on several grounds. Gifts have been traditional for services in the past; the distinction between the public and private realms has been much less precise than in European societies; and the machinery of administration would be even more immobile without this simple method of lubrication. None the less, the very acceptance of faction, graft and corruption renders the growth of a mature citizenship morality exceedingly difficult. The pursuit of personal or sectional advantage in state business, after all, runs utterly counter to the ideal of the civic conscience. This is by no means to suggest that mature Western states are innocent of such questionable standards. Indeed, it was from the USA that the terms 'gerrymandering', 'pork-barrel' and Tammany Hall entered the political vocabulary. But they were scandalous excrescences on the body politic rather than an integral part of its physiology.

Citizenship education in developing countries

Politicians in the new states have been very alert to the difficulties of nurturing an effectively mature style of citizenship. They have placed great faith in the power of education to accomplish this. However, the complexities of the problem have not always allowed the setting or achievement of clear objectives. Differences of emphasis have sometimes been evident as between politicians and between politicians and educationists. Furthermore, practical difficulties have on occasion proved more impervious to the civic educational policies than the planners have anticipated. Whether complementary or mutually at odds, the total array of objectives in programmes of education for citizenship may be listed as: comprehension, integration, participation, obligation and 'conscientisation'.

Just as the various imperial powers made different assumptions about the speed and fashion of their colonies' journey to self-government, so their educational policies also differed. The French concentrated on civilising an élite by immersion in French culture. The Belgians, with a much longer time perspective, stressed elementary schooling. The British were theoretically committed to a preparation for indigenous citizenship for the masses; in practice they only really managed an Anglocentric education for an élite. The liberal ambitions of the British Colonial Office are vividly displayed in a series of reports on African education. The last of these, published in 1948, was entitled *Education for Citizenship in Africa*. It proclaimed one of the functions of education in the British territories to be the production of 'men and women as responsible citizens of a free country', but reminded its readers that 'good citizenship may be described as a way of living rather than as a body of knowledge'.[82] No imperial power provided anything like an adequate training in citizenship for their colonial peoples in preparation for independence. As a consequence, the new states were presented with a massive task of 'nation-building' and civic education that had to be accomplished at great speed with exiguous financial and trained human resources. The Europeans and Americans have discovered how difficult the task was even in far more propitious circumstances. The widespread disappointment expressed by so many Asian and African commentators at the slenderness of their achievements so far should not necessarily therefore be read as condemnations of their efficiency.

One of the most famous blueprints for such an ambitious educational policy was Julius Nyerere's speech, 'Education for Self-Reliance', delivered in 1967. He laid down a programme for the transformation of schooling so that pupils would be trained in the skills of efficient farmers and the behaviour of good citizens. Young people, he declared, must have instilled into them,

. . . a sense of commitment to the total community . . . co-operative endeavour . . . concepts of equality and responsibility to give service . . . Our education [he continued] . . . must encourage [in a person] . . . a basic confidence in his own position as a free and equal member of society.[83]

The starting-point had inevitably to be huge programmes to raise the literacy rates — at both child and adult levels. Furthermore, it was precisely those countries with low standards of education that have experienced the fastest population increases. Literacy campaigns have therefore become a race between education and demography. Nevertheless, the vastness of the problem has not blunted determination to tackle it. Governments, local administrators, the people themselves, not to mention UNESCO, have all shown steadfast commitment to the task. Perhaps the most remarkable success was the campaign in Cuba in 1961, during which year, it was claimed, the illiteracy rate was slashed from 23.6 to 3.9 per cent. Much of the motivating drive has been the desire for the economic efficiency of a literate workforce. On the other hand, the political need for a literate citizenry has also been a weighty consideration. The correlation seemed self-evident to both outside observers and indigenous planners. During a tour of the USA in the late 1950s, the Kenyan politician, Tom Mboya reported, 'I was told that the high illiteracy rate would make it impossible for Africans to operate a democracy successfully.'[84] At much the same time the Indian politician and academic K. L. Shrimali in a speech entitled, 'Mass Education and Democratic Ideals', said,

A person who is illiterate, has to accept only that information which is given to him and, therefore, is unable to exercise discrimination as to what is good and bad. He becomes easy prey to all kinds of propaganda. In a democratic society, people should be able to discriminate between truth and falshood.[85]

The political motives for literacy campaigns have not been confined to the ideal of a critically aware citizenry. Governments have also sought by the teaching of the vernacular as opposed to the imperial language to reinforce a sense of national identity and cohesion. And upon the foundation of linguistic control has been built nationalist education via school ceremonies and subject teaching, notably in History. Central governments have striven to enforce the nationalisation of school curricula against formidable odds. These have included: the traditional function of the family of socialising their children into local customs; the regional demands for the preservation of ethnic, linguistic or religious distinctiveness; the cultural pull of the former imperial power, the source of and inspiration for modernisation; the dearth of teachers and textbooks for transmitting reformed curricula; and in many societies, especially Islamic, a particular opposition to civic education for women.

The speed and determination with which schools were used as institutions for political socialisation in the new states has varied from country to country. For example, the process was particularly marked in the 1960s in Indonesia, Guinea and Egypt. The cultural consciousness of Arab states helped the process in the Middle East. The French scholar, Jean-Jacques Waardenburg, noted in 1966,

Of all the factors which influence education in the Arab countries nationalism is the major ideological factor in the education of children. The Arabic language and its potential are emphasized, the past notably after the coming of Islam, is taught . . . . Even when teaching subjects as far removed from politics as biology or psychology the spirit is stamped with this nationalist Arab fervour.[86]

At times, indeed, the indoctrination has become quite crude. For instance, the Egyptian critical newspaper *Al-Ahram* commented in 1971 that 'the poor Egyptian child does not learn anything that is not accompanied by either insults or praise, as if he were reading a paper or listening to the radio.'[87]

The need to use the schools to infuse a sense of national cohesion is, naturally, more intense in some states than in others. The fratricidal quasi-genocidal war of the Biafran secession in Nigeria (1968–70) provides one of the most grievous examples. Prior to the war the potential of the schools for building a national consciousness had been totally neglected. Its shock brought a reassessment of this negative policy. The issue was quite clear, as the educationist, F. A. Adeyoyin, explained eight years after the end of the war:

To redefine the school's role, we only need to recall the war experiences of most adult members of our society to see the great need for the schools to contribute to the social and emotional development of the child. Embittered by their own experiences of war, most parents pass these onto their children who on arrival at school cling only to those of their tribe and watch others with suspicion and distrust. When the home therefore fails, for one reason or another, to develop the right attitude towards nationalism, it is the role of the school to do so.[88]

In 1976 the Ministry of Education produced a guiding document, *Federal Republic of Nigeria Policy on Education*. It leaves no doubt about the national purpose of education. Section 1, for example, refers to 'the inculcation of national consciousness and unity'; while section 4, on secondary education, declares that education should 'foster Nigerian unity, with an emphasis on the common ties that unite us in our diversity . . . . Education should help develop in our young a sense of unity, patriotism and love of country. It is essential that everything possible be done to foster in them a sense of national belonging.'[89] There has, however, been a considerable difference in the pace of implementation as between urban secondary schools and remote rural primary schools.

Egypt and Nigeria are relatively wealthy and modernised states. But even the most impoverished have had their programmes of civic education. Thus a government official of the People's Republic of the Congo was able to report in 1975, a time of low and static GNP, along the following lines:

. . . there is a programme of ethics and history in primary teaching, to instil a sense of citizenship in those of our children who receive a primary education, that is from 6 to 14–16 years of age.[90]

Admittedly, primary-school enrolment was then below 50 per cent. However, supplementary political education, albeit of an ideological kind, has been available through the Pioneer Movement and the Young Marxist Clubs.

References to the Islamic culture of Arab states and the Marxist ideology of the Brazzaville regime serve as reminders of the political heterogeneity of the countries clustered here under the label of 'new states'. In some, education for citizenship has been a matter of replacing the History of the metropolitan country with indigenous History and the singing of patriotic songs. In others, quite sophisticated syllabuses have been drawn up, identifying objectives, concepts and methods of evaluation. In Pakistan, for example, such a syllabus was devised for an eighth grade course on 'Civic Life in Pakistan'. With proper allowance for cultural differences, it would not look out of place in a western school. Nevertheless, in many of the poorer countries, especially in Africa, the concept of citizenship and hence education for that role has a slightly different connotation from the western form. The social and economic duty to work, as in European Communist states, is given particular priority. The eminent African scholar, Ali Mazrui, has produced a succinct formula:

In my opinion there are only three politically significant values which can be inculcated in the educational system and retain relevance regardless of the regime in power. I call these values 'the three T's of training in nationhood'. The T's I have in mind are 'tolerance', 'toil' and 'teamwork'.[91]

Citizenship education involves cultivating a sense of national cohesion and loyalty and a sense of obligation and duty to the community and one's fellow-citizens. It also requires the qualities of initiative and willingness to participate. But the development of these civic qualities has been slow. Part of the reason has been the difficulty of overcoming the inertia bred of the subservience required by the colonial systems. Partly, too, the post-independence governments have recognised the potential ambivalence of education for active citizenship. For the process can undermine that very political cohesion it is designed to promote. In many states, programmes of civic education have not by any means been implemented in a balanced manner. Some regions have been favoured over others; towns have benefited more than rural areas; the middle class, more than the peasantry. Active civic involvement by a new educated citizen élite has tended therefore in some states to exacerbate divisions. This élite overshadows the still passive and poorly educated majority; and by engagement in local or regional political activities its behaviour sharpens the differences between these identities and loyalties at the expense of an overarching national coherence. Even so, faith in the politically beneficent power of education remains. With typical English moderation, Lord Bryce voiced what has become a virtually universal belief. Writing about South America at the beginning of the century, he declared that 'education, if it does not make men good citizens, makes it at least easier for them to become so.'[92]

It is from South America much more recently that a radical challenge has been thrown down to conventional styles of citizenship education. In 1972 the Brazilian, Paulo Freire published his *Pedagogy of the Oppressed*. Through this book he broadcast his concept of 'conscientisation'. He argues that no form of education is politically neutral. Since most people in Third World countries, and certainly the peons of the Noreste province among whom he worked, suffer from oppression, their education should take this condition into account. The purpose of education for the politically, socially and economically oppressed is to render them critically aware of this reality and so strengthen their will to exact reform. Part of the educational task is to combat illiteracy. This has been particularly relevant in Brazil where, at the time of Freire's work, the illiteracy rate was 40 per cent and illiterates were barred from voting. And yet Freire believes that literacy is a superficial accomplishment. Conscientisation must build rather on the wealth of knowledge and understanding in the possession of even the most 'uneducated'. The process of education enables the oppressed both to appreciate the significance of this vernacular knowledge and to use the self-confidence thus unlocked to overcome the 'culture of silence'. For oppression depends on sustaining the oppressed ones' belief in their own powerlessness. To overcome this inhibition teachers and students must work in collaboration; and then

. . . the presence of the oppressed in the struggle for their liberation will be what it should be: not pseudo-participation, but committed involvement.[93]

'Citizenhip' is not a word that interests Freire. None the less, his messages are most germane to the evolution of the status, particularly in Third World countries. For teachers are enjoined to alert the millions of underprivileged to assert their rights to a more just order. The concept of citizenship does not allow for passive 'pseudo-participation' in obedience to an oppressive state. It requires, as a balance to obedience, 'committed involvement' for a just social and political order. Wherever, therefore, the duties of citizenship are emphasised to the virtual exclusion of the rights, Freire's educational programme is both a relevant and urgent corrective.

Or perhaps the very concept of citizenship is so alien to the native traditions of the Third World countries that the political and educational tasks of fostering its development are fundamentally misconceived? The concept took centuries to mature in its European context. Are the difficulties like political instability and confused political identity merely the growing pains of extremely young polities? Or is the attempted forced growth of European institutions, including citizenship, quite artificial and evidence that the transplantation will not take? If the concept of national citizenship is unnatural in the new states, it may be that their inhabitants will be less resistant than are so many in the northern hemisphere to the idea of world citizenship.

3.4 WORLD CITIZENSHIP

Perhaps the most vital element in our peace crusade is the adequate education of the young in world citizenship. For if we are to achieve a lasting peace based on the system of collective security, the whole conception of citizenship must be changed.

Arthur Henderson, MP,[94]

The reasons for wanting to pin down that elusive concept 'world citizenship' have, in our own century, intensified, accelerated and multiplied. The basic uneasiness of the ancient cosmopolitans at the artificiality of sub-dividing the human race into distinct political units has persisted. This motive for advocating a world citizenship has subsequently been reinforced by new 'layers' of concerns – the desire to end war, then the wish to honour human rights and, most recently, worries about preserving the biosphere. Already in the age of the Enlightenment (pp. 53–56) plans for pacification by political federation, hitherto confined to bellicose Europe, were being extended in imagination to a global scope. As the nineteenth and twentieth centuries piled up the horrors of martial conflict, so the need for a truly planetary sense of civic, eirenic responsibility appeared to many to be of mounting urgency. The belief in a universal code of conduct in conformity with basic human rights and transcending particular state laws came more gradually. Moral revulsion against slavery had helped to condition world opinion to question the right of sovereign states to persist in this offensive institution. However, it was not until the bestiality of Nazism that attempts were made to codify international law to incorporate the principles of overarching human rights. Finally, though the consciousness of the fragility of our ecosystem was already evident to a few before the Second World War, it was not until the 1970s that the cry arose to the effect, 'Citizens of the world unite, you have everything to lose!'

Hopes in the shadows of the world wars

Yet we still lack an adequate political theory of cosmopolitanism. Kant led western philosophy to the brink of such a system. But the nation-state has remained too solid an institution for any further speculation to rise much above the level of rhetoric or paper constitutions. It is an ironic commentary on the malign strength of the modern state that the unnecessary and bloody First World War should have been fought at a time of growing realisation that the sovereignty of the state needed abridgement for the sake of peace. The creation of the international court of arbitration at The Hague following the 1899 conference, however cynically viewed by governments, gave a great boost of optimism to the peace movements which had come into enthusiastic existence since c. 1860. The period 1899–1914 witnessed numerous peace con-ventions. Their objectives were primarily to reduce the power of the arms manufacturers and the propensity of governments to warlike actions. In 1910 the American psychologist William James spoke of the need to channel man's pugnacity into creative social endeavours by the cultivation of 'the moral equivalent of war', so that 'on the ruins of the old morals of military honor' would be built 'a stable system of morals of civic honor.'[95] Although James conceived of this new civic duty as relating to the global community, much of this activity did not necessarily, however, imply a loyalty to the world as a whole at the expense of the state. On the other hand, some commentators were questioning the usefulness of the state in practice and the tenability of the theory of the state to explain reality. For example, one British political scientist could write in 1914 that,

Most of the recent dissatisfaction with the State . . . arises from the failure of the State to meet the new problems with which the extraordinary increase in the inter-connectedness of mankind in the last fifty years has presented it.[96]

A follow-up article was entitled 'The Discredited State'. At the same time Sir Norman Angell, the distinguished peace campaigner, wrote:

Save only in a narrow juridical sense, which . . . does not affect the vital functions of society, the nations which form the European community are not sovereign, not independent, nor entities.[97]

During the inter-war period half-hearted attempts were made through such institutions as the League of Nations and the Kellogg-Briand Pact to restrain the absolute right of the state to wage war. Much more significant from our point of view were the efforts to persuade ordinary citizens to think in global terms. The need to educate as well as mobilise public opinion characterised the most significant organised movements ever to have been created in support of world order. These were the League of Nations societies and most notably the British League of Nations Union (LNU), which flourished after the First World War. '. . . in a democratic age everything depends on public opinion,'[98] declared Lord Robert Cecil, the Chairman of the LNU. He believed that by creating a mass organisation the British government would be forced to adhere to the principles of the Covenant of the League and to ensure that other member states did also.

However, for those commentators who were especially horrified at the prospect of a repetition of world war, the limitations of the League provoked intense impatience. Some, like Count Coudenhove-Kalergi, sought salvation in reviving yet again the notion of European unification. Others, like Bertrand Russell and Leonard Woolf in Britain, looked to a fully global solution. No one worked with a more energetic pen to popularise the idea of world order and thus create a mental climate for world citizenship than H. G. Wells. Already in the 1890s he was pleading for world government. As the Second World War became inexorably a rising threat and then a hideous reality, so he importuned his readers with a flood of appeals – *The Fate of Homo Sapiens*, *The New World Order*, *The Rights of Man* and innumerable short pieces – to see and act upon his kind of reason. He called for a revolution in political thinking and behaviour with a view to establishing a new World Order based upon broadly socialist principles. He discerned, however, that

The new order cannot be brought into existence without a gigantic and more or less co-ordinated effort of the saner and abler elements in the human population.[99]

In other words, by pressure from individuals behaving as world citizens. Wells was, nevertheless, vague about the political structure of this new order, placing his faith in global-functional administration rather than world government. In this respect he differed from the Federalist movement, which nevertheless in some moods he supported.

The idea of a federation of at least a portion of the states of the world was in the air during the 1930s. Hopeful support crystallised round *Union Now*. This book by Clarence K. Streit, Geneva correspondent of the *New York Times*, was published in 1939 and was warmly received in both the USA and the UK. In Britain an organisation called Federal Union was established to propagate the plan, and such bodies themselves subsequently federated to become the United World Federalists. The scheme involved the creation of a US-style federal system of government among the democratic states of the world as a nucleus and to which would adhere others as their political systems became compatible. Crucial to the whole project was the readiness of the individual to act responsibly in his dual citizen role — as a citizen of his state and as a federal or world citizen. Streit explained:

The knife edge is removed from disputes between states in a union because the citizens of each state are also citizens of the union, have the same control over both, and inevitably rate higher the citizenship that opens the wider field to them . . . and gives them their standing in the world . . . .
If each who profits from the Rights of Man gives now his mite as he sees best for the cause that made these Rights possible, he will soon have world union, and its greater rights for men.[100]

The Second World War, far from crushing the spirit of the proponents of world citizenship, stimulated further activity, which spilled over into the immediate post-war years. More books were written, most notably Emery Reves' *The Anatomy of Peace* (1947), J. Middleton Murray's *The Free Society* (1948) and Stringfellow Barr's *Citizen of the World* (1952). But perhaps the influence of some of these volumes among the reading public was inversely proportional to the likelihood of their ideas being implemented. For when Wendell Wilkie stood as the Republican candidate in the 1940 US Presidential election, campaigning under the slogan of 'One World', he was soundly beaten by the incumbent, F. D. Roosevelt. Moreover, when he attempted to broadcast his message of 'one world or none' in book form, it was derided as 'Gullible's Travels'!

The really great world-citizen traveller of this period was Gary Davis, who dubbed himself 'First World Citizen'. His exploits, though of little historical significance, provide a fascinating commentary on the cosmopolitan ideal. Guilty about his actions as an American bomber pilot and discontented with the exclusive loyalty demanded of its citizens by the nation-state, Davis made the following resolve:

I would bring about world government . . . precisely as all other governments had been brought into being: simply by declaring myself an actual citizen of that government and behaving like one.[101]

On 25 May 1948 at the American Embassy in Paris he formally swore the oath of Renunciation of US citizenship. For ten years he lived and travelled as a stateless 'world citizen'. He was denounced as a crank, imprisoned as an illegal resident, but gained immense publicity and the approval of many distinguished figures. The French intellectual Camus was especially supportive;

the Australian statesman Dr Evatt and the Indian prime minister Pandit Nehru commended his campaign. Davis' most significant symbolic actions were journeys he undertook on his 'world passport' – a do-it-yourself document. Amazingly this gave him at least temporary admission to some countries and thus partial evidence that nationality status was not essential for international travel.

But the gesture bore no permanent fruit. Perhaps because popular interest was so limited. For, as Einstein stated in a telegram of support to Davis, popular opinion was crucial. He declared:

A supra-national institution must have enough powers and independence . . . to solve the problems of international security . . . . Only the unbendable will of the people can free the forces which are necessary for such a radical break with the old and outlived traditions in politics.[102]

True, in part stimulated by Davis' exploits, World Citizens' Clubs sprang up, individuals registered themselves as world citizens and several towns declared themselves 'mondialised'. In Britain, J. B. Priestley proposed the creation of an Order of World Citizenship. But the moment of enthusiasm and commitment soon passed.

Gary Davis' dream was to build a world communtiy from the grass-roots up. An alternative strategy was to produce a constitution for a world government and gradually work for its acceptance. While Davis was in the process of renouncing his US citizenship, the *Preliminary Draft of a World Constitution* was being produced by a committee convened at the University of Chicago. Whereas almost all previous schemes derived solely from a desire for peace, the *Preliminary Draft* is based on the belief that peace is in any case unattainable without a prior foundation of social and economic justice. This is clear from its Declaration of Duties and Rights of world citizens, which gives primacy to:

. . . release from the bondage of poverty and from the servitude and exploitation of labor, with rewards and security according to merit and needs.[103]

The drafters were very conscious that any definition of world citizenship had to embrace the Marxist socialist tradition as well as the liberal, if it were to have any claims to universal application.

None of this had the slightest ring of realism about it for most people who nevertheless wished in a general way to promote a tighter sense of world community. For the pragmatically minded in the post-war years, building on the United Nations Organisation and international law appeared the only practical way forward. Some foresaw the potential of the UN to become a quasi-supranational government dispensing a universally accepted code of world law. The most detailed blue-print for the evolution of the UN along these lines was drafted by the American lawyers, Grenville Clark and Louis B. Sohn in their *World Peace Through World Law*. This book shows how the UN Charter should, in their view, be amended. In the course of this analysis the authors grapple specifically with the issue of citizenship:

The new Article 4 deals with a new subject, namely United Nations citizenship. This citizenship would be extended to all the citizens of all the member Nations. The reason for this new feature is that the revised Charter would not only grant certain rights and privileges to individuals, but would also impose definite obligations on individuals. For example, individuals as well as governments and organisations, would be bound by many regulations concerning disarmament and might be punished directly by the United Nations for violating them.[104]

The individual and international law

How far in fact have individual states and the world community as a whole accepted that citizens have rights in respect of and duties to obey a universal moral code, even if it dictates actions contrary to the interests of the state as perceived by any given government? The greatest strain in the event of such a clash of codes of conduct is likely to occur in times of war. This is so because it is simultaneously a time when the state needs maximum loyalty of its citizens and when the brutal treatment and killing of human beings is likely to raise doubts in the consciences of both individual citizens and the community of nations about the justification of such contraventions of human rights. Two quite conscious sets of legal decisions in our own century confirm that some states at least do indeed recognise a moral code over and above their own judicial and authority systems. These have been the concession by liberal states of the status of conscientious objection and the concept of crimes against humanity. Thus the British Conscription Acts of 1916 allowed tribunals to hear appeals based on 'a conscientious objection to the undertaking of combatant service'. The state conceded the principle that the individual had the right, usually on religious grounds, to refuse to defend the state by killing other human beings. In the USA the Supreme Court has similarly recognised the validity of such a plea.

The second set of legal decisions, namely the concept of crimes against humanity, was established by the Nuremberg trials of Nazi war criminals in 1945–46 (and the parallel trials of Japanese in Tokyo). Henceforth, neither obedience to the orders of a superior nor pursuit of state policy could be cited as justification for individual criminal behaviour. It is true that the justice of the proceedings at Nuremberg was questioned on very plausible legal grounds. Nevertheless, the point for our purposes is to note that crimes against the principles of universal moral conduct were now codified in the London Charter, which provided the legal framework for the trials. Article 6 of the Charter specified three:

(a) Crimes against peace: namely planning, preparation, initiation or waging a war of aggression, or a war in violation of international treaties. . . .
(b) War crimes: namely, violations of the laws and customs of war. . . .
(c) Crimes against humanity: namely, murder, extermination, enslavement, deportation and other inhumane acts committed against any civilian population. . . .[105]

Now until the Second World War it had been generally assumed that an individual could not be deemed guilty of a crime if that crime was committed in pursuance of orders from a superior. Indeed, such a convention was written into the disciplinary codes of most armies. However, the London Charter stated categorically:

That international law imposes duties and liabilities upon individuals as well as upon states has long been recognised . . . . The very essence of the Charter is that individuals have duties which transcend national obligations.[106]

The fact that the Allies chose not to execute the Nazi leaders explicitly as an act of retribution by victors in war, but as an act of justice, was by itself an assertion that the individual has an obligation to international law based upon universal principles of human morality. The message was that if the state orders its citizens to violate these principles, the citizen's responsibility is to disobey the state in favour of the higher code. To act, in short, as world citizens.

The Nuremberg Tribunal was of course an exceptional court established in exceptional circumstances. Nevertheless, there have been some subsequent attempts to call upon the principles it created. Most obviously have been the follow-up arrests and trials of numerous former Nazis notorious for their active prosecution of the 'Final Solution' policy. Then in 1985, to mark the fortieth anniversary of the opening of the Tribunal, 400 lawyers from the USA, West and East Europe met to reiterate the validity of the Nuremberg Principles. However, their greatest practical test was presented by the Vietnam war. As the chief US prosecutor at Nuremberg has noted,

The claim that American intervention in Vietnam is itself an aggressive war and therefore criminal − the so-called 'Nuremberg defence' − has been put forward by draft card burners, draftees facing induction and soldiers about to be shipped to Vietnam.[107]

In retrospect one may view the trial of war criminals as part of a broader revival and development of the concept of human rights. We have seen (pp. 47−49) how the American and French Revolutions of the eighteenth century produced their own statements of the rights of man and the citizen. However, the universalist potential of the concept of the rights of man was totally at odds with the doctrine of nationalism which was, paradoxically, triggered by that same French Revolution. By 1945 nationalism was abhorred in Europe as the major cause of the appalling suffering of the 'second Thirty Years War' of 1914−45. The mood was therefore propitious for a revival and reinvigoration of the idea of human rights but in universalist form. The basic document is the United Nations Universal Declaration of Human Rights of 1948. Admittedly, the term 'world citizen' does not feature. None the less, the social and political rights listed in the document are declared to be universally applicable irrespective of the state of which the individual is citizen: no state may legitimately deprive its own citizens of these rights; the state therefore cannot claim absolute sway over its citizens. What is more, the last paragraph of the preamble makes it clear that the individual has a universal political obligation beyond his obligation as a citizen of a state:

Now therefore the General Assembly proclaims this Universal Declaration of Human Rights as a common standard of achievement for all peoples and all nations, to the end that *every individual* and every organ of society, keeping this Declaration constantly in mind, shall strive by teaching and education to promote respect for these rights and freedoms and by progressive measures, national and *international*, to secure their *universal* and effective recognition and observance . . ..

It is quite evident from the words emphasised here that the intention of the Declaration is to accord the individual universal political responsibilities – in other words, a modicum of world citizenship.

Furthermore, as the century has progressed the matter of human rights has become a very live practical political issue. In 1946 the UN accepted that 'it is no longer contrary to the law of nations that a state shall intervene in the territorial sphere of another state to uphold basic standards of human rights.'[108] Most notably President Carter elevated the issue of human rights to a major feature of his foreign policy. As he has written,

Whenever I met with the leader of a government which had been accused of wronging its own people, the subject of human rights was near the top of my agenda.[109]

The most remarkable achievement of this policy was persuading the Soviet government to accept the proposals at the Helsinki conference in 1979 for monitoring improvements in the honouring of human rights in the USSR (p. 258). Much more dramatic was the military intervention by the altruistic President Nyerere in the same year to rid neighbouring Uganda of the repugnantly homicidal Idi Amin. The implication is clear. An individual can now justifiably expect to have his rights protected against the actions of the state of which he is a citizen by the intervention of a foreign state implementing a universally recognised code of human rights. Moreover, some individuals who suffer abridgement of these rights have not remained passive. The dissidents in the Soviet Union, the Charter 77 group in Czechoslovakia, the African National Congress in South Africa, the relatives of the *desaparecidos* in Argentina have all appealed for intervention in the name of human rights. These appeals could be construed as political acts justified by the status of the appellants as world citizens – or novice world citizens at least.

Modes of thought outside the western tradition

The concept of human rights which has provided the framework for these developments has, it is true, been criticised by both Communist and Third World régimes as being western liberal rather than truly universal in assumptions, priorities and style. This is a matter for later consideration (p. 287). However, the problem of cultural conditioning serves to remind us that the notion of world citizenship, based upon the recognition of a universal natural moral law, has in fact evolved in separate distinct forms outside the European-Atlantic tradition of juridico-political thought. We have already noted the cosmopolitan strain in Confucianism (p. 8). The Indian *Advaita* doctrine, which Mahatma Gandhi embraced, has similar characteristics, and indeed certain affinities with Stoicism. Gandhi spoke of 'world citizenship', of 'the essential unity of God and man and for that matter of all lives', holding that 'All mankind in essence are alike'.[110] Contemporaries of Gandhi, the political-activist-turned-philosopher, Sri Aurobindo and the statesman-philosopher, Rajagopalachari, were perhaps more concerned than Gandhi about bellicose international relations and the obsolescence of the nation-state as seen through borrowed western spectacles. However, their solutions, like Gandhi's, were typically oriental: they believed that a genuine feeling of human oneness was a precondition of any form of political unity and that this could be achieved only through religious conviction. In the case of Aurobindo he believed in a religion of humanity, a faith that mankind is the most highly developed vehicle for the fulfilment of a divine reality and that only by brotherly collaboration can the human race reach its potential for perfection. Such ideas, including the political concept of the cosmopolis, are so remote from the practicality of twentieth-century politics that few eminent politicians are ready to commit themselves publicly to their achievement. A notable exception was the Indian prime minister, Nehru. He combined the Gandhian conviction of the achievement of peace and justice by non-violent thought and action with a world federalist certainty that world government must eventually be constructed. In a radio broadcast in 1948 he said,

. . . so long as we do not recognise the supremacy of the moral law in our national and international relations, we shall have no enduring peace. So long as we do not adhere to right means, the end will not be right and fresh evil will flow from it. That was the essence of Gandhiji's message and mankind will have to appreciate it in order to see and act clearly. When eyes are bloodshot, vision is limited.
I have no doubt in my mind that World Government must and will come, for there is no other remedy for the world's sickness.[111]

Indian thought generally tends to philosophical holism. More specifically focussed on the political issue of world citizenship is the Bahá'í religion. This faith was developed in the late nineteenth century. Its founder, Bahá'u'lláh declared, 'The earth is but one country, and mankind its citizens.' He conceived a New World Order, 'in which,' in the words of the Guardian of the Bahá'í Faith in 1931, 'the fury of a capricious and militant nationalism will have been transmitted into an abiding consciousness of world citizenship.'[112]

Nor did the orientals lose, as western industrialised man so fatally did, an awareness of the interdependence of humankind with the rest of nature. None the less, that understanding is returning to the northern hemisphere. Indeed, Biology is now helping to shape political thought — just as Christian theology shaped that of Aquinas, mechanistic physics that of Locke and classical economics that of Marx. A rapidly increasing number of the world's population are becoming conscious of the preciousness and vulnerability of the earth's ecosystem. Similarly an increasing number are recognising their duty to take whatever action they can to stem the plundering and pollution of the global environment. Moreover, in this task national boundaries and so-called national interests are meaningless. Brazilian and non-Brazilian citizens alike have a right and duty to condemn the felling of the Amazonian rain-forest; Soviet and non-Soviet citizens, the negligent management of nuclear power stations; British and non-British citizens, the acidification of the atmosphere. Thus do the environmentally concerned adopt the habits of thought and consciences of world citizens. At the same time philosophers of Biology have been endeavouring to explain their growing sense of man's unity both within his species and with the planet he inhabits.

The Jesuit palaeontologist, Teilhard de Chardin, believed that the God-driven process of evolution was leading mankind inexorably to a unity of thought. He argued that this linking of all humanity through the shared mental processes of the 'noosphere' (as he called it) was the very apogee of the evolutionary process. In his posthumously published, *The Phenomenon of Man* (1959), he wrote:

How can we fail to see that after rolling us on individually – all of us, you and me – upon our selves, it is still the same cyclone (only now on the social scale) which is still blowing over our heads, driving us together into a contact which tends to perfect each one of us by linking him organically to each and all his neighbours.[113]

More recently there has been propounded the secular Gaia hypothesis. This suggests that the whole planet is one gigantic organism. Moreover, since mankind alone of all species is both aware of the nature of the ecosystem and capable of annihilating it, then the totality of mankind has a responsibility for preservative action. And the necessary activity is civic, political activity:

Our diversifying power structure, with ever-multiplying special interest groups, village organizations, regional groupings, and transnational bodies, means that we can *effect action*, all at once and globally, to a concerted aim and by a diversity of means . . . .
It is time for humanity to use this power, and use it well. We must have the courage to face ourselves, to admit our power of life and death, and bring it under permanent, watchful control.[114]

Can this feeling of moral responsibility for our ecosystem be undergirded by international law? In 1970 the American Arthur Galston argued that 'ecocide' should be rated alongside genocide as a crime against humanity. The implications for world citizenship are interesting. Individuals who failed to disobey orders for the serious degradation of the environment would be as guilty as those tried at Nuremberg. For they would be in breach of the prime requirement to obey the most imperative of all moral laws, namely to preserve a life-sustaining planet for future generations.

The League, the UN and education for international understanding

The erosion of state sovereignty, even in the face of impending catastrophe, has been an extremely slow process. Governments and the people they represent have been reluctant to surrender their autonomy and power. Similarly, governments have been hesitant to encourage any form of citizenship education other than nationalist in tone. None the less, educationists themselves started effectively to rebel against such political narrowness at the beginning of the century. Three movements of significance in the history of education for world citizenship originated c.1900. One was the start of schools committed to 'Progressive' or 'New Education', founded by such educationists as Maria Montessori in Italy and Rabindranath Tagore in India. It can be argued that this movement provided a necessary liberation from traditional ideas, without which no effective World Studies could have developed. The freeing of young people from state-directed syllabuses (usually of a catechistic mode) was a precondition for a more positive form of learning. The New Education tended to emphasise instead the development of the imagination, the fostering of toleration and the cultivation of collaborative methods of learning. These styles of education are more likely to generate an empathetic understanding of other peoples than the dogmatic jingoistic teaching which often characterised popular education in the nationalistic era. Indeed, Maria Montessori viewed the child unspoiled by formal education as a 'teacher of peace'. Furthermore, this close relationship between the New Education and internationalism was to be reflected in the inter-war years by the work of the New Education Fellowship. This worldwide network of teachers advocated the teaching of school subjects in such a way as to illustrate what they believed to be civilised man's natural propensity to co-operate.

Secondly, in the work of van Vollenhoven in the Netherlands we have the earliest example of the revision of textbooks with a view to erasing national bias. It was a process that was to be eagerly pursued later under both League of Nations and United Nations auspices. And thirdly were the movements for promoting Peace Studies inspired by the Second Hague Conference of 1907. The following year School Peace Leagues were founded. These were particularly active in the USA, Britain, France and the Netherlands, where Peace Day was celebrated in many schools – 18 May, the day the first Hague Conference had been inaugurated in 1899. The US Office of Education gave enthusiastic support to the activities of its League; and even President Taft himself encouraged attempts at international educational links. The varied work of the British League has been described by an American scholar in the following way:

Its aims were to promote, through the schools, international peace, arbitration, and friendship; to study, in meetings and conferences, the problems of racial relationships and the best means of eliminating prejudice; to study the history of the international peace movements; to promote, through lessons in civics, the development of a rational and humane national life and patriotism, and a sense of the corresponding duties to humanity; to print and circulate literature bearing upon these points among teachers of all kinds; to foster courage and devotion in the pacific spheres of industry and social service; and to work in connection with similar organizations abroad for the establishment of an international organization.[115]

The reader may justifiably object that these trends were neither enjoyed by anything but a tiny proportion of the world's children nor intended to produce fully-fledged world citizens in any case. But all three movements did at least begin to raise serious questions about the nationalistic, often xenophobic style of education common at the time and to show the way to forms of learning designed for a global sense of responsibility. The educational emphasis mirrored the contemporary political purpose – namely the desire for peace.

The shock of the First World War gave added weight to this argument. Yet the Covenant of the League of Nations, the international instrument devised to prevent the recurrence of such horrific conflict, was silent on the matter of education. A group of ladies, led by the indefatigable American educationist, Fannie Fern Andrews, urged the inclusion of education, but to no avail. Indeed, even when subsequent pressure persuaded the League Assembly to create an International Committee on Intellectual Cooperation (ICIC), the reference to education had to be deleted from the original resolution because of continuing opposition: member states feared it might lead to external interference in their school systems. The remit of the Committee had to be confined to the ivory tower to the exclusion of the chalk face. However, from 1926 some work related to schools got under way. In that year the League was persuaded to create a 'Sub-Committee of Experts for the Instruction of Children and Youth in the Aims of the League of Nations' (which later, not surprisingly, changed its name). By 1932, 33 of the 58 member-states reported that they had included teaching about the League in their curricula. During the rest of that decade the Committee broadened its concern to the teaching of world citizenship through all appropriate subjects and media. A particular effort was made to encourage the elimination of nationalist bias from textbooks, especially in History. This move started in 1925 with the Casarès Resolution, which suggested

that one of the most effective methods of bringing about the intellectual *rapprochement* of peoples would be to delete or modify passages in school textbooks of a nature to convey to the young wrong impressions leading to an essential misunderstanding of other countries.[116]

In a number of states the associations established to support the League developed some activities in schools to promote international understanding. By far and away the most successful of these was the Education Committee of the British League of Nations Union. The LNU built up considerable enthusiasm in schools and youth movements for education in world citizenship (a term by then in vogue) through classroom work, school and youth clubs and camps. At the height of its influence 1400 schools were members. Local education authorities and teachers' professional associations had become deeply committed to this cause by the late 1920s. However, even in Britain the attitude of central government throughout this inter-war period was generally luke-warm. The 1937 edition of the *Handbook of Suggestions for Teachers* sums up official hesitancy admirably. Teachers were advised to teach about the circumstances which 'have made it necessary that peoples of the world should combine with their natural sense of local patriotism a conception of their common interests and duties.' But they were sternly warned to 'avoid troublesome details'![117]

On the continent of Europe attention to international studies was much weaker even than in Britain. A French report compiled in the mid-1930s is characteristic:

In secondary education the direct study of international questions has found no place except for some extra-curricular conferences which have been able to be provided in the Lycees by the associations for the League of Nations and the importance of which, in fact, has been extremely feeble.[118]

The frailty of the academic discipline of International Relations contributed to the weakness of the more elementary work in schools. In this respect more progress was being made in the USA. Here too nationalist opposition was strong, in some areas so powerful that it could not be overcome by teacher commitment to the internationalist cause. The National Council for the Social Studies did their best to encourage such work especially by broadcasting the success of well-prepared programmes, most notably the Glens Falls Project.

Perhaps one of the reasons for the uncertain progress of education for world citizenship in the inter-war years was the lack of firm and committed leadership from the intellectuals. True, the French novelist Anatole France addressed the French teacher in 1919 with the following demand:

He must make the child love peace and its works; he must teach him to hate war. He must exclude from his teaching every appeal towards hatred of the foreigner.[119]

Thirteen years later the English philosopher, Bertrand Russell argued that, if

. . . the elimination of large-scale wars . . . were achieved by the establishment of an international authority, the teaching of militant nationalism would no longer serve a purpose . . . Moral training would no longer have homicide as the apex of a virtuous life.[120]

Interestingly Anatole France was advocating a proper education to achieve international peace, while Russell was pleading for international peace to achieve a proper education. But in any case, neither attracted widespread support. The Frenchman was famously and bitterly hostile to the vindictiveness of the Versailles Settlement; the Englishman, famous for his 'advanced' opinions and his pacifism. Neither was therefore accepted as a coolly dispassionate advocate.

During the Second World War the ideal of education for global responsibility was kept alive in Britain by the Council for Education in World Citizenship, a body which evolved from the LNU Education Committee. What is more, it was able to involve in its work a number of distinguished refugees from occupied Europe. Inspired by the classical scholar and League enthusiast, Professor Gilbert Murray, CEWC pressed for the creation after the war of an International Organisation for Education (the objective which Fannie Fern Andrews had failed to achieve). As a result of parallel thinking in the USA and the work of the Committee of Allied Ministers of Education a body of this kind was created. This was UNESCO, founded on the proposition

. . . that since wars begin in the minds of men it is in the minds of men that the defences of peace must be constructed.[121]

But has the UN generally and UNESCO specifically been committed to education for world citizenship? The main thrust of the UN system is the promotion of collaborative endeavours between governments. Moreover, initially UNESCO saw its function as merely 'advancing the mutual knowledge and understanding of peoples'. But, of course, citizenship requires more; it involves commitment, loyalty and participation by individuals. By the 1970s the organisation was moving gradually in that direction. A great deal of work had been accomplished before that date to promote education for international understanding through textbook revision and the Associated Schools Project. However, recognising the limitations of these activities, UNESCO issued in 1974 a *Recommendation concerning education for international understanding, co-operation and peace and education relating to human rights and fundamental freedoms*. Not only did its extraordinarily cumbersome title reveal an appreciation of the complexity of the task, the document also contained a section specifically on 'Ethical and civil aspects'. This contained the following advice:

Member States should urge educators . . . to prepare [children and adolescents] to exercise their rights and freedoms while recognizing and respecting the rights of others and to perform their social duties.

Member states should promote . . . an active training which will enable every person to gain a knowledge of the method of operation and the work of public institutions . . . and to participate in public affairs. Wherever possible, this participation should increasingly link education and action to solve problems at the local, national and international levels.[122]

The actual term 'education for world citizenship' is not favoured by the UN. Indeed, it was rarely used in the post-war decades, though a certain revival could be detected in the 1980s. Fear that it denoted impractical idealism or an undermining of national loyalty, or both, were powerful inhibiting factors among educationists committed to the cause. For example, when the Council for Education in World Citizenship was launched in Britain, its members were shocked by the hostility of *The Times Educational Supplement*, which warned its readers that the new body might well be

. . . the beginning of yet another attempt to coax children into wide and vague loyalties, to give a visionary slant to the teaching of history.[113]

The priorities from c.1940 were more restrained: in the first place, education for peace, as had been urged episodically ever since Comenius; and, in the light of Nazism, education in tolerance and respect for human rights.

Global education in recent decades

In an age of nuclear weapons and of psychological and sociological interest in the nature of human aggression, Peace Studies have come to assume an even greater urgency and to provoke even greater controversy than hitherto. The development of multidisciplinary academic Peace Studies from the late 1960s revealed the naïvety of the earlier beliefs that international peace could be sustained by spreading knowledge about foreign peoples and cultures. This research also undermined the simplistic equation of Peace Studies with Nuclear Disarmament Studies. True, since nuclear weapons do pose a threat to civilised life, even all life, on this planet, it is quite clear that no one pretending to the status of world citizen can ignore the problems they present. Furthermore, since states in possession of these weapons have believed in their necessary deterrent value, governments have been sensitive to any teaching in schools which has emphasised the global threat at the expense of national security. None the less, the proponents of Peace Studies insist that their educational case is much more comprehensive. It is also even more germane to the issue of world citizenship. Peace is threatened not just by the proliferation of weapons, conventional and nuclear, but by 'structural violence' – by the existence of injustices of so many kinds. When the Sahelian states of Africa are suffering from environmental degradation and the distortion of international markets by multinational companies, nuclear weapons, like conventional systems, are relevant to these peoples more for their obscene absorption of wealth than their destructive potential. The education of the true world citizen would aim to produce an individual knowledgeable about, sensitive to and determined to act to abate the sufferings endured by fellow human beings from all forms of violence. In the words of one English academic in the field,

In the end we may be discussing a new educational manifesto, a new pedagogy – both content and methods, means and ends – and its linkage with social and political action.[124]

By concerning itself with the violence done to human dignity and welfare by poverty and the violence done to the environment by unrestrained economic expansion, Peace Studies impinge upon two other facets of World Studies, namely Development Education and Environmental Education. Citizenship involves a sense of responsibility for the welfare of one's neighbours and one's environment. In today's 'global village' all are our neighbours, to whom, as in the parable of the good Samaritan, we should be prepared to 'show mercy'. In the modern context this has expressed itself in charitable work for the Third World countries by organisations which, by the 1960s, had evolved supporting educational activities. This was especially so in Britain where Oxfam was a vanguard movement. The widening gap in wealth between the northern and southern hemispheres was emphasised by the international Brandt Commission as not only a crying injustice but also as portending hazardous global tension. They appealed to schools to strive to avert this peril:

The Commission feels that schools all over the world should pay more attention to international problems so that young people will see more clearly the dangers they are facing, their responsibilities and the opportunities of cooperation.[125]

But citizenship is about equal rights, not charity; about responsibility as a moral duty, not as a response to fear. As Development Studies evolved in the 1970s the concept did come to be interpreted in a fuller, multi-dimensional sense, a sense more closely related to the ideal of world citizenship. Development, it came to be appreciated, involved so much more than expanding the wealth of poor countries by pumping in indiscriminate aid.

Development Studies have therefore involved bringing young people to a comprehension of the interplay of environment, economy and culture and an understanding that there is room for progress to a more just and satisfying life for the more unfortunate members of so-called 'developed' as well as 'developing' countries. In schools where the stress has been placed on empathy and constructive help, pupils have been learning to behave as young world citizens. UNESCO has provided a conspicuously successful scheme called the Gift Coupon Scheme, in 1976 renamed Co-Action (the Co-operative Action Programme). Schools in the more affluent countries are enabled to forge links with less fortunate communities and to raise money for very specific self-help projects for improving, for example, agricultural production or health or educational services.

The price of northern hemispheric wealth is threatening ecological catastrophe; the price of attempts by the southern hemisphere to catch up is also accelerating ecological catastrophe. Widespread realisation of the vulnerability of the biosphere in face of demographic and technological pressures has come recently and rapidly. The UN Conference on the Human Environment and the associated publicaton, *Only One Earth* in 1972 was a significant landmark which attracted considerable attention in the teaching profession. Five years later UNESCO convened the first Intergovernmental Conference on Environmental Education. Then in 1987 the international commission chaired by the Norwegian prime minister, Gro Bruntland, conflated development and environmental issues quite consciously in urging a policy of 'sustainable growth'. Furthermore, they emphasised that they were

. . . addressing the young. The world's teachers will have a crucial role to play in bringing this report to them.[126]

As issues of a global scale have impinged on the world's consciousness, so appeals have been transmitted to the schools to alert the rising generation to its responsibilities for alleviating the crises. Given the sensitising of the world's conscience on the issue of human rights by the evidence of Nazi atrocities, it is somewhat anomalous that almost four decades elapsed before really systematic attempts were made to persuade schools to engage in human rights education. These initiatives were made most notably by UNESCO and the Council of Europe. In 1985 the Council of Europe Committee of Ministers adopted a Recommendation encouraging schools to teach about human rights as an essential 'part of social and political education', involving as it does 'intercultural and international understanding'.[127] Even so, much of the stress was placed on the need to underpin democratic values in a domestic political context. This, of course, was a perfectly valid concern in an age of prejudice, intolerance and violence. It nevertheless prevented the recommendation from being an eager commitment to a global civic consciousness.

The educational systems of the world have received since 1945 more entreaties from more diverse and authoritative sources to nurture a global perspective in their pupils' thinking than at any other time. Simultaneously many educationists have themselves, as alert citizens, been deeply conscious of the world issues pressing for solution. Partly in response to appeals from outside the education service and partly from their own initiative curriculum developers and classroom teachers have adapted school programmes to reflect the interdependence of the modern world. A number of tactics have been adopted. One has been to broaden the syllabuses of traditional subjects. Most notably this has been undertaken by the introduction of elements of World History alongside conventional national History — in the USA, UK, West Germany, for example. Other subjects have also responded, most having at least some potential in this regard. A second approach has been the forming of units of work on facets of world affairs — for instance, teaching about the UN, Development Studies, Peace Studies.

Nowhere have attempts been more energetically made to provide some form of global studies in schools than in the USA. In 1966 President Johnson lent his authority to the strengthening of educational efforts for international understanding. Congress responded with the International Education Act and two years later there was created the Institute of International Studies in the Office of Education. With this encouragement a number of American educationists produced influential statements about the global dimension to education. Two were especially significant: the report compiled in 1969 by Becker and Anderson on the direct invitation of the Office of Education; and Hanvey's *An Attainable Global Perspective* (1982). Such writers were at pains to recommend not just cognitive learning about the world but the development of appropriate attitudes and skills. The practical effects of all this political and intellectual activity was, none the less, superficial. Let the despairing voice of the President of the National Council for the Social Studies in 1984 bear witness to this condition of inertia:

The traditional image of citizenship education persists. The belief that one should train young people to be good citizens by giving them lots of information about their country is everywhere. Just observe a typical classroom or examine a typical textbook . . .. Listen to the members of state boards of education and state legislatures talk about citizenship education — 'What our students need are more courses about America,' many of them say.[128]

Yet even much of what had been advocated for global studies in the USA until the mid-1980s has been considered unacceptably half-hearted by those fully committed to World Studies. Such educationists have been seeking a comprehensive model of teaching global-mindedness. In the 1980s certain strands of academic and creative thought in the USA assisted this search. In particular the insight that the world in political, economic and ecological terms is a collection of dynamic and self-organised systems naturally favours the interdisciplinary study of interconnections. Secondly, arguments that much academic and popular thinking is hidebound and excessively national lends added insight to educational processes which emphasise self- and empathetic awareness. An agenda for holistic global studies and deriving much of its inspiration from American influences has been drawn up by two English educationists, Pike and Selby. They have identified 'five aims which together constitute the irreducible global perspective.' In skeletal form these are listed as:

Systems consciousness
Students should: acquire the ability to think in a systems mode; acquire an understanding of the systemic nature of the world; acquire an holistic conception of their capacities and potential.

Perspective consciousness
Students should: recognise that they have a worldview that is not universally shared; develop receptivity to other perspectives.

Health of planet awareness
Students should: acquire an awareness and understanding of the global condition and of global developments and trends; develop an informed understanding of the concepts of justice, human rights and responsibilities and be able to apply that understanding to the global conditions and to global developments and trends; develop a future orientation in their reflection upon the health of the planet.

Involvement consciousness
Students should: become aware that the choices they make and the actions they take individually and collectively have repercussions for the global present and the global future; develop the social and political action skills necessary for beoming effective participants in democratic decision-making at a variety of levels, grassroots to global.

Process-mindedness
Students should: learn that learning and personal development are continuous journeys with no fixed or final destination; learn that new ways of seeing the world are revitalising but risky.[129]

This very extensive quotation has been reproduced (though highly abbreviated from the original) because it so clearly states the most recent formula for education for world citizenship. If a world order of some kind is a useful way of picturing the direction in which our swiftly changing planet is moving, then a responsive and responsible education must be constructed along lines which at least approximate to this set of aims. One of the crucial and novel elements of recent thinking in World Studies is insistence on future projections. But this is professionally unnerving. Teaching History is hazardous enough. Yet by what right does the teacher foretell the speedy decline into irrelevance of the nation-state which employs him? And by what right does he prepare the younger generations for a cosmopolis which has existed for two and a half millenia only in mankind's imagination?

REFERENCES

1. K. Mannheim, *Freedom, Power and Democratic Planning*, quoted in Brennan, *Political Education and Democracy*, p. 106.

156

2. Woodrow Wilson, 'Fourteen Points' speech, 8 January 1918, quoted in Macartney *National States and Minorities*, p. 189.
3. Woodrow Wilson, speech before Congress, quoted ibid., p. 190.
4. Polish Minorities Treaty, Article 7, reprinted ibid., p. 504.
5. H. J. Laski, *The Recovery of Citizenship* (Benn, 1928), pp. 3 & 12.
6. Leo XIII, *Rerum Novarum*, reprinted in M.Oakeshott (ed.), *Social and Political Doctrines of Contemporary Europe* (Basis Books, 1940), p. 57.
7. Pius XI, *Quadragesimo Anno*, reprinted ibid., pp. 59 & 58.
8. John XXIII, *Pacem in Terris* (trans. H. Waterhouse, Catholic Truth Society, 1980), paras. 24 & 73.
9. G. D. H. Cole, *Labour in the Commonwealth*, quoted in Pateman, *Participation*, p. 38.
10. Quoted in G. & D. Cohn-Bendit, *Obsolete Communism: The Left-Wing Alternative* (Penguin, 1968), p. 254.
11. *Social Insurance and Allied Services* (Beveridge Report), quoted in R. B. Jones, *Economic and Social History of England 1770–1977* (Longman, 1970), p. 260.
12. T. H. Marshall, *Citizenship and Social Class and Other Essays* (Cambridge University Press, 1950). pp. 25 & 26.
13. Ibid., p. 29.
14. J. Rawls, *A Theory of Justice* (Oxford University Press, 1973), p. 96.
15. Quoted in L. Hansberry, *A Matter of Colour* (Penguin, 1965), p. 116.
16. Quoted in W. J. Weatherby, 'Rosa has still to overcome', *Guardian*, 8 February 1988.
17. T. Renton, 'Firm but fair controls', *Guardian,* 13 November 1987.
18. Dewey, *Democracy and Education* (Macmillan, 1916, 1961 ed.), pp. 99 & 120.
19. Durkheim, *Education and Sociology*, quoted in T. Englund, *Curriculum as a Political Problem* (Chartwell-Bratt, 1986), p. 166.
20. Mannheim, *Freedom, Power and Democratic Planning*, quoted in Brennan, *Political Education and Democracy*, p. 107.
21. Althusser, *Education: Structure and Society*, quoted in T. Tapper & B. Salter, *Education and the Political Order* (Macmillan, 1978), p 57.
22. Quoted in H. Entwistle, 'Antonio Gramsci and the School as Hegemonic' (University of York Open Seminar Documentation Service, n.d.), p. 8.
23. J. Morrissett, 'The Needs of the Future and the Constraints of the Past' in H. D. Mehlinger & O. L. Davis (eds.), *The Social Studies* (National Society for the Study of Education, 1981), p. 39.
24. G. Z. F. Bereday (ed.), *Charles E. Merriam's The Making of Citizens* (Teachers College Press, Columbia University, 1966), pp. 217–18.
25. J. V. Torney *et al.* (eds.), *Civic Education in Ten Countries* (Halsted Press, 1975), p. 67.
26. Reprinted in J. A. Muñoz, *La educación politica camo función de gobierno en el Estado* (Ediciones Universidad de Navarra, 1982), pp. 426–7 (author's translation).
27. Reprinted ibid., p. 432 (author's translation).
28. Reprinted in B. Crick & A. Porter (eds.), *Political Education and Political Literacy* (Longman, 1978), p. 252.
29. Department of Education and Science, *Education (No. 2) Act 1986* (HMSO, 1986), Ch. 61, Sects. 44 & 45.
30. W. C. Sellar & R. J. Yeatman, *1066 And All That* (Methuen, 1930, 1984 ed.), p. 5.

31. See R. E. Gross, 'Citizenship Education' in *Encyclopedia Americana*, vol. 6 (Grolier, 1981), p. 746.
32. Bereday, *Merriam's The Making of Citizens*, p. 254.
33. J. Jarolimek, 'The Social Studies: An Overview' in Mehlinger & Davis, *Social Studies*, p. 7.
34. Reprinted in L. L. Snyder (ed.), *The Idea of Racialism* (Van Nostrand, 1962), pp. 184–5.
35. Swann, *Education for All* – Cmnd. 9453 (HMSO, 1985), pp. 335–6.
36. A. S. Neill, 'Freedom Works' in P. Adams *et al.*, *Children's Rights* (Granada, 1972), pp. 137–8.
37. W. Langeveld, 'Political Education: Pros and Cons' in Heater & Gillespie, *Political Education in Flux*, p. 41.
38. Quoted in Englund, *Curriculum as a Political Problem*, p. 78.
39. M. Ozouf, 'Histoire et Instruction Civique', quoted in J. Carduner, *'Making of French Citizens'*, p. 93.
40. J. P. Patrick, 'The Reconstruction of Civics Education in American Schools', quoted in M. J. Turner, 'Civic Education in the United States' in Heater & Gillespie, *Political Education in Flux*, p. 53.
41. D. G. Dufty (ed.), *Teaching about Society* (Rigby, 1970), p. 11.
42. R. Stradling, 'Political Education: Developments in Britain' in Heater & Gillespie, *Political Education in Flux*, p. 100.
43. George Orwell, *Nineteen Eighty-Four* (Penguin ed., 1954), p. 50.
44. *History of the Communist Party of the Soviet Union (Bolsheviks)* (Foreign Languages Publishing House, 1951), p. 527.
45. Reprinted in Snyder, *Nationalism*, p. 163.
46. Quoted in R. Omond, *The Apartheid Handbook* (Penguin, 1985), p. 102.
47. Quoted in Z. Medvedev, *Ten Years After Ivan Denisovitch* (Penguin, 1975), p. 247.
48. Quoted in *History of the CPSU* (Bolsheviks), p. 527.
49. C. Milosz, *The Captive Mind* (Penguin, 1980), p. 217.
50. Quoted in R. A. Brady, *The Spirit and Structure of German Fascism* (Gollancz, 1937), p. 181.
51. A. Rosenberg, *Deutsches Kulturrecht*, quoted ibid., pp. 105–6.
52. K. Mehnert, *China Today* (Thames & Hudson, 1972), p. 104.
53. B. von Schirach, *Revolution der Erziehung*, quoted in K. D. Bracher, *The German Dictatorship* (Penguin, 1973), p. 330.
54. Quoted in R. F. Price, *Marx and Education in Russia and China* (Routledge & Kegan Paul, 1977), p. 70.
55. Quoted in Joseph J. Zajda, *Education in the USSR* (Pergamon, 1980), p. 207.
56. Quoted ibid., p. 30.
57. Quoted in R. H. Samuel & R. Hinton Thomas, *Education and Society in Modern Germany* (Routledge & Kegan Paul, 1949), p. 83.
58. Quoted in N. Grant, *Soviet Education* (Penguin, 1964), p. 65.
59. Quoted in R. F. Price, *Education in Modern China* (Routledge & Kegan Paul, 1979), p. 294.
60. M. Gorbachev, *Political Report of the CPSU Central Committee to the 27th Party Congress* (Novosti Press Agency, 1986), pp. 69, 72, 76.
61. Quoted in *Guardian*, 1 February 1986.
62. Quoted in W. K. Cummings, 'Samurai Without Swords' in Gumbert, *In the Nation's Image*, p. 21.

63. Quoted in J. E. Thomas, *Learning Democracy in Japan* (Sage, 1985), p. 50.
64. Reprinted in M. Balfour, *Four-Power Control in Germany and Austria, 1945–1946: I. Germany* (Oxford University Press, 1956).
65. S. Duczek, 'Political Education in Germany' (University of York Political Education Research Unit, October 1977), p. 9.
66. A. Hitler, *My Struggle* (abr. edn, Paternoster Library, 1933), p. 174.
67. S. Rushdie, 'Midnight's real children' in *Guardian*, 25 March 1988.
68. Horace, *Epistles*, III, i.
69. M. MacDonald, quoted in J. D. Hargreaves, *The End of Colonial Rule in West Africa* (Historical Association, 1976), p. 7.
70. Quoted in H. Grimal, *Decolonisation: the British, French, Dutch and Belgian Empires, 1919–63* (Routledge & Kegan Paul, 1978), p. 53.
71. Quoted in R. Segal, *African Profiles* (Penguin, 1962), p. 63.
72. Quoted in Grimal, *Decolonisation*, p. 61.
73. J. K. Nyerere, *Man and Development* (Oxford University Press, 1974), p. 108.
74. Quoted in V. Mehta, *Mahatma Gandhi and His Apostles* (Penguin, 1977), p. 250.
75. Reprinted in K. Nkrumah, *I Speak of Freedom* (Heinemann, 1961), p. 206.
76. Quoted in T. Hodgkin, *African Political Parties* (Penguin, 1961), p. 36.
77. J. Timerman, *Prisoner Without a Name, Cell Without a Number* (Weidenfeld & Nicolson, 1981), pp. 16–17.
78. J. K. Nyerere, '*Ujamaa*': *the Basis of African Nationalism*, reprinted in A. Luthuli *et al.*, *Africa's Freedom* (Allen & Unwin, 1964), p. 70.
79. Quoted in B. Moore, *Social Origins of Dictatorship and Democracy* (Penguin, 1967), p. 373.
80. Quoted in R. Iyer, *The Moral and Political Thought of Mahatma Gandhi* (Oxford University Press, 1973), pp. 256 & 257.
81. Reprinted in Nkrumah, *I Speak of Freedom*, p. 23.
82. Quoted in W. F. Connell, *A History of Education in the Twentieth Century World* (Curriculum Development Centre, Canberra, 1980), pp. 325–6.
83. Quoted in K. Prewitt (ed.), *Education and Political Values* (East Africa Publishing House, 1971), p. 56.
84. T. Mboya in *New York Times*, 28 January 1959 quoted in A. A. Mazrui, *Political Values and the Educated Class in Africa* (Heineman, 1978), p. 55.
85. K. L. Shrimali, *Education in Changing India* (Asia Publishing House, 1965), pp. 15–16.
86. Quoted in J. S. Szyliowicz, *Education and Modernization in the Middle East* (Cornell University Press, 1973), p. 47.
87. Quoted ibid., p. 281.
88. F. A. Adeyoyin, 'The Role of the School as a Politicizing Agent through Citizenship Education', *International Journal of Political Education*, April 1979.
89. C. Harber, 'Schools and National Awareness in Nigeria', ibid., April 1982.
90. Reprinted in Muñoz, *La educación política*, p. 425 (author's translation).
91. Mazrui, *Political Values*, p. 190.
92. J. Bryce, *South America*, quoted in S. M. Lipset, *Political Man* (Heinemann ed., 1963), p. 56.
93. P. Freire, *Pedagogy of the Oppressed* (Penguin, 1972), p. 44.
94. A. Henderson in *The Schoolmaster*, November 1934, quoted in LNU, *Teachers and World Peace* (League of Nations Union, 5th edn, 1937), p. 23.
95. W. James, 'The Moral Equivalent of War' reprinted in Mayer, *Pacifist Conscience*, p. 188.

96. A. D. Lindsay, 'The State in Recent Political Theory', *The Political Quarterly*, February 1914.
97. N. Angell, *The Foundations of International Polity* (Heinemann, 1914), p. xx.
98. Quoted in D. S. Birn, *The League of Nations Union 1918–1945* (Clarendon, 1981), p. 20.
99. H. G. Wells, The *New World Order* (Knopf ed., 1940), p. 93.
100. C. K. Streit, *Union Now*, quoted in W. B. Curry, *The Case for Federal Union* (Penguin, 1939), pp. 131 & 211.
101. G. Davis, *My Country is the World* (Macdonald, 1961), p. 19.
102. Quoted ibid., pp. 218–19.
103. E. Mann Borgese (ed.), *A Constitution for the World* (Center for the Study of Democratic Institutions, Santa Barbara, 1965), p. 27.
104. G. Clark & L. B. Sohn, *World Peace Through World Law* (Harvard University Press, 1958), p. 15.
105. Quoted in L. Kuper, *Genocide* (Penguin, 1981), p. 21.
106. Quoted in W. Maser, *Nuremberg: A Nation on Trial* (Allen Lane, 1979), p. 268.
107. T. Taylor, *Nuremberg and Vietnam* (New York Times, 1970), p. 15.
108. L. R. Beres, *People, States and World Order* (F. E. Peacock, 1981), p. 49.
109. J. Carter, *Keeping Faith* (Collins, 1982), p. 150.
110. Quoted in Iyer, *Thoughts of Mahatma Gandhi*, pp. 91 & 92.
111. Reprinted in A. Appadorai (ed.), *Documents on Political Thought in Modern India*, vol. 2 (Oxford University Press, 1976), p. 811.
112. Bahá'í World Centre, *Promise of World Peace*, pp. 13 & 19.
113. P. Teilhard de Chardin, *The Phenomenon of Man* (Collins, 1959), p. 334.
114. N. Myers (ed.), *The Gaia Atlas of Planet Management* (Pan, 1985), p. 257.
115. D. G. Scanlon (ed.), *International Education: A Documentary History* (Teachers' College, Columbia University, 1960), pp. 7–8.
116. Reprinted in D. Heater, *World Studies* (Harrap, 1980), p. 171.
117. Board of Education, *Handbook of Suggestions for Teachers* (HMSO, 1937), pp. 418 & 428.
118. *Les Sciences sociales en France*, quoted in S. H. Bailey, *International Studies in Modern Education* (Oxford University Press, 1938), p. 141, (author's translation).
119. Quoted in B. J. Elliott, 'The League of Nations Union and History Teaching in England' in *History of Education*, vol. 6 (1977).
120. B. Russell, *Education and the Social Order* (Allen & Unwin, 1932, 1977 edn), p. 145.
121. Preamble to the Constitution.
122. *UNESCO Recommendation* Section V, paras, 12 & 13.
123. *Times Educational Supplement*, 13 April 1940.
124. N. Young in J. Thacker (ed.), *Perspectives II: Peace Education* (School of Education, University of Exeter, 1983), p. 23.
125. Independent Commission on International Development Issues, *North-South: A Programme for Survival* (Pan, 1980), p. 11.
126. World Commission on Environment and Development, *Our Common Future* (Oxford University Press, 1987), p. xiv.
127. Council of Europe, *Recommendation* No. R(85)7 (1985), Appendix, para. 1.1.
128. C. Hahn, 'Promise and Paradox: Challenges to Global Citizenship', *Social Education*, April 1984.
129. G. Pike & D. Selby, *Global Teacher, Global Learner* (Hodder & Stoughton, 1988), pp. 34–5.

CHAPTER FOUR

Historical Legacies

4.1   THE ORIGINS

[England, France and the USA] draw their ideas of citizenship (including their acceptance of the ideal of citizenship) from a common ancestry, that of the Graeco-Roman city state modified by Hebraeo-Christian ethical biases or dogmas. It is this idea of citizenship which is loose in the world today, so powerful that it is imitated — and counterfeited — in societies where the idea has no deep historical roots.

Denis Brogan[1]

The foundations of citizenship and citizenship education

Citizenship has been a persistent human social need. During the two and a half millenia from the emergence of the Greek city-state to the consolidation of the modern nation-state the concept was invented and defined, re-invented and redefined in five distinct contexts. The Greek city-state, the Roman Republic and Empire, the medieval and Renaissance city, the nation state and the idea of the cosmopolis each produced its own distinct interpretation of the basic idea. What forces underlay this episodic urge? The political needs of participation and loyalty cannot be the sole explanation since so many other methods of government and cohesion have been adopted in the course of human history and have been successful in their own terms. The evidence of the period from the Greek city-state to civil-war England shows that three other factors must be accommodated in any explanation.

One is the philosophical. Theories of citizenship contain assumptions and beliefs about the nature of man. The fundamental political nature of man is, of course, most forcibly expressed by Aristotle: he considered any man who is either unable or has no need 'to share in the benefits of political association [to be] . . . either a beast or a god.'[2] All theories of citizenship based on the notion of popular sovereignty assume that the exercise of power by any individual or group is legitimate only if, in the last resort, it is sanctioned by the people as a whole. No human being has a right totally to dominate another (slavery always excepted, whether in Periclean Athens or antebellum

USA). Citizenship evolved as a means of institutionalising this basic belief. Citizenship of a city or nation also takes for granted the human need to identify with a political unit, the state. In contrast, the idea of world citizenship denies this narrow view – in the belief that man has an urge and a need to recognise the moral and social oneness of his species.

The second explanation for the emergence of citizenship is the military. The Greek *polis* or city-state was originally defensive in purpose. *'Polis'* at first meant citadel, a meaning which survives in the Acropolis in Athens. Citizens were those who bore arms in defence of their city. Roman citizens had a similar responsibility and the early extension of the status to the inhabitants of Latin cities was an integral part of the absorption by military and diplomatic means of the province of Latium. In the imperial era dilution of the quality of citizenship went hand in hand with the dilution in quality of the cohorts. In more recent periods, the conferment of citizenship on the inhabitants of a medieval city-state originated in their recruitment into its defensive system, while the Machiavellian concept of civic virtue, drawn from his reading of Roman history, depended upon an armed citizenry. Similarly the modern nation-state universally requires, when necessary, the duty of military service of some kind from its citizens.

The third element is the economic. Theorists from Aristotle to Harrington worried round the question whether citizenship should be confined to the propertied classes. In all four of the cases of citizenship evolving in practice *ab initio*, it was the economically privileged classes who held the status in the early phases. At first, the sole right to citizenship or full access to its privileges was confined to that stratum of society that had a considerable economic stake in the orderly conduct of its affairs. Weber commented on this constant:

In the first period of development of the city communities, the similarity between the ancient and medieval city was very great. In both cases it is those of knightly birth, the families leading an aristocratic existence, who alone are active members of the group, while all the remaining population are bound to obedience.

Similarly, he noted that the modern nation-state, born in internecine war, required money to pursue these conflicts. This was available only from the capitalist class. And so,

Out of this alliance of the state with capital, dictated by necessity, arose the national citizen class, the bourgeoisie in the modern sense of the word.[3]

When these three factors – the philosophical, military and economic – coincided with the political abolition or decline of monarchical power, citizenship evolved. In Greece the circumstances became propitious with the decay of the Homeric monarchical system; in Rome, with the expulsion of Tarquinius Superbus and the creation of the Republic. In the Middle Ages the process was facilitated by the seizure of independence by the cities from the local prince: Venice showed the way in its renunciation of Byzantine tutelage. The pattern in the modern nation-state was the erosion of royal power by the capitalist and bureaucratic classes. The origins of world citizenship are, naturally, rather less precise because of the lack of a political framework within which it could be made real. However, insofar as Alexander consciously tried to implement the ideal, there were powerful military and economic factors in his policy. He integrated Persian and Hellenic troops and military techniques and sought to consolidate the economies of the Mediterranean, Nile, Tigris and Indus into one unified commercial network. Perhaps the ingredients of at least a partial world citizenship were assembled in a potentially cosmopolitan army and mercantile class? But the essential catalyst was unable to complete his work. In the words of Arnold Toynbee,

If Alexander had lived to ally himself with Zeno and Epicurus, it is conceivable that the Hellenes might have succeeded in stepping straight out of the city-state into the *Cosmopolis*.[4]

Although the social environment was sufficiently fertile for the theory and practice of citizenship to grow and flourish in several different periods, it has failed to blossom to its full potential. No society has yet educated its young people to a full appreciation of their potential roles as citizens of their own states and of the world and, at the same time, provided a full range of opportunities for these roles to be performed on reaching adulthood. Even so, by c.1700 all the basic issues in the shaping of a complete citizen had been illuminated, either by practical experience or theoretical advocacy. Very early in its history the term already contained a cluster of meanings related to a defined legal or social status, a means of political identity, a focus of loyalty, a requirement of duties, an expectation of rights and a yardstick of good social behaviour. Thousands of Greeks and Romans lived such a definition. No subsequent discussion of the topic has required any more components nor would have been complete with any fewer.

The element of status needs further comment. Is citizenship a status which sets the freeman apart from the serf or slave? If so, in a society where servitude no longer persists are all men citizens? If not, is citizenship then a status reserved for a select segment of society? Or yet, further, should there be gradations of citizenship? Again, all these issues were raised in the early centuries. It may appear that these issues are no longer relevant in the modern world. Both law and rhetoric presuppose the universality and equality of citizenship. And yet in all honesty can we accept that second-class citizenship does not exist? In the real world women, the unemployed, the minorities who are discriminated against or persecuted actually experience such an underprivileged existence. At least the theory and practice of earlier centuries had the merit of honesty: either the distinctions were clearly drawn or at least were worried about as problems. The crucial question has been, are the lower orders more likely to be a destabilising influence if they are admitted to or excluded from full citizenship status? Maybe the question is as pertinent in contemporary Johannesburg or even Liverpool as it was in fourth-century Athens or seventeenth-century Putney.

A review of the early history of citizenship may also lead us to question the modern assumption that the status necessarily adheres to the sovereign nation-state. As we have seen, the concept can be associated with any geographical unit from a small town to the whole globe itself. If participation is the priority, then the intimacy of the Greek or medieval city seemed essential. If loyalty to a moral code, then the whole of humanity must be embraced. If legal status is the essence, the Romans revealed the flexibility of dual city and imperial citizenship. Only if the nation-state is sovereign, commands the complete loyalty of its inhabitants and is the sole source of rights and duties must citizenship necessarily be exercised in that particular geographical context. The possibility, even wisdom, of a more flexible concept is perhaps a lesson to be learned from the experience of the past.

Without the consciousness of history we assume with too much certainty that we know what citizenship is or should be. This consideration bears with equal force on citizenship education. Present-day opponents of schools engaging in any formal preparation for this adult role may draw some comfort from the limited evidence that this was ever widely advocated let alone practised in these early periods. Not, of course, that the issue was ignored. The major aspects of the question often so emotionally debated in our own day are all reflected in the past. Can children be expected to understand the essentially adult practice of politics? Insofar as a training in good civic behaviour is desirable, should this be the function of the family or the state? Should the learning be theoretical and indirect, through History or Rhetoric, for example; or practical, by visits to the forum and law courts, for instance? And what should be the basic objective of such learning: should it be primarily civic participation or social obedience? In the intimate atmosphere of the city-state or the élitist society of the early nation-state, education for citizenship could be safely left to the civic environment and the family. Political socialisation was osmotic rather than didactic. In a geographically rapidly expanding polity like Rome, however, the state felt it prudent to provide more formal instruction.

The transmission of early ideas

Some quite specific messages echo with remarkable clarity across the centuries. Let us record just four examples. Spartan education has sometimes been likened to the Hitler Youth. The distinction between active and passive citizens written into the French Constitution of 1791 was a close parallel to the Roman distinction between full citizenship and *civitas sine suffragio*. When we read Kipling's 'The English Flag', particularly the line 'And what should they know of England who only England know', might we not be reminded of Montaigne's appreciation of the need for comparative knowledge for proper self-understanding (p. 15)? And finally, what a splendid syllabus Hobbes provides for training people in conservative citizenship! Adults are to be taught with religious overtones their duty of obedience (p. 33). There is little that would have been discordant with the New Right philosophy of Reaganite America or Thatcherite Britain.

In addition to repetitions of ideas in different historical circumstances we may also find precise conscious debts owed to the thoughts and practices of the past. We have already had occasion to sketch the revival of Aristotelian thought in the Middle Ages. The men of the Renaissance, of the English, American and French Revolutions were steeped in Roman History and deeply admired the Roman concept of civic virtue, especially as transmitted through the lucid prose of Cicero. In his old age Jefferson, writing about the Declaration of Independence, stated that:

All its authority rests then on the harmonizing sentiments of the day, whether expressed in conversation, in letters, printed essays, or in the elementary books of public right, as Aristotle, Cicero, Locke, Sidney and Co.[5]

In the 1790s the speeches of Robespierre and the canvases of David were alike shot through with classical allusions. Similarly, the writers of the Renaissance and Enlightenment made conscious reference to the Hellenistic idea of the cosmopolis. In 1850 there occurred the Don Pacifico affair, in which the institution of Roman citizenship was most famously invoked. Although of Portuguese Jewish parentage and living in Athens, Pacifico claimed British citizenship by virtue of having been born in Gibraltar. And on this rather flimsy basis the British prime minister, Palmerston, bullied the Greek government when they refused to meet the demand of Pacifico, an extortionate money-lender, for compensation for the pillaging of his house by an angry crowd. When criticised in the House of Commons, Palmerston boldly asserted that,

. . . as the Roman in days of old, held himself free from indignity, when he could say *Civis Romanus sum*; so also a British, subject, in whatever land he may be, shall feel confident that the watchful eye and strong arm of England will protect him against injustice and wrong.

Gladstone, morally horrified at this abuse of British power, retorted:

What then, Sir, was a Roman citizen? He was the member of a privileged caste: he belonged to a conquering race, to a nation that held all others bound down by the strong arm of power.[6]

An interesting contrast in the lessons of History. In the field of education we may note the recognition accorded to Comenius in our own century. From 1926 his birthday was marked each year by a lesson devoted to Peace Studies in all the secondary schools of his native Czechoslovakia. More recently, his scheme for a College of Light has been interpreted as foreshadowing the need for a body such as UNESCO, which accordingly celebrated the tercentenary of his death in 1970.

The period surveyed in Chapter 1 witnessed a remarkable accumulation of experience and theoretical speculation and judgement on citizenship and citizenship education. But how far was there conscious and continuous development over the period? And what legacies were transmitted to the modern age? The geographical context of the city-state and the underpinning of Roman law persisted throughout virtually the whole two and a half millenia, surviving the culture shock of the barbarian invasions. There survived too the concept of popular sovereignty of the Roman *lex regia* and the Roman practice of civic education through Rhetoric.

What is of greatest interest, though, is the revival of the classical ideal of civic virtue. Resuscitated in the civic humanism phase of the Italian Renaissance, the concept was transmitted by the writers of the Enlightenment over broad geographical areas, and subsequently through the classical curriculum of schools to the educated élites of Europe and the USA. Sociological questions were of considerable interest. Were citizens made virtuous by stringent laws? Until the nineteenth century there was a tendency to accept that this was so and, in consequence, Sparta was held up as the model rather than Athens. The assumed correlation between civic or 'republican' virtue and the ownership of property and the bearing of arms we have already noticed. But a new factor relating to wealth worried the thinkers of the eighteenth century. What concerned such writers as Montesquieu in France, Hume and Ferguson in Scotland and Hamilton in America was the relationship of trade to the qualities of citizenship. Although the *ownership* of wealth might well be a precondition for citizenship, the *making* of wealth was an entirely different matter. Might not the commercial ethos be detrimental to the selflessness required of the good citizen? Alexander Hamilton was particularly convinced that commerce would lead to the pursuit of empire and the destruction of the delicate balance between citizen and government. He wrote:

. . . as riches increase and accumulate in few hands; as luxury prevails in society; virtue will be in a greater degree considered as only a graceful appendage of wealth, and the tendency of things will be to depart from the republican standard. This is the real dispositionof human nature . . . . It is a common misfortune, that awaits our state constitution as well as all others.[7]

The thought is not without its relevance today.

Hamilton may be taken as an exemplar of American thought at the time. Steeped in the classical republican tradition as mediated through such commentators as Machiavelli, Harrington and Montesquieu, the intellectuals among the colonists clung to the belief that civic virtue was essential to resist corruption, from whichever side of the ocean it threatened. This republican tradition has remained a significant ingredient in the style of American politics ever since. In the eighteenth century it vied with the newer, contractual theory. The basic notion that citizens have rights vis-à-vis the state as well as duties was consolidated by the theory of virtual contract. The American colonists were creating an embryonic national citizenship on this basis, while on the other side of the Atlantic Locke expounded his thinking in his *Second Treatise on Government*. Lockean theory was to have a powerful influence on eighteenth-century thought, on the American and French Revolutions and, via these upheavals, on much of the subsequent history of citizenship. This new style of citizenship was, however, based upon the mechanism of representation – a considerable dilution of the classical ideal of the active citizen.

Greek and Roman citizenship were remarkable inventions. And yet little progress in practical terms can be recorded after these initiatives much before the eighteenth century. None the less, the political theory over the period was both rich and flexible. It proved itself quite capable of accommodating the needs of both Christianity and the nation-state. In contrast, neither the theory nor practice of cosmopolitanism made much headway. Man and citizen were conceived as utterly dichotomous moral entities, while the rise of the nation-state rendered any universalist expansion of the concept of citizen well-nigh impossible. Similarly, education for citizenship lagged behind both political fact and theory. And yet is it not an immature, even unstable, polity that neglects the civic function of education? Plato, as we saw on p. 2, certainly had no doubt of this as a basic truth.

4.2 CONSOLIDATION OF THE MODERN STATE

The good citizen is one who will have sense enough to judge of public affairs; discernment enough to choose the right officers; self-control enough to accept the decisions of the majority; honesty enough to seek the general welfare rather than his own at the expense of the community; public spirit enough to face trouble or even danger for the good of the community.

Lord Bryce[8]

Factors in confirming the citizenship idea

Citizenship was highly suitable for adaptation to the democratic era ushered in by the age of revolutions in the late eighteenth century. During the period from the American War of Independence to the First World War the principle was so consolidated in both thought and practice that it has been inconceivable since for it to be expunged from the structures of social, legal and political relationships. What, we must therefore ask, were the overall forces that shaped the ideal and practice during this crucial age; and what in consequence were the characteristic features of citizenship transmitted to our own century?

Not of course that the contributions of 'the long nineteenth century' (Eric Hobsbawm's term for the period c.1780–1914) were written on a *tabula rasa*. The classical ideals remained powerful influences, most evidently in Rousseau's thinking. There is more than a little of Roman civic virtue in the definition of citizenship by the British jurist and politician, Viscount Bryce, cited at the head of this section; and perhaps even more in his earlier catalogue of hindrances to good citizenship, which he listed as indolence, personal interest and party spirit. Closer to the time was the defence of the English in the seventeenth century of their traditions of political freedom and the role of parliament in government. England provided a model for envious commentators on the continent in the eighteenth century, especially as mediated through the pen of Voltaire. He noted that,

. . . the outcome . . . of the troubles in England [was] liberty. The English nation is the only one on earth . . . in which the people share in the government without confusion.[9]

The notion of a social contract, such a common feature of seventeenth-century

167

political thought, was also a vital idea for the development of citizenship. The basic principle of a balance of rights and duties in the relationship between citizen and state is, after all, contractual in nature.

It is nevertheless extremely doubtful whether citizenship would have made any discernible progress had it not been for the impact of the three great revolutions of the late eighteenth century – the American, French and Industrial. The French and Industrial Revolutions in particular fatally undermined the legitimacy of the old social and political order. This structure comprised Divine Right monarchy atop a hierarchical society which was politically represented in an Estates system dominated by aristocracy and Church. That arrangement, however gamely its beneficiaries fought back in counter-revolutionary endeavours, was rendered obsolete by the great upheavals. The concept and status of citizenship was needed to provide an alternative means of stability. It was this need that was so lucidly understood by Tocqueville, and which his younger compatriot, the statesman Georges Clemenceau, was wont to refer to as 'solidarity'.

But what were the specific forces at work in 'the long nineteenth century' which provided the evolving institution and moral ideal of citizenship with its particular traits? It is possible to discern five. The first is the growing strength of the middle classes. The professional men such as lawyers, teachers and writers took the lead in the revolutionary crises in demanding a juster, freer and more participative political system. They may or may not (usually not) have had faith in what Edmund Burke called 'the swinish multitude'. Nevertheless, their demands in the name of popular sovereignty could not in principle be limited, as disadvantaged groups in our own century have continued to argue. The contribution to the development of citizenship of the capitalist middle class was rather more complex. Capitalism acted as a positive force in helping to sweep away traditional institutions with the object of making room for the unconstrained operation of the market mechanism. By infiltrating the institutions of representative government the mercantile and industrial classes were able to use them to their own advantage and provide both a lesson and justification for the working class when they demanded similar opportunities. On the other hand, capitalism encourages the worship of Mammon – the accumulation of private wealth and the selfish pursuit of private interests. These features are not conducive to an altruistic frame of mind, which is intrinsic to the very concept of citizenship. The tension in the relationship between capitalism and citizenship, was a crucial feature of nineteenth-century practical politics and was present in different ways in both the thinking of Marx and Tocqueville on the topic. Furthermore, it has surfaced as a matter of cardinal interest in more recent discussions (pp. 265–272).

The expansion of capitalism and the extension of citizenship particularly required new answers to the age-old question of the relationship between citizenship and property. With the partial exception of the Levellers (p. 32), from Aristotle to the late eighteenth century it was generally agreed that it is 'the greatest blessing for a state that its members should possess a moderate and adequate property'.[10] The asumption was that the commitment required of citizenship could be realistically expected only of those with a tangible stake in maintaining stability. The argument drawn from this premiss by nineteenth-century laissez-faire liberals was that the state should protect the property of its citizens that they might be free to enjoy its fruit and by their consequent contentment contribute to the harmony of the polity. For a brief while in the USA Jefferson was able to suggest that in his vast land all could be potential citizens in this sense since all could become property-owners. This did not happen; and so in America as well as throughout Europe during this period liberals could find themselves constricting citizenship by, for example, defending property qualifications for the suffrage. Furthermore, the basic attitude of mind has been rejuvenated in recent years by the neo-liberal Hayekian philosophy of the New Right especially in Britain and the USA (p. 101).

The contrary attitude towards property and citizenship was not really fully developed until the twentieth century. Nevertheless, its origins can be clearly discerned in the nineteenth, especially in the thinking of the English Idealists. This view is that the state has a responsibility to deprive the wealthier of some of their property and redistribute it to the poor so that they might be brought to the minimum level of welfare necessary for their role as citizens. The debt of modern social democracy to this nineteenth-century concept may be vividly illustrated by the excerpt from the Beveridge Report quoted on p. 100. But whether the poorer classes and disadvantaged groups in society could rely for improvements in their condition on their steady incorporation into the status of full citizens was thrown into doubt by Marx's analysis of capitalist-dominated society and bourgeois-controlled state. And so the nineteenth century passed on an inheritance of vigorous dispute concerning the relationship between citizen and the distribution and ownership of goods. Liberal, social democrat and Marxist priorities are still in contention.

Closely related to the strengthening of capitalism at this time were the combined processes of urbanisation and industrialisation. These major developments assisted the evolution of citizenship in two ways. In the first place, by shifting the focus of economic power away from the landed aristocracy, they considerably advanced the destruction of the old socio-political order. Secondly, by increasing the urban population, they expanded the artisan and labouring classes, whose alertness to their rights counterbalanced the traditional deference of rural communities. Through various forms of organisation the urban workers were able to exert a leverage on governments for concessions of those rights. Furthermore, by attracting labour to their factories the burgeoning industrial cities induced greater geographical mobility in the population. This in turn weakened the grip of local loyalties and enabled a sense of national identity to grow in concomitant strength.

The third factor was the modernisation of the state. Industrialisation was, of course, part of this, bringing in its turn rises in population and improvements in transport. As life became more complex, so did the administrative machine of the state. This then raised questions about the relationship between the citizen and the bureaucracy. Interestingly Hegel and Mill took opposite points of view on this issue. Hegel believed that government officials would themselves have a civic consciousness sufficient to encourage a full development of citizenship virtue among the populace of their states. Mill, in contrast, warned of the need for a vigilant protection of freedom by the citizen against the heavy dampening hand of bureaucracy. But not only did the citizen of the nineteenth-century state have to find ways of relating to the civil service, in many countries he had little choice but to perform his own military service. The traditional close relationship between citizenship and the right and duty to bear arms, which marked the status from Greek to Renaissance times, was revived. Citizenship rights were extended either to buy a more ardent loyalty in war or as a recompense afterwards. Total war, as initiated by the French Revolution, required the mobilisation of the hearts and muscles of the citizenry. The more complete the interpretation of citizenry could be, the more militarily powerful would be the state. This facet of citizenship was epitomised by the slogan used during the campaign in Sweden to extend the franchise: 'One man, one vote, one gun.'

But could the state rely on the loyalty of citizens if they were simultaneously Christians? The question was, of course, as old as the Roman Empire. It was raised again in dramatic form by the French Revolution. Clerics and lay citizenry alike were split asunder when the state attempted, against papal opposition, to force an oath of allegiance on the clergy. In consequence, some revolutionary leaders felt driven to an attempted campaign of dechristianisation or, as in the case of Robespierre, the substitution of a Rousseauesque civic religion. Such extreme measures did not catch on. Nevertheless, the steady secularisation of society and the reduced political influence of the Church in many states undoubtedly helped the development of citizenship.

Yet the very fact that citizenship involves more than the mechanical exercise of rights and obligations raises the issue of commitment. Citizenship could not have been the substitute legitimising and stabilising factor the post-revolutionary states were seeking if it had not contained within it a substantial moral and emotional element akin to religion. Rousseau comprehended this with great clarity. The thought led him to insist on a 'civil profession of faith', which he defined as 'a body of social *sentiments* without which no man can either be a good citizen or a faithful subject'.[11] Can there be much doubt that, insofar as the nineteenth-century citizen found such faith, he discovered it in the synthetic secular religion of nationalism?

The unfinished business of the long nineteenth century

The shape and style of citizenship at the beginning of the twentieth century had been moulded by these influences. What inheritance of unresolved issues was then transmitted from the nineteenth century to its successor? In the first place, it has to be appreciated that in 1914 the idea was still evolving. In many ways it was more an ideal which was flexibly interpreted than an ideological blueprint. The basic principles were universal, but they were implemented with varying emphases depending upon the traditions and circumstances operating in different states. For example, in states with powerful traditions of urban citizenship, the institutions and loyalties of that mode can be found to have survived during the period under review. For instance, Hamburg retained a system of local government in which inhabitants could participate, through a Citizens Assembly only if they paid a substantial citizenship fee. In England, the habit of local government by amateurs and the persistence of deep social cleavages gave citizenship a different quality from that which developed in the centralised bureaucratic system of France. Different again were the developments in the USA where citizenship has sometimes been caricatured as the practice of voting for everyone from town rat-catcher to national President. And so by c.1914 two very significant features had become imprinted on citizenship: its absolute necessity for the political health of the modern state; yet its malleability to conform with particular circumstances. As a consequence, it has been possible for this concept, which evolved in the liberal régimes of Europe and North America, to be adapted in the twentieth century to fit states of quite different configurations. Neither the totalitarian Fascist and Communist states nor the new nations of Asia and Africa have felt that they can do other than rely, and rely heavily, upon the institution and morality of citizenship. Yet in the one case it might be argued that the pattern has been contorted by the powerful ideologies, and in the other only shallowly impressed for want of conducive traditions.

In so far as citizenship evolved in this period in response to commonly experienced political ideas, these were nationalism and democracy. Nationalism not only provided the emotional adhesive, it led to the virtual identification of citizenship with nationality. It became difficult for an individual to claim the desired legal and political identity without accepting the required cultural identity. It meant too the almost complete extinction of the parallel concept of world citizenship. Following the revitalisation of this classical ideal by the Renaissance and Enlightenment, its near annihilation by the force of nationalism could scarcely have been predicted c.1780. Those who have attempted its resuscitation in the twentieth century have consequently faced the daunting task of breathing life into an almost moribund ideal.

Indeed, insofar as the nineteenth century can be said to have transmitted any legacy regarding world citizenship it is a collection of confused ambiguities. Darwinian biology was vulgarised into the doctrine of 'the survival of the fittest' and so helped to propagate the concept of mankind not as potentially unified but as violently racially divided. That such an interpretation was the very reverse of Darwin's own beliefs did not prevent the widespread acceptance of this parody. For, in his *Descent of Man*, he had in fact written:

As man advances in civilisation . . . the *simplest* reason would tell each individual that he ought to extend his social instincts . . . to all the members of the same nation, though personally unknown to him. This point being once reached, there is only an artificial barrier to prevent his sympathies extending to the men of all nations and races.[12]

Marxism too was ambiguous. Although foretelling the eventual evolution of

171

a harmonious world society, nineteenth-century Marxists were highly suspicious of schemes for European federation designed to enhance, at least partially, the sum of human harmony. These were denounced as bourgeois frauds. Engels poured scorn on the 'sentimental fantasies of universal brotherhood of peoples . . . and eternal world peace'.[13] In fact, the very educated liberal middle classes whose peace projects the Marxists derided were caught in their own nationalist bind. No one reminded them more of the potent force of millenia of social and cultural conditioning than Herder:

The savage in his hut has room for any stranger . . .. The saturated heart of the idle cosmopolitan is a home for no one.

The citizen of the world, he declared, is 'a human ghost'[14] Nor did nineteenth-century education have much truck with cosmopolitan ideals. Democracy highlighted the question of education for citizenship – or rather four questions. The first was whether the lack of a basic education, that is, bare literacy, should be a bar to enfranchisement. The problem worried some intellectuals, notably John Stuart Mill, who commented in the 1840s:

We were now much less democrats than I had been, because so long as education continues to be so wretchedly imperfect, we dreaded the ignorance and especially the selfishness and brutality of the mass.[15]

The question of literacy persisted into our own century. It was used as a means of depriving American Blacks of the vote and has presented political parties with the challenge of alternative means of communication in democracies with a low literacy rate such as India. The second educational question was the utility and propriety of using schools to produce 'good' citizens. The problem that has become very evident today can already be glimpsed in the nineteenth century. It is that governments have willingly encouraged, even directed, schools in this function so long as the objectives are harmonious social behaviour, deferent political attitudes, cohesive national feeling and loyal patriotic fervour. Both specific subject teaching and the 'hidden curriculum' of school 'tone' were used in the nineteenth century to achieve these ends. But citizenship in the sense of critical thinking and independent judgement was dependent on the, probably rare, teacher who would not accept such regimentation. Yet was this a more honest version of education for citizenship? Was state manipulation in the education of young citizens not a contradiction in terms? The third facet of education for citizenship related to the growing belief that part of the citizen's duty was to ensure that his children received an education, so as to enhance their usefulness to the state. Factory workers and soldiers need at least a modicum of education if they are to obey instructions and perform their functions efficiently. And fourthly, the complementary argument came to be deployed that the state owed it to its citizens to provide schools for their children as part of the social or welfare aspects of citizenship. In combination this pair of views relating to obligation brought legislation for compulsory school attendance in Europe and the USA in the nineteenth century and in Afro-Asia nations more recently.

The gradual advance of democracy also had a political impact, the implications of which are still being worked through in the world today. For it raised questions concerning the breadth and depth of citizenship. If the status was to be open on equal terms to all, this objective had very evidently not been achieved by 1914. Large proportions of the populations of most states were disadvantaged by reason of education, social class, sex or race. A sense of individual worth preceded political enfranchisement. Figaro set the scene by having the spirit to answer his own question about the Count: 'What have *you* done to deserve such advantages? Put yourself to the trouble of being born — nothing more!'[16] Political rights have had to be extended in response to this kind of self-confidence for the past two centuries. Then, as the enfranchisement and provision of opportunities for association and participation in public affairs were conceded for some, this process raised expectations in those left behind. This century, therefore, has witnessed a continuation and intensification of the nineteenth-century attempts by these second-class citizens to catch up on their rights: the impoverished, the feminists and the racially disadvantaged have all sought social, legal and constitutional redress for this civic deprivation.

But even those relatively secure in their citizenship status have felt that the state has insufficiently catered for their need and right to participate in public affairs. From Rousseau onwards the argument in favour of participation has been twofold. The first is that only by the committed involvement of the citizens will decisions be made by government in the interests of the community as a whole. The second is that if citizenship involves a sense of responsibility, it is only by being trusted with some involvement in civic affairs that the citizen will develop this quality. These views were revived and became powerful stimulants to active demands throughout the western world in the 1960s, most dramatically in the student demonstrations in 1968, especially the May *évènements* in France.

In 1914 there were many uncertainties, reservations and loose ends about the matter of citizenship. Even so, it is unlikely that many politicians and commentators (except Marxist-Leninists) could have been found to deny that the symbiotic relationship between state and citizen was anything but fundamentally mutually advantageous and morally valid. From the perspective of the late twentieth century this belief can be questioned. The liberal can abhor the manipulation of citizens by totalitarian régimes. The Marxist can regret the subversion of the citizen's class-consciousness by the bourgeois state. The New Right can deplore the selfish abuse of rights by the citizen while neglecting his obligations. And the cosmopolitan can fear the consequences of the citizen's blinkered loyalty to a nation-state to the perilous detriment of the needs of the world as a whole. As a consequence of these complications, just as school systems were settling to an education of young citizens for an acceptance of the social and national status quo of their respective states, these objectives were thrown into serious question.

4.3   THE TWENTIETH CENTURY

Perhaps in a modern society there are not many *citizens* in Rousseau's sense of the word, that is, men who are concerned about the public good as such and willing to sacrifice their own interests for it.

Raymond Aron[17]

The diversity of the age

In no other period of history has citizenship been so universally accepted as a fundamental status yet interpreted in so many diverse ways as in the twentieth century. What have been the characteristic contributions to the theory and practice of citizenship and citizenship education of our own age? The most dramatic change, of course, has been the huge increase in the number of people with the right to vote. Universal suffrage has become the norm in every continent. Mass electorates have raised difficult questions concerning modes of communication between politicians and citizens. These have been tackled in some measure by an unprecedented enhancement of the literacy rate and partly by the technology of broadcasting. The latter has rendered irrelevant Aristotle's question, 'who can .give [a state of large population] orders, unless he has Stentor's voice?'[18] The volume of Stentor's fifty-voiced bellow was puny compared with the power of the modern radio transmitter. But technology has yet to cope with the problem of mass participation. Pressure for opportunities for realistic political involvement has been episodic rather than persistent. However, the spread of universal enfranchisement has for the first time opened up the possibility of legitimate demands, which the current institutional structures might be unable to satisfy. On the other hand, the number of individuals displaying citizenship as a moral quality, as the French sociologist Aron has reminded us, has by no means kept pace with citizenship as a legal and political status.

Nor indeed have the rights and privileges of citizenship been as equitably distributed as the legal and political status. We have seen how large portions of nominally democratic societies have, by reasons especially of race or sex, been consigned to a second-class category. This is, of course, no twentieth-century novelty. What is new is that the condition runs counter to the prevailing theory and rhetoric; and thus foments just resentment. The poor — the unemployed, underemployed, ill-paid — have also come to feel that they do not enjoy their citizenship status to the full. The problem exists alike in relatively rich capitalist states, Communist societies and underdeveloped countries. Before the present century it was generally true (with the partial exception of the USA) that the privilege of political citizenship was denied to the poor in any case. The disjunction between theoretical and practical status was consequently not so very stark. Only in relatively recent decades has the question come to be posed, How far can the state expect the conscientious and loyal discharge of duties by citizens for whom the state makes inadequate welfare provision? Does not the very concept of citizenship entail some realistic *quid pro quo*?

But the twentieth century has also witnessed such a diversification of political régimes that generalisations about citizenship are perhaps as unreal as Aristotle believed them to be. Should we not say with him rather that the good citizen is he whose behaviour corresponds with the needs of the particular constitution under which he happens to be living? If that is so, the twentieth century has raised the question in a particularly acute form. Were the Germans who enthusiastically supported the Nazi régime 'good' citizens? And if so, what are we to understand by that epithet? What of the view that a citizen is someone capable of independent judgement, mentally impregnable to manipulative propaganda? Moreover, by a similar, if not entirely the same, token, are citizens 'good' who accept without demur the threats to life and the planet posed by policies of their own states? Again the twentieth century has come to appreciate this dilemma with an acuteness unknown to previous ages. Has a truly world citizenship become for the first time an imperative state of mind rather than, as hitherto, a philosophical luxury?

The expansion and consolidation of universal suffrage has been accompanied by the state provision of universal education, at least to an elementary level. The possibilities of using the schools for political education have been lost on neither the state nor the teaching profession. What has been in dispute has been the level of political understanding that can be expected of young people and the objectives that should be pursued. Should the schools be nurturing deferent and loyal national citizens? Or active and questioning democratic citizens? Or broadly concerned world citizens? Priorities have naturally differed from person to person and with the particular circumstances. In those societies where the government has accorded primacy to ideological conformity open civic education has given way to indoctrination. The following gem from the Soviet Union in 1929 indicates the frame of mind:

Confirming the [Central Committee] resolution on the voluntary character of the political education, the CC at the same time considers it an error to interpret the principle of voluntariness as permission to refuse political education.[19]

As in such manner the term 'political education', in Oakeshott's phrase, fell 'on evil days'[20], so one is forced to suggest a distinction between it and citizenship education. A citizenship which is not a counterfeit of the true article requires sturdy independence and self-confidence (among other qualities); it cannot be manufactured by government or party *diktat*.

Yet despite the geographical and social spread of citizenship, twentieth-century political theory has had remarkably little to say on the subject. To some extent this can be explained by the general dearth of great theoretical statements on a par with the classic texts. But even as interest in normative political theory has revived with scholars like Rawls, the topic of citizenship has not captured their attention as it did Aristotle or Rousseau. The absence of any deep consideration of world citizenship in international theory is even more striking.

Explanations of citizen behaviour

Two facets of citizenship have stimulated some academic interest, each of which will be considered more fully in Chapters 5 and 7. One is the relationship of its evolution to the existence of a capitalist mode of production, a debate prompted by Marshall's lectures (pp. 100–101). The other is the matter of citizenship behaviour embraced in the related concepts of civility and socialisation. The American scholar Edward Shils revived the Renaissance idea of civility in order to argue that the prime duty of the good citizen is the maintenance of political stability. Citizens reveal the virtue of civility when they accept the community as a moral entity and the right of the government to exert authority to sustain its cohesion. Two other Americans, Gabriel Almond and Sidney Verba, sought to discover empirically how variable this quality was in a sample of democratic countries. Their work, *The Civic Culture*, was part of a huge quantity of mainly American studies in the 1950s and 1960s, which attempted to understand how citizens are socialised, that is, acquire their political attitudes; but the methodologies and findings have been brought into question.

One of the variables which this socialisation research weighed was education. The results generally showed a significant correlation between the level of education received and a sense of political efficacy, a belief that interest and involvement are worthwhile because the ordinary citizen can exert influence. But educationists have been slow to marry this insight (or truism?) concerning *level* of education with the teachings of Dewey concerning democratic *styles* of learning. Indeed, twentieth-century educational theory has failed to grapple with the full and complex range of relationships, attitudes and behaviour-patterns encapsulated in the term 'citizenship'.

The twentieth century has raised as many questions as it has solved about citizenship and citizenship education. No society has revealed the problems more vividly than the Germany of the 1920s and 1930s. The constitutional lawyer, Hugo Preuss, the most influential draughtsman of the Weimar constitution, provided Germany with the fairest and freest system the world had yet known. The constitution incorporated a list of rights and duties. Men and women over 20 were enfranchised. Voting was by proportional representation. Economic democracy was also provided for by a network of works councils linked to a Reich Economic Council. Even citizenship education in a broad sense was required by Article 148:

In all schools effort shall be made to develop moral education, civic sentiments, and personal and vocational efficiency, in the spirit of the German national character and of international conciliation.[21]

But of course, fairness, freedom, morality and international conciliation were soon to be cast aside by the Nazi régime. The reasons for the failure of Weimar have been investigated most thoroughly. One crucial factor was the unpreparedness of the Germans for their new democratic mode of civic life. The novelist Thomas Mann expressed this view with some acidity. He wrote of

. . . a certain regrettable and unearned dispensing of civilian freedom from all restraint, the degeneration of a national structure so long held together by discipline into debating groups of masterless citizens.[22]

In other words, the German citizens lacked the necessary qualities of citizenship. And in large measure this was due, in the opinion of the German sociologist Ralf Dahrendorf, to the traditional deficiencies of the educational system:

. . . all important influences of the education of the German child originate even today in the family . . . the superordination of the family to the school in Germany may further explain the predominance of private virtues in the values of German society and thereby the pathology of democracy in Germany.[23]

In other words, German children lacked a proper education for citizenship. Even Article 148 of the Weimar constitution could not compensate overnight. It could not compete with the familial or the military traditions so ingrained in German, especially Prussian, society. And the lack of a powerful form of education for civic autonomy and responsibility rendered easy the Nazi moulding of their own style of citizenship by indoctrination and propaganda.

The twentieth century draws to a close with so many questions related to citizenship still not satisfactorily answered. Four main problems remain on the agenda. What is the appropriate balance between active independent-mindedness and deference? What is the relationship between citizenship as status and as good civic behaviour? Are national and world citizenships compatible in some kind of multiple loyalty? What is the role of education in assuring satisfactory resolutions to these problems?

4.4   THE PERSPECTIVE OF HISTORY

It is the State that has rescued the child from patriarchal domination and from family tyranny; it is the State that has freed the citizen from feudal groups and later from communal groups; it is the State that has liberated the craftsman and his master from guild tyranny.

Emile Durkheim[24]

Citizenship in history

No State, no citizen? The history of citizenship would suggest that the concept and status have real meaning and vigour only when the impersonal notion of the state is a paramount political idea. Primitive societies have recognisably political modes and rules of behaviour, but have neither state apparatus nor citizen status. When monarchs hold sway by personal or divine right, citizenship, even if it exists as a legal status, is empty of real meaning. If, as in Marxist theory, the state is but a tool of the dominant class and is doomed as an institution to wither away, then citizenship must be conceived as a

subjective and temporary condition. This apparent necessary relationship between state and citizenship has had a marked influence on the history of both
cosmopolitanism and education for citizenship. In the case of cosmopolitanism
it has severely inhibited the burgeoning of the nascent concept of world
citizenship: a world state has very evidently not been a fact; nor has it been,
in the judgement of even many of the world-minded, a desirable arrangement
for which they would be willing to strive. In the case of education, school
programmes have been largely determined by the state. If the health and
stability of the state has been dependent on the supportive attitudes and behaviour of its citizens, then at a young age their minds and habits must be
shaped accordingly. A manipulative political socialisation, not a true open
political education, has been the norm. The American political scientist and
statesman, Robert Pranger, commenting on the historical rarity of the true
from has written,

Political education emphasises above all the artificiality of political order and the
citizen as a creative actor within this order. In the history of practical politics there
have been only infrequent periods when political education of this sort has triumphed
over narrower, more disciplined socialization, most notably, during sporadic intervals
in ancient Athens from the fifth-century Sophists to the Hellenist cosmopolitans in
the fourth and third centuries BC.[25]

The evidence of history should provide clues about the circumstances which
have been propitious for the expansion of the condition of citizenship, both
in terms of the extent of rights and of the proportion of the population thus
embraced. Several socio-economic conditions have been suggested as causing
these developments. One is immigration. Clearly this was an important factor
stimulating the development of American citizenship. But it can hardly be
accepted as a perennially crucial motor force. Industrialisation has been canvassed as another cause. Britain is evidently the model here. On the other
hand, insofar as citizenship was a claim to equality of status against the practices of a hierarchically ordered society, it can be argued that the acceptance
of that principle was a precondition for industrialisation as much as a consequence of the process. And in any case, the ancient world hardly fits this
pattern. Similarly the relationship between citizenship and capitalism is complex and controversial – so controversial indeed for contemporary interpretations
of citizenship that the issue will be discussed separately in Chapter 7.

We are left with the role of political violence – of revolution and war. We
have already noticed that military service has been a common duty attached to
the status of citizenship (p. 162). What has also been common is for the
status to be demanded and/or conceded at a time of domestic or international
crisis for a state. When the Roman Empire or medieval city-state wanted more
troops, they opened up their citizen-registers. When the American and French
republics were being born in revolution, they pronounced an egalitarian
citizenship. The First World War prompted women's emancipation in the
USA and Britain. The Second World War had widespread effects: for example,
in Britain, the concept of social citizenship was consolidated in the Beveridge
Report; in the USA, Blacks who had been enlisted in the armed services un-

derstood clearly and bitterly the anomaly of military duty without civil rights; while the recruitment into the fighting forces of men from European, especially British colonies, raised expectations of similar concessions of political freedom. Part of the phenomenon is the raising of political consciousness in times of violent stress. And there is nothing quite so effective as a mode of political education as throwing men together in military units. The barrack-room lawyer is a ubiquitous personality.

World citizenship in history

Furthermore, the fluctuating fortunes of the cosmopolitan ideal have been closely related to both violent conflict and the development of citizenship in the state. The idea of world citizenship has sprung to life on four main occasions. In the Hellenistic period discontent with the internecine strife which characterised the declining years of the city-state paved the way for the first flowering of the alternative idea of the cosmopolis. Nevertheless, a century after the death of Alexander, Greece and Asia Minor were absorbed into the expanding Roman domains. Roman citizenship was proffered to the leading inhabitants and cosmopolitanism was consigned to the level of ethical speculation whence it came.

In the seventeenth century AD the horrors of recently experienced religious wars spurred on the international lawyers to formulate some tangible expression of the universalist ideal. However, the internal torment suffered by France for similar reasons had already led to the erection of the theory of sovereignty to firm up the structure of the state. By consolidating the state as a political entity, the concept of sovereignty undermined *pari passu* the re-emerging cosmopolis. For the legal theorists, torn in their pursuit of contradictory political ideals, it simply transferred the principle of sovereignty, as devised to describe internal relationships, to the global plane, as a means of describing international relationships. Hard on the heels of these developments came the further resuscitation of cosmopolitanism by the men of the Enlightenment in reaction to the dynastic wars of the age. But this revival too was still-born, smothered by the overwhelming power of state citizenship massively strengthened by the democracy and nationalism unleashed in the age of the French Revolution.

Finally, in our own century there has arisen a yearning for peace and the preservation of the planet, both sorely damaged and even further threatened by lethal technologies. Thoughts have consequently turned yet again to the ideal of world citizenship. The fate of this latest hesitant renascence we cannot yet, of course, know. There are, however, stirrings in some societies, which bear comparison with the observations of Dr Pranger quoted above. As in the fifth-third centuries BC some educationists are emancipating themselves from the conformist traditions of political socialisation and are teaching their pupils to be questioning and critical as well as responsible citizens, and in both the national and global senses. Has education the power to break the historical rhythm of emergence and submergence of cosmopolitanism? And if it has that power, would its successful employment produce a more politically effective and a morally enhanced style of citizenship? Answers to these questions can

179

only be usefully framed in the conscious appreciation of the current historical circumstances of the world as set against some notional citizenship ideal.

REFERENCES

1. D. W. Brogan, *Citizenship Today* (University of North Carolina Press, 1960), p. 7.
2. Aristotle, *Politics*, p. 6.
3. Weber, *Citizenship*, pp. 323 & 337.
4. A. Toynbee, *A Study of History* (Abridgement of Volumes I–VI by D. C. Somervell) (Oxford University Press, 1946), p. 318.
5. Letter to Henry Lee, 8 May 1825, reprinted in Williams, *Revolutions,* p. 54.
6. Reprinted in M. E. Chamberlain (ed.), *British Foreign Policy in the Age of Palmerston* (Longman, 1980), pp. 125–6.
7. Quoted in G. Stourzh, *Alexander Hamilton and the Idea of Republican Government* (Stanford University Press, 1970), p. 71.
8. Viscount Bryce, *Promoting Good Citizenship* (Macmillan, 1913), p. 3.
9. Voltaire, *Letters on England* (trans, L. Tancock, Penguin, 1980), pp. 44–5.
10. Aristotle, *Politics,* p. 182.
11. Rousseau, *Social Contract*, bk. IV chap. 8 (E. Barker ed., Oxford University Press, 1947), p. 437.
12. C. Darwin, *Descent of Man,* quoted in J. Laurent, 'More sex please, we're vicarious', *New Scientist*, 22 January 1987.
13. Quoted in F. Parkinson, *The Philosophy of International Relations* (Sage, 1977), pp. 146–7.
14. Herder, *Ideas for a Philosophy of the History of Mankind,* quoted in J. Dunn, *Western Political Theory in the Face of the Future* (Cambridge University Press, 1979), p. 77.
15. J. S. Mill, *Autobiography*, quoted in A. Arblaster, *Democracy* (Open University Press, 1987), p. 48.
16. Beaumarchais, *The Marriage of Figaro* (trans. J. Wood, Penguin, 1964), Act V, p. 199.
17. R. Aron, *Progress and Disillusion* (Penguin, 1968), p. 238.
18. Aristotle, *Politics,* p. 292.
19. Quoted in *International Affairs* (Spring 1988), p. 304.
20. M. Oakeshott, *Rationalism in Politics and Other Essays* (Methuen, 1962), p. 112.
21. Quoted in Bereday, *Merriam's The Making of Citizens,* p. 127.
22. T. Mann, *Doctor Faustus* (trans. H. T. Lowe-Porter, Penguin, 1968), p. 328.
23. R. Dahrendorf, 'The Tradition of Authority, Democracy and Social Structure in Germany' (n.d.).
24. Durkheim, *Professional Ethics and Civil Morals*, quoted in R. Bendix, *Nation-Building and Citizenship* (University of California Press, new edn 1977), p. 61.
25. R. Pranger, *The Eclipse of Citizenship* (Holt, Rinehart & Winston, 1968), p. 44.

PART TWO

Analysis

CHAPTER FIVE

The Feeling of Citizenship

5.1 CITIZENSHIP AS IDENTITY

The proposition is that those who share an interest share an identity; the interest of each requires the collaboration of all . . .. Those who share a place share an identity. Prima facie this is a fair statement, whether 'the place' is taken to be 'space-ship earth'; or a beloved land; or a desolate slum or public housing scheme.

W. J. M. Mackenzie[1]

Political identity

Citizenship is more than a label. He who has no sense of a civic bond with his fellows or of some responsibility for civic welfare is not a true citizen whatever his legal status. Identity and virtue invest the concept of citizenship with power. The social or political ties which hold an individual in community with his fellows is the essence of human nature, said Aristotle; it is an intrinsic psychological need, says the modern social scientist. Durkheim wrote,

Man is the more vulnerable to self-destruction the more he is detached from any collectivity . . . . wars, in quickening the sense of patriotism, subordinate preoccupation with self . . .; consequently, the bond between individual and society is strengthened, and, at the same time, the linkage to life is also re-inforced. The number of suicides declines.[2]

So basic and universal is this human need to belong to a community that hermits might be said to exist in order to provide proof of the rule by their exceptional life style.

Social identity requires the reciprocal processes of integrating oneself with others of like kind and of that consequent collectivity differentiating itself from those of other kinds. A sense of togetherness derives from a sharing of common interests, territory and pride. The interests which unite a group are often cultural – a sense of tradition, ethnicity or way of life. Futhermore, consciousness of political identity is usually heightened by systems of beliefs, ceremonies and symbols. Professor Mackenzie has written that

. . . myth, symbol, ritual and ideology . . . [are] of extreme importance in the attempt to give a workable meaning to talk about social and political 'identity'.[3]

Just think how impoverished the nature of Athenian citizenship would have been without a vision of the protective and wise goddess of the city, Athena. Or US, citizenship without 'Old Glory' present and paraded on every conceivable occasion. The examples could, of course, be multiplied endlessly. In a primitive society an individual's social identity is simply mapped out by his membership of a family and tribe. In our own confusing age the matter of integrating oneself with others of like kind and differentiating oneself from those unlike is a much more complex business. Race, nationality, religion, class may all contribute to the rich amalgam. And for different purposes and different occasions each of these primary elements in a given individual's identity will determine more than the others the overall colouring. Thus a denizen of the Ardoyne area of Belfast might have considered himself primarily of British nationality in 1939 but first and foremost a Roman Catholic thirty years later. Indeed, it can often happen that different identities within the compounded colouration of the complete social individual are incompatible with each other. The consequent clash of loyalties can of course be psychologically most uncomfortable and is a matter taken up in Part Three below. Nevertheless, however often the kaleidoscope is shaken, the urge to make a pattern of some shape remains constant.

One form of identity is citizenship. It differ from others in two important regards. In the first place, as so many political theorists in the liberal tradition have emphasised, the exercise of citizenship is crucial for the development of the individual's moral maturity. The person grows as a social being: judgement requires thought; participation dispels inertia; and consideration of the common good nurtures altruism. A citizen is someone who has political freedom and responsibility. In the words of Mill,

The maximum of the invigorating effort of freedom upon the character is only obtained when the person acted upon either is, or is looking forward to becoming, a citizen as fully privileged as any other . . . [Also] It is not sufficiently considered how little there is in most men's ordinary life to give any largeness either to their conceptions or to their sentiments . . .. Giving them something to do for the public, supplies, in a measure, all these deficiencies.[4]

A citizen is a different kind of person from the vassall of a feudal lord, a landowners's serf or the subject of a divine-right monarch. The distinction lies primarily in the moral autonomy and high level of moral behaviour which characterises at least the 'good citizen' in his ideal form. But this is to encroach on the next section of this chapter.

The second particular feature of citizen-identity is the way in which it overlays the other social identities the individual inevitably feels. A male Hindu of high-caste Indian origin living in London may think of himself as sexually, religiously, socially, racially and culturally different from a Roman Catholic working-class Scotswoman in Glasgow. But they are both British citizens. These other identity-feelings can often generate intense emotions, even dangerous antagonisms; hence the melancholy history of the subjugation of women, religious wars, racist persecution, nationalist conflict and class hatred. Citizenship can help satisfy the human need for identity without arousing the perils of such animosities. For, despite the persistence of second-class levels of treatment for many citizens, at least the accepted model is for the status to be egalitarian and all-embracing, not hierarchical and divisive. Moreover, the attitudes and behaviour expected of citizens involves the disciplining of emotions by rationality. Necessary feelings, such as tolerence, charity, conscience and patriotism must not be expressed unthinkingly. Citizenship is political identity par excellence; and by emphasising the political virtues of the responsible conciliation of conflicting interests (to use Professor Crick's definition), citizenship helps to tame the divisive passions of other identities. A word of caution, however; citizenship must not be allowed to swallow up or blanket out all other social identities; that way lies totalitarianism. We must take heed of Aldous Huxley's warning. The motto of his Brave New World State was 'Community, Identity and Stability'.[5] The alpha-to-epsilon conditioned inhabitants assuredly had identity, but in no sense were they citizens. The inhabitants of Nazi Germany who were not Jews or inmates of concentration camps were citizens in a legal sense – but at what cost in terms of the essential citizen right of freedom.

History, nationality and fraternity

In the modern world, citizenship identity has a special relationship with history, nationality and fraternity. Let us take each in turn. History, both as the repository of facts about the past and as the provider of myths, is a society's collective memory. Without some knowledge of history the citizen knows nothing of the traditions of his state – is a political amnesiac. The English positivist philosopher, Frederic Harrison, pondered on the fate of a society with no historical consciousness:

. . . suppose a race of men whose minds, by a paralytic stroke of fate, had suddenly been deadened of every recollection . . . . [Can we] imagine a condition of such helplessness, confusion and misery?[6]

History is a need of all societies; yet its civic function is formed of two incompatible styles. It can be cogently argued that the more sophisticated the society, the greater the need and the greater the importance that the record be an accurate and an honest one.

History is the sextant and compass of states [wrote the American historian Allan Nevins], which, tossed by wind and current, would be lost in confusion if they could not fix their position.[7]

On the other hand the myths of distorted history provide the necessary emotional adhesive for such civic feelings as pride and patriotism. However, transmogrified as myth, Clio gives treacherous guidance to the ship of state. If history is to be, to use A. F. Pollard's phrase, 'a treasury of responsible citizenship'[8], then the myths must be delicately adjusted by sound factual knowledge. So, enough with metaphor. A citizen's identity is an awareness of his relationship to his state and to his fellow citizens. This relationship is not static; and since it changes over time, it cannot be properly comprehended without some understanding of the historical context. A citizen of France and a citizen of the Ivory Coast have both similar and dissimilar identities because they share the Gallic 'civilisation' and republican traditions and yet have states of very different ages. In order to know himself a citizen must know his state; that knowledge includes an understanding of how it has become what it is.

The second closely associated mode of identity is nationality. One must distinguish this term from nationalism as a political ideology and from nationality as a legal status. Nationality as a feeling of cultural togetherness is a mental construct. Objective tests such as a common language all collapse beneath the weight of accumulated exceptions. We are therefore forced to accept, with the Dutch historian, G. J. Renier, that,

Outside men's minds there can be no nationality, because nationality is a manner of looking at oneself − not an entity 'an sich'.[9]

One can, of course, have a clearly conceived sense of nationality without being a citizen in any effective political or legal sense. Let one example serve to illustrate this point. In 1832 Count Uvarov (later minister of education) presented an official report to Tsar Nicholas II recommending that Russia should be based upon the three principles of Autocracy, Orthodoxy and National-mindedness. The very formula, by associating autocracy with nationality, scarcely made provision for citizenship in any true sense. Moreover, since nearly half the tsar's subjects existed in a condition of serfdom akin to slavery, again any assumption of citizenship attaching to this principle of cultural nationality must be anachronistic.

However, as nationality became associated in the ideology of nationalism with the doctrine of popular sovereignty, it became important that cultural nationality and legal citizenship should correspond. Cultural homogenisation of provinces, cultural assimilation of ethnically heterogeneous peoples and cultural consciousness of the whole population have been policies pursued with varying degrees of intensity hand-in-hand with the opening up of citizenship rights for some two centuries. In our own age the equation of nationality and citizenship has been the keystone in the construction of political stability in new states. Chaos has supervened so often where that crucial building block has been lacking. And where the policy has been successful, the educational power of broadcasting has been of fundamental importance. In the words of one authority,

It opens up the hearts and minds of emerging nations to the mental and spiritual resources which nourish a dignity and purpose as citizens within their nation . . .. Without radio and television tribal peoples would not have developed the modern understanding of nationhood they need to survive.[10]

The national culture must come to embrace, though not suffocate, the group culture. Or to make the point rather differently, can anyone who does not speak English, let alone who has never consumed fish-and-chips or complained about the weather, be a true British citizen whatever his ethnic or regional origin?

Thirdly, fraternity is an emotional force which binds a group to a common identity. The word can be used to represent a cluster of near synonyms: 'brotherhood' as a literal translation (and its awkward feminine form 'sisterhood'); the more flaccid 'co-operation'; 'solidarity', originating in France at the beginning of the century and popularised in the 1980s by Polish trade unionists; and the more nearly equivalent 'communalism'. Fraternity implies a respect for others with whom one collaborates. Fraternity means that the group bound together by the feeling have a common sense of purpose and are engaged in a common activity. A sense of fraternity may or may not be associated with citizenship, depending on circumstances. Rival gangs, whether supporters of Montagues and Capulets or of Chelsea and Tottenham Hotspur football clubs, have fraternal identity; but their consciousness of citizenship, involving essentially surely responsible behaviour, is exceedingly dull. Even so, small group fraternity can also be a school of citizenship. Fellow-feeling in a small and local group can be related to and expanded into a sense of civic consciousness on the national (or indeed global) scale. Moreover, the political freedoms, which are the bedrock of citizenship, must be of uncertain security if undefended by communal vigilance. Victor Hugo, thinking on both national and supranational levels declared in 1870, 'Liberty is saved through fraternity'. [11] Citizenship is but a pale imitation of its true self if not embellished by the collaborative sense of purpose and activity which we call fraternity.

As we shall see in the next section of this chapter citizenship has a significant moral content. It can consequently be argued that a vivid sense of citizen identity is beneficial for both the individual and the state. It can counteract the more selfish and mutually antagonistic identities which inevitably exist in any given society. Sadly, the alternative scenario is all too familiar. If a state contains a significant proportion of economically deprived or racially or religiously harassed or ethnically subordinate, how can these inhabitants experience a proper sense of citizen identity? Such people will tend to identify with those fellow beings who share the experience of being discriminated against and outcast. And by turning inwards to their group their sense of resentment and fear of the seemingly unjust society of which they are a part is strengthened. Thus are the bonds of group identity tightened and those of common citizenship made slack. The state therefore has both a moral and pragmatic duty to pursue and encourage policies which, while preserving the richness of cultural identities within an overarching culture, enhances citizenship as an egalitarian and just style of political identity.

Cosmopolitan identity

Citizenship, it is suggested, is a shadowy identity if it lacks the substance of a common tradition and nationality and the feeling of fraternity. Does this mean that a sense of identity as a world citizen is impossible of achievement?

Identity involves an appreciation not just of similarities I share with my fellows, but also of the dissimilarities which mark us off from those with different identities. Surely this means that the little green men from outer space must materialise before the whole of mankind can be said to have a common identity. Yet this negative face of identity can be ugly. It can so easily degenerate into animosity and hatred towards those outside the group. If identity as a world citizen must rest solely upon positive feelings, should mankind not rejoice in this circumstance? We have suggested that citizenship is a form of identity which overlays and subsumes other forms which have the potential to cause dissension. World citizenship must therefore be considered the ultimate integrative and placating identity, incorporating as it does, the scores of state citizenships as well as other social and cultural group feelings. True, the idea of world citizenship is short on symbols of belonging. And yet, one particular image has seized the collective human consciousness. It is that of our own Earth, floating in space, seen thus for the first time through the eye of a space-craft's camera. This beautiful, small and vulnerable planet was immediately recognised as the home and life-giver of all mankind; the photograph, the symbol of this common homeland.

Furthermore, where state citizenship has the envigorating forces of history, nationality and fraternity to sustain it, so world citizenship can call upon similar related emotional bonds. Although, since the nineteenth century History has frequently been written in a national frame of reference, this has not always been so, nor is it a necessary feature of the subject. Indeed, many a great master from the Greek Herodotus and the Chinese Ssu-ma Ch'ien have sturdily shown by precept their belief that historical explanation must be universal in scope. No less an authority than the father of modern historical scholarship, Leopold von Ranke, was quite certain of this:

The final goal – not yet attained [he wrote in the 1860s] – always remains the conception and composition of a history of mankind . . . . there does exist the danger of losing sight of the universal, of the type of knowledge everyone desires. For history is not simply an academic subject: the knowledge of the history of mankind should be a common property of humanity . . ..[12]

It must be emphasised that when historians refer to World or Universal History they mean something very different from an accumulation of national Histories. What is of interest and importance is rather the accumulated experience of the human race – the constants of that experience. For, over and above the myriad stories of the rise and fall of communities, states, civilisations even, the history of mankind is, in a broad sense, the tale of basic experiences and endeavours shared over the millenia. This we see if we focus on the broad sweep of Social and Economic History rather than the minutiae of political and military conflict.

We have already argued that a sense of shared identity is well-nigh impossible without a shared tradition. World citizenship is therefore dependent upon a global perspective to historical understanding. Not only is it necessary in its own right, World History must also perform a corrective function in face of the nationalist distortions of much traditional History. An individual has small chance of achieving an awareness of himself as a world citizen if he harbours jingoistic and xenophobic thoughts implanted by a nationalistic interpretation of his own state's past. UNESCO recognised this and so produced its *History of Mankind*, though it is but an imperfect approximation to what Ranke must assuredly have had in mind. And so, as the nation-state has called upon the professional historians (not to mention the teachers of History in the schools) to confirm the national identity of their citizens, so any world community or cosmopolis worthy of the name must be able to rely upon similar assistance.

What, then, is the cosmopolitan's equivalent of nationalism itself? Nationality is a feeling of relative cultural homogeneity. 'Relative' is an important modifier. A mature nation-state is capable of containing a medley of cultures, yet all consciously sharing a capacious nationality. It would not be difficult to find in the USA, for example, New Yorkers, Californians and Texans, Protestants, Catholics and Jews, Blacks, Latins and Whites, all of whom have an unshakeable conviction that they are Americans by cultural nationality in addition to and even taking precedence over their provincial, religious and ethnic particularities. By analogy therefore there is no reason to doubt the sincerity of professed world citizens who, by virtue of their origins and lives, retain national identities. Gradual submergence of national identity in favour of identity as a 'terrestrial', to use Teilhard de Chardin's term, is in fact becoming easier. An ever-increasing proportion of the world's population is able to communicate in a common language (English) and to use the products of modern technology (electrical and electronic). Marshall McLuhan's 'global village' is swiftly becoming a tightly-knit community.

For some people, thinking as world citizens, by virtue of the conditions of their lives and work, comes much more easily than for others. People who work for transnational organisations, whether UN, charitable or business, not only mix with others of many different nationalities, but, by working away from their own homeland, experience a dilution of national sentiment. By drawing on a diversity of cultures, they create for themselves their own personalised cosmopolitan cultural identity. Indeed, a conscious rejection of too deep a national identity is essential for the impartiality of international civil servants. Thus, despite Khrushchev's bitter personal assault and his assertion that 'there are no neutral men', Dag Hammarskjöld as UN Secretary-General probably came nearest in recent years to having the complete identity of a world citizen. He laboured unremittingly to be impartial. And were not the Meditations of the cosmopolitan Stoic Emperor, Marcus Aurelius, his favourite bedtime reading?

Thirdly, is any real meaning to be attached to the idea of universal fraternity? Certainly when the concept was popularised during the French Revolution it was used in a transnational sense some months before the slogan of 'liberty, equality and fraternity' became popular in the national context. In November 1792 the Convention issued a decree declaring that it would 'accord fraternity and help to all peoples wishing to recover their liberty.'[13]

If fraternal feelings require a common sense of purpose and engagement in a common activity, then our contemporary world affords expanding needs and opportunities for such feelings to flourish. The really fearful dangers which threaten, threaten the whole planet, are appreciated worldwide and require global action for their solution. Universal fraternity may well be essential for human survival. Indeed, the very practically-minded American-based World Order Models Project (WOMP) has recognised the need for a sense of global identity as a crucial part of any programme for tackling global issues. In defining a kind of highest common factor of agreed perils, they reported:

We were able to agree that humankind faced five major problems: war, poverty, social injustice, environmental decay and alienation. We saw these as social problems because we had values — peace, economic well-being, social justice, ecological stability and positive identity which no matter how vaguely operationalised, we knew were not being realised in the real world.[14]

As individuals are coming to appreciate that a sense of national fraternal identity strengthens the selfish activities of their state at the expense of the wellbeing of the world as a whole, they are steadily forging global fraternal links and feelings.

In his book *Person/Planet* the American historian Theodore Roszak has propounded the thesis that the interests of the person and of the planet are at one in face of the psychological and physical depredations of modern industrial society. He reminds his reader that man identified himself with the planet well before he identified himself with any segment of it. Thus, if to share an identity is to share a space, for millenia mankind consciously shared Earth. And just as nation-states have been personified — by Marianne, John Bull, Uncle Sam, for example, — so primitive man personified and indeed often deified Mother Earth, the White Goddess, Gaia.

I shall sing of Gaia, universal mother
firmly founded, the oldest of divinities,

wrote Homer.[15]

Education for citizenship identity

Even so, it may well be protested, the average citizen feels his identity these days in a national not a global sense. The sublimation of this consciousness is not easy. But is this not because of socialisation and educational forces which should not be assumed to be immutable? How powerful are these forces? Common sense would suggest that the individual does not acquire his identity as a citizen suddenly on attaining the age of majority. The minor frog does not metamorphose in the twinkling of an eye into a princely citizen. Nor is the transition from the child's family identity to the adolescent's civic identity solely achieved by the efforts of the schoolteacher.

Research in the field of political socialisation has shown that children from the age of about 4 to 7 develop clear national identities. This process of identification seems to be achieved largely by means of symbols, particularly the flag, and by stereotypical contrasts with other nations. This sense of national identity has usually been expressed in the form of preferences: the Union Jack is the best flag, the USA is the best country. The connection between preference and identity is the implicit, if not always stated, pride in the young respondents in belonging to what they fervently believe to be the best. An international study has summed up the evidence from a number of countries as follows:

Most studies have found that the child's attachments are to his political community, his nation, his tribe or some other basic polity. He learns, for instance, that he is a Swede or a New Zealander and that this makes him different in some respects from citizens of other systems who may speak a different language. His initial emotional reaction to the system is predominantly positive, but is not based on much information or reasoning. [16]

At this stage clearly the family is a strong influence. However, there is some evidence in industrialised states, most notably the USA, of the power of television in this regard even at this early age. The 'nationalisation' of sport, fostered by television coverage, has also probably been a significant factor in recent years in consolidating national identity particularly among boys addicted to football.

When the child enters school he is subjected to a plethora of messages designed to confirm these early impressions. The American authority in this field, Jack Nelson, has argued that the nation-state commonly seeks to use its school system to develop a belief in national values by the

. . . development of positive feelings toward those rituals, ceremonies, symbols, ideas and persons that express or incorporate those values . . . and [the] development of negative feelings toward countries, ideologies, symbols and persons considered contra-national. [17]

Thus is the basic process of integration and differentiation, essential to the creation of a national identity, initiated at a tender age.

This general pattern of socialisation into a national, not to say nationalistic, awareness is still underpinned by the very common practice of teaching national History. We have already argued that History is a form of collective memory without which a collective identity is impossible. Whereas an individual's memory is the recollection of past experiences, collective memory is possible only by the vicarious recollection through historical evidence. An introduction to this mental activity of imaginative recall is an important function of the schools. A citizen of a nation-state has both the need and the right to be equipped with this memory. Though he also has a right to be provided with an honest picture. There have been plentiful examples of the blatant distortion of national History and the consequent indoctrination of young minds. Both teachers and textbook writers are today more aware of the dangers of bias; and in many countries they are less controlled by the state than was the case fifty to a hundred years ago. (p. 175) Nevertheless, even if young people are not consciously being instilled with a false memory, the teaching of national History to the exclusion of any geographically broader material can have a blinkering effect on an individual's political identity. Distortion by omission may appear less culpable than distortion by commission. It is distortion just the same. The teaching of Imperial History presents a telling example. Lessons about the Spanish in Central America, the French in West Africa or the British in India may be essential portions of the historical preparation of young citizens of Spain, France and Britain respectively. But without counterbalancing knowledge of the Mayan, Mali and Mogul empires the implanted memory is partial.

The story of the efforts to cultivate an imperialistic civic identity in Britain is a clear example of the process at work. The late Victorian era witnessed an extraordinarily comprehensive outburst of imperialistic patriotic pride, which lasted into the middle of the present century: advertising, the theatre, the cinema, children's literature and youth 'movements all exuded this pervasive message. One authority has judged that the games and patriotic cults, so common in schools and youth movements,

. . . not only promoted social discipline and 'good citizenship', but also fostered a national conceit, a sense of Social Darwinian superiority, elaborated equally in all juvenile literature, every geography and history text, and the manuals of the uniformed youth organisations.[18]

Indeed, Baden-Powell's *Scouting for Boys* has been described as 'a crude and insistent expression of Tory imperialism.'[19] Interestingly, the Geography and History textbooks, rapidly compiled for the expansion of popular education after 1870 and coinciding with this welling up of imperialistic sentiment, cast their influence over two to three generations. Some continued to be reprinted decades after their original publication; replacements were written in similar vein. The identity of the British citizen was cast definitely in an imperial mould. Moreover, despite the humiliation of the Suez escapade of 1956, the rapid retreat from Empire and the production of syllabuses and textbooks also liberated from the imperial tradition, the Falklands war of 1982 vividly showed that this layer of civic identity was still very close to the surface.

These deliberate policies of creating a self-contained national civic identity continues to inhibit the efforts of educationists bent on unmasking the identity of the world citizen, which they believe resides in us all. Indeed, insofar as such an educational endeavour involves the pupil coming to an understanding of the nature of humanity, the purposes of liberal education and of world citizenship might be considered virtually identical. Robert M. Hutchins, former Chancellor of the University of Chicago, has written in such terms:

If education becomes in practice the deliberate, organized attempt to help people to become human, then it will inevitably promote the world community . . . the civilization we seek will be achieved when all men are citizens of the world republic of law and justice and of the republic of learning.[20]

Since school ceremonies and curricula have for several generations now been designed to imprint national civic identity, alternative ceremonies and curricula are necessary if a world civic identity is to be nurtured. Recognition of various United Nations 'days', such as UN Day itself or Human Rights Day can be used to complement national days like 4 July in the USA and 14 July in France.

We have seen in Chapter 3 how courses in Global or World Studies and World History have been devised in recent years. By emphasising our common habitation of the planet and broadly common historical evolution, such courses are bound to underscore the concept of species identity as opposed to national identity. World Studies courses are probably more successful in this enterprise than World History. There are two reasons for this. One is that History teachers, trained primarily in national History or at most national Histories, are ill-equipped to perceive and interpret the universal constants of World History. In contrast World Studies courses tend to focus on contemporary issues, which are self-evidently global in origin and effect in any case.

Not only do World Studies tend to be focussed on the present, they also project into the future. And this is their second advantage. Citizenship identity is obviously easier to acquire, both cognitively and affectively, if it can be associated with a consolidated reality. The nation-state is such a reality — in the eyes of international law, in the operation of political institutions and, in the maturely established states, in the existence of homogeneous cultures and traditions. However, although the cosmopolis does not exist in any of these concrete senses, young people can grasp the idea that powerful unifying trends are already operating. By intelligent extrapolation of the trajectories of these forces, the notion of world citizenship can assume a greater degree of practicable relevance. Kant understood this most lucidly. He wrote:

Children ought to be educated, not for the present, but for a possibly improved condition of man in the future; that is, in a manner which is adapted to the idea of humanity and the whole destiny of man . . .. Neither [parents nor sovereigns] have as their aim the universal good and the perfection to which man is destined, and for which he has also a natural disposition. But the basis of a scheme of education must be cosmopolitan.[21]

How much more valid is such an insight two centuries later?

5.2 THE GOOD CITIZEN

I suppose that the happiest people, and those who reach the best destination, are the ones who have cultivated the goodness of an ordinary citizen — what is called self-control and integrity — which is acquired by habit and practice, without the help of philosophy and reason.

Plato[22]

Civic virtue

Socrates was suggesting that, with the transmigration of souls, the virtue of good citizens would be rewarded by reincarnation as social and disciplined creatures like bees, wasps or ants — 'or even back into the human race again, becoming decent citizens.' One need not, of course, accept Socrates' reasoning or John Gay's later formulation that 'virtue is its own reward' in order to recognise how vital the moral elements in citizenship are for its true realisation. The trouble is that so many philosophers and politicians over the past two and a half millenia have commended civic virtue or good citizenship and have accorded the term so many different meanings that it has become virtually impossible to know what any given advocate has in mind without knowing the context. Aristotle defined the good citizen as someone who lived in harmony with the constitution; for Cicero, civic virtue implied public duty; for Machiavelli, *virtu* is almost translatable as 'valour'; Robespierre spoke of incorruptibility; while T. H. Green gave it a Christian connotation. And when today's conservative speaks of good citizenship he usually emphasises deferent and orderly behaviour, while the liberal stresses active involvement in public and community affairs.

The truth is that the ideal good citizen must be a paragon of multiple virtues, who brings to the fore different qualities according to circumstances. To assume, as so often happens, that certain components of civic virtue are the totality is to emasculate the word. One may realistically accept that the truly good citizen exists only as a perfect model laid up in a Platonic heaven; but one still needs a term to define that ideal. An individual who is deficient in some of the necessary qualities or who is unable to keep them in proper balance is nothing but an unsatisfactory approximation. Most of us *are*, of course, unsatisfactory approximates. The danger occurs when, for ideological objectives or party political advantage, the part is passed off as the whole. Of what does this whole consist? In basic terms, the answer is simply given — namely, loyalty, responsibility and respect for political and social procedural values. However, each of these virtues contains a complex cluster of personal qualities, positive attitudes and beneficent behaviour. These virtues are expressed in the good citizen's relations to the state and his fellow citizens; and insofar as the term is applicable on a global level, to the world and mankind as a whole.

Loyalty

Let us take loyalty first. Loyalty is an emotional attachment to an institution, land, a group or a person. This attachment is closely related to identity. The two are linked through the sense of fraternity. Loyalty also derives from belief in the values which the object of loyalty stands for. One can, of course, be loyal in many contexts which do not involve citizenship. But a person who displayed disloyalty or even uncaring apathy towards his country and his fellows would scarcely warrant the title of 'good citizen'. Despite its etymology, loyalty does not require law for its expression. During his trial for treason in 1916 the Irish nationalist, Sir Roger Casement, emphasised this important distinction:

Loyalty is a sentiment, not a law. It rests on love, not on restraint. The government of Ireland by England rests on restraint and not on law; and since it demands no love, it can evoke no loyalty.[23]

He thus provided an interesting echo of Montesquieu, who wrote two centuries earlier, 'Customs always make better citizens than laws.'[24] Loyalty involves a sublimation of selfish feelings. This ability to feel a moral bond with and allegiance to the object of one's loyalty can be generated in a variety of ways. They include a rational approval of the values upheld; an emotional feeling akin to love; a quasi-religious reverence; or a fierce pride in achievements. The archetypal loyal man was Virgil's 'pious Aeneas', loyal to the gods, homeland, friends and family.

With the rise of the modern state it is the state itself which has come to expect the citizen's prime loyalty. Hegel pronounced unequivocally the right of the state to subsume all other loyalties. 'Loyalty' has been a vibrant watchword in recent American history. In the neurotic atmosphere of the early Cold War, President Truman created a comprehensive structure of Loyalty Commissions and Loyalty Boards. Citizens were required both to be loyal and to test loyalty:

The government's loyalty program was a vast undertaking that took the time and work of many of the top men in the government. Commissions to help in this program were composed of leading citizens of both political parties.[25]

The issue of loyalty then collapsed into the obscenity of McCarthyism. But loyalty remains absolutely central to the Americans' self-image of themselves as citizens.

It is interesting therefore to note that the Americans who take such pains to display their loyalty score so high on tests of pride. When, in the early 1980s samples from various countries were asked in a Gallup Poll to state whether they were 'very proud' of their country, Americans responded to the tune of 80 per cent. Other scores included British, 55 per cent; French, 33 per cent; West Germans, 21 per cent. These figures would suggest that Americans are especially patriotic; the West Germans, very much not. But this begs the question whether patriotism is a desirable sentiment. Patriotism is a close cousin to loyalty; it involves loyalty to the *patria*, the fatherland. Should one therefore expect a good citizen to be a patriot?

There is no gainsaying the power of patriotism, especially in times of danger. Writing at the time when Britain alone stood against Hitler, George Orwell wrote,

One cannot see the modern world as it is unless one recognises the overwhelming strength of patriotism, national loyalty . . . . as a *positive* force there is nothing to set beside it. Christianity and international Socialism are as weak as straw in comparison with it.[26]

Within months, indeed, Stalin was appealing to Soviet citizens ([*sic*], not peasants and workers) to resist the German invaders in the Great Patriotic War − for all the world as if he were Alexander I in 1812 and Marxism had never been. Patriotism is that love and generosity of spirit which will rally with enthusiasm and courage when the fatherland is under threat. It is the readiness to bear arms with valour, the classical civic virtue, rendered into modern terms. Patriotism is thus an essential ingredient of good citizenship. And so too is that mode of citizenship transposed into more tranquil times. Patriotism which is a just pride in the honest and benign achievements of one's country is a sentiment to be applauded in the citizen. It cements social identity and encourages new generations to emulate their forebears.

Problems arise, however, when citizens wish either, on the one hand, to voice legitimate criticisms of their motherland or, on the other, to press their laudatory assertions to the point of blindness to her failings and to others' merits. The critical patriot may love his homeland dearly for all his consciousness of its imperfections. But he must beware expressing his honest feelings lest he be dubbed a bad citizen or, in times of tension, even traitor. And those who would treat him so give patriotism a bad name. Furthermore, such people make their views so conspicuously felt that the bad name is often well deserved. When the patriotism of citizens degenerates into the swaggering arrogance personified by the Napoleonic soldier, Nicholas Chauvin, governments may be persuaded to adopt intolerant and bellicose policies. Conversely, of course, governments bent on such aggressive behaviour can rouse a chauvinist temper in their people.

But since the Napoleonic Empire was an expansionist state, was not Chauvin an exemplary citizen for reflecting this mood? For Napoleon himself declared that 'The love of country is the first virtue in a civilised man'.[27] If one criterion of good citizenship is to stand with Stephen Decatur and pronounce, 'our country, right or wrong!'[28] – then the good citizen should not attempt to place restraints on patriotism. If, however, the citizen has the responsibility of monitoring the morality of his state's actions, then the patriotic duty may well be to rein in any bullying tendencies for the good of his state's reputation in the eyes of the world. In other words, the virtue of the good patriotic citizen is not gauged by a state-prescribed morality, but by reference to more universal precepts. Reflex patriotism is therefore, on this view, a badge not so much of civic virtue as of a stunted morality and psyche. In the words of the psychologist, Havelock Ellis, patriotism is 'a virtue – among barbarians'.[29] Or, in Dean Inge's formulation of the case,

. . . an arrest of development in the psychical expansion of the individual, a half-way house between mere self-centredness and full human sympathy.[30]

If verification of this interpretation is needed, one has only to cite the hooligan antics of some English football supporters in various European countries. Brazenly clad in union-jack underpants and other garments, their uncouth and violent display of jingoistic patriotism makes a mockery of any suggested equation between this sentiment and good citizenship.

If the truly moral patriot must judge his country against a universally applicable ethical code, is he not by that assessment acting as a world citizen? Patriotism is love of and loyalty to one's own state and one's fellow-citizens. It involves the Christian precept to love one's neighbour as oneself by interpreting 'neighbour' currently in a national sense. Many, as we saw on pp. 56–57 especially, have doubted the wisdom or practicality of expecting such an expansion of cohesive sentiment. Is it possible to feel an attachment to Mother Earth as one can to one's motherland; or to one's fellow humans as to one's fellow countrymen?

There is nothing inherently difficult nor indeed particularly uncommon about an expansion of loyalty. International civil servants, whether working for the UN or its specialised agencies or for regional bodies, most obviously the European Community, manage to grow a supranational sense of fidelity. Since the eighteenth century many who have sought revolutionary change have committed their loyalty to a transnational ideal rather than a national state. In the 1770s and 80s the Florentine Philip Mazzei was involved in the revolutionary events in America and Poland; in the mid-nineteenth century Marx preached the solidarity of the urban working classes world-wide; in the mid-twentieth century the Argentine Che Guevara fought against oppression in Guatemala, Cuba and Bolivia and became an international cult figure with the young. But the commonest experience – for we are not all by any means either functionaries or insurgents – has been the growth over time of the level of loyalty by the growth through accretion of the state. Venetians and Neopolitans have over the generations been transformed into faithful Italians; Shona and Matabele, with some discomfort it is true, are becoming loyal Zimbabweans. The examples could be multiplied over the centuries. And so why not a fully cosmopolitan loyalty? A state citizen experiences a respect for values, love, reverence and pride when contemplating his nation (as land and people). Cannot then the cosmopolitan experience similar responses when contemplating the world (as planet and mankind)?

Loyalty can attach to institutions, land or people. In the absence of a world state, fidelity to global institutions is difficult. Nevertheless, those, admittedly few, people who work for transnational organisations, pre-eminently the UN, can display this kind of transnational loyalty. Not only do they have the opportunity, they have the responsibility. When he was Secretary-General, Dag Hammarskjöld was unequivocal on this matter. He declared that 'UN officials should sever all their ties of interest or loyalty with whatever may be their home country.'[31] Their loyalty must be concentrated on the UN, its Charter and the ideals of international co-operation for which it stands. In the absence of a world state, loyalty comparable with that owed by the national citizen to the nation-state is, naturally, impossible for the mass of human beings. But is not a conscious attempt to be faithful to the principles of the UN Charter and other documents such as the Universal Declaration of Human Rights a loyalty of sorts? The ideals and principles enacted therein can touch at least some of the springs of loyalty – respect for the values enshrined in the institutions and pronouncements and pride in their achievements against so much national self-interest.

Loyalty in the shape of patriotism is most conspicuous when the motherland and one's fellow citizens are in danger. But mankind and the only planet he has *are* in danger. A universal rallying of human support may well therefore seem not only feasible but necessary. In July 1792 the French Legislative Assembly made provision for issuing a declaration: 'Citizens, the country is in danger'. It was to be a call for all citizens to respond to the state of emergency in the face of internal and external threat. The loyalty of citizens of the world is just as desperately needed today in the face of the current multiple global emergency. A world citizen is one who displays a faithful commitment to preserve and protect the planet against the threatening nuclear, demographic and environmental disasters.

Responsibility

A feeling of loyalty may nevertheless be a very passive experience. There are innumerable armchair patriots and sensitive television watchers of global tragedy. The good citizen has more than loyalty; he has a sense of responsibility to take positive and supportive actions. Responsibility is itself a container of other moral qualities. A good citizen intelligently understands and gladly accepts his legal duties and moral obligations. The good citizen performs his legal duties, such as paying taxes or military service, not for fear of the consequences for himself of avoidance but for fear of the consequences for his country. He also recognises his moral obligations to be a good citizen in return for the benefits he receives. The state provides protection and services; his fellow citizens also help by their beneficial social and civic behaviour. The good citizen is he who gives at least as much as he takes – both vertically to the state and horizontally to his fellows. To put the matter negatively, the bad citizen is the selfish individual. In his Inaugural Address, President Kennedy urged,

. . . my fellow Americans, ask not what your country can do for you; ask what you can do for your country.
My fellow citizens of the world, ask not what America will do for you, but what together we can do for the freedom of man.[32]

The good world citizen treats the whole planet in the same way. He appreciates that he owes his very existence to the life-sustaining Earth; that as one human being he has no more moral right to greater dignity than any other. The good world citizen therefore recognises his obligation to serve in his own small way the world and its peoples. Clearly duty and obligation presuppose conscience. The citizen who behaves selfishly, who lets slip an opportunity to perform a duty or meet an obligation will be worried by the lapse. The bad citizen, in contrast, will congratulate himself on his good sense, fortune or skill in managing to dodge the responsibility.

There are, it is true, exceptions to these generalisations: those who believe the *Fable of the Bees*. In 1714 the English poet, Bernard Mandeville, published this celebration of hedonism, with the sub-title 'Private Vices, Public Benefits'. He slated civic virtue as paraded hypocrisy; and argued that the colony benefits incidentally by the individual bee's amoral task of making honey for itself (with doubtful entomological accuracy in distinction to

Socrates' interpretation). The human parallel was obvious — and became very popular!

Then leave complaints: Fools only strive
To make a great and honest hive.
T'enjoy the World's Conveniences,
Be fam'd in War, yet live in Ease,
Without great Vices, is a vain
Eutopian seated in the Brain![33]

In modern guise, Mandeville turns up as the New Right's justification for their 'trickle down' theory. The pursuit of economic self-interest will expand the economy and even the least successful will benefit more than if the fortune-makers had acted with conscious civic morality. The hedonist need suffer no pangs of conscience.

A citizen's conscience may remain unsullied or be rendered spotless white by the cleansing power of good intentions. He will none the less not qualify for entry into the pantheon of good citizens if he lacks the necessary qualities to put his intentions into effect. He needs the participatory equipment of political knowledge, skills, judgement and initiative. Without these, state and planet, fellow-citizens and human beings stand precious little chance of benefiting from the sense of responsibility. What in fact do we in liberal democratic states expect of the good citizen? The answer must be given in four parts with an added rider. The good citizen must be helpful to his fellows. He must participate in public affairs. He must have integrity and honesty. And he must be law-abiding. However, in all these activities a sense of moderation and balance is essential — an appreciation of Horace's *aurea mediocritas*, the golden mean.

At its easiest and most effective level good citizenship is neighbourliness, the boy scout ethic of doing a good deed every day. It is, of course, helpfulness, not nosiness or busy-bodiness. It is helping old ladies to cross the road, but only when they really want to reach the other side! Let us take a detailed example. In London in March 1986 two girls were invested with young citizens' awards, one for helping police trace three armed robbers, the other, for launching an appeal for hospital equipment after surviving horrific injuries inflicted by a stolen car. Each year the civic virtue of British youth is recognised in this way. Millions of people worldwide are good citizens in this community sense, most in more humdrum fashions, though vigilante groups in US cities risk personal safety in the execution of their self-imposed duty. In terms of the proportion of the population engaged in voluntary community work, Britain has a splendid record, as the following two statements bear witness. The first was written by Dr Alec Dickson, who founded Community Service Volunteers; the second from the chief executive of Business in the Community:

Active citizenship means doing; it is practised daily by Scouts and Guides, by the WRVS, by pupils in hundreds of secondary schools (to an extent unparalleled in any other country in Europe).

Active citizenship and involvement in community work are encouraged by [over 3,500 companies], who allow employees the time they need to be school governors, justices of the peace, regional health authority members, or to counsel in local enterprise agencies and voluntary organisations.[34]

Voluntary work falls into three main categories: administration to ensure the smooth running of facilities (e.g. being a governor of a school); assisting law and order (e.g. participating in a neighbourhood watch scheme); or working for the less fortunate (e.g. collecting money for UNICEF).

None of these activities is political in any strict sense. The good citizen must also discharge his responsibilities as a political participant. Why is participation a virtue? In the first place, a right to have a say in the government of one's own country is a precious gift, handed down in varying degrees of security, from former years. It would be irresponsible to past and future generations to allow this right to atrophy or to neglect to strengthen it. Political participation, by shouldering some share of responsibility for decisions, is also a crucial component of being a morally autonomous person. By discussion, voting, membership of political organisations, demonstrating, one is discharging one's obligation to help shape the general will. Even airing views is an important contribution to sustaining political freedom: in the words of the British political philosopher, J. R. Lucas, 'Democracy can flourish only in a land of pubs.'[35]

Secondly, governments cannot, without constant surveillance, be trusted to pursue the most just policies. It is surely part of civic morality to try to ensure that justice prevails. The good citizen makes judgements; and when he discerns injustices, he tries to bring pressure to bear for change — whether this be at local, national or international level. For example, in a discussion on the hideous problem of Third World debt, the British Economics journalist William Keegan, has written,

There is a vast gap between what citizens who support Live Aid or turn out for demonstrations feel should be given or lent to developing countries and what their governments actually do.[36]

In this case the good world citizen keeps up the pressure because his conscience tells him that only by his action and by others of like persuasion will right prevail. The third argument is the one high-lighted by J. S. Mill (p. 73). In the process of acting as a participative citizen the individual becomes a better person. Civic participation enhances autonomy and altruism: autonomy from self-government; altruism from judging the interests of the community.

This is the contentious part. Supposing that the responsible citizen judges that the interests of the community are best served by vigorous opposition to the government? Is the good citizen the one who supports the government for the sake of stability and because, in a democratic polity at least, it has been duly elected? Or is civic virtue rather to be displayed by demanding justice and arguing that loyalty is due to the state and political rectitude? The posing of alternatives makes sense only if the interests of the state and the government are distinguishable. One might think that this distinction is a basic principle of political theory. In fact it was unequivocally denied by the judge in the Clive Ponting trial in England in 1985. Ponting, a civil servant in the Ministry of Defence, passed on to an Opposition MP evidence which cast doubt on the government's explanation of the sinking of the Argentinian cruiser *General Belgrano* during the Falklands war. His action was clearly against the interests of the government. But since he believed that the sinking and consequent loss of lives was unjustified and damaged Britain's reputation for integrity, he considered it his duty as a citizen to help in uncovering the truth. Brought to trial under the Official Secrets Act, Ponting was acquitted by the jury, who by that verdict rejected the judge's guidance concerning the identification of state with government.

Governments and especially right-wing governments are naturally prone to define good citizenship as deferent and supportive behaviour towards the government in office. It is at least a definition which makes the citizen's task easy: understand what the government wants and uphold it in the implementation of its policies. Moreover, it is an interpretation which can be justified by all the ideologies. In representative democracy the government has a mandate from the people. An authoritarian régime wields power to prevent collapse into anarchical conditions. Totalitarians claim allegiance from their citizens in their pursuit of the millenium. There is no civic morality in challenging the will of the majority, the upholders of civilised order or the navigators on the route to utopia.

Yet, although such an interpretation accords with Aristotle's concept of good citizenship, it contains a massive contradiction. A citizen by very nature of his status is a morally free and autonomous person. Neither subject nor serf, he is vested with the responsibility of using his sense of right and his political judgement. If he must refrain from deploying these qualities in opposition to his government, in what sense is he still a citizen? Are his virtuous qualities to be packed away in some amoral cupboard, to be taken out and dusted down only on special occasions like elections and referenda? Surely not. And if not, then the good citizen must be constantly measuring government pronouncements and actions against the benchmark of what he gauges to be the good of society, his state and the planet.

The good citizen not only distinguishes between state or planet on the one hand and government on the other. He also distinguishes between self and the collectivity. The good citizen must therefore be endowed with integrity. He must struggle with the temptations of selfishness and dishonesty. Both capitalism and socialism have been accused of corroding citizenship values. Both, it is suggested, encourage the attitude, 'I care not for you, Jack, I'm all right!' Capitalism is guilty because it fosters the making and accumulation of wealth and therefore the sin of greed. Socialism is guilty because it fosters dependence on the state provision of welfare and therefore the sin of sloth. Both greed and sloth are civic sins because they are facets of egoism. Charity not greed, industry not sloth are the characteristics of the good citizen.

The good citizen is also a keen upholder of law and order. Complaints may be heard from so many countries – from the USSR as well as the USA – of youthful lawlessness. Gang fights, vandalism, violence against property and peaceful citizens seems so ubiquitous as to cast doubts over the depth to which the citizen ideal has succeeded in digging its roots. Hooligan behaviour has been endemic throughout the centuries: the Blue and Green Hippodrome factions in sixth-century Byzantium; Montagues and Capulets in Shakespeare's Verona; the *jeunesse dorée* in post-Thermidor France; the *stilyagi* in Khrushchev's Russia. Not to mention the dire reputation of Britain which, in the eighteenth century was 'one of the noisiest, most aggressive, brutal and bloodthirsty nations . . . in the world'.[37] This lack of self-discipline and social conscience is the very reverse of good citizenship and the behaviour is abhorred by the good citizen. The good citizen obeys and upholds the law and practises civilised and orderly behaviour in public places.

We must, however, distinguish between social lawlessness and political protest. Gangs of youths smashing their way through a town in an orgy of drunken vandalism is a different matter from politically incensed youths demonstrating against an unjust government and defending themselves in clashes with riot-police. The motives and the nature of the violence are quite dissimilar. The participants in a hooligan rampage can never be considered as acting as good citizens; those in a political demonstration may well be. In the latter case, it all depends on the justice of their cause and on whether they have truly and patiently exhausted more pacific forms of protest. The British political scientist, David Marquand has made this point:

. . . the politically competent potential protester is a blood-brother to the good citizen of liberal-democratic theory. He is likely to turn to protest, not because he does not understand the system or accept its norms, but because he has been disappointed in it: because he comes to feel that it has let him' down.[38]

The distinction between hooliganism and political protest is sometimes not easily drawn; and the task is not facilitated by the muddying of issues by propaganda. When the British women camped at Greenham Common, were they bad citizens because they were trespassing, damaging RAF property by cutting fences and marring the environment of the Newbury citizens by the untidiness of their camp? Or were they good citizens because they sincerely believed the presence of cruise missiles there was a dangerous escalation of the nuclear arms race and rendered Britain an increasingly provocative target for the Soviet Union? They were certainly sincere in holding to these beliefs. But is it good enough to identify with Charlie Brown in the 'Peanuts' cartoon and believe that sincerity is a sufficient test of civic virtue?

Justice of cause, sincerity of belief and altruism of motive are valid indices of good citizenship. We must add to this the test of civility. The term, originally used to denote good, stable government, has been adapted by modern social scientists to describe the socially virtuous behaviour of 'good citizenship'. One of the most distinguished exponents of the concept, Edward Shils, has provided the following comprehensive definition:

Civility is a belief which affirms the possibility of the common good; it is a belief in the community of contending parties within a morally valid unity of society. It is a belief in the validity or legitimacy of the governmental institutions which lay down rules and resolve conflicts. Civility is a virtue expressed in action on behalf of the whole society, on behalf of the good of all the members of the society to which public liberties and representative institutions are integral. Civility is an attitude in individuals which recommends that consensus about the maintenance of the order of society should exist alongside the conflicts of interests and ideals. It restrains the exercise of power by the powerful and restrains obstruction and violence by those who do not have power but who wish to have it. Civility is on the side of authority and on the side of those over whom authority would rule.[39]

If civility is virtually synonymous with good citizenship, then that virtue is recognised by a Janus-like ability to support authority and to challenge its abuse. It is an ability to keep a nice balance and is an influence for moderation.

Indeed, not only does the good citizen use his influence in the quest for common-sense political solutions, he must exercise a common-sense moderation on his own tendencies to excessive involvement. Oscar Wilde said that 'the trouble with being a socialist is that it requires too many free evenings'.[40] The conscientious citizen can experience the same trouble. Aristotle also emphasised the need for time to perform civic duties (p. 3). A citizen who undertook all his potential responsibilities with the required zeal would paradoxically be a bad citizen. His life would be lop-sided. Because of his business in public affairs he could not prevent himself from neglecting his family, his work and his need for relaxation. And this very distortion of his life would be liable to warp his experience and his overall sense of responsibilities to such an extent as to render suspect his judgement as a citizen.

Citizenship and procedural values

In taking a moderate, common-sense view of his role, and by eschewing fanaticism, the good citizen will comport himself by reference to Bernard Crick's list of procedural values: freedom, toleration, fairness, respect for truth and respect for reasoning.[41] Although Crick compiled this list as objectives to be aimed at in educating a person to be politically literate, we may readily approximate 'political literacy' with 'good citizenship' and adapt his procedural values for our own purposes. Their pertinence can be thrown into particularly sharp relief if we turn them into their negative forms. It is inconceivable that one would accord the title of good citizen to someone who advocated a condition of servitude, who was intolerant, unfair, lied and refused to engage in rational discussion. Many of the procedural values are at least implicit in much of the preceding discussion. Rather more needs to be made here of toleration.

Toleration (or tolerance) is the willingness to allow people to hold and express views and to take actions of which one disapproves. The stance is most forcibly expressed in the aphorism attributed to Voltaire: 'I disapprove of what you say, but I will defend to the death your right to say it.'[42] It is evident that toleration has no place in a totalitarian state. What part does it play in the citizen's make-up in liberal-democratic societies? Citizenship is an egalitarian status, at least in theory and intention. No one should suffer diminished rights because of sex, political opinions, religious belief or ethnic origin. Now if citizen A refuses to extend a tolerant understanding to citizen B, the former will be liable either actively to promote the abridgment of B's rights or at least connive at their abridgment. A will in consequence not be a good citizen because he will not be treating B with the equal respect and dignity which is his due as a fellow citizen.

Intolerance is bad citizenship in another sense too. It emphasises and intensifies differences. The dream of the good citizen should be a harmonious state; that of the good world citizen, a harmonious planet. Intolerance, prejudice and discrimination make for discord. Ethnic prejudice both within and between countries is rife throughout the world, often further embittered by religious differences. Whites and Blacks fear each other in South Africa; Tamils and Sinhalese loathe each other in Sri Lanka; some British dislike their continental Community partners . . .. The list could be almost endless to prove the frailty of the citizenly virtue of tolerance.

Is the expectation of tolerance in the ideal good citizen limitless? Should the intolerant themselves be tolerated? It is, of course, the classical liberal dilemma. How valid were Voltaire's principles to the Canadian citizen in c. 1970 when the Front de Libération du Québec used terrorist methods with the aim of securing the secession of the province? Can, indeed should, the citizen be tolerant towards violence and threats to the political unity of which he is part? Again, the answer must lie in the pragmatic judgement of the citizen. He must measure the relative damage that will be caused, on the one hand, by the destructive policies of the dissentients and, by the oppression of a possibly just cause on the other.

Education for good citizenship

Life in the modern state and the modern world is a complicated business. Being a loyal, responsible and virtuous citizen of one's state and of the world is no easy matter. Though the burdens be heavy, the discomforts that would attend their relinquishment would be even more acute. The education of young people to become good citizens is therefore a matter of some consequence. But politicians who blame schools for their failure to produce 'good' citizens are either ignorant of the problems entailed or are guilty of humbug. The difficulties attending the education of young people as good citizens are threefold. In the first place, one must ask the question whether teaching social and political values is the purpose of the school at all. It is perfectly legitimate to hold the purist view that History and Politics should be taught in such a way that values do not intrude. The purpose of these disciplines is to understand, not to pass moral judgements, still less to absorb moral lessons from them. In this sense an important distinction must be made between teaching Politics and political education. The former is the study of a social science; the latter is a preparation for real life in which facts, interpretations, opinions and judgements are used to shape a personal value-position. In practice, of course, schools have always purveyed values and no doubt always will. The modern taxonomic analysis of learning into cognitive, affective and psycho-motor domains is a recognition that the education of feelings, both moral and aesthetic, is a significant component of the learning experience. Schools have taught their pupils to be good citizens in one of three ways. One is by the, often unconscious, selection of material so that it conveys a biassed message: nationalist History is an obvious example. Another is by the very deliberate identification of teaching objectives to ensure a particular moral outcome: traditional styles of Religious Education clearly fit this category. Thirdly, there is the 'hidden curriculum' – the daily almost subliminal messages which pupils absorb from the school assembly, the relationships with teachers, the organisation of class teaching, extra-curricular activities. Much of the ethos of a school contains assumptions about the nature of the good citizen. The balance of competitiveness and co-operation, teamwork and individual initiative, self-assurance and deference, imposed discipline and personal responsibility all contribute.

The fact that one can cite these opposed choices raises the second difficult question, namely, who is to decide what social and political values are to be taught? While there might be a general agreement that the Physics syllabus is best left to the Physics teacher, many other interested parties claim a legitimate voice in the education of the young citizen – central government, school governors and children's parents most obviously. But supposing their priorities clash? It should be clear from the analysis in this section that the notion of the good citizen is exceedingly complex. As we shall argue in later chapters the task of constructing a self-consistent, comprehensive, acceptable and practicable definition of citizenship, though urgent, is by no means simple. In the meantime we have either disagreements or government-constructed guidelines, depending on the effectiveness of educational centralisation in different states.

Even without this confusion concerning the delineation of objectives, there is room for considerable doubt about the effectiveness of schools in moulding attitudes. And this problem contains at least three sub-questions. The first concerns the aptness of teaching techniques. Traditional approaches have tended to the style of the 'full-frontal' didactic instruction in the classroom or the headteacher threatening to punish any pupil who is found dropping litter. Recent work, especially in the fields of Peace and Global Studies, has raised serious doubts about this manner of citizenship education. If good citizenship requires any particular personal qualities these must surely include self-discipline, initiative, co-operativeness. Traditional teaching techniques are hardly designed to foster these characteristics. The doyen of peace researchers, Johan Galtung, has pointed to the challenge:

204

One could not teach democracy forever in school without practising at least some of it, and the *idea* of peace goes much further . . . . Young people today have heard many *words* . . . – and they may be more interested in the teacher's *life-style* and how peace is *practised* in everyday reality than in a million or two extra words.[43]

It is not easy to meet the challenge. Do enough teachers have the skills to adapt their teaching? Do the relaxed, co-operative styles presuppose an inner discipline which most pupils do not possess?

And are such learning styles effective? It is easy enough to test whether a class has successfully learned by rote a list of dates. How does one test progress in the affective domain? Attitude tests have been administered by the thousand, especially in the USA. In Britain, teaching techniques to reduce colour prejudice have become a particular concern. The personality and style of the teacher seem significant influences. On the other hand, behaviour outside the school may reveal little change; and the difficulties of longitudinal research would seem insuperable. Of course, how far adult citizens are measurably the products of their schools is a controversial issue. How many former members of British cadet force units became militarists? Pacifists were also produced by reaction to the same system. Other influences are, of course, recognisably powerful. Children no doubt acquire attitudes from parents, juvenile literature and television as much as, if not more than, from school.

This fog of uncertainty does not necessarily mean that the teacher should give up the task of trying to produce good citizens. What it does mean is that he must understand how best he can complement or counteract these other influences. Schools as institutions need to know what attitudes and feelings their pupils bring with them from extramural influences, be clear what their strategies are, and ensure that governors and parents are in sympathy with these strategies. Teachers must then fully comprehend how children develop moral understanding. They must appreciate the significance of the researches of Jean Piaget and particularly Lawrence Kohlberg, namely the sequential nature of moral learning. This means that, however propitious the child's environment and level of intelligence might seem to be for sophisticated moral teaching, progress can only be made in a step-by-step manner. For instance, the child must learn that rules are imposed by force before he can understand that they incorporate principles of justice. The teacher too must understand how the child progresses from a comprehension of moral principles to an emotional commitment to their value.

In discussing the recent practices in human rights and global education, the American authority on the psychological aspects of this teaching has written,

Some of the same timing principles delineated for human rights education, such as the importance of middle childhood and adolescence, probably also apply in [citizenship education for global perspectives] . . . . The major conclusion to be drawn, however, is that concern for the psychological and pedagogical issues of sequence and timing has not been adequately considered in the design of international education programs.[44]

205

The general message is that in the teaching of social and political moral values the process must be started earlier than has usually been the case so that the ideals of responsibility may be consolidated before the onset of adolescent alienation and cynicism.

Let us now turn our attention to some of the educational policies and pedagogical practices which have been designed to produce good citizens. If we look at the dominant attitudes over the past century in western states, it is possible to discern a fluctuating pattern. At the start of the process of mass education, as we have seen (pp. 80–86), the aim was to train young people to be loyal, law-abiding, temperate and deferent citizens. By the 1960s, particularly under the influence of the American 'New Social Studies', academic objections to such manipulation led to an advocacy of a social scientific approach. This in turn was displaced or supplemented by greater attention to citizens' rights and world consciousness. Most recently, in reaction, demands to make young people more conscious of their civic obligations have been heard. For example, the American Morris Janowitz has argued that in western democracies and especially the USA, 'The long-term trend [in civic education] has been to enhance citizen rights without effective articulation of citizen obligations' with a consequent 'widespread criticism of organised education – public and private.'[45] The patterns in the Communist states and in the newly independent nations have been different. In Communist régimes, deference and duty have been combined with the Marxist form of social scientific analysis. In the new nations, identity and loyalty have naturally been given precedence.

Let us now glance at a few examples of the common methods used in schools to inculcate good citizenship. The most ubiquitous efforts are those devised for fostering national loyalty and pride. The techniques used are most usually ceremonies and the teaching of national History. In the USA, for example, millions of school children each day take the Pledge of Allegiance to the flag, the sanctity of which ceremony became a serious issue between the two candidates in the 1988 Presidential election. Nationalist History textbooks are epitomised by that brilliant send-up of the genre, already cited (pp. 110–111), *1066 and All That*, which concluded that 'History is now at an end' because after the First World War 'America was . . . clearly top nation.'[46] Furthermore, old historical prejudices and stereotypes have extraordinary staying power. For example, even in a Communist state like Hungary, where History has been substantially rewritten, the influences of the traditional textbooks have persisted. György Čsepeli has reported most perceptively on this phenomenon:

Reviewing a study on the high-school historical textbooks used in Hungary before 1945 a striking similarity was found between the cognitive and affective patterns of contemporary public national attitude and those of [sic] taught in schools long time ago. . . .

The reasons are partly connected with the effectiveness of the old curriculum, partly with the shortcomings of the new curriculum ignoring relevant aspects of the national history. There is no vacuum in the social consciousness, if there is a need unsatisfied it will seek for its satisfaction and won't care with [sic] the ideological nature of the material to fill the vacuum in.[47]

Civic duties and social obligations are commonly taught in a factual manner in Social Studies lessons. However, practical experience is more important in this sphere. If social studies lessons do not stimulate a desire for community service, they have failed in their good citizenship objective; if they do stimulate the demand for practical opportunities and do not provide them, then the school has similarly failed in that objective. It is true that various youth and voluntary organisations may be able to compensate for such failings. Nevertheless, the school is the proper body to arrange these activities so that theory and practice can be mutually reinforcing. Institutions which take the task of preparing young world citizens very seriously in this manner are the United World Colleges. Admittedly they are highly selective in their intakes of 16-year olds and are generously endowed. They may nevertheless be taken as models of what can be achieved. The Student Prospectus for the original, Atlantic College, in Wales explains:

United World Colleges offer students of all races and creeds the opportunity of developing international understanding through a programme which combines high academic quality with activities which encourage a sense of adventure and social responsibility. ·· .
All students are asked to join a programme of service to the local community . . . . In most services the student can only become effective after a period of intensive training.[48]

The teaching of personal moral values has traditionally been the responsibility of the churches and Religious Education teachers, as well, of course, as the home. (In Communist countries, for 'churches' read 'the Party' and for 'R. E. teachers' read 'teachers of Marxist ideology'.) The emphasis of the catechisms, homilies and admonitions vary, inevitably, from country to country. Morality may be based on class solidarity, reverence for God, respect for the law, inter-cultural tolerance, abstinence from drugs. Breaches of such standards, depending on the society, would be considered evidence of bad citizenship. But it is precisely in this area that the responsibility and efficacy of the school may be most seriously questioned. Home and other socialising forces are so powerful. And yet most societies expect the schools to make the effort and even blame them for low standards of civic behaviour. The ethos of the school in any case is probably much more effective than this kind of textbook writing:

A citizen . . . must have a sense of social responsibility − a sense of belonging to the community. The citizen may have to sink his own immediate interests and the interests of his small group in the common good . . . . Tolerance towards others is perhaps the greatest need of society today. A citizen must respect the individualities of others . . . .[49]

And how many readers of the present book would guess the source of this extract? It is taken from a History textbook in use for seventh-grade pupils c.1970 in South Africa!

Some school systems, it is true, have drawn up comprehensive Social Studies syllabuses which aim to furnish young citizens with all their basic requirements, including fundamental civic virtues. For instance, the syllabus for Elementary Social Studies for Class V in Pakistan lists three affective objectives, namely, '1. Service to the people; 2. Co-operation; 3. Preservation of Pakistan's ideology.' And for Class VIII, '1. Love for humanity; 2. Consciousness of social welfare; 3. Respect for those working for others.'[50]

If those educationists in the vanguard of citizenship education can be observed to share a set of special considerations, they may be said to be threefold. In the first place, they are forward-looking. They recognise the need to educate for change; that change will accelerate with increasing rapidity; and that teachers have been too complacent in their use of old material and methods. Secondly, a global dimension must be incorporated in this work. And thirdly, that young people must learn to face up *critically* to moral issues. The Canadian teacher-educator, Ken Osborne, has sharply contrasted the differences between what he calls 'Traditional Civics' and 'Recent Approaches to Political Education'. The former, he claims, 'tends to avoid normative questions of what might be; avoids value-issues.' The latter 'emphasizes values-issues; raises normative and ethical concerns.'[51] Even so, the questions remain. Who is to determine the ingredients of good citizenship? And how can the so common problem of inertial time-lag be combatted? At both state and world levels these questions require urgent answers.

REFERENCES

1. W. J. M. Mackenzie, *Political Identity* (Penguin, 1978), pp. 124 & 130.
2. E. Durkheim, *Moral Education* (1925, Free Press of Glencoe edn, 1961), pp. 68–9.
3. Mackenzie, *Political Identity*, p. 157.
4. J. S. Mill, *Representative Government*, p. 216.
5. A. Huxley, *Brave New World* (1932, Penguin edn, 1955), p. 15.
6. Quoted in A. Marwick, *The Nature of History* (Macmillan, 1970), p. 13.
7. Quoted ibid., p. 245.
8. A. F. Pollard, 'History and Citizenship', *Factors in Modern History* (Constable, 3rd. 1932), p. 228.
9. G. J. Renier, *The Criterion of Dutch Nationhood* (Allen & Unwin, 1946), p. 16.
10. G. Heptonstall in *RSA Journal*, January 1988, p. 151.
11. From a speech made in 1870 and used as a legend on the UNESCO medal commemorating the centenary of Hugo's death.
12. Reprinted in F. Stern, *The Varieties of History* (Macmillan, 2nd., 1970), pp. 61–2.
13. Decree of 19 November 1792, reprinted in J. M. Thompson, *French Revolution Documents 1789–94* (Blackwell, 1948), p.213 (author's translation).
14. S. Mendlovitz (ed.), *On the Creation of a Just World Order*, quoted in S. Smith (ed.), *International Relations* (Blackwell, 1985), p. 104.
15. Quoted in T. Roszak, *Person/Planet* (Gollancz, 1979), p. 38.
16. J. V. Torney et al., *Civic Education in Ten Countries*, p. 29.

17. J. L. Nelson, 'Nationalistic political education', *Cambridge Journal of Education*, vol. 8(1978), pp. 142–3.
18. J. M. MacKenzie, *Propaganda and Empire* (Manchester University Press, 1984), p. 249.
19. Quoted in A. Warren, 'Citizens of the Empire' in J. M. MacKenzie (ed.), *Imperialism and Popular Culture* (Manchester University Press, 1986), p. 235.
20. R. M. Hutchins, *The Learning Society* (Penguin, 1970), pp. 76–7.
21. Kant, *Education*, quoted ibid., pp. 74–5.
22. Plato, *Phaedo* (trans. H. Tredennick, Penguin, 1954), p. 108.
23. See R. Stewart (ed.), *The Penguin Dictionary of Political Quotations* (Penguin, 1986), p. 30.
24. Montesquieu, *Lettres persanes*, quoted in A. Cobban, *In Search of Humanity* (Cape, 1960), p. 104.
25. H. S. Truman, *Memoirs, Vol. 2: Years of Trial and Hope* (1956, New American Library edn, 1965), p. 331.
26. G. Orwell, 'The Lion and the Unicorn', reprinted in 'My Country Right or Left 1940–1943' (Penguin, 1970), p. 75.
27. Napoleon, Speech to the Polish deputies, 1812; see Stewart, *Dictionary of Political Quotations*, p. 120.
28. S. Decatur, Toast proposed at a dinner at Norfolk, Virginia, 1816; see ibid., p. 46.
29. Quoted in W. R. Inge, 'Patriotism', *Outspoken Essays* (Longmans, Green, 1920), p. 35.
30. Ibid.
31. Quoted in J. P. Lash, *Dag Hammarskjöld* (Cassell, 1962), p. 286.
32. J. F. Kennedy, Inaugural Address, January 1961, reprinted in T. C. Sorensen, *Kennedy* (Pan Books, 1965), p. 277.
33. Mandeville, *Fable of the Bees*, quoted in Cobban, *In Search of Humanity*, pp. 80–1.
34. Letters to *The Times*, 14 October 1988.
35. J. R. Lucas, *Democracy and Participation* (Penguin, 1976), p. 264.
36. W. Keegan, 'In My View', *Observer*, 2 October 1988.
37. H. Perkin, *The Structured Crowd* (Harvester, 1981), p. 29.
38. D. Marquand, *The Unprincipled Society* (Cape, 1988), p. 196.
39. E. Shils, 'Observations on Some Tribulations of Civility', *Government and Opposition*, vol. 15 (1980).
40. Cited in B. Barber, *Strong Democracy* (University of California Press, 1984), p. 236.
41. Crick & Porter, *Political Education and Political Literacy*, pp. 66 et seq.
42. S. G. Tallentyre, *The Friends of Voltaire*: see *Oxford Dictionary of Quotations* (Oxford, 3rd edn, 1979), p. 561.
43. J. Galtung, 'What a Challenging Issue Peace Education Is!', *Bulletin of Peace Proposals* vol. 5 (1974).
44. J. V. Torney-Purta, 'Applying the Perspectives of History and of Psychology to Three Models of International Education' in Heater & Gillespie, *Political Education in Flux*, pp. 285–6.
45. M. Janowitz, *The Reconstruction of Patriotism* (University of Chicago Press, 1983), p. ix.
46. Seller & Yeatman, *1066 And All That*, p. 123.
47. G. Csepeli, 'National Belongeness [*sic*] As a Result of the Socialization Process',

Perspectives in Political Education in 1980s (Research Committee on Political Education, 1982), pp. 132–3.

48. United World College of the Atlantic, *Student Prospectus*.
49. A. N. Boyce, *Legacy of the Past*, reprinted in Muñoz, *La educatión political*, pp. 460–1.
50. Reprinted ibid., pp. 466–7 (author's translation).
51. K. Osborne, 'A Canadian Approach to Political Education', *Teaching Politics*, vol. 17 (1988).

CHAPTER SIX

The Political Citizen

6.1 THE POLITICAL CITIZEN OF THE STATE

. . . the ability of individual citizens to understand, much less actively to influence the decisions of central government appears to be diminishing. Thus there has been a rapidly increasing pressure for participation in smaller, often local, units of decision-making . . . . The school curriculum would be wise to recognise this and to increase the likelihood of *responsible* participation by supporting it with knowledge and an informed understanding of the potential, and the limitations, of the contribution of individuals to their own government.

John Slater and R. A. S. Hennessey[1]

Varieties of political participation

Benevolent absolutism can provide civil rights while denying the political. Benevolent absolutism can, hypothetically, create a just society. Albert Schweitzer's description of the French Revolution as a 'fall of snow on blossoming trees' was such a benign judgement of the policies of enlightened despotism, which was so common a feature of European régimes in the late eighteenth century. But the inhabitants of these states are not true citizens because they are precluded from having any authentic voice in the framing of policy. The exclusion of the mass of the people from politics is now widely considered unacceptable – an infringement of human rights. The Universal Declaration specifies that,

Everyone has the right to take part in the government of his country, directly or through freely chosen representatives . . . . The will of the people shall be the basis of the authority of government.[2]

This statement may be helpful as a proclamation, but it leaves unanswered a number of difficult questions concerning citizen participation and education for that function.

The great difficulty, not always overtly admitted, in devising school programmes for educating young citizens to political competence is the need to achieve agreement on prior social and political questions. The style of political education will be affected by the perceived purpose of the school system as a whole. This in turn may well be determined by the accepted purpose of the political régime. This purpose itself will be related to the kind of involvement in politics expected of the individual. And this expectation will be shaped by basic assumptions concerning the way people can and should behave in society. All classifications are in danger of being oversimplifications. Nevertheless, it is helpful to examine each of these five levels of political and educational thought and practice under the headings of five main political doctrinal positions. The following table provides an abbreviated overview of this analysis. Clearly policies pursued by any given government, party, pressure group or school may incorporate more than one of these positions. Even so, it is useful when examining any policies to be aware how the amalgam is constituted.

There are many drawbacks to the Left-to-Right spectrum view of politics. It is none the less helpful for reminding us that there is a distinct difference between the political philosophies of those who view human nature with an optimistic vision and those whose perception is pessimistic. A caveat must also be entered about the dangers of making a straight connection between the entries against 'political education policies' and the corresponding political doctrines (p. 339). What we have in this table is a set of variations on the theme of participation. The term 'citizenship' is meaningless without some kind of participation in public affairs. There have, however, been enormously diverse interpretations of this function. What advantages are thought to accrue from citizen participation? How much participation and of what kind is desirable? And how practicable? What are the educational implications of the different answers to these queries? It is these questions which underlie much of the following discussion.

The totalitarian citizen

In treating the matter sketched in the table it is useful to deal with totalitarianism first; then the other four categories fall neatly into two pairs of mirror images for contrast and comparison. Totalitarianism can be dismissed here fairly briefly: it has already been discussed as a self-contained topic in Chapter 3; and the claim of the inhabitants of totalitarian states to citizenship in the full sense of the term may be questioned because of their lack of opportunity for autonomous political judgement. By attempting to politicise the whole of life, totalitarianism stands outside the mainstream European tradition. For this tradition accepts a distinction between the public and the private life. The individual is not expected to behave *qua* citizen for twenty-four hours a day and in all his or her activities. (It is likely that most Victorian brides were spared the advice to think of England in the most private of situations. Given their lack of citizen status, such an appeal to selfless patriotism would surely have been a trifle ironic in any case!) Totalitarianism, in contrast, demands the complete absorption of the human personality. Mussolini expressed this objective succinctly in his definition of Fascism:

	Participatory/ Democratic	Conservative/ Elitist	Totalitarian/ Manipulative	Nationalist/ Integrative	World/ Universalist
Assumptions re individuals	Commonsense of the masses – beneficial	Only an élite is wise and altruistic	Duty to support ideology	Personality dependent on national identity	Human identity more significant than national
Political involvement	Maximum use of opportunities for participation	Minimal participation – to support élite	Enthusiastic mass support of leadership	Support for national cohesion and 'greatness'	Duty to raise consciousness about world issues
Purpose of politics	Maximise individual freedom and equality	Preservation of traditional values through process of change	Achievement of the 'ideal' society	National integration and differentiation	Subordination of national to HCF of world interests
Educational policies	Development of individual child's aptitudes but social homogenisation	Distinction between élite and mass education	Politicisation of whole school system	National rather than sectional provision	Co-operation and tolerance
Political education policies	Knowledge and understanding of the system and participative skills	Deference from the masses, loyalty from all	Indocrination and regimentation	National consciousness and patriotism	Empathetic understanding of other peoples and global problems

It wants to remake, not the forms of human life, but its content, man, character, faith. And to this end it requires discipline and authority that can enter the spirits of men and there govern unopposed.[3]

In totalitarian régimes the individual is either a citizen or a non-person. The function of the schools is to ensure the perfection of this dichotomy. To draw from Italian Fascism again, Gentile wrote that,

The essential task of education is to produce good citizens, and the good citizen is one who hears the voice of 'the State' within him.[4]

The individual who cannot or will not become a political animal in this un-questioning sense is no true totalitarian 'citizen' in his heart. And when the political police open a window into that most secret place the false 'citizen' will pay the penalty.

Totalitarian régimes, at least in theory if not wholly in practice, resolved the problem of the relationship between the power to govern and the power of the governed. The complete authority of the leadership was strengthened and justified by the artificially stimulated zeal of the citizenry. Liberal democracies, holding a formula of this kind to be sham, degrading and, above all, dangerous, have failed to solve the riddle. In both prescriptions of the ideal and descriptions of the real two contrasting models continue to vie for acceptance. The one is based on minimal citizen participation; the other, on the maximum of such civic activity.

Elitist v. participative ideals

The natural Conservative has a low and gloomy opinion of the average human being. He (the average human being, that is, not the natural Conservative) is born to sin and copes with the temptations of evil by submission to them whenever lucky enough to have the opportunity. The conviction that most people are ruled by their baser instincts is as old as Plato. This élitist tradition holds that, so far from the mass of slothful and ignorant individuals playing a major role in government, government is a device to keep them apathetic lest their positive propensities to selfishness and violence undermine communal life. Edmund Burke expressed the point of view memorably:

Society requires not only that the passions of individuals should be subjected, but that even in the mass and body as well as in individuals, the inclinations of men should frequently be thwarted, their will controlled, and their passions brought into subjection. This can only be done *by a power out of themselves;* and not, in the exercise of its function, subject to that will and to those passions which it is its office to bridle and subdue.[5]

Another way of expressing the same basic worry is that the more politically conscious the mass of people become the more deeply society will be divided by their different needs, ambitions and demands.

Moreover, because the bulk of citizens will always be politically ignorant and naïve, they fall easy prey to the demagogues. The democratic options are not in reality between the formulation of policy by an elected representative élite or by a constantly interventionist citizenry. If the latter alternative were ever to come to pass, the real decision-makers would be the articulate minority or unaccountable manipulators. George Bernard Shaw, no élitist himself, nevertheless impishly expressed the idea through the mouth of Boanerges, the trade union official in *The Apple Cart*:

I talk democracy to these men and women. I tell them that they have the vote, and that theirs is the kingdom and the glory. I say to them, 'You are supreme: exercise your power.' They say, 'That's right: tell us what to do'; and I tell them. I say, 'Exercise your vote intelligently by voting for me.' And they do. That's democracy . . . .[6]

The Conservative élitist would rather emphasise the right of the individual to exercise his freedom *not* to participate. His ideal is the private, not the public, citizen.

For government is the business of governors. It is a task requiring hard work to grasp the problem and the capacity to take the tough decisions among a number of frequently almost equally unpalatable options. The expectation that policies for the good of all emerge from the General Will of right-thinking public opinion is a Rousseauistic mystical delusion. Efficient and just government is the task for a small group of politicians and bureaucrats. It remains to the citizen merely to express an overall judgement on this performance when the politicians episodically present themselves for election, and by that action to legitimise the élite who govern on his behalf.

This élitist theory of democracy rests not only on assumptions and intuitions about human character and behaviour. A number of political scientists have set out to substantiate these views empirically (the Americans Berelson, Kornhauser, Lazarsfeld, Lipset, Schumpeter most notably). These studies seem to reveal that the majority of citizens are politically ignorant and apathetic; and, moreover, when they are on occasion roused to political involvement, the effect is almost invariably unfortunate. Participation is a difficult term to define. If it means voting in general elections, then in Britain, for example, the turn-out is quite high — about three-quarters. But that is a feeble kind of political citizenship. And when a more vigorous definition is adopted, such as membership of a political party or pressure group or taking the initiative in raising an issue with the local council then the proportion drops to perhaps barely a quarter of that figure. Not only do the majority of citizens not wish to become politically involved, surveys suggest that they lack the necessary knowledge to make any involvement either practicable or desirable. Some evidence of the most basic political ignorance would seem to explode the comfortable democratic theory of government by representatives judiciously selected by well-informed and rational citizens. A survey of British youth conducted in 1979–82 is typical in revealing that,

Time and again the young people reported that they had little interest in and knew nothing about politics. Their responses to questionnaire items about political knowledge confirmed their ignorance. Many were unable to identify the policies of any party except the National Front's commitment to the enforced expulsion of non-whites.[7]

Faced with such dispiriting evidence, little wonder the élitist prays that the masses remain politically somnolent. Since a little political learning can be a dangerous thing, their arousal must be feared. Moreover, empirical evidence would appear to support this gut reaction. Two basic findings are pertinent. One is that a high rate of participation is often an index of a régime that is unhealthy by democratic criteria: either that the citizenry is provoked to activity by discontent with the democratically elected government (as in Weimar Germany) or that it is prompted to a show of support to legitimise a totalitarian government (as in Nazi Germany). In the last free elections of the Weimar Republic $11\frac{3}{4}$ million people voted for the Nazis. The second set of findings relates to the characteristics of that segment of the citizenry who are the most apathetic. This is revealed to be composed of the cynical, ignorant, intolerant and authoritarian individuals. They are, in short, the very people whose increased participation to render democracy more whole and wholesome would by that very action infect it with diseases which could well prove, indeed in some instances have proved, lethal. Did not Aristotle warn against mass political involvement, which he termed 'ochlocracy' or mob rule?

But then Aristotle also warned against a self-perpetuating and self-interested oligarchy. The right-wing democrat places his trust in two devices to prevent an élite from becoming entrenched and abusing its authority. One is the ultimate power of the citizenry to replace unacceptable members of the élite; the other is that the ranks of the élite should be permeable to constant fresh recruitment.

These guarantees do not satisfy those on the left of the political spectrum. They see human nature in a more kindly light — through pink-tinted spectacles, if you wish. One may contrast Burke's contempt for the 'swinish multitude' with Rousseau's famous flash of insight while resting one summer on the road to Vincennes:

Oh Sir, if I could ever have written one fourth of what I had seen and felt under that tree, ... With what force I should have exposed all the abuses of our institutions! With what ease I should have shown that man is naturally good, and that it is through these institutions alone that man becomes bad.[8]

It follows that the more the mass of people can be cleansed of the corrupting influences of unjust institutions, the more their natural social virtue will shine through; and the more truly democratic participatory institutions can be brought into play, the more that virtue will be able to express itself in co-operative civic behaviour to the greater good of the individual and society alike. A modern version of this faith may be read in a statement written by two members of the British Labour Party in 1988 in an attempt to clarify the party's aims and values:

Britain should be far more democratic . . .. We believe that a democratic society and a socialist society will be the same thing, one in which popular participation is maximised and people are helped not just to help themselves but to help others.[9]

Once an optimistic portrayal of human nature is adopted, then the case in favour of substantial citizenship participation can be constructed. While the role requires an element of altruism and empathy, those qualities can only be developed by practice. To put the point slightly differently and more familiarly: people only learn to act responsibly by being given responsibility. If only more accessible participatory institutions relevant to ordinary citizens' interests and needs were made available, their civic consciousness, understanding and common sense would be more fully discerned and appreciated. The liberation of the people to political involvement is, moreover, crucial for efficiency. 'How many men work in this factory?' Khrushchev was once asked. 'About half,' he replied. Gorbachev's reforms are attempts to release popular initiative and undermine the élitist bureaucracy which led to these conditions. The problem is universal. That the expert knows what is good for the ignorant so-called citizens is a myth. The remote so-called expert does not understand what the ordinary citizens need and want. And it is the frustration and cynicism which this condition breeds that inevitably engenders the apathy so cheaply jibed at by the élitist critic of participation.

Participatory democracy is also safe. The more citizens are involved in the making of policies and decisions, the more protection they have from the abuse of power by 'the authorities'. Indeed, the process of participation can measurably help to soften the hard 'them' and 'us' distinction. Participation is also a safety-valve. It ensures that all have at least a fair opportunity to share in decisions. As a result, the difficulties of government and administration become more fully appreciated and if wrong decisions are made, all share in that responsibility. When power is concentrated in the hands of an élite, there is always the danger that channels of communication and levers for the exertion of popular pressure are ineffectual. These circumstances, vividly demonstrated for instance in Poland during the 1980s, lead to widespread feelings of alienation. When sufficiently pent up they explode in demonstrations of popular violence. The harmony of the citizen-state relationship modulates into the cacophony of civil discord and the citizen is transformed into a revolutionary.

Finally, there is the argument from human rights. By what right does a government not involve the masses of citizenry, the very people who are affected by political and administrative decisions? The citizen-state relationship is, or should be, a moral relationship, sustaining the dignity and worth of the individual. Participation is a vital means of giving proper effect to that relationship. The surrender of this right of direct involvement entirely to a small group of representatives, as élitists require, is a renunciation of the very core of political citizenship.

So much for the theoretical arguments. What now of the empirical evidence for the case in favour of participation? The defenders of participative democracy can draw upon an interesting body of evidence that reveals a level of civic willingness and ability, albeit often latent, that can be marshalled against the élitists. It depends how the questions are posed. If a sample of citizens are presented with a list of pre-formulated questions their total scores on knowledge and interest criteria, as the élitists assert, are likely to be dismally low. But ask the same group if they have worries and irritations, if there are matters which they would like to see handled differently, then individually these people are most likely to reveal a political consciousness about particular issues that impinge on their lives. Following a comprehensive survey in the USA the researchers reported in 1972:

Our data on the content of citizen initiated contacts show a citizenry involved with the government in ways that are highly salient to them, on issues that they define, and through channels that seem appropriate. What we are suggesting is that on matters of the politics of everyday life, citizens know what they want.[10]

Levels of interest naturally vary as between countries. As part of their famous early 1960s survey the American political scientists Almond and Verba asked respondents whether they thought they could do something about an unjust local regulation, whether they thought they would make the effort to protest if they felt strongly, and whether they had in practice attempted to influence their local authority. In Italy the percentages were 51, 41 and 13; in Britain, 78, 50 and 18 respectively. Since the 1960s in a number of the more mature liberal democratic states citizen participation has been notably on the increase, especially in hitherto unorthodox ways. In Britain in the 1960s community politics became the fashion. Neighbourhood or Community Councils were created to grapple with all local issues which exercised the population of the particular area.

Furthermore, discontent with and alienation from representative systems is widespread. Not only are the morality and competence of elected politicians often questioned, especially in the less politically mature states, but so also is the very suitability of the parliamentary system, untempered by the availability of other lower-order decision-making bodies. Representative institutions, it can be claimed, are not even efficient at representation. In Britain, for instance, second-class citizens suffer numerically second-class representation (or perhaps that correlation is an index of efficiency?). Following the 1987 election, although more black and women MPs were returned than ever before, these representatives of 4 and 51 per cent of the population respectively amounted to only 0.6 and 6 per cent of the membership of the House of Commons.

Significant, though not always consistent, lessons can be drawn from these arguments and scraps of evidence. First and simplest is that the lack of constant participation by the majority of citizens may be an indication of satisfaction rather than apathy. Low-key monitoring of public affairs should not be mistaken for passivity. Secondly, willingness to participate may well be a function of the perceived utility of participation. If most citizens appear apathetic, the fault may well lie with the system and not the individual. If the reward for the effort of involvement is impotent frustration before an immovable and faceless bureaucracy, then apathy will supervene – or violence. The greater the expectation of efficacy, the greater the incidence of participation. Thirdly, if the interests and concerns of citizens are diffused among a myriad of particular issues, then participation requires a very diverse range of institutions for the articulation and canalisation of those interests and concerns. The formal institutions of town hall and parliament are too irrelevant and forbidding for many. If 'personalised' institutions are what the average citizen wants, then clearly they must operate on a small scale. And finally, if there is a felt need for more appropriate styles of participation, if the formal structures fill the citizen with a sense of alienation rather than commitment, then the denial and discouragement of participation, which is the policy of the élitist, could be dangerous. These last two considerations were voiced by E. F. Schumacher, the author of *Small Is Beautiful*, in 1974:

I know that on a small scale people's power can be mobilised and that, when the scale becomes too large, people's power becomes frustrated and ineffective . . . . The discovery and mobilisation of people's power may be nothing less than the condition of survival for the hitherto affluent societies of the West.[11]

A footnote needs to be added to this outline of the case in favour of the citizen as political participator. It concerns the possibility of dividing this school of thought into two sub-categories. Let us conveniently label them centre and left. The former tends to emphasise the moral justification for allowing citizen participation, while expecting, even just hoping with crossed fingers, that such political activity will be directed to the better running of the liberal democratic system basically as it is. The more radical position is that the mass of citizenry should be conscious of the continuing inequalities and injustices which persist in most, if not all societies, and use their political power for reform. Moreover, since many so-called democratic institutions make a mockery of those very democratic principles they are supposed to encapsulate, then citizens must devise more honest ones.

Elitist v. participative civic education

The knowledge and skills required for truly active participation are naturally rather different from those needed if the citizen is to perform a more quiescent role. The style of political education advocated and devised will therefore differ according to the assumptions one holds about human character and democratic processes. Since throughout the whole span of recorded history any form of democracy, let alone a fully participative democracy, has existed but rarely, it is the élitist style of civic education that has inevitably been predominant. The knowledge purveyed has most often been historical, sometimes legal-institutional, though of a mechanical kind. For centuries skills were confined to rhetoric, stylised for an equally educated élite audience. Critical questioning of the status quo, the skills to render the system more dynamic, an understanding that citizenship could be a group as well as an individual function – all these requirements of education for participation were for centuries totally lacking.

The élitist style of political education has been typified by English courses in Civics or British Constitution. These consisted largely of rote learning about the machinery of British government, brought to life in the better programmes by visits to the town hall and Westminster and visits to the school by the MP and someone involved in local government. The conservative-minded believe that a brief series of lessons along these lines is certainly sufficient for young people. In their capacities as politicians, school governors, academics and parents they have voiced their protests when teachers have ventured beyond these confines.

A variety of arguments has been deployed and they may conveniently be illustrated by reference to comments made in Britain. Temperamentally the Conservative wishes to reduce political activity to the minimum; consequently, to teach young people both that there are better things in life than politics and that, in any case, the limits of political competence are exceedingly confined. If unrealistic expectations are raised in the minds of citizens, then the inevitable frustration of their hopes could well spark a dangerously angry reaction. In his Inaugural Lecture, the Conservative philosopher Michael Oakeshott, expressed his hopes concerning political education. These included his belief that,

. . . the more thoroughly we understand our own political tradition . . . the less likely we shall be to embrace . . . the illusion that in politics there is any safe harbour, a destination to be reached or even a detectable strand of progress. [12]

The politically Right are fearful of the urge they see among the Left, not just to introduce more political studies into the schools, but to politicise the whole of school life. Moreover, when we consider the average adolescent, there is little that he can truly understand about the complex, technical and essentially adult nature of politics. This opinion, stated with clarity by Aristotle, has been echoed by a number of academics in more recent years. Thus, the political scientist, Professor J. D. B. Miller said:

A man who has seen a few elections go by, who has tested the promises of political parties against their performance . . . is better equipped to see politics whole than an ex-schoolboy who may know nothing but what his teachers have taught him about the need to serve his country (or not serve it, depending on the teacher). [13]

But attempting to teach about political matters to the young is more than a waste of time. Since, by the law of the conservation of the curriculum there is only a finite amount of time available to the teacher, the incorporation of a course on Politics must inevitably displace something that does have positive worth. Professor Scruton (another Conservative philosopher) has voiced this view most pungently:

For several years now, enlightened educationists have been telling us that this or that subject of the old school curriculum . . . is of only antiquarian interest . . . . This cant . . . has been responsible for the virtual extinction of classical and religious education in schools, and for the growth of subjects like sociology and politics . . . which (unless tempered by some other, more rigid, form of study) can introduce nothing but confusion into the minds of the child. [14]

If the young are to acquire political knowledge at all, the proper place for this learning to happen is the home. Politics are controversial matters, matters involving opinion and belief, essentially therefore concerns of the private mind and conscience. The Conservative politician, Rhodes Boyson, a junior Education Minister at the time, declared,

I am suspicious of all forms of political education . . . . Politics, like sex education, is something that should be left to the family.[15]

After all, is it realistic to expect teachers to be able to avoid indoctrinating their pupils? The more a teacher wants to increase the political content of the curriculum, the more he is likely to have a decided political commitment himself and the less he will be able to prevent that bias from colouring his teaching. This abuse, one Conservative paper published in 1985 argued, has become endemic. The authors wrote:

It is a commonplace to suggest that British educational institutions are increasingly losing sight of the distinction between education and indoctrination, or even rejecting the first of these purposes in favour of the second.[16]

Certain local education authorities, most notably Inner London, were accused of openly fostering this unprofessional activity. The issue of indoctrination will also be discussed elsewhere. The point here is to note the part it plays in the élitist's objection to what they see as the dangers of too heavy a concentration on the political preparation of young people for citizenship.

Each of these shots in the élitist locker can be matched by equal calibre ammunition in the armoury of the defenders of an active citizenship education. Against the Conservative argument that political education should be a minor component to correspond with the peripheral nature of politics are ranged two arguments. One is that those who present the apolitical case are covertly defending the status quo. If politics is a process for the reconciliation of differences, then political activity occurs only when differences are allowed to surface; that is, when the consciousness of what might be challenges the acceptance of what is. That consciousness could well be dormant without effective political education. It is consequently in the interests of the beneficiaries of the status quo to dissuade schools from a proper democratic education; and perhaps therefore their objections are not as altruistic as they sound. Conversely, those who would benefit from changes in society would benefit from political education. The second arm of the argument is that élitists tend to assume a very narrow definition of politics. For them, the term generally means what transpires in cabinet and representative assembly. The advocates of participation, as we have seen, have a so much broader view. Similarly proponents of education for participative skills view their task as a preparation of young people for engagement in debate and negotiation in work and community affairs more than in parliamentary elections. One may quote Bernard Crick, Professor of Politics and self-defined 'extreme moderate', to the effect that,

. . . there are overwhelmingly clear grounds for saying that societies are bad which prevent or even merely discourage popular participation, and there are reasonably clear grounds for thinking that distaste for or distrust of politics can threaten any kind of just and tolerant life . . . the first task of any possible political education that is of educational value is to convey some sense of the naturalness and variation of politics.[17]

The second task is to show that politics is an area of experience and study perfectly accessible and comprehensible to young people, if only handled with professional skill. The ignorance and cynicism, which without doubt can be found in abundance among adolescents and which some commentators have interpreted as evidence of the inappropriateness of political education for young people, can be explained in other ways. There is, after all, weighty evidence of positive reactions by quite young children. Summing up her research in primary schools one educationist concluded:

The age of approximately nine years appears . . . to be significant in the development of political concepts. A spurt of understanding, interest, and the ability to articulate ideas appears to take place for many children at about this age:[18]

If, then, by the age of 14–16 many teenagers have appeared to 'switch off', this attitude could well be part of the familiar pattern (in Britain and other 'advanced' countries) of general adolescent alienation from society and school as part of that society. Far from political education being unimportant, it is therefore crucial. If courses are properly shaped, capitalising on the budding interests of the nines-to-tens, then a realistic appreciation of what the citizen can achieve could be taught. Indeed, the Conservative's prophecy is self-fulfilling. Teach about constitutional machinery and not about political controversies because the former is dull and safe. Because it is dull and safe, it will be uninteresting. Because it is uninteresting, young people will turn away from their role as citizens and leave political matters to an élite who 'know about these things'.

The argument relating to the displacement of 'proper' subjects in the curriculum can similarly be turned on its head. The persistence of difficult and abstract academic subjects at the expense of the socially relevant can be interpreted as a method of creating a sense of failure among working-class children. For they may well see little point in a style of learning that is so remote from their own current and likely future lives. If practical and relevant work in, for instance, Political Studies were more commonly undertaken, both interest and standards could well improve. When preparations for raising the school-leaving age in Britain were being made in the mid-1960s the word 'relevant' was on everyone's lips. Thus, the Schools Council Working Paper, *Society and the Young School Leaver*, declared that

A frequent cause of failure seems to be that the course is often based on the traditional belief that there is a body of content for each separate subject which every young school leaver should know. In the least successful courses this body of knowledge is written into the curriculum without any real consideration of the needs of the boys and girls and without any question of its relevance.[19]

Finally, there is the matter of indoctrination. Four points may be made to suggest that the fear of the Conservative-minded has little foundation. The first is that there has always been bias in schools and quite gross attempts at indoctrination: traditional Christian Religious Studies, 'drum and trumpet' nationalist History and cadet forces are just three obvious examples. Political education, if it is handled in a biassed way, represents nothing very different. Secondly, young people are really not so naïve as to soak up every opinion expressed by their teachers. Indeed, the very decline in respect, of which the Conservative so complains, ensures that a teacher's views are now subject to even more critical assessment by his pupils than hitherto. Thirdly, stories of overt attempts at indoctrination in Britain have in all probability been colourfully exaggerated. For example, considerable press coverage of Government concern in the mid-1980s was followed by legislation to cover the issue (p. 110). A year after the new law came into force the Education Correspondent of the *Guardian* undertook an investigation. He reported:

With the whole country alerted to the danger, only six complaints had been made to the Department of Education . . .. Of the year's crop of six, the DES said . . . that five had been 'resolved'.[20]

In the sixth case, one paragraph in teachers' notes for a teaching pack were rewritten. And fourthly, teaching young people to detect bias and to protect themselves against indoctrination is a vital facet of programmes of political education advocated by the supporters of participative democracy. For as adults they will be subjected to a barrage of distortion from advertisers, politicians and tabloid press.

From the late 1960s a number of developments encouraged the evolution of this liberal style of political education in many Western countries. These developments included the following. The findings of research in political socialisation revealed a capacity for political learning in the young hitherto unsuspected. The research also concluded (whether justifiably or not) that fundamental political attitudes are formulated at an early age and then remain basically unaltered. If a keenness by citizens to support democratic values is central to their continual existence, then political education in this style is of critical importance. Democratisation of both political and particularly educational systems was vociferously urged in a number of quarters, and was thought to be just by many in positions to concede the demand. Support among the younger generations for extremist political ideologies antipathetic to liberal democracy frightened some politicians. In Britain, neo-Nazi racism seemed to be taking hold following the substantial coloured immigration of the 1960s. Education for tolerance and empathy became a priority on the sheer pragmatic grounds of social and political safety. And finally, the general lowering of the age of majority to 18 so reduced the gap between school-leaving and full citizenship that the argument against political education on grounds of immaturity was significantly undermined.

What was the response in Britain to these pressures and opportunities? The creation of a professional organisation, the Politics Association, in 1969 was an important spur to new thought and action. From this grew the Programme for Political Education, under the leadership of Bernard Crick, the central concept of which was 'political literacy'.

A politically literate person [the project report stated] will . . . know what the main political disputes are about; what beliefs the main contestants have of them; how they are likely to affect him, and he will have a predisposition to try to do something about it in a manner at once effective and respectful of the sincerity of others.[21]

The fleshing out of the term, hitherto used in only a generalised sense, led to the widespread acceptance of the programme, among British politicians across a broad doctrinal spectrum and by many teachers, not only in Britain but several other countries too (most notably Australia). Here at last was a formula for making the kind of citizen which the theory of participative democracy required, but which, to the chagrin of its more honest proponents, existed in fact in but paltry numbers.

Had, then, the devisers of political literacy outmanoeuvred the élitists and rallied a remarkable rainbow of supporters to the need for effective political education in school? Those who initially believed this to be so perhaps failed to recognise the incipient division within the camp of the participant democrats, between those of the centre and those of the left (p. 219). What is more, the left-wing critics took their attack into what should have been the invulnerable heart of the project, namely its pretended academic objectivity. The objections were expressed by a clutch of Social Scientists, who argued along the following lines. If the political literacy programme were intellectually honest, it would allow for full opportunities to question the established British political culture and institutions. Also, insofar as social education should cultivate a sceptical and questioning cast of mind in young people, Political Education could not now be relied upon to fulfil this need because it had sold the pass in its bias towards understanding and operating the capitalist and parliamentary systems. In the words of one of the most trenchant writers,

There is . . . a fair amount of prima facie evidence that the success of the political education movement in mobilising support from politicians is associated with their belief that it could assist in preserving the status quo and in bolstering respect for it. . . .
the struggle for a genuinely open and critical education must go far beyond political education periods in school.[22]

The Programme for Political Education, and its central concern to produce participative, politically literate citizens, was sniped at from both sides. It would produce 'demonstration fodder . . . [and] the sort of ill-considered reforming activism which has been the curse of Britain over the last quarter of a century'[23] was a view from the Right. From the Left came the accusation that 'participation implies acceptance' and therefore to teach it as a priority is to 'neutralise the teaching of alternative values and systems.'[24] Does all this then mean that it is quite impossible to achieve a reasonable measure of agreement on education for political citizenship?

Foreign affairs and defence − special cases?

If the Conservative wishes to protect political affairs from too great an intrusion by the *profanum vulgus*, the unhallowed throng, how much more does he wish to shield the special arcane and secret matters of foreign affairs and defence from any vulgar influence? At a time when nuclear weapons are deployed on British soil and in British waters and when peace studies are taught in some British schools, the matter has become heatedly contentious. Three considerations in fact need to be balanced in determining the appropriate level of citizen-involvement. One is the right to help shape policies which may literally be a matter of life or death. Secondly, there is the problem of the average citizen's lack of interest and/or expertise in these areas. And thirdly, there is the need for security of information.

The close association of citizenship with military service in so many ancient and medieval city-states helped to ensure that participation in decision-making about foreign and defence matters was taken for granted. One may cite, for instance, the famous description by Thucydides of the debates in the Athenian Assembly concerning the Sicilian expedition:

The Athenians held an assembly and listened to what the Egestaeans and their own delegation had to say. . . .they voted in favour of sending sixty ships to Sicily and appointed [three] commanders. . . .
Five days later another assembly was held to discuss the quickest means of getting the ships ready to sail and to vote any additional supplies that the generals might need for the expendition.[25]

Quite obviously this level of detail cannot possibly be handled by the citizen body of a modern nation-state. On the other hand, foreign and defence policies are plainly defined and communicated through the news media by politicians. In recent years in Britain, for instance, there have been clear party differences over major issues like membership of the European Community, the provision of overseas aid and the possession of nuclear weapons. Furthermore, pressure groups (e.g. Britain in Europe, Oxfam, CND) have existed to inform and mobilise public opinion on these matters. Keeping to these three examples, a citizen might be expected to formulate considered viewpoints on these questions touching respectively his identity, conscience and security. An individual might well be considered a mere semi-citizen if he surrenders these wide areas of public policy as being beyond his competence.

In a democratic society such civic self-denial might also be judged as positively damaging to the body politic. One reason is that a rigid distinction between domestic and foreign affairs is impossible to sustain. How would one categorise an increase in defence spending at the expense of social services? Or lax regulation of heavily pollutant industries? In Western Europe are Community decisions foreign or domestic to the constituent states they affect? But in any case, all democratic politicians pay lip-service to the theory that citizens have a legitimate interest in foreign affairs, witness election manifestos and government broadcasts at times of crisis. If real opportunities are denied to citizens to develop and express this interest, the democratic process will be imperilled by the hypocrisy of circular, self-fulfilling argument: the public should be kept in ignorance in case it demands undesirable policies, which are bound to be undesirable because of its ignorance.

Maybe there is good logic in witholding the status of special category to foreign and defence policies. But is it practicable to expect ordinary citizens to cope? The extraordinary technicalities of contemporary international relations and weapons systems must defy any attempts by all except the experts to comprehend. If Palmerston believed that only three people had fully understood the Schleswig-Holstein question (viz, the Prince Consort, who was dead; a German professor, who was mad; and himself, who had forgotten), how much more mythical must be the modern citizen's grasp of the intricacies of nuclear disarmament? No wonder there is more evidence of citizen apathy about foreign than domestic affairs. Professor Holsti has estimated that even in highly literate societies about 70 per cent of the population are 'apathetic, uniformed and nonexpressive' on most foreign issues.[26] In Britain, the affairs which the mass circulation tabloid newspapers keep their readers, so to say, abreast of, are rarely foreign or defence. Walter Lippmann, the shrewd American observer of public opinion, argued that matters of great moment, like war and peace

. . . can be answered with the only words that a great mass *qua* mass can speak — with a Yes or No . . . .
The unhappy truth is that the prevailing public opinion has been destructively wrong at the critical junctures . . .
It has shown itself to be a dangerous master of decisions when the stakes are life or death.[27]

And yet there is a dormant interest and, arguably a commonsense competence, which awaken when the emotions of fear, aggression or compassion are aroused. Let us take a few examples from recent British experience. In 1954 Sir Edward Boyle, MP received 150 letters from his constituents, but only one on foreign affairs. When the Suez crisis broke (and provoked his resignation as a junior minister), he received 37 on the issue. When thermonuclear weapons were first being tested and deployed in the late 1950s and when intermediate-range missiles were being deployed in Europe (including Britain) in the early 1980s, CND recruited more members than any other pressure-group had achieved in recent decades. Fear was the stimulant. In contrast, patriotism marred by ugly xenophobia flared with the Falklands war; and the fortunate success of the British expeditionary force propelled Mrs Thatcher's reputation from the most unpopular to the most popular of postwar prime ministers. Yet altruism too can find expression in the contemplation of Third World poverty and disaster. Financial support for charitable organisations raises millions of pounds annually; while particular events like the publication of the Brandt Report and the Live Aid concert for Ethiopian famine relief have intermittently tapped further wells of humane compassion and feelings of justice. Although it is obviously difficult to prove the exact weight these expressions of popular opinion carry with government, it is at least surely true that they are by no means totally ignored. In practice therefore the political role of the citizen is certainly not confined to domestic issues.

There none the less persists, in Britain most notably of democratic states, an almost paranoiac concern for secrecy in foreign and defence matters. The contrast between the typical American and British attitudes is tellingly revealed in an exchange between Livingstone Marchant and Sir Evelyn Shuckburgh. The former, an Assistant Secretary of State in the US State Department, described the current public questioning to which he was subjected. The latter, Eden's Private Secretary in the early 1950s, was shocked to learn of this, expressing fear that 'democracy could not survive if *issues,* as opposed to personalities, were to be put before the public . . .. You can fool the public about issues, but not . . . about the character and quality of leaders.' Marchant expressed his belief that 'Even the English would have to give up the "old-fashioned" idea of entrusting vital secrets to experts.'[28] A generation later the Thatcher government exerted pressure on civil servants, the BBC and elements of the quality press to try to prevent the revelation of confidential information about defence and security matters which, in the opinion of the government, was damaging to the national interest. Moreover, when the government started in 1988 to reshape the Official Secrets Act, they planned to make an indictable offence not just of revelations of defence secrets but any 'official' information regarding relations with foreign states. Informed citizen involvement in the formulation of foreign policy was evidently not considered a particularly high priority.

There is no more difficult nor more heatedly argued area concerning citizen participation than the problem of nuclear weapons. To argue the citizen's right to such involvement from the classical principles laid down by city-states of old will not do. Whether to invest in a new galley or a couple of extra ballistas was scarcely of the same order as a decision about continuing Britain's policy of nuclear deterrence by replacing the obsolescent Polaris with the substantial numerical increase of the Trident system, itself designed for counter-force rather than blunt deterrent strategy. The effects of the use of such weapons and the engineering and strategic technicalities involved, of course, bear no comparison whatsoever − and require a moral and technical understanding of an utterly different complexity and profundity.

Yet the conclusion which is drawn by some, namely that nuclear policies must be left in the expert hands of a technocratic élite, is faulty on two major grounds. One is that there is no reason to believe that the members of any such élite are capable of sounder moral judgement than ordinary citizens. The very notion of deterrence is based on convincing the other side that there are some circumstances in which you would be willing to press the button. The consideration of and preparation for such circumstances raise moral as well as technical questions. There is no reason at all to think that a prime minister or a general is better equipped than the average citizen (provided he has basic information) to make decisions on ethical grounds. The slogan, 'No annihilation without representation' is a powerful moral statement. Moreover, and this is the second objection to technocratic control, the specialist is liable to be blinkered. Obsessed with technicalities and the competition of an arms race, the technocrat may lose sight of the moral considerations − the Dr Strangelove syndrome. In the film version of that story, when the Soviet ambassador reveals that his country has the ultimate life-destroying deterrent, General Turgidson's aside is, 'Gee, I wish we had one of them Doomsday Machines.' Nor is such a mentality confined to celluloid fantasy. The chairman of the presidential commission on the near-disaster at the Three Mile Island nuclear power station noted:

I kept running into scientists whose beliefs border on the religious and even occasionally on the fanatical. . . .
This is incompatible with the fundamental nature of science, and it creates an atmosphere in which there is serious mistrust of experts.[29]

Even so, proper judgement cannot be made in a knowledge vacuum. If the citizen's voice is to be heard, the justification for listening must rest not merely on moral right and competence, but on the expectation that his judgement is underpinned by something more substantial than an ignorant hunch.

The coverage of foreign and defence policies in the news media in often somewhat skimpy. There are a number of reasons for this. Some relate to the general arguments against popular participation in these affairs already discussed. There is also the factor that policies are continuous in their operation and rarely surface as 'newsworthy' dramatic incidents. The case for schools educating young people in these aspects of public affairs is therefore particularly strong. Yet more often than not they have been neglected. An understanding of his country's position in the world has usually been indirectly provided for the pupil through History. Since this subject became commonly part of the curriculum a century or so ago it has been blatantly distorted for nationalist purposes. As facts and dates rapidly faded in memory the young citizen took with him into adulthood the firm conviction that his country's relations with others have always been conspicuous for the justice and valour with which they have been conducted. His own attitude was as like as not therefore to be 'My country, right or right'. Textbook revision in recent decades has helped, it is true, to rectify this bias.

So too has the advent of Third World or Development Studies and Peace Studies. In a number of Western countries these programmes have questioned the rectitude and prudence of their own state's economic and defence policies. This outcome is by no means the main purpose of such studies. On the other hand, insofar as a global perspective and an empathetic understanding of other people's points of view are prime objectives in these courses, they cannot avoid presenting any given nation's policies in a more critical light than traditional teaching.

Nuclear weapons are a major factor in the need to keep the peace between those who possess or are affected by them. It is not surprising therefore that the problems of nuclear war and deterrence should feature in Peace Studies. Indeed, the development of such courses owed a great deal to the onset of the New Cold War, c.1980. Teachers were faced with the dilemma of how to cope with the interests and fears expressed by their pupils. One English teacher explained the situation:

228

'Sir, would you tell us if the bomb was going to drop?' When the first-former raised his hand at the beginning of the drama period, I had not expected his question to render me speechless.[30]

But having accepted the professional responsibility of handling the issue, are teachers liable to indoctrinate their pupils against established government policy? From San Francisco to Stuttgart this worry has led to pressures upon teachers to reconsider the validity of this teaching at all. Thus in Britain in 1984 two academics published a pamphlet in which they attacked Peace Studies as 'immensely damaging to our national interests, and favourable to those of the Soviet Union.'[31] A year later Devon County Council banned teachers from displaying CND badges or car-stickers. A Peace Studies syllabus became a red rag to a John Bull.

It is highly likely that in Peace Studies as in other controversial areas of the curriculum the accusations of bias have provoked explosions of outrage utterly disproportionate to the scale and danger of the problem. The controversy has rather been an expression of shock by the traditionalists, who have become aware that schools are moving beyond their previously accepted boundaries of social education. The modern state has provided education for the masses partly at least to ensure that the citizenry, endowed now with political rights, should contribute to the cohesion and strength of purpose of their nation. The legitimacy of any lessons which erode the unswerving patriotism required by these objectives must therefore be in question. It is this widely-held view that also helps sustain the rooted objections to the idea of world citizenship as a form of political activity.

6.2   THE POLITICAL CITIZEN OF THE WORLD

About 'world citizenship'. . . . I do not quite like the phrase. It seems to profess too much. On the other hand, it is fairly exact in describing the ideal that we wish young people to get into their heads . . . it is a comparatively new idea which needs hammering in, though of course it is as old as the Stoics.

Gilbert Murray[32]

Arguments against world citizenship

World citizenship is nonsense; active world citizenship is nonsense on stilts. Thus would those who will have no truck with the idea would no doubt wish to adapt Bentham's aphorism. The logic of the argument against world citizenship is soon summarised. The state (in its present form, the sovereign nation-state) is a reality, performs vital functions and therefore its preservation is in the interests of mankind. Conversely, world government has neither reality nor expedience. And since world government would be incompatible with the existence of separate sovereign state governments, world citizenship would be incompatible with state citizenship. It follows that world citizenship is neither real nor expedient. The key to the debate over world citizenship is sovereignty. Does absolute state sovereignty exist in a really meaningful sense? Does it benefit the citizen? Would its transfer to a world authority be possible or desirable? For sovereignty, in Hobbes' imagery, 'is an Artificiall *Soul*, as giving life and motion to the whole body' of Leviathan.[33] A number of consequences follow from this analogy. A state cannot concede a portion of that sovereignty to another state or to a supranational institution without undermining its own true nature. Nor can it brook any allegiance by its citizens to the authority of another state or a supranational institution without similar consequences.

Some commentators argue that this undermining process is already evident as transnational and supranational institutions grow in strength. But, in truth, the announcement of the death of the sovereign state, like that of Mark Twain, has been exaggerated: there is sound clinical evidence of vigorous life. Even the United Nations Organisation, once viewed by some as an embryonic world goverment, 'is based on the principle of the sovereign equality of all its members'.[34] In the first place, all states still claim and exercise extensive jurisdiction over their own citizens. For example, as recently as 1986 the arm of the English criminal law was extended by new extradition arrangements with both the USA and Spain. On the other hand, the principle of the non-intervention of one state in the political affairs of another remains a principal facet of the international code of behaviour. International law sets out a precise definition of 'intervention'. Even so, one statesman's perception of unjustifiable intervention is another's justifiable rendering assistance to an ally or to freedom-fighters. The point is, however, that the principle of non-intervention is frequently appealed to in the event of the involvement of one state in the domestic affairs of another. What is more, the moral is often drawn of the evil consequences of transgressing the code. The outcry against the involvement of the USA in Vietnam and Nicaragua, of the Soviet Union in Hungary and Afghanistan and of Britain in the Suez adventure all provide vivid examples of the continuing belief in the validity of the principle.

A second clue that the sovereign state remains alive and well is the continuing conviction that it should retain the monopoly of the legitimate use of force, both domestically and externally. Once again it is instructive to remember that the founding fathers of the UN failed to breach this principle. The proposed Military Staff Commitee (Article 47) was stifled soon after birth. And again, as with non-intervention, the strength of feeling for retaining the principle of the monopoly of force has been loudly voiced: in this case through widespread condemnation to terrorism. Anarchist groups like Baader-Meinhof; nationalist separatist organisations like ETA; and the virtually *sui generis* Palestinians have all dramatically challenged the convention – only to prove how vital it remains.

The third piece of evidence for the continuing health of the sovereign state is its common rejection of any binding international moral principles in favour of adhesion to the practice of *Realpolitik*. Even when paying lip-service to international morality and obligations, governments still primarily seek to protect and advance the interests of their own states. Sometimes remarkably blatantly. In 1986 the US-Iran-Contra affair provided a particularly telling double exemplification of the reality. The US government committed itself with sanctimonious whole-heartedness to the principle of never negotiating with terrorists. Yet in an attempt to obtain the release of US hostages held by Iranian-backed terrorists in Lebanon, war materiel was secretly transported to Iran to help that country in its prolonged conflict with Iraq. What is more, some of the money from these sales was fraudulently diverted to the Nicaraguan Contra rebels, thus reinforcing the US policy of intervention in the domestic affairs of that Central American republic.

It is sometimes conceded by those who argue the endurance of the sovereign state that admittedly it has less vitality as an institution than it had in the eighteenth and nineteenth centuries. But is even this true? In some ways the institution is stronger than it has ever been. To cite the UN once again, the number of its sovereign state members has more than trebled from the 51 at its inauguration. The right of national self-determination has not only been claimed by former colonial territories, but in addition threatens further frag-mentation as independent statehood is demanded, for instance by Basques, Kurds and Tamils. Internally too the grip of the state over its citizens has tightened. Of course, Hayek and his disciples of the New Right have deplored what they perceive as the peril of creeping totalitarianism in Western states and have striven to shorten these Stalinist shadows. Here is not the place to make a judgement on this issue. The purpose is rather to record the fact that through the state control of education, welfare state provision and nationalisa-tion – not to mention the computerisation of a wealth of data about its citizens – even in so-called free societies, the state's influence on its citizens is far greater today than it was a century ago.

If the sovereign state is still such a powerful political institution, it can surely be argued with some cogency that the idea of world citizenship has little hope of effective realisation. It is the state that continues to provide welfare and protection for its citizens. It is the state that continues successfully to demand loyalty and duties from its citizens. Neither incentives nor oppor-tunities are therefore effectively available to the citizen to seek a higher political relationship. Moreover, insofar as such insubstantial dreams may be entertained, they are misbegotten. For even if the sovereign state were moribund, would we not be wise to mourn rather than rejoice in its passing? Has it not been one of the most significant and useful political inventions of mankind? Let those who sneer at the defects of the modern state consider what other choices are available. There are basically four. One is the dissolu-tion of, particularly, large and medium states into smaller units. But these tiny entities could still consider themselves sovereign and behave in the same way as large nation-states. There are many so-called micro-states in the world already. The opposite process could be amalgamation into regional blocs. But these could well turn out to be magnified sovereign states, as Orwell warned in *Nineteen Eighty-Four*. These options would be changes without a difference. Confederal or Community arrangements, as in Switzerland and the EEC respectively, perhaps have the potential to be truly different. In practice, how-ever, such arrangements tend to polarise to create or preserve sovereign behaviour. Since the *Sonderbund* war of 1847 the Swiss cantons have had no real opportunity or desire to exercise any thorough independence from Berne. And there has been much foot-dragging to retard the federal implications of the Single European Act within the Common Market, not least in Britain. In both cases attempts to undermine the sovereign state – the one by fission, the other by fusion – proved extraordinarily feeble. The fourth option is world government. We need to consider the objections to world government in rather more detail. For, accepting that citizenship is a relationship between the individual and the state, then there is a powerful case against world citizenship if a world state can be shown to be undesirable and/or imprac-ticable. The citizen of a state exercises his citizenship within a clearly defined framework of standards of moral behaviour, codes of law and political institu-tions. But on a global scale it is evident that codes of morality differ as between cultures; international law concerns primarily the relations between states as legal entities, not individuals; and world government does not exist. Cosmopolitan theories have consequently been of necessity extremely vague, with appeals to reason and conscience to discern certain desirable laws of human conduct and to abide by them. But since those so-called laws are neither codified nor supported by the coercive power of a world government, it is exceptionally difficult for the individual to learn and sustain a pattern of 'civic' behaviour in defence to them. Moreover, if, as was shown above, a crucial feature of citizenship is participation, then political institutions in which to participate must exist. It follows that world citizenship cannot exist because such world political institutions are lacking. Now if the proponent of world citizenship concedes these arguments, he often shifts to the position of asserting that the world citizen is he who works for the creation of a world government, in which he recognises we are so sadly deficient.

However, the practical obstacles to both the creation of a world state and to its subsequent administration are assuredly insuperable. Hypothetically a world state could be created in three possible ways. One is by some kind of spontaneous generation. It is envisaged that by the exercise of the collective will of governments and peoples, mankind declares, 'Let there be a world state'. Short of an imminent threat of extraterrestrial invasion, such a scenario can hardly be taken seriously. It belongs to the realm of utopian and science fiction writers. The second hypothetical way of achieving world union is by stealth: that is, by the gradual accretion to a core of states committed to the ideal of others increasingly disillusioned with the perilous disadvantages of a fragmented world. Perhaps. Nevertheless, neither a broad view of history nor an analysis of the contemporary scene suggests that this method is at all plausible. The pattern of world political history as interpreted by some 'world statists', as a gradual, if uneven, evolution from city-state through nation-state to empire, culminating in a truly ecumenical polity, is utterly fallacious. The sizes of states have waxed and waned throughout history. True, numerous cases may be cited of groups of states voluntarily submitting to an overarching authority. Examples may be gleaned from the original Greek amphyctionic league of the seventh century BC to the European Community today. However, they have all had three features in common, namely, restricted geographical area, cultural homogeneity and a jealous retention of a generous measure of individual state autonomy. This insistence by already established states, of whatever size, of retaining considerable independent control over their own affairs has also of course seriously hobbled the potentially truly universal institutions, the League of Nations and the United Nations. If anything, the expansion in membership of the UN has so diversified the range of interests represented as to reduce rather than increase its effectiveness as a world authority over the years. Currently the best example of the process of accretion is the European Community, which has doubled the number of its member-states since its establishment. But can anyone seriously imagine it attracting to its membership the USA, USSR, China and Japan, for example? And other attempts at regional integration, such as the Arab League and the Organisation of African Unity have failed to achieve any effective collaboration even within themselves. And so we come to the third method: conquest. This is admittedly the least difficult to imagine. Alexander, the Romans, Napoleon and Hitler all made passable attempts at creating quasi-universal states by force of arms. Insofar as weapons- and transport-systems inhibited the ancient empires from further geographical expansion, these are, of course, no longer serious difficulties. The balance of power is. The bi-polar nuclear balance of fear between the United States and the Soviet Union can indeed be partially explained by the concern of each that the other would in fact take over the world, if not thus held in check. Moreover, the speedy growth of China to become a third super-power suggests that world conquest by an overwhelmingly powerful state is unlikely in the foreseeable future.

Yet even if, by some concatenation of events, however unlikely, a world government were to be instituted, could it remain in being? The chances seem slim. In both technical and psychological terms the centrifugal forces would surely be so much more powerful than the centripetal. The task of administrating such a vast political unit would be daunting if not impossible. Nevertheless, unity would have to be imposed by effective administration since a sense of global community would be unlikely to burgeon automatically among the diverse peoples of the planet (pp. 182–186).

If both history and the current condition of the world alike cast grave doubts on the practicality of world citizenship becoming a reality through world government, should not the ideal be kept alive as a desirable, if remote objective? The opponents of world citizenship continue to give a negative reply on the grounds that world government is in any case wholly undesirable. The very act of creation, if by military conquest, is horrific to contemplate in a nuclear age. The result would be a global hell rather than a world state. And even if mankind did survive and an ecumenical political structure were erected, the dangers posed by such a world government would be potentially awesome; its advantages, highly dubious. Government means power. World government, however federally conceived, means the centralisation of ultimate power. How would that power be used? There is no reason to suggest that the experience of mankind in the use of state power would not be repeated at the global level. And history has more than enough examples of the corrupting influence and malign use of political power. Could not a world dictator lust for power and seek tyrannically to extirpate the last remnant of local political, religious or cultural autonomy? After all, a world government would mean little if it did not enjoy a monopoly of military strength, command over which would provide splendid opportunities for the seizure of political power by a would-be global Bonaparte. By definition a world dictator could not seek to *extend* his imperium, unless he coveted the planets of course. None the less he could well seek to sate this lust by *intensifying* his power. A global Big Brother is an awful prospect. Orwell's models, Hitler and Stalin, were horrific enough; but at least there were several other regions of the earth during their lifetimes which enjoyed humane régimes. Such havens of sanity and hope would not exist under a world government. Or if they did, the attempts by the central government to quell them would lead to global civil war. So much for the preservation of the happiness, freedom and dignity of the individual human being!

It may be argued, of course, that such a dismal scenario is unlikely, that checks and balances would be built into a world constitution. But even if the emergence of a world dictator is accepted as improbable, there would still be no guarantee that such a government would not be dominated by the rich and privileged regions of the world. Despite the Marxist belief in the international solidarity of the proletariat and the coming of a world revolution, adherents of the doctrine have been suspicious, and perhaps justly so, of the motives of the proponents of cosmopolitanism. Already in 1849, as we have seen (p. 172), Engels worried about this problem, warning that any scheme of international federalism would be a bourgeois fraud if it was put into effect before the proletarian revolution. At the height of the Cold War these suspicions were voiced in the Soviet Union in almost hysterical fear of American expansionism and defence of Russian culture. A definition of cosmopolitanism in a 1952 philosophical dictionary, for example, stated that the idea

. . . is being cultivated by American imperialists who are striving at world-hegemony. It aims at inducing peoples to renounce their struggle for national independence and sovereignty and set up a 'world government' which will be at the service of imperialism.[35]

Two years later the Secretary-General of the Congress of Soviet Writers described cosmopolitanism as 'the repulsive ideology of the war-mongers'. More recently, such a message has found a resonance in the fears of neo-colonialism among the poorer nations of the Third World. For instance, the Indian scholar, Rajni Kothari, has written scornfully of

. . . the hollow sounds of comfortable, angry men from the Northern hemisphere, hopping from one continent to another in a bid to transform the whole world — the latest edition of the white man's burden.[36]

Arguments in favour of world citizenship

Is the sovereign state so immutable? Is its persistence so desirable? And does the idea of a political world citizenship really depend upon a world state wielding an absoluteness of sovereignty torn from the nation-state? There are compelling arguments for answering all these questions negatively. Even if the state retains considerable signs of vigour, there is nevertheless no reason to think it immortal. Already at the beginning of the century, as we have see (p. 141) scholars were remarking on the obsolescence of the state. Given the multiplication of matters which the state cannot cope with because of their transnational or global extent, how much more of an anachronism is the state today? Now if the sovereign state is anachronistic, so also therefore is the idea of exclusive loyalty to it. Any notional social contract the citizen may be thought implicitly to have with the state may be seen to have loopholes if the state does not completely adhere to the commitments in its side of the deal. Furthermore, even on utilitarian grounds of sheer self-interest, the case for a sense of citizenship stretching out well beyond the confines of the state now appears extraordinarily compelling. This perspective has been dramatically presented by Barbara Ward in the context of the huge gulf between the affluent minority and the poverty-stricken masses of the world:

Given the openness of planetary communications, the established contacts between extremists on a world-wide basis, the proven impatience and violence of potential despair, it may be that if the underpinning of greater solidarity is not found through compassion and responsibility, we cannot rule out more cataclysmic possibilities.[37]

Whether the modern state is truly losing its grip on the sovereign exercise of power and authority, which it has enjoyed for some centuries in Europe, is a matter of hot dispute among political scientists. Nevertheless, a cogent case can be made for such a loss of power and authority on a number of grounds. One may discern four elements. The first is the twin concept of transnationalism and functionalism. The second is the phenomenon of the interdependence of states. Thirdly, one may argue the uselessness of the sovereign right to wage war in a nuclear age. Finally, all these arguments render the concept of sovereignty in a nationalistic sense dangerously outmoded. Where the theory of sovereignty provides a very simple picture of the world divided 'vertically' into states, the alternative functionalist theory emphasises the significance also of 'horizontal' divisions. These divisions operate across national boundaries by virtue of the existence of interest groups and organisations for whom the state is at best an irrelevance and at worst an encumbrance to their activities. The international system is not, in this view, a collection of billiard balls but an intricate cobweb of interconnecting interests and functional bodies. Commerce provides obvious exemplification of this theory. Clearly trade has been pursued for centuries often with little reference to the presence in the world of separate political entities. Multinational companies like Exxon and IBM are prominent today. Yet they are by no means novel phenomena, witness the operations of the East India Companies and the Hanseatic League in past centuries. What is new is the extraordinarily large number of transnational companies and administrative and professional bodies which currently operate and affect so many individuals' lives. World-wide services are provided by bodies like the World Meteorological Organisation and other Specialised Agencies of the UN. And increasingly people in different countries meet and communicate in pursuit of their shared profession, sport, artistic activity or even hobby. It may be argued that most if not all of these multifarious bodies are non-political in nature and consequently neither subtract from the sovereignty of the state nor detract from the citizen's loyalty to the state.

Yet the potential of these transnational and functional trends for undermining the exclusive citizen-state relationship must surely be recognised as considerable. In the first place, much transnational activity is economic, an area of activity inextricably linked with the strength of a state in political terms. Secondly, many functions performed by the state in the heyday of sovereignty are no longer under its exclusive control. Even the exchange-rates of the currencies of nations in the capitalist system are at the mercy of the levels of confidence exuded in the money markets of London, New York and Tokyo. These fluctuations, or even merely fears of fluctuations, can affect the fiscal policies of the governments of so-called sovereign states many thousands of miles away. Thirdly, on some occasions transnational bodies are able to exert leverage on governments, either directly or indirectly. International terrorist groups provide the most dramatic examples of such power. But of course the steep increases in oil prices in the 1970s arranged by OPEC have had the most far-reaching effects. As a result, many poor states had no option but to slow down their industrialisation programmes and/or to contract cripplingly burdensome loans. Individuals are affected by these trends, particularly insofar as any given state is powerless to insulate its citizens from the actions of transnational agents. What price the status of citizenship for the victim of terrorist assassination or kidnapping when his state is impotent to protect or liberate him?

Other actors on the world stage are thus performing functions which might otherwise be thought to belong to the state and which in other ages have. At the same time, individual states are finding that they are dependent on others for certain crucial activities. This is the second element in the argument against sovereignty. For example, in Europe, the cradle of the sovereign state, two sets of defence and economic organisations bind the states of each of the two halves of the continent interdependently together. In the West, the very existence of NATO and the EEC makes a nonsense of any claims to absolute sovereignty on the part of their members. The same is true of the Warsaw Pact and Comecon in the East. And if the modern state can no longer exercise total independent control even of its economy and defence, precious little remains of its vaunted claim to sovereignty. Moreover, from the point of view of the individual citizen, he must recognise that his welfare and life are no longer solely guaranteed by the state, but are dependent on the contributions of other states and institutions in the systems of which his own state is but a part.

As an illustration of the circumscription of state sovereignty in the modern world, let us look at the case of Britain. In currency and economic affairs many a government's room for manoeuvre is constrained by membership of such international and supranational bodies as GATT and the Common Market and by the operations of multinational businesses and transnational currency speculators. Indeed, these last-named have so reduced Britain's control over its 'own' sterling that Harold Wilson when prime minister denounced them in his impotent frustration as 'the little gnomes of Zurich'. In defence matters most of Britain's forces are integrated into NATO commands. It may be argued that Britain voluntarily entered into such relationship as the EEC and NATO by the exercise of its free sovereign will, and by the same token could extricate itself from them if so desired. In practice, however, most commentators agree that such a hypothetical possibility would prove in some cases to be virtually literally impossible and in others extremely damaging to the national interest.

It may appear therefore that British governments are outmoded and hypocritical when they occasionally struggle to assert what remnants are left of the nation's sovereignty. Thus Britain delayed membership of the European Community and still does not participate in the European Monetary System. She has refused to sign the UNCLOS III treaty (United Nations Conference on the Law of the Sea: among other provisions this attempted to place mining of the deep sea bed under international supervision). And most dramatically in her conflict with Argentina over the Falklands Islands Britain hesitated about conceding absolute sovereignty before the 1982 war and has since determinedly refused to negotiate with a view to modifying the islands' status in that respect. Some commentators view these examples as Britain properly standing by her legal sovereign rights. Some politicians, most notably Mrs Thatcher, have believed also that the attitudes thus adopted are morally highly principled. Others believe that the constant harping on sovereignty by Britain (and other states, it is true) on such issues retards and inhibits co-operation and heightens tension in a world that is desperately needful of the former and endangered by the latter.

The third and fourth elements in the case against sovereignty are arguments which show the idea not only to be shabbily outmoded but positively dangerous. One is the traditional relationship between sovereignty and war. Defence of sovereignty has been continually used as a justification for war. Perhaps therefore the retention of the principle has become unacceptably dangerous as the effects of war have become increasingly horrific, especially with the proliferation of nuclear weapons. The right to be incinerated in defence of one's sovereignty is scarcely an attractive justification of the principle. The related objection dates back to the age of the French Revolution when the concepts of sovereignty and nationality became fused. With the rejection of monarchical government sovereignty was transferred from the king to the people. But, further, the people were defined as the nation; and the will of the sovereign nation was asserted to be absolute. The Declaration of the Rights of Man and the Citizen pronounced that 'The principle of all sovereignty rests essentially in the nation'; while Sieyes, the theoretician of the Revolution, asserted that, 'The Nation exists before all things and is the origin of all. Its will is always legal, it is the law itself.'[38] Even God, to whom at least most monarchs were considered answerable, was evicted from any role as moral monitor. As a result, sovereignty came to be regarded as both absolute and untrammelled by any political or moral constraints and identified with nationality. The concept of national sovereignty smothered the burgeoning cosmopolitanism of the Enlightenment. The simultaneous emergence of the ideas of popular sovereignty and of nationalism was an historical accident. They became the Siamese twins of modern political ideology, accepted as the natural political order throughout the world. Yet the concept of popular sovereignty could well, on its own, have been interpreted very differently — in a universal sense. As it has turned out the sovereignty of the people has not been absolute: it has been artificially constrained by the principle of nationality. The theoretical possibility of the sovereign people to declare a global citizenship for all mankind was thus blocked by a chance coincidence of political theories. For, as indicated below (p. 323), there is nothing natural or self-evident about nationalism.

Evidence of the decline of the state as an entirely autonomous sovereign institution may clear the way for an acceptance of world citizenship as a political role. But it is evidence of a negative kind. Are the will and opportunities to hand to enable the role to be practised in any realistic sense? Four sets of indicators suggest that the idea should by no means be totally dismissed. The dream of a world government is not such a nightmare to some even hardheaded politicians. Down-to-earth Englishmen like Macmillan and Attlee urged serious consideration of the concept. Harold Macmillan, speaking as Minister of Defence, in the House of Commons on the need for nuclear disarmament, asserted:

The control must provide effective international, or if we like supranational, authority invested with real power. Hon. Members may say that this is elevating the United Nations, or whatever may be the authority, into something like world government; be it so, it is none the worse for that. In the long run this is the only way out for mankind.[39]

In more general terms Lord Attlee wrote in 1958:

An increasing number of people in many countries are realising that the only way to prevent the destruction of our civilisation is to substitute for the anarchy of States claiming complete individual sovereignty a world organisation with an authority to lay down, a court to decide, and a force to sanction a system of world law.[40]

Bevin, Gaitskell and Heath have all spoken or written in a similar vein. True, world government is a less popular ideal than it was c. 1945–60. Yet the variety and seriousness of global problems and the inability of the nation-state to cope with them are even more evident. The risk of world government may again soon appear to be less of a peril than continuing to stand aloof from its implementation in some form.

In the meantime, ordinary people are coming increasingly to behave as world citizens. If, as was suggested in the previous section, participation is the true political mark of the citizen, then there is mounting evidence that this is happening in total disregard of state frontiers. There are now many opportunities for individuals to work loyally for transnational institutions – the UN Secretariat, the World Health Organisation, the World Bank, the International Civil Aviation Organisation, for instance. What the UN in its pi of alphabet nomenclature calls NGOs (Non-Governmental Organisations) exist in their hundreds. People employed by these bodies are pledged to work in the interests of what is at least an embryonic global community, not the states of which they are national citizens. Collectively they form a rudimentary cosmopolitan civil service.

Much wider oppotunities are available in our third trend, that is, participation in pressure groups with global objectives. The multiplication of grass-roots and interest-group organisations devoted to an amelioration of the world's condition has been a most remarkable recent phenomenon. Because it has been both widespread and spontaneous, it has also been extraordinarily complex. These organisations providing for world citizenship action may be divided in a simplified manner into six clusters on the basis of whether their membership is local/national or global; whether they operate by pressure that is persuasive/humanitarian or provocative/hostile; and whether their actions are focussed on/mediated through national governments or are designed to have a *direct* impact on a global problem. The distinctions may best be presented in tabular form:

	Persuasive/humanitarian	Provocative/hostile
Local/national via governments		
Global via governments		
Local/national direct		
Global direct		

Three small footnotes to this table. First, those movements which do not have international membership are sometimes said to work on the principle of 'Think globally, act locally'. None the less, and this is the second point, organisations of international scope often operate by pin-pointing specific local issues which illuminate their general concern. Thirdly, since resistance to global ameliorative actions can only effectively be made by states, it is possible to contemplate provocative/hostile action only when attempting to operate via governments, not when tackling an issue directly and where nation-states have no individual axes to grind.

This attempted classification may be clarified by an example of each. A number of countries have Green Parties, which pursue their policies through their parliamentary systems. Most successful in terms of seats gained and keeping environmental issues in high profile, at both *Land* and federal levels, has been the West German Green Party. Activities of a more provocative style, on the very edge of legality, have been conspicuously undertaken by anti-nuclear weapons groups. These have included most famously the British women at Greenham Common, protesting at US cruise missiles, and the American Ground Zero group in Washington State, protesting at the Trident submarine system. The latter have suffered imprisonment for their obstructionist tactics but have nevertheless won important supporters, including the Archbishop of Seattle. Perhaps the most distinguished body working in a persuasive, humanitarian style transnationally is Amnesty International. Started in a small way in 1961 by Peter Benenson, a Catholic lawyer of Jewish Anglo-Russian descent, AI can now boast workers in most states. Through its unremitting endeavours to free prisoners of conscience, it is a constant reminder of the precious value of human rights. More militant on an international plane is the environmental body, Greenpeace. Fearless in their attempts to prevent French nuclear testing in the South Pacific, the organisation became involved in a most sensational incident in 1985: their vessel, the *Rainbow Warrior*, was blown up by French secret agents while in a New Zealand harbour.

Nation-states do not often take such drastic action to protect what they conceive as their national interest against the operations of pressure groups. And when it comes to work of a charitable nature, the nation-state system is happy to have its efforts supplemented by the direct involvement of voluntary bodies. The people of the least developed countries, especially in times of calamities like widespread flooding or famine, have good cause to be grateful for the financial, material and human assistance afforded by a variety of organisations. In these categories are national groups like Oxfam based in Britain and *Médecins sans frontières* in France; international organs like the Red Cross, and fund- and consciousness-raising activities such as Bob Geldof's. The dedication of this Irish pop-singer in the mid-1980s raised $120 million to ease poverty and famine in Africa.

In one way or another millions of people have been involved over the past generation in one or more of these manifold organisations and have thus acted in however small a way as world citizens. All interests are catered for. The scientists concerned about nuclear weapons have their Pugwash movement. Even politicians, so often nationally-minded, have Parliamentarians for World Order, who seek 'to promote the cause of world peace through enforceable world law for the peoples of the world as a single community, through parliamentary action.'[41] However, although this plethora of organisations has in common the mobilisation of public opinion and effort to create a more unified, peaceful and just world, there is little else that conjoins them. Some have very practicable, immediate objectives; others are more ambitious, long-term, even utopian. Some are world-wide in their membership and activities; others, national, even local. Some focus on very precise issues; others, on big, all-embracing themes. The American Richard Falk wrote in 1987,

The organisational vehicles of citizen/pilgrims [i.e. world citizens] are generally not yet connected, in visible and familiar patterns, except by way of convergent lines of macro-historical interpretation . . . . It is quite striking, for instance, that communities of nuclear resisters that have taken shape in the main cities of the United States during the last decade are often out of contact with one another despite their shared agendas and similar tactics.[42]

The difficulty surrounding more effective progress lies perhaps in the orthodoxy of thinking of the frustrated prospective world citizens. Working conventionally means working in isolation. Commentators like Marilyn Ferguson, whose *The Aquarian Conspiracy* has been so influential, have argued that mankind is on the threshold of radically new insights about how life, the world and the universe are to be understood. In politics, she has suggested, the network is becoming the tool for replacing worn-out institutions. The basic idea is that people with a common interest and concern should form a group for mutual self-help, exchange of information and experiences and social action. The concept is germane to world citizenship because no geographical frontiers in principle prevent transnational membership, especially in this age of easy and rapid communication. Furthermore, the very system involves overlapping and connections between the groups. The idea originated in England at the turn of the century with the prediction by Edward Carpenter that such a system would revolutionise the world:

Networks of individuals would slowly form; widening circles would meet, overlap and finally close around a new centre for humankind . . .
This ultimate connection would be like the linked fibres and nerves of a body, lying within the outer body of society. The networks would move towards that elusive dream, 'the finished, free society.'[43]

By the mid-1970s the practice of networking in and outward from the USA was involving thousands of groups. This mode of participation seemed both necessary and practical. It is necessary because, in the words of Marshall McLuhan, 'There are no passengers on Spaceship Earth. Everybody's crew.'[44] Networking is practical because the system is eminently flexible, responsive to felt needs and immune to bureaucratic arthritis. On the other hand, from the perspective of the late 1980s the momentum of the early enthusiasm seems not to have been sustained.

Education for world citizenship: for and against

Some educationists believe that networking is so potentially beneficial that teachers should actively promote the practice. Those who adopt this view do so because they consider teaching facts, even when undertaken with the partial objective of shaping attitudes, is a responsibility only half discharged. In educating for citizenship, including world citizenship, the ultimate goal must be to nurture in young people the will and equip them with the tools for action. What are the skills needed by young people for this purpose? Clearly as a first step they need knowledge and powers of judgement in order to decide what action is desirable and practicable. The matters discussed in the above pages need to be taught at the appropriate level. They also need information, particularly related to participatory activities. They should know which public figures (such as elected representatives) can be usefully approached, what pressure groups exist, what work is undertaken by charitable organisations. The practical skills which can be developed by careful teaching are the persuasive and the organisational. The former include the lucid marshalling of evidence and argument, both orally and in writing. Simulation and gaming have proved useful methods here, and have the additional advantage of training in empathy: action is so much better undertaken in the light of an appreciation of the feelings of others. Organisational skills relate to participation in or the founding of a pressure group. All these skills can be practised initially in the classroom; then by projects outside the school.

Ideally, pupils should be given the opportunity to work to some social purpose in a country different from their own. This, of course, can rarely be arranged. Most activities are necessarily locally based with the objective of having some effect beyond the pupil's own nation. This distinction between direct and what one might term telekinetic impact may be simply illustrated from two schools in England. One, in Milton Keynes, has actually sent pupils to Tanzania to work alongside their peers. Pupils in the other, in Leicestershire, refurbished old tools to send to Tanzania. True, these examples are not overtly political. More apposite would be joining a youth branch of Amnesty International or writing to the local member of parliament so that he should reveal his position on a particular global issue.

The number of schools engaged in even community-based activities designed to provide young people with experience as political world citizens is very limited. There are a number of reasons for this. Teacher training, until recently and in many institutions still, has not prepared the profession for this style of teaching. Furthermore, syllabuses and school organisation are often too inflexible to accommodate such active modes of learning. In addition to these practical obstacles, there are hostile intellectual and professional arguments. Some opponents have insisted that to expect of school pupils an understanding of other cultures or the big contemporary world issues is naïve. In the one case, the beliefs and life-styles are too remote; in the other, the problems are too complex. And encouragement to action on the foundation of faulty understanding is irresponsible: young people will come to accept that they can protest whenever it takes their fancy, irrespective of the superficiality of their grasp of the issues at stake. A little learning, as Pope warned, is a dangerous thing because 'shallow draughts intoxicate the brain'.[45] It is particularly dangerous when, inebriated by ill-considered enthusiasm, young people demand inappropriate action – and, what is more, carry this frame of mind into adult citizenhood.

Even more basic is the opposition deriving from the conviction that schools have no business teaching political skills at all, and least of all, those related to global issues. This criticism has two prongs. One is the argument that the purpose of schooling is to teach a core of intellectual skills — the 3Rs and the disciplines built upon them — and to provide some vocational training. Educating young people to be actively participant world citizens is a diversion of the precious resources of time and pedagogical expertise from the proper job in hand. Furthermore, behind this objection lies a denial of the validity of teachers' motives. In arguing his case for the teaching of English History, Sir Geoffrey Elton, lately Regius Professor at Cambridge, wrote:

I find the frequent attacks on English history . . . hard to understand; or rather, I should find them hard to understand if I thought that the attackers were pursuing intellectual ends rather than political and social ends — were concerned to train reasoning intelligences rather than produce supposedly desirable beings — [e.g.] worthy citizens of the world . . ..[46]

The pedagogical call to participation, the dissatisfaction with knowledge as sterile if it leads to no action, has too a suspect ideological ring to it. For the cautious and conservative it is uncomfortably close to the Marxist concept of praxis: the purpose of theory is action; effective action must be underpinned by theory. Teachers who train their pupils for political action must consequently be suspected of being destablising influences.

The matter of social education for the twenty-first century, runs the counter-argument, is far too pressing to be constrained by these out-dated sensitivities. Whether we like it or not, young people in many countries are aware of the wider world — through parents, radio, television and films. The days of sitting pupils in serried rows of iron-bound desks to learn off lists of capes and bays as an introduction to the planet they inhabit are, or should be, gone. To put the matter negatively, what is the reaction of pupils likely to be if they are not introduced to realistic activities? There is plenty of evidence that young people feel a paralysing helplessness coloured by doom-laden fear when contemplating the world. For example, in reporting a study undertaken in Berlin about children's and adolescents' fear of nuclear war, Gabriele Kandoza has commented on the pervasive atmosphere of worry among the young:

Apart from the fear of atomic war, the children are vexed by anxieties about further destruction of the environment, about hunger, unemployment, and the possible explosion of a nuclear power station.[47]

If the reaction of 'dropping out' is to be counteracted, a sense of efficacy even before these awesome problems needs to be instilled.

Passivity before problems which impinge directly upon our lives breeds fatalism and depression; and fatalism and depression are corrosive of the citizen ideal. Citizenship requires involvement. And the involvement cannot be considered freely given if it is forced artificially to halt at a national frontier. In the words of two of the most distinguished American advocates of Global Studies,

In a global age where worldwide interdependence makes itself felt in the daily lives of most human beings, it is critical that individuals learn how they might exercise some measure of control and influence over the public affairs of global society, as well as over the public affairs of their local communities and nations.[48]

However, global politics, even more so than Bismarck ever conceived at the state level, is the art of the possible. The teacher, in striving to counteract the enervating sense of powerlessness, must guard against raising excessive expectations of influence. For when the modest grain of his pupils' compassionate action is seen to weigh so lightly in the vast scales of the world's problems, they must not be dispirited and disillusioned. Realistic objectives must be set; and a consciousness of being a part, however small a part, of a growing and spreading responsiveness must be cultivated in the minds of young people. For teaching too is the art of the possible.

REFERENCES

1. J. Slater & R. A. S. Hennessey, 'Political Competence', reprinted in Crick & Porter, *Political Education and Political Literacy*, pp. 252–3.
2. Article 21.
3. Mussolini, *La Dottrina del Fascismo*, reprinted in Oakeshott, *Social and Political Doctrines of Contemporary Europe*, p. 168.
4. Quoted in Connell, *Education in the Twentieth-Century World*, p. 251.
5. Burke, *Reflections on the Revolution in France*, reprinted in F. O'Gorman, *British Conservatism* (Longman, 1986), p. 67.
6. G. B. Shaw, *The Apple Cart*, Act. I.
7. H. McGurk (ed.), *What Next?* (Economic and Social Research Council 1987), p. 50.
8. Rousseau, Letter to Malesherbes, quoted in L. J. Macfarlane, *Modern Political Theory* (Nelson, 1970), pp. 12–13.
9. D. Blunkett & B. Crick, 'The Labour Party's aims and values', *Guardian*, 1 February 1988.
10. S. Verba & N. H. Nie, *Participation in America*, quoted in M. Margolis, *Viable Democracy* (Macmillan, 1979), p. 88.
11. E. F. Schumacher speech, quoted in T. Gibson, *People Power* (Penguin, 1979), p. 9.
12. Oakeshott, *Rationalism in Politics and Other Essays*, p. 133.
13. J. D. B. Miller, *The Nature of Politics* (Penguin, 1965), p. 286.
14. R. Scruton, 'Why teach philosophy to children who can't add up?', *Daily Mail*, 3 February 1984.
15. Quoted by A. Stevens, 'War on Peace Studies', *Observer*, 27 June 1982.
16. R. Scruton *et al.*, *Education and Indoctrination* (Education Research Centre, 1985), p. 5.
17. Crick & Porter, *Political Education and Political Literacy*, p. 4.
18. O. Stevens, *Children Talking Politics* (Martin Robertson, 1982), p. 170.
19. Schools Council, *Working Paper No. 11*, reprinted in Schools Council, *The New Curriculum* (HMSO, 1967), p. 25.

20. J. Fairhall, 'Who is brainwashing whom?', *Guardian*, 29 December 1987.
21. Crick & Porter, *Political Education and Political Literacy*, p. 33.
22. G. Whitty, 'Political Education: Some Reservations', *The Social Science Teacher*, vol. 8, 1979.
23. K. Minogue, 'Can One Teach Political Literacy?', *Encounter*, quoted in A. Porter, 'Political Literacy' in Heater & Gillespie, *Political Education in Flux*, pp. 203–4.
24. C. Brown, 'Social Studies' in T. Brennan & J. Brown (eds.), *Teaching Politics: Problems and Perspectives* (BBC, 1975), p. 74.
25. Thucydides, *Peloponnesian War*, pp. 371–2.
26. K. J. Holsti, *International Politics* (Prentice-Hall, 2nd edn, 1974), p. 383.
27. W. Lippmann, *The Public Philosophy* (New American Library, 1956), pp. 23–4.
28. Quoted in A. Adamthwaite, 'Eden and the Foreign Office', *International Affairs*, vol. 64 (1988).
29. J. G. Kemeny, 'Saving American Democracy', *Technology Review* (1980), quoted in R. Dahl, *Controlling Nuclear Weapons* (Syracuse University Press, 1985), p. 98.
30. M. Reidy, 'What shall we tell our pupils?', *Times Educational Supplement*, 31 October 1980.
31. C. Cox & R. Scruton, *Peace Studies: A Critical Survey* (Institute for European Defence & Strategic Studies, 1984), p. 7.
32. Gilbert Murray, Letter 21 April 1944, Murray papers (Bodleian) box 240 fol. 157.
33. Hobbes, *Leviathan*, Introduction, p. 1.
34. UN Charter, Art. 2.1.
35. Quoted in R. N. Carew-Hunt, *A Guide to Communist Jargon* (Bles, 1957), p. 37.
36. R. Kothari, *Footsteps into the Future*, quoted in H. Bull, *The Anarchical Society* (Macmillan, 1977), p. 304.
37. B. Ward, *Progress for a Small Planet* (Penguin, 1979), p. 170.
38. Quoted in A. Cobban, *A History of Modern France*, vol. 1 (Penguin, 1957), p. 161.
39. Quoted in B. Russell, *Has Man a Future?* (Penguin, 1961), pp. 72–3.
40. Quoted in H. Usborne, *Prescription for Peace* ('Minifed' Promotion Group, 1985), p. 85.
41. *Parliamentarians for World Order*, leaflet (n.d., but 1982?).
42. R. A. Falk, 'The State System and Contemporary Social Movements' in S. H. Mendlovitz & R. B. J. Walker (eds.), *Towards a Just World Peace* (Butterworths, 1987), p. 38.
43. M. Ferguson, *The Aquarian Conspiracy* (Granada, 1982), p. 49.
44. Quoted ibid., p. 205.
45. Pope, *Essay on Criticism*, l. 217.
46. G. R. Elton, *The Practice of History* (Collins, 1967), p. 198.
47. G. Kandzora, 'Peace Education between Repression and Capability of Acting', *Research Committee on Political Education Bulletin*, November 1986.
48. L. Anderson & J. Becker, 'Education for Involvement,' *The New Era*, vol. 58. (1977).

CHAPTER SEVEN

The Status of Citizenship

7.1 CIVIL AND LEGAL DEFINITIONS

CITIZENSHIP is a relationship between an individual and a state involving the individual's full political membership in the state and his permanent allegiance to it . . . . the status of citizen is official recognition of the individual's integration into the political system.

Murray Clark Havens[1]

Equality of status

Citizenship has a tendency to mutate from being an agent of segregation to an agent of association. Within the state, it began as a means of differentiating between inhabitants; it is now a means of equalising their status. Internationally, citizenship has become a device for distinguishing the members of one nation-state from another; world citizenship could become a device for recognising the homogeneity of mankind. The education of young people for their social and political functions has reflected these trends. Initially civic education was a privilege reserved for an élite. Then the reality of second-class citizenship was mirrored by the differential civic messages in the school systems. Now education for citizenship is widely recognised as a necessary facet of the schooling of the mass. Gradually, also, teachers are bringing their students to an understanding of their status as budding world citizens.

Citizenship has many meanings. But the notions of political participation, of social and welfare rights, of communal identity and civic responsibility could not have grown so luxuriantly without the sturdy root of a clearly defined civil and legal status, which each state has laid down and adapted to changing pressures and circumstances. Yet even the fundamental concept of citizenship as a legal status has itself become very complex and today carries with it many unresolved questions, not least in the United Kingdom. As a consequence, it may be confidently argued, no citizen is likely properly to appreciate the nature of his role if his education has lacked this element.

The civil and legal condition of citizenship is indistinguishable from the

246

rights which that status defines. Indeed, the great American Chief Justice Earl Warren declared,

Citizenship *is* man's basic right for it is nothing less than the right to have rights. Remove this priceless possession and there remains a stateless person, disgraced and degraded in the eyes of his countrymen.[2]

A citizen is someone who possesses rights which are denied in a legally stratified or segmented society to non-citizens and in all societies to resident aliens and foreigners. Moreover, at least in theory or as an ideal, civil rights are equally conferred upon and enjoyed by all who bear the status of citizen. This objective is succinctly propounded by the philosopher Rawls.

The position of equal citizenship is defined by the rights and liberties required by the principle of equal liberty and the principle of fair equality of opportunity. When the two principles are satisfied, all are equal citizens, and so everyone holds this position.[3]

By extension, a step towards effective world citizenship rights could be made if Rawls' principles were universally applied by serious acceptance and implementation of the International Bill of Rights (i.e. the Declaration and two Covenants). A full world citizenship would, however, require the rights to be accessible regardless of state frontiers. The necessary abolition of migration controls could, however, have unacceptable destabilising effects.

Let it not be thought that the waving of a magic legislative wand to ensure the application of the Rawlsian principles, either nationally or globally, would inaugurate a utopia. Rights may have to be enunciated and protected; they must also be exercised with responsibility. It may be that the moral quality of citizenship as discussed in Chapter 6 is a sufficient guarantee of such behaviour. However, it may also be the case that the duties of citizenship as well as the rights need to be more fully defined than is currently the general practice. The second reason to pause is that the sudden blanket application of civil rights may cause tension in a society unused to such egalitarian practices. The problem is caricatured in the following, apocryphal, anecdote from the French Revolution. An agent of the Committee of Public Safety challenged a certain nobleman. 'What is your name?' he asked. 'The Marquis de Saint-Ange,' replied the nobleman. 'That cannot be,' declared the revolutionary, 'for we have abolished the Christian Church and all titles of nobility: there are no more Saints or Angels; and no more Marquises − all are citizens now.' 'In that case,' responded the *ci-devant* nobleman resignedly, 'register me as *"Citoyen Personne"* (Citizen Nobody)!'

Citizenship as legal status

In practice most states have defined and extended the civil rights of citizens by a combination of specific enactment and gradual implementation. Political turning-points from the Athenian crisis of c.600 BC to the achievement of independence by former European colonies have occasioned such codifications. Solon drafted his reforms; new Afro-Asian states have drawn up constitutions, many with bills of rights. The British experience has been unusual. For centuries the English were a by-word for the freedoms and justice they enjoyed. Magna Carta, the Habeas Corpus Act and the Bill of Rights preceded any comparable enactments in other states. Furthermore, English common law, antipathetic to the concept of the concentration of power, retained its strength. Whereas on the continent the sixteenth century witnessed the 'reception' of Roman civil law as an undergirding of absolutist monarchical sovereignty, England by and large successfully resisted such encroachments. And the failure of Philip II's 'Enterprise of England' in 1588 together with the 'Glorious Revolution' a century later ensured that England was not forcibly absorbed into the dominantly continental system. Yet the very specificity of the English style of case-law has hindered the promulgation of any generalised statement such as a bill of citizens' rights. The lack of any real revolutionary trauma in the country's history has also had the same effect.

The evolutionary character of the British state has led to the retention of the doctrine of the sovereignty of the Crown-in-Parliament. This derived in essence from the 1688 Revolution and contrasts significantly with the doctrine of the sovereignty of the people in those states whose constitutional theory is based on the revolutions which broke out a century or so later. The British tradition has had a restraining effect on the development of a clear concept of state citizenship. There are two basic problems. In the first place, the rights and will of the body of British citizens can, hypothetically, be ignored or overturned by Parliament. For, in the classic prescription of Dicey, Parliament has 'the right to make or unmake any law whatever.'[4] Secondly, the continued incorporation of the Crown in the theory of sovereignty raises complications. As a consequence, British nationals retain the status, obsolete in most other states, of subjects of the monarch – a station of subordination rather than equality; a relationship with a person, not an abstraction (like the state). Moreover, the monarchy, by virtue of its visibly privileged position at the apex both of society and of the 'dignified' part of the Constitution, can be interpreted as sustaining a hierarchical type of society inimical to a fully-fledged style of citizenship.

Even so, recent governments have been forced to try to define British citizenship in a basic legal sense. This action has been prompted by the felt need to stem immigration from former colonial territories, not by any regard for the protection of rights as has been the normal motive in other states. It is indeed becoming increasingly doubtful whether the tradition of civil liberties and the defences of the common law remain sufficient protections for citizens' rights in the United Kingdom at the turn of the twentieth century. There is, however, little point in codifying citizens' rights and providing more effective institutional safeguards if the bulk of the body of citizenry remain in ignorance of those rights and bereft of the skills for bringing those safeguards into play. Education must complement legislation. More, education concerning the civil nature of citizenship should be a civil right in itself. The negative 'ignorance of the law is no excuse' should be substituted by 'knowledge of the law is a civil right'.

In any examination of legal and civil citizenship the first problem is to understand how the status is defined and acquired and to ask whether one is satisfied with the current position. Two basic conventions must be distinguished: *ius sanguinis* and *ius soli*, citizenship by parentage or by place of birth. Aristotle provided the classic description of Greek convention:

For practical purposes, it is usual to define a citizen as 'one born of citizen parents on both sides' . . . .; but sometimes this requirement is carried still further back, to the length of two, three, or more stages of ancestry.[5]

Most European states base their law of nationality today on the principle of *ius sanguinis*; whereas most states of the American continents follow the *ius soli* rule. Citizenship may also be conferred by naturalisation. The great volume of both voluntary immigrants and refugees during the course of the last century or so has forced states to define their criteria for naturalisation, both in terms of qualifications and numbers. For example, within six years of the erection of the Statue of Liberty with her welcoming torch on Bedloe's Island, an immigration station was established on neighbouring Ellis Island to filter out 'undesirable' would-be American citizens. Current South African law must be mentioned for its sheer novelty. After five years' residence an individual has South African citizenship imposed upon him, whether he wishes it or not! This is a device for increasing the white manpower available for military service and thus adds a new twist to the old equation of citizenship with the bearing of arms. Applications for naturalisation are sometimes couched in the form of a desire to become a 'national' of a given state. Indeed, the terms 'nationality' and 'citizenship' are often currently used interchangeably. For example, on the descriptive page of a British passport one finds the entry: 'National status/nationalité: British Citizen'. Yet they are not strictly synonymous even in these days of egalitarian enfranchisement and ubiquitous nation-states. For instance, only an individual has citizenship; a corporation can have nationality. A minor or a convicted criminal have defined nationality without being citizens in any effective sense of the term.

What is the current situation in Britain? The naturalisation regulations are comparable with those of many other states – for example, a period of residence, good character, a simple language test, payment of a fee; though the Home Secretary has wide powers of discretion. It is the constant shifting of position in the various immigration and nationality acts from 1948 to 1981 that has caused concern (p. 104). There have been two main worries. One has been the belief that legislation in the mid-to-late 1960s sacrificed the civil rights of some potential immigrants with valid claims to British citizenship to the pragmatic fears of racial prejudice. Secondly, the 1981 act breached the age-old principle of *ius soli*, which had formerly been a fundamental tenet of English common law on the matter. Henceforth, children born in Britain and knowing no other country have for the first time been denied British nationality. And yet there remains the peculiar anomaly whereby nationals of the Irish Republic have the right of quasi-British political citizenship to vote in elections in the UK if resident there.

Precise definitions are crucial in our present age, in which the state has such all-embracing functions. A person who lacks citizenship status is doomed to exist in the uncertainty of a Dantesque limbo. A person who cannot be categorised as belonging to any state is an awkward anomaly. It afflicts a few accident-prone individuals like Spike Milligan, who, by chance of birth and domicile, slip through the interstices of international law. Much more serious is the condition of refugees. By the current UN-defined principle of non-refoulement, people who have fled in genuine fear of their safety may not be repatriated against their will. But unless and until they can be accepted as citizens of their country of asylum, they are civic non-persons. In the 1980s, for example, many thousands of Vietnamese boat-people sailed the south-east Asian seas seeking sanctuary, some suffering the purgatory of their unwholesome vessels, others a similar suffering when accommodated in cramped and forbidding camps in Hong Kong. Yet they represented but a tiny proportion of the many millions who at any one time in the contemporary world make up that most wretched of all 'nations' – the refugees. *De jure* loss of citizenship is the fate of far fewer and is common only in authoritarian states (p. 116). It rarely occurs in Britain, for example. Nevertheless, a British citizen who obtained that status by naturalisation is more vulnerable than one who enjoys the status by right of birth. Citizenship by naturalisation may be removed if it was obtained by fraud, if the citizen receives a prison sentence of more than a year or if he is disloyal to the monarch. This law became relevant in 1987 in the matter of unmasking former Nazis who were thought to have obtained British citizenship by falsifying their past.

Civil rights

A stateless person is at risk because he has no right to call in aid the authority and power of a state to defend him against any enemies. Protection of one's person and property against internal or external assault is, after all, the prime function of the state on behalf of its citizens. And in return the citizen must perform certain duties. Legal requirements have varied over the ages and still do as between different countries. Nevertheless, ever since the Greek city-state four basic duties have been commonly demanded: participation in the political process; involvement in the administration of the law; enrolment in military service; and the payment of taxes. The first two of these categories may, of course, also be seen as rights to be protected as well as duties to be (in some societies) enforced.

In contemporary Britain, there is no legal requirement for political participation, not even to vote. However, the replacement of domestic local rates by the community charge or poll tax has raised awkward questions about the relationship between the franchise and taxation. Some commentators have expressed the fear that the electoral register might be used for drawing up the lists of eligible poll-tax payers. The introduction of the new tax may present a temptation to citizens to disenfranchise themselves by non-completion of the register as a means of avoiding the charge. Failure to return an accurately completed electoral register form is illegal. But how seriously immoral is the arrangement of such civic invisibility depends on one's perception of the justice of the poll-tax in the first place. It may be seen as regressively unfair on the poor and part of a political attack on the autonomy of local government (p. 297). Those who hold such a view consider this means of tax-avoidance as venial and the government culpable of tempting such citizens into a renunciation of their basic political right.

The abolition of rates is the abolition of a centuries-old English system. The jury is even more venerable. The duty of the eligible to serve as jurors, the right of the accused to be tried by jury and the convention that the jury's verdict must be held to be true have been cherished as quintessential features of English justice and freedom. The abolition of property qualifications for jury service in 1974 was therefore a significant step in the broadening of citizenship. On the other hand, by the mid-1980s the wisdom of some verdicts was being questioned by a number of right-wing politicians. Most famously in the trial of Clive Ponting (p. 200), the jury, in acquitting him, were asserting rights and duties of citizenship: their own right to make an independent judgement and Ponting's duty as a citizen to alert an elected representative about what he considered the falseness of government statements to Parliament. Other verdicts of a less political nature were also thought to be questionable. Were juries therefore sometimes composed of unsuitable people? Should the lower age limit of 18 be raised? Should a property qualification be reintroduced? Or some other stringent test be applied? But if such changes were effected, they would reverse the process of the broadening of citizenship rights. Would that not be a retrograde step? And supposing that were generally thought to be desirable, if the changes were introduced for political motives, they could undermine confidence in the independence of the system and strike at the very heart of English freedom. Every since Magna Carta enshrined the right of trial 'by the lawful judgement of his peers'[6], the jury has become, in the words of the distinguished judge, Lord Devlin, 'the lamp that shows that freedom lives.'[7] As in ancient Athens, so in modern Britain, one must take care not to underestimate the precious organic relationship between the judicial duties of citizenship and the preservation of civil liberties.

Those liberties are primarily the ones which citizens are deemed to enjoy as a right in the first place against interference or oppression by the state and its agents, and secondly as a means to self-improvement. In the former category we may include the right of assembly and freedom of speech; in the latter, the right of association and to own property. What is meant by saying that an individual or a collection of individuals has rights? How are they to be discerned and justified? Is there a distinction between rights which a person enjoys as a human being and rights which he enjoys as a citizen? Furthermore, if certain rights are thought to be universally applicable, how does such an idea relate to the concept of world citizenship?

It could be argued that general civil rights (as opposed to any specific political enfranchisement) can and do exist independently of the concept or institution of citizenship. We have seen, for example, that it would be quite anachronistic to associate the citizenship idea with pre-Civil War England (except in the urban sense). And yet the Petition of Right of 1628 is a formidable catalogue of rights, mainly relating to protection against arbitrary taxation and imprisonment, conceded by medieval monarchs and which Charles I was accused of violating. And when the French Revolutionaries drew up their Declarations in 1789 and 1793, they made no evident attempt to distinguish between rights which adhered to man and those which adhered to the citizen. The rights of *man* are described as 'natural and imprescriptable.'[8] Similarly, the UN Declaration a century and a half later speaks of 'the equal and inalienable rights of all members of the human family.'[9] Insofar as the status of citizenship is relevant to the matter of rights it is perhaps only in a watchdog capacity. The reason for the publication of the 1793 Jacobin Declaration, for instance, was given as follows:

. . . in order that all citizens, being able constantly to compare the actions of the government with the end of all social institutions, should never allow themselves to be oppressed and debased by tyranny.[10]

On the other hand, perhaps there is a deeper distinction. For example, is there not a difference between the negative freedom of a man not to be unjustly imprisoned for any reason and the positive freedom of a citizen to speak and write in criticism of the law or the government? Karl Marx, that great authority on the history of the French Revolution, certainly recognised a significant distinction between the rights of man and the rights of the citizen (p. 74). The former were the realistic, selfish rights: 'The practical application of the rights of man to freedom is the right of man to private property.'[11] The civil, political rights of the citizen, such as freedom of speech, were those enjoyed in concert with fellow-citizens. But, Marx argued, whenever citizen rights conflicted with the rights of man, by threatening instability for instance, then it is the communal citizen's rights that will be abridged.

Defining the exact nature of the civil and legal rights of citizens is no mere historical or philosophical exercise. It became a practical, live issue in Britain during the 1980s for example. In 1987 Mrs Thatcher made her famous remark, 'There is no such thing as Society. There are individual men and women and there are families.' It is sometimes suggested that comments like these reveal a total denial of citizenship by the New Right. Their position is in fact more complex than that (p. 101). It might be more useful here to think of Thatcherite ideology as emphasising the French Revolutionary rights of man to property and security at the expense of the rights of the citizen to (political) liberty and resistance to oppression. The function of the state is to stand aside to allow the growth of a property-owning citizenry and to stand strong in their defence against external attack and 'the enemy within' (i.e. Socialists and trade unionists). In practice this has led to the consolidation of the wealth of the more fortunate citizens by the privatisation of state-owned industries and income-tax reductions; the strengthening of police powers *vis-à-vis* the liberties of the ordinary citizen; insistence on the preservation of state confidentiality against the citizen's right of access to political information;

and the weakening of the citizen's right to protection of employment conditions by trade unions. This agenda may well have been prudently designed to improve the prosperity and happiness of the British people. That is not the issue here, however. The question we need to address is the effect of such policies on the civil rights of citizenship.

The problem was expressed succinctly by the journalist Harold Jackson in 1985 from the perspective of a seven-year absence in the USA.

I find . . . that I have started to worry about what previously I would have thought far-fetched – that as an Englishman I stand a good chance of being deprived of my ability to go about my lawful occasions, to have my children educated, to register my vote, and to be protected against arbitrary government. These rights seem much more endangered in this country than I could have thought possible when I left – and far more than they could ever become in the United States.[12]

The very essence of the citizenship style of polity is that there should be a nice balance between the honouring of the rights of the citizen by the government and the ability of the government to wield authority over its citizen body. The policy of the Thatcher governments has been consciously to adjust that balance in favour of authority (p. 297).

Four areas of activity may be cited as revealing this trend. One was a reduction of the rights of trade unions, even the withdrawal of negotiating rights from two categories of state employees: teachers and, most completely, communications intelligence-gathering officers. Secondly, one may note the insistence on secrecy in government affairs – a deepening of a tradition which had already set Britain apart from most other liberal democracies. This revealed itself in pressure on producers of revelatory television programmes and most dramatically in the famous trials of Ponting, already mentioned, and the attempt to suppress the book *Spycatcher* written by the former secret agent, Peter Wright. For certain people, it looked as though George Theiner's aphoristic comparison between Czechoslovakia and Britain might be at risk: this editor of *Index on Censorship* was wont to say that in both countries there was freedom of expression, but only in Britain was there freedom *after* expression. Nor were the critics of the notorious blanket Section 2 of the Official Secrets Act and of the government's handling of affairs satisfied when that Act was replaced in 1989. A freedom of information act, such as exists in the USA and several Commonwealth countries, was not forthcoming. Two categories of citizens suffer restrictions on their civil rights because of this stance on secrecy. One is the individual – usually, by the very nature of the situation, a government employee – who has information which he believes it his duty as a citizen to divulge. He cannot for fear of prosecution. The second is the ordinary citizen, who is deprived of information that might well be necessary for making a judgment on public matters. For if the government's case in the Ponting and *Spycatcher* affairs was the need to protect the guardians of the realm from inquisitive probing, the democrat's response must be to ask, with Juvenal, 'But who is to guard the guardians themselves?' For freedom of speech is a muted right if censorship is too readily applied as a gag. Thirdly, police powers have been increased. From 1979 to 1988 their manpower was strengthened by an additional 16,000. Both police practice and legislative enactments during the 1980s reduced the civil liberties of the citizen. For example, the Prevention of Terrorism Act enables officers to hold and interrogate without explanation any citizen travelling to or from Ireland, while the Public Order Act increased the powers of police against the traditional right of assembly for peaceful demonstrations.

Very good reasons can be adduced for this policy and there is little doubt that the government has had considerable public support for each (and for the many more undertaken in the same vein). After all, does the citizen not have as much right to security as to freedom; and in a perilous age should not the former be accorded priority? What worries the defenders of civil rights is the cumulative effect of so many subtractions from the sum of hard-won citizens' rights. Is there a danger − and this is the fourth category − that the state may be attempting to place itself above the law? The process may involve tiny steps, each of which may be plausibly justified, but the end result none the less dangerously destructive of civil freedom. If a minister can cite national interest for his agents taking the law into their own hands and refuse to provide even Parliament with a detailed explanation on the same grounds, that destruction may be said to have begun. Suspicions that members of the security services did indeed act outside the law in planning to undermine Harold Wilson's government and in adopting a shoot-to-kill policy against the IRA in Northern Ireland and in Gibraltar were voiced in the 1980s. Most notoriously, Wright described how, from the early 1970s there was

. . . a decisive shift inside M15 toward domestic concerns . . .. Intelligence on domestic subversion became the overriding priority . . .. The F Branch people wanted a relaxation in the restrictions governing the use of telephone taps and letter intercepts . . .. The enemy [sic] was diffuse, and its communications so widespread, that this was the only way they could get to grips with the problem.[13]

Yet the concept that the state must act in obedience to the law is the keystone of British constitutional theory. One of the major charges against James II listed in the Bill of Rights was that he

. . . did endeavour to subvert and extirpate . . . the laws and liberties of this kingdom:-
1. By assuming and exercising a power of dispensing with and suspending of laws, and the execution of laws, without consent of Parliament.[14]

That the notion of 'state necessity' was utterly unrecognised by British constitutional law was, it is significant to add, firmly established in the following century.

If, then, the rights of the British citizen are being eroded, should they not be unequivocally defined in a new consolidated Bill of Rights? The French seem to love changing their system of government every so often, by revolution or other means, in order to have the excuse of drafting new constitutional documents. The British go to the other extreme, avoid revolutions and refuse to encapsulate their constitutional laws in general principles. This characteristic is famously summed up by Jeremy Bentham's tetchy dismissal:

Natural rights is simple nonsense, natural and imprescriptable rights, rhetorical nonsense, – nonsense, upon stilts.[15]

Bentham's scornful dismissal of the American and French revolutionary lists highlights objections to two particular assumptions. One is the idea that rights can be thought of as 'natural' rather than pragmatically acquired through political pressure and concession. The other is that a list of rights can without inconvenience be so solidly 'entrenched' in the constitution as never to be overridden even in dire crises. In Britain the latter objection is reinforced by the theory of the sovereignty of parliament. For a bill of rights which could never be repealed would hobble all future parliaments and thus impede the exercise of their putative sovereign authority. There are several other objections too, most notably concern about the suitability of British judges to pronounce on infringements. For judicial machinery analogous to the function of the US Supreme Court would be necessary if such a bill were to be effective. It is also argued that English common law is already sufficiently tough to cope with any genuine complaints. It has, after all, not only defended freedom but worked on the simple and generous principle that the citizen has a right to any action not expressly forbidden by law. However, those who have suffered at the hands of security force interrogators in Northern Ireland and those who have been compelled to use the extraordinarily clumsy procedures of the European Commission and Court of Human Rights would deny this. Indeed, more British citizens have brought more successful cases before these Council of Europe institutions than citizens of any other member-state. Merely incorporating the European Convention into British constitutional law would surely be of considerable benefit?

As a young man Tennyson wrote of England as the land

That sober-suited Freedom chose;
The land, where, girt with friends or foes,
A man may speak the thing he will;
A land of settled government,
A land of just and old renown,
Where Freedom slowly broadens down,
From precedent to precedent.[16]

But c.1980 the land was girt with a foe armed to the teeth with conventional, chemical and nuclear weapons; and settled government was being shaken by violently striking trade unionists and threatened by constant acts of terrorism. Little wonder then that in defensive reaction the government doubted whether in every circumstance a man may still be allowed to speak (or print) the thing he will. The result, however, was that the land's old renown became distinctly tarnished. Moreover, precedent could perhaps no longer be relied upon. Britain's arrogant superiority in standing aloof from the constitutional practices of other liberal democracies, justified by centuries of more beneficent habits, was no longer warranted. The separation of the judicial from political powers, long the bedrock of British civil liberties, has become a barrier to the defence of rights. In the absence of special administrative courts resistance to the infringement'of rights is a task exhausting of both funds and patience. A bill of rights as a check-list of the civil liberties a citizen should expect to enjoy would at least restrain Parliament from the legislative expression of too much panic and prejudice and the Executive from too much abuse of its power. Whereas absolute power corrupts, absolute rights protect.

Besides providing a general codification of rights such a bill could have the important secondary effect of lifting the burden of discrimination from the numerous categories of second-class citizens. Throughout the world civil rights enjoyed by the dominant sectors of any given society are denied to an equal degree to others by discrimination and prejudice. Religion, for centuries a bar to equal treatment, no longer consigns the adherents of particular faiths to subordinate status quite so automatically. True, Buddhists in Tibet, Jews in the Soviet Union, Muslims in Israel, and perhaps still Catholics in Northern Ireland have sound reason to complain that they continue to suffer a denial of equal rights with their atheist, Jewish and Protestant fellow-citizens respectively. Nevertheless, the main concern today centres on the denial of rights by reason of race or sex (or gender, to use the inaccurate vogue word).

Although it is now rare for discrimination still to be sanctioned by the law, some notable examples do exist. Much of the apartheid legislation in South Africa, despite recent alleviation, remains intact. Marriage law in many Third World countries places women at a considerable disadvantage compared with their husbands in regard to the ownership of property. Writing about Blacks and women in the same paragraph helps to emphasise the similarities of their predicament, first noted by women in nineteenth-century USA, where they were sometimes treated as little more than their husband's chattels. Indeed, the Women's Lib movements which have grown up in most western societies since the late 1960s originated in American women's bitterness at being omitted, even positively scorned, in the era of Civil Rights consciousness. One can appreciate the anger generated by the notorious comment of Black Panther Stokeley Carmichael about the contribution women might make to the movement: 'The only position of women is prone.'[17] Even so, important race discrimination and equal opportunities legislation was forthcoming. As early as 1969 for instance the US Equal Opportunity Commission declared that there were only three occupations where sex was relevant – acting, modelling and wet-nursing. There is, however, some evidence of a decline in some countries in the effectiveness of the feminist campaign. One of the reasons is the split between socialist and liberal feminism. The damning of the family as an oppressive institution by Engels a century ago has been rediscovered by women of a radical turn of mind. But it is the liberal emphasis on rights rather than the ideological argument which gains most sympathy in male-dominated establishments.

In Britain discrimination in practice, of course, remains widespread and second-class citizenship is a reality. The Scarman Report into the Brixton riots revealed police prejudice. Twice as many convicted Blacks as Whites are given prison sentences. Evidence of the psychological and physical harassment of

Asians by Whites abounds. Employment prospects are grim: the rate of unemployment among black youths has been twice the average. Blacks and women alike undertake a disproportionate share of low status and low-paid work.

Stereotypical slogans are, of course, common: 'Blacks are lazy'; 'A woman's place is in the home'. These are often based, however unconsciously and spuriously, on supposed biological differences. In a European Community opinion poll conducted in 1988 only 40 per cent of respondents believed in complete equality between the sexes. The fact that there are black youths who are less than conscientious in seeking and undertaking work and that there are women who prefer a domestic life may be of sociological interest. It is not germane to the issue of citizen's rights. Neither legal barriers nor social resistance should prevent them from enjoying equal treatment at the hands of the law or in employment opportunities if and when they seek the implementation of the egalitarian principle of citizenship. Second-class citizenship should not only be more widely recognised as an injustice; it should be more widely recognised as a contradiction in terms. Citizenship loses its very meaning if it allows itself to contain caste distinctions. The persistence of formal caste in India makes the point trenchantly: in what sense is an untouchable a citizen when he is condemned to a lifetime of begging or clearing human excreta? Legislation, even a bill of rights, can achieve only a limited rectification. It is public opinion that must change. More than that, legislation which is too far in advance of popular attitudes can provoke a backlash of more virulent prejudice against the supposed beneficiaries of the new laws. Opinion does change. It would be rare in Britain today to hear the coarse comments which so muddied the reputation of Mary Wollstonecraft (p. 70). Perhaps a more sympathetic appreciation of the ideal of equal citizenship could be accelerated by more effective education?

World citizenship in international law

However, before addressing this issue, it is necessary to examine the idea of civil and legal citizenship in a world context. There is much to be said for the argument that neither international theory nor international law recognises the status of world citizen. The actors on the international stage are corporate entities: primarily states, but also transnational companies and international institutions. The individual has legal status *qua* citizen of a state. Insofar as he has a relationship with the world at large it is expressed in the moral duty to recognise the dignity and rights of other human beings and to have his own dignity and rights reciprocally recognised. Thus to extend the term 'citizenship' to the global is unhelpfully confusing. The traditional distinction in political theory since Aristotle between 'man' and 'citizen' is crucial. Martin Wight expressed the point with characteristic lucidity. Even the Pope, he pointed out, needs the Vatican; even he cannot operate in the secular world as a world citizen, only as the prince of a state. And in general terms:

Since the sixteenth century, international society has been so organized that no individuals except sovereign princes can be members of it, and these only in their representative capacity. All other individuals have had to be subjects or citizens of sovereign states.[18]

Two examples may help to confirm this view. One is that for a century now it has been virtually impossible to travel without a passport, a document which categories a person by national citizenship. Secondly, even United Nations human rights documents are largely concerned to provide yardsticks for judging the way people in their capacity as human beings should be treated by their own states.

And yet the case against world citizenship status in legal terms is really not quite so complete as it might at first seem. In the first place, a powerful philosophical tradition may be traced from the seventeenth century, which exhibits unhappiness concerning the attitude encapsulated in the slogan, 'My country, right or wrong'. If there is a universal moral code of law which is superior and exists prior to the solidification of the authority of the state, then the individual must be conceived as having some obligation to that law; and it is an obligation which, at least hypothetically, takes precedence over state law. Moreover, the undermining of that universal law in one place endangers the whole moral code and must be resisted by all who can. It is interesting to compare the following: 'a violation of right in one place of the earth is felt all over it.'[19] And,

The participating states recognize the universal significance of human rights and fundamental freedoms, respect for which is an essential factor for peace, justice and well-being. . . .[20]

The first was written in 1795, the second, anagramatically, in 1975.

In concrete terms, one may note the small attempts at issuing 'international passports' during this century to an important category of stateless persons, namely, refugees. In the 1920s thousands of refugees were able to travel on League of Nations identity documents, called eponymously 'Nansen Certificates'. Since 1951 the UN Convention on the Status of Refugees has provided for the issue of temporary international travel permits so that the stateless might seek asylum in a country of their choice. Indeed, the very acceptance by the international community that a refugee has rights, even though through fear he has renounced by flight his national citizenship, is an implicit statement of world citizenship. For if an essential part of citizenship is to have certain basic rights protected by political and legal institutions, then refugees have that status – vis-à-vis the UN High Commission for Refugees and the community of a hundred states which have ratified the UN Convention on the Status of Refugees, for example. And one of the crucial rights is that, while they are seeking permanent settlement, refugees are guaranteed security by the principle of non-refoulement (p. 250).

It is not only refugees who in recent decades have had their rights upheld by the international community. There are many circumstances in which the individual can be deemed to be appealing to his rights *qua* world citizen when his rights *qua* national citizen have been circumscribed by his own state. The most obvious examples are those in which continental rather than global institutions have acted. Most conspicuous have been the activities springing from the European Convention on Human Rights (p. 255). Since 1955 individual petition to the investigatory Commission of Human Rights has been allowed and nineteen states recognise as binding any rulings consequently made by the European Court of Human Rights. The facility is certainly used: 3,000 applications, for example, in 1984. The following is a brief summary written in 1985 of the use of the Commission and Court by British citizens:

The rights which have been upheld in the British cases have always been fundamental and often far-reaching. Two bills in the present Parliament – applying new restrictions to telephone-tapping and corporal punishment – stem directly from rulings of the European Court.
Other cases . . . include . . . undue interference with a free press in the *Sunday Times* Thalidomide campaign against Distillers and the inhuman treatment of suspected terrorists in Northern Ireland.[21]

Rather more dramatically the Inter-American Court on Human Rights put the Honduran government in the dock in 1988: it was charged with using death squads to eliminate leading civilian opponents of the régime.

One way in which a citizen's rights are protected is by the punishment of those who imperil those rights. The police and courts exist to preserve a citizen's person and property against attack. The means of protection and sanctions available to the world community are of course so much more limited than those available to the state. None the less for centuries the basic principle has been accepted that individuals who infringe the universal moral law may be punished by authorities other than their own state. From the dawn of international law pirates have been classified as *hostes homini generis* (enemies of mankind). A pirate has had no right to claim protection or redress from his own state in the event of another state's exacting punishment for his plundering activities. If refugees are people who have had honorary world citizenship bestowed upon them out of respect for a universal moral law, then pirates have had that status stripped from them for the same reason. There are few pirates in the world today. But there are many torturers. Since they assault some of the most precious rights of their victims, depriving them of dignity and physical and psychological peace, should they not be similarly categorised as enemies of mankind? The case of *Filártiga* v. *Peña-Irala* has certainly set a precedent. The case, against a Paraguayan torturer, was brought in the USA, and the American judge made precisely the analogy with the outlaw status of pirates.

Finally, the Nuremberg trials provide the most famous setting down of rules of conduct whereby individuals are recognised as having a duty as world citizens (pp. 144–145). Yet although it took the commission of Nazi atrocities to enshrine the principle in international law, the principle itself had been quite lucidly enunciated by the great Dutch international jurist, Hugo Grotius, over three centuries earlier:

. . . if the authorities issue any order that is contrary to the law of nature or to the commandments of God, the order should not be carried out.[22]

To suggest that the legal status of world citizen is as fully developed and institutionalised as the status of national citizen would naturally be folly. But conversely, an utter denial of any validity to world citizenship status is not a mark of intelligent understanding. Although, as we shall see (p. 287), there are still problems relating to the universal acceptance of a code of human rights because of ideological and cultural differences of emphasis, considerable progress has been made since 1945. Paradoxically it is not the strength of nation-states that prevents a more widespread adoption of the kind of system developed by the Council of Europe, but their weakness. It is the maturity, stability and self-confidence of the West European polities that allows them to concede such latitude to their citizens. The growth of this legal facet of supra-national citizenship to a more truly world citizenship therefore awaits the spread of such political conditions.

Education in civil and human rights

The civil and legal rights of citizenship are defined by laws, which are interpreted and upheld in courts of law. And since the core of the citizenship ideal is that each citizen should be fully alive to his status and its implications, one would expect to find some basic teaching of constitutional, civil and international law to feature as a major component in courses of civic education. Contrary to much of the practice of the ancient world, this has not been so in modern states. A comment by a British authority in the late 1980s would probably be typical of the situation in most countries:

. . . our efforts to educate young people about the ways in which the law affects them have not significantly changed in a hundred years of compulsory education.[23]

Those efforts have been devoted largely to the historical dimensions: Magna Carta in England, the 1789 Declaration of Rights in France, the Bill of Rights in the USA. In younger educational systems syllabuses do include references to elements on the 'rights and responsibilities of citizens'. But these are interpreted most frequently as political rights (i.e. voting) and civic responsibilities (i.e. paying taxes and military service). Civic rights such as equality before the law and freedom of speech seem to receive less attention. The fourth grade Social Studies syllabus in Thailand, for example, has the following entry: '7. Rights and duties of Thai citizens with special emphasis on taxes, security and unity of the nation.'[24]

This widespread neglect of teaching about the civil and legal nature of citizenship may be explained by three contributory factors. One is the academic background of teachers engaged in education for citizenship. Until quite recently in most countries it has been the History teacher who has taken the major responsibility for this work. Only comparatively recently, first in the USA then increasingly in other countries, have teachers with qualifications in the Social Sciences, including Politics, entered the classrooms. Teachers who have studied Law are rare in schools. Secondly, Law has a forbidding, technical sound to it, with the result that many have believed it an unsuitable subject for schools. And thirdly, many governments and school authorities have had a conservative nervousness about introducing the notion of rights in any truly practical sense into schools: it could have an 'unsettling' effect on pupils' consciousness of their status, let alone on what they might come to demand as mature citizens. More obedience and discipline are demanded in many western schools rather than rights.

A change of climate can, however, be discerned. As has so frequently happened in the field of Social and Civic Education the USA was in the vanguard. In 1981 one distinguished American authority identified law-related studies as one of three areas most likely to receive particular attention. He cited two reasons for this: the huge increase in crime and the mounting intrusion of law into social relationships. By 1987 another scholar reported that elementary pupils using the *Law in a Free Society* programme read simplified versions of the landmark Supreme Court cases dealing with free speech, the freedom to assemble, freedom of religion, and the procedural due process issues relating to arrest, detention and trials.[25] Two other factors have been a growth of consciousness that the various categories of second-class citizens need help to improve their lot; and the promotion of human rights education by UNESCO and the Council of Europe. Again, some US educationists were quicker to try to introduce human rights education into schools than their colleagues in other countries. Now, of course, not all this pedagogical activity has been directly related to enhancing an understanding of the status and rights of citizenship. Some of the objectives clearly relate to improving the level of law-abiding civic behaviour.

Let us outline recent developments in England that are specifically germane to our present considerations. As we shall see below (pp. 305–306), the 1980s witnessed a tense political debate over the teaching of History. True, a Right-wing minister of Education, Sir Keith Joseph, with typical personal honesty, provided a balanced statement:

It is particularly salutary that pupils are brought to realise that the ideas and values . . . which they take for granted were acquired through processes which were often painful and difficult and that the institutions we most value were won at a price in human endeavour.[26]

Nevertheless, the pressures for a core of British History in the National Curriculum awakened fears among many History teachers that a biassed, Whig interpretation of History might be reintroduced into the schools.

The concern that overt law education might be biassed towards the study of duties at the expense of rights was raised by the incorporation of a strange clause in the 1986 Education Act. This required governing bodies, when considering the secular curriculum, '. . . to have regard . . . to any such representations which are made to them by the chief officer of police and which are connected with his responsibilities.'[27] Much-needed objective and balanced guidance for teachers and materials for pupils has, happily, been forthcoming from 'Law in Education', a project jointly initiated in 1984 by the Law Society and the School Curriculum Development Committee. Some of the subject-matter relates directly to citizen rights, though the whole project is carefully balanced with material on responsibilities too. The general response of teachers and pupils was confirmation that this subject has been almost totally neglected and enthusiasm for the interest and utility of the subject-matter provided. One wonders, nevertheless, how many of those involved appreciated the irony of the reaction of some fifth-formers in an Essex secondary school. The teachers reported that, 'All pupils became very interested, to the extent that some individuals attended law lessons when truanting from other subjects.'[28]

The issue of human rights is handled in the project through an examination of the Nazi persecution of the Jews. This episode more than any other prompted the founding-fathers of the UN to commit the organisation to promoting 'universal respect for, and observance of, human rights and fundamental freedoms' (Article 55 of the Charter). UNESCO encouraged schools to engage in work to support this objective, providing a definitive set of aims in 1980:

(i) Fostering the attitudes of tolerance, respect and solidarity inherent in human rights;
(ii) Providing knowledge about human rights, in both their national and international dimensions, and the institutions established for their implementation;
(iii) Developing the individual's awareness of the ways and means by which human rights can be translated into social and political reality at both the national and international levels.[29]

By the same date the Council of Europe was similarly active.

It is likely that one of the major motives for this teaching was to draw attention to cases of deprivation of rights, with teachers using their favourite bogey-states as illustrations. To be sure there are examples enough to be spoiled for choice. In Britain the favourites are probably Nazi Germany and South Africa. What these two régimes have had in common, of course, is deprivation of civil rights by the test of racial classification. This form of injustice has a resonance for teachers concerned about the incidence of racial prejudice and discrimination nearer to home. The issue of immigrants' civil rights has rendered the whole topic, in some quarters, urgently relevant. Pupils certainly recognise its topicality, as this extract shows. It is taken from the Swann Report, *Education for All. The Report of the Committee of Enquiry into the Education of Children from Ethnic Minority Groups*:

Our own discussions with secondary pupils from a range of ethnic backgrounds have left us in no doubt that the majority of them have strong views on issues which can be perceived as 'political' and have definite opinions on 'racial' questions such as immigration, discrimination and the respective 'rights and responsibilities' of the ethnic majority community and ethnic minority groups in this society.[30]

Although such work is valid in terms of importance and relevance, it has had the unfortunate effect of tending to equate human rights education with teaching about race discrimination, when the topic is, of course, so much broader.

It has also had the unfortunate effect of attracting accusations of left-wing bias to this work. What, ask these critics, about the severe violations of civil rights in Communist states? Human rights education has indeed been subjected to a variety of criticism, much of it related to the basic hesitations concerning the very nature of human rights agendas themselves (p. 287).

Yet the potential benefits of this teaching require educators to persevere. The director of the French National Educational Research Centre expressed her firm conviction in the crucial role human rights education can play in the preparation of young people for democratic citizenship:

Human rights as a universally recognised and applicable standard can be the core or the heart of this new civic and moral education. Human rights embody the respect that all human beings owe to each other above and beyond any differences of ethnic, cultural or political allegiance.[31]

Many of the problems which both friendly and hostile critics of human rights education have voiced might well be resolved if these courses were incorporated in clearly defined and fully developed programmes of education for citizenship, including world citizenship. Complaints that human rights education emphasises rights at the expense of responsibilities would be met since citizenship clearly presupposes a balance in the behaviour of citizens. Complaints that the published international human rights documents are culturally biassed and teaching about them is similarly skewed would be met by the cosmopolitan principle of the superficiality of cultural differences.

In this section we are focussing on the status and rights of citizenship. How should these be defined and taught in both national and world contexts? Clearly the status of national citizenship is fundamental to an individual's legal-political identity. Whatever one thinks about the desirability and significance of any form of supranational status it is the national status that is in reality most relevant to most people. School pupils should understand this basic fact of political life. The somewhat abstract concept can be rendered more vivid by reference to situations which may affect their own lives: for example, the citizenship law regarding immigration for ethnic minority groups and the consular services for those whose families take overseas holidays.

The matter of rights can be tackled in schools at four levels: an understanding of what is meant by having rights; knowledge of the civil rights which exist in national and international law; the development of the skills necessary to use the existing machinery for the exercise of rights and redress of grievances; and, for the most advanced, a critical appreciation of the problems surrounding the whole issue of civil and human rights. As a social being there is little that is dearer to the heart of the young than rights. The present author has suggested elsewhere that complaints commonly heard in every home and classroom reveal a very keen understanding at their own level of a variety of rights which at the political level have forbidding abstract labels. The point is best made in tabular form.[32]

'I've got my rights'	Rights
'That's not fair!'	Justice
'He's/she's your favourite!'	Equality
'You're always picking on me!'	Discrimination
'Why can't I stay up late/go out tonight?'	Freedom to
'Why do I have to wear these clothes/visit these boring relations?'	Freedom from
'We want to choose our own team/class captain'	Self-determination

In states with written constitutions enshrining codes of civil rights these primitive concepts can be equated with particular articles. In Britain, the European Convention might be most usefully employed for this purpose. This would be a convenient teaching device partly because a number of supporters of a British bill of rights have suggested its incorporation into British law to achieve this end; and partly because British citizens have successfully pleaded their causes from this document. A study of the Convention provides a dozen rights: right to life; freedom from torture; freedom from slavery and servitude; liberty and security; fair trial; no retroactive laws; privacy; freedom of thought, conscience, religion; freedom of expression; freedom of assembly and association; right to marry; right to effective remedy if these rights are violated. For more advanced students the absence from the European Convention of the Lockian right of property (also included in the UN Declaration) could be considered. The criticism that such a study would so magnify in the pupil's mind the idea of rights as to obscure legal duties and moral obligations must be taken very seriously. Civil duties are few, but must not be forgotten, for instance, jury service, payment of taxes, military service when required. A weightier balance is provided by the whole area of moral obligations discussed in the next chapter. The budding rights and duties of individuals as world citizens is probably best dealt with mainly historically by reference to the Nuremberg principles both in their origin and as advanced by American conscientious objectors to the Vietnam war.

Educationists have become increasingly aware that knowledge is indeed inert if its possessor remains lacking in the skills necessary for its application. And so it may be considered no more pointless to be able to draw a woodwork plan without being able to handle a chisel than it is to know you have a right of assembly without being able to handle the police monitoring of such an event. Pupils must consequently be taught how to use channels of communication both to secure rights and to seek redress in case of their violation. Part of the skill is itself knowledge — of the roles, for example, of local councillors and MPs. It also involves the skills of presenting one's case orally or in writing and the mobilisation of support of people of like mind or in like condition. An understanding of how to use organisations like the National Council for Civil Liberties and Amnesty International should also be part of the course.

The more advanced students could be encouraged to take a broad historical view of the topic. An understanding of the way the status of citizen has evolved throughout the centuries would help to place the present position in context and to encourage a questioning of the most desirable and practicable ways in which the status and rights might develop in the foreseeable future. The issue of a British bill of rights and the possibility of a legal strengthening of the concepts of European Community citizenship and world citizenship could fruitfully be discussed.

The teaching profession, certainly in Britain, is insufficiently alert to its responsibilities for undertaking this work. The civil status of citizenship – the enjoyment of a just legal system and freedom from arbitrary state oppression for the ordinary citizen – preceded political enfranchisement. The average subject of George III could lay quite a firm claim to citizenship status in this civil sense when his political right to vote existed only in the dreams of radical pamphleteers and members of radical societies. Yet school syllabuses still tend to focus on the political facet of citizenship. Civil rights are too precious to be thus taken for granted. The consciousness of each new generation of citizens to their value is crucial to their preservation and enhancement.

7.2   SOCIAL CITIZENSHIP

. . . the modern drive towards social equality is, I believe, the latest phase of an evolution of citizenship which has been in continuous progress for some 250 years.

T. H. Marshall[33]

Citizenship, welfare and capitalism

Nothing quite so absorbs the attention of scholars and politicians when contemplating the nature of citizenship today as the social rights which adhere to the status. Can a citizen by virtue of being a citizen expect a certain social status and a secure level of welfare? If so, by what right? And if so, what becomes of the relationship of citizenship to its modern historical evolution out of capitalism and the class system? Also, what are the implications of citizenship for other means of defining social status such as class and sex? Attention to such questions was particularly drawn by T. H. Marshall (pp. 100–101) and much of the substantial subsequent literature has taken his lectures as its starting-point. There is space here only to indicate the major features of this facet of the citizenship question. Readers wanting a fuller discussion will find particularly helpful Bryan S. Turner, *Citizenship and Capitalism: The Debate Over Reformism* (1986).

Plato and Aristotle established that the cardinal function of the state is to ensure that justice prevails. It was Aristotle who distinguished between 'corrective' and 'distributive' justice. By the latter he meant the principles and practices of sharing out offices, honours and wealth. The guideline he laid down was that of proportionate equality, that is, basically equal shares adjusted according to the 'merit' of the recipients. We are still struggling to achieve agreement on a definition of 'merit' and on a measure for determining the size of the adjustment. Nevertheless, during the past century (pp. 99–101) the belief that the state has a duty to ensure social justice and an adequate level of welfare for all its citizens has rapidly gained ground. The guiding principle of the policies commonly implemented has been Robin Hoodism: the taxation of the rich to provide for the poor. The state funds thus raised have been used for educational and health services and the cushioning of citizens from the impoverishing effects of illness, unemployment and old age. The immense suffering of and effort made by many European peoples in the Second World War strengthened the belief that states owed it to their citizens to interpret the principle of distributive justice in a generous way. It was in embattled Britain, in 1941, that the term 'welfare state' was coined – by the Archbishop of Canterbury.

If a defining feature of citizenship is the recognition of reciprocal rights and responsibilities, then the notion of social citizenship must be discerned in this way. The state has an obligation to provide basic welfare to its citizens; the rich particularly and all citizens generally have an obligation to contribute funds for social welfare; the beneficiaries of the welfare state have an obligation not to abuse these rights and services. In practice, until quite recently, the need to build, enhance and maintain welfare states has been so pressing that it has seemed necessary to insist more on the honouring of rights than the concomitant obligation not to abuse the facilities.

In a sense, the state provision of welfare is unrelated to the specific status of citizenship. One does not need to be a Thomas Hobbes to recognise that for millenia human beings have clustered together and organised political systems to advance their collective economic, cultural and security interests as an improvement on the nasty, brutish and short existences of primitive life. In the succinct definition of Edmund Burke, 'Government is a contrivance of human wisdom to provide for human *wants*.'[34] Burke, arguing the pragmatic case, was rejecting the view that the individual has a natural right to this kind of provision, though such a case can be sustained. Other justifications for the state provision of social welfare include the principle of distributive justice and the cynical/realist belief that some state relief of poverty is necessary to ward off an insurrectionary response of the downgraded to their condition. Or there is the citizenship argument: that gross social and economic inequalities are incompatible with the civic and political egalitarianism inherent in the status.

Because social welfare is so intrinsic to the very purpose of political association and because so many justificatory arguments can be advanced, the wealth of historical evidence for such provision should occasion little surprise. The methods and priorities, admittedly, differed widely. Although there is some evidence of social welfare in the Greek city-state, it is not far from the mark to suggest that, 'The ancient Athenians, for example, provided public-baths and gymnasiums for the citizens but never provided anything remotely resembling unemployment insurance or social security.'[35] In the medieval and early modern periods of European history, apart from ecclesiastical charity, citizens enjoyed some welfare provision as members of guilds. In England, the state recognised its obligation in the Tudor legislation defining parochial responsibilities for the poor, though in truth out of a sense of fear more than of charity. The right of the disadvantaged to state-provided welfare was written into the French Constitution of 1791:

There will be created and organised a general establishment for public welfare to bring up abandoned children, to relieve the poverty of the infirm, and to provide work for the poor who are fit but otherwise unable to find employment.[36]

In both Tudor England and Revolutionary France the confiscation of Church property raised the issue of alternative, state provision. But, in the case of England certainly, the rapid demographic changes of the Industrial Revolution undermined the old Poor Law system. Moreover, the amended arrangements which were in place from 1834 to 1929 were bitterly resented as an insult to the dignity of persons, who were increasingly conscious of their pretended status of citizen in legal and even political senses.

We need to be clear about what is meant by the term 'social citizenship'. It is the belief that, since all citizens are assumed to be fundamentally equal in status and dignity, none should be so depressed in economic or social condition as to mock this assumption. Therefore, in return for the loyalty and virtuous civic conduct displayed by the citizen, the state has an obligation to smooth out any gross inequalities by the guarantee of a basic standard of living in terms of income, shelter, food, health and education. Essential standards in these facets of life should be enjoyed as a right of citizenship irrespective of wealth, bargaining power, sex, age or race. Furthermore, no stigma should attach to the communal source of provision.

What has all this to do with capitalism? The answer has several components. In the first place, it can be plausibly argued that a capitalist organisation of the economy is a necessary precondition for the emergence of a true citizen status. Personal subservience, social hierarchy and provincially fragmented economic units were alike anathema to capitalism: it is an economic mode which requires personal initiative, social fluidity and open access to markets. By undermining medieval institutions and social structures to achieve its own purposes, capitalism provided the very conditions in the Atlantic world in which citizenship could evolve. It may well be that the political struggles for citizenship chronicled in Chapter 2 would have enjoyed less success, or indeed would not have occurred at all, if the socio-economic context in which they were fought had itself not been subjected to such revolutionary changes.

And yet, although capitalism and modern citizenship may be said to have emerged in double harness, the yoke chafed for both. Citizenship has developed in ways which render capitalism a most inconvenient companion. Capitalism generates economic inequalities, exacerbates class differences and encourages selfish acquisitiveness – all antitheses of the citizen ideal. In the context of the fear which preachers and theologians expressed of the perils of covetousness inherent in early capitalism, Tawney remarked,

It was against that system, while still in its supple and insinuating youth, before success had caused it to throw aside the mask of innocence, and while its true nature was unknown even to itself, that the saints and sages of earlier ages launched their warnings and their denunciations.[37]

In the seventy years since Tawney wrote those words, the capitalist mentality has become even brasher. And language too has suffered a sad deterioration from his elegance so that we now describe that same phenomenon as the loadsamoney society'.

At the same time, capitalism has found it equally uncongenial to be paired with citizenship. As citizenship has taken on a social colouration, it has demanded that its principle of equal status and dignity be supported by an amelioration of the effects of unbridled market forces. Some of the wealth from profits must be diverted, via taxation, to welfare and educational provision for the less fortunate. Thus, in the name of social citizenship the state intrudes on the liberty of the capitalist to enjoy all the profits he accrues from the operation of the free market.

The decision of the state to intervene in such a way is clearly a political action and raises the question of the relationship of capitalism to democracy. One of the principal tenets of capitalism is the prudence of separating economics from politics: the market must not be distorted for political purposes. But by that very separation capitalism, it can be argued, has set up a tension in the process of formulating citizenship in a holistic sense. The egalitarian civil and political forms of citizenship are consonant with the aims of capitalism; egalitarian social citizenship is not. The former provide the freedom necessary for the expansion and diversification of economic activity; the latter diverts the profits therefrom. In fact, this model of the relationship is historically rather too simple. In practice, it was the professional rather than the capitalist middle classes who spearheaded the legal and political reforms. The lower classes (and later women, ethnic minorities and colonial subjects) benefited by the illogicality of their exclusion from civic and political citizenship. And from these platforms of civic and political rights, by means of trade union and parliamentary activity, they extended their hold on citizenship into the socio-economic sphere. But many a bourgeois, capitalist or professional, has contemplated the whole process of the extension of citizen rights with barely concealed misgivings.

In the contemporary world, however, the social effects of naked capitalism have not supervened to generate the proletarian revolutionary despair which Marx predicted. For even in the states with the purist capitalist policies, like the USA and UK in the 1980s, the working classes have been allowed to enjoy some of the fruits of capitalism − either by using the services of the welfare state or by incorporation into the commercial and rentier classes. This process of ameliorating the impact of capitalism on the working classes by absorbing them into the system can be viewed in three different ways. To the purist Marxist who rejects the strategy of reformism in favour of hard-line revolution, the proletarian who enjoys these benefits is betraying the true interests of his class. To the liberal, the enjoyment of property and welfare has been extracted as a right in hard-fought struggles against the privileged classes. To the conservative, the status of social citizenship has been grudgingly but prudently conceded to blunt the revolutionary anger of the lower orders. It is interesting to note how widespread has been the view that universal property-ownership rather than safety-net welfare should be the ideal form of social citizenship. It is scarcely surprising to find this in Aristotle given the social conditions of the time. It is of greater wonder that one can juxtapose Jean-Jacques Rousseau and Margaret Thatcher by this means. Rousseau defined property as 'the most sacred of all rights of citizenship.[38] How faithfully is this sentiment echoed in the 1987 Conservative Party manifesto, which spoke of 'A capital-owning democracy . . . . a profound and progressive social transformation – popular capitalism.'[39]

The alternative of involving the majority of people in capitalist activity rather than expecting them to be reliant on state provision of services is attractive to many on the grounds that the individual suffers from the welfare state. Individualism is sacrificed to equality; privacy, to bureaucracy; and, furthermore, security is bought at the price of stigma and the loss of that very dignity of citizenship it was designed to enhance. That these features of the welfare state lead to an undesirable attenuation of true citizenship has been recognised over a broad political spectrum. And the canvassed solutions have been correspondingly diverse. The New Right virtually denies the validity of social citizenship. This Reaganite policy has been adopted in many other states besides the USA – in countries as different as the UK and Pakistan. The principle is to raise the general level of personal wealth by liberating market forces and reducing taxation. The latter involves reducing welfare provision. But then the implication is that those who fail to take advantage of the new opportunities 'to stand on their own two feet' deserve to fall into an 'underclass' of a sub-citizen category in any case. The British Secretary of State for Social Services, John Moore, explained the philosophy in a speech in 1987:

Of course we believe real distress must be alleviated and help given to those who cannot help themselves. But as in medicine where the aim is, so far as possible, to *cure* someone who is sick, not just contain the illness, so welfare measures, if they are to *really* promote economic and social welfare, must be aimed ultimately at encouraging independence, not dependence.[40]

The snag has been that, with persistently high unemployment (well over two million in Britain when the speech was made), it has been extremely difficult for many of the dependent to 'cure' themselves.

In states with a powerful Social Democratic tradition since 1945 – notably Sweden, Norway and Austria – the emphasis has been placed on training and economic management to ensure a high rate of employment rather than expending money on large numbers of unemployed. The problem of relating dependency with citizenship is consequently of much more manageable size. For those who do still need welfare assistance, the Swede, Gunnar Myrdal has urged

> . . . the relevance of the Utopian, decentralised and democratic state where . . . the citizens themselves carry more and more of the responsibility for organising their work and life by means of local and sectional co-operation and bargaining . . .[41]

This insistence on emancipating the needy citizen from the clutches of centralised bureaucracy relates directly, of course, to the principle of participation. Thus the political and social citizens meet in their roles as active participants.

The dignity of equal citizenship is still none the less endangered if the needy participate as suppliants for charity, which is ultimately funded by the state. The British sociologist Richard Titmuss has tackled this problem through his concept of 'the gift relationship'. He sees the real threat of the welfare state as the destruction of the spirit of altruism. All citizens, poor and rich alike, have something to contribute to communal welfare – time and energy, if not always money. State provision must complement not smother this civic benevolence.

At the very heart of the issue of social citizenship lies a conflict of ideals between Right and Left on the political spectrum. For the New Right the concept of social citizenship barely exists, for all citizens in an ideal world should be socially independent and autonomous. To cite John Moore again, 'society's aim for all its citizens' is that they should be 'independent, self-reliant . . ., able to participate in life and gain satisfaction from it.'[42] The few who, despite all their best efforts, fail to reach or fall out of this category of 'proper' citizens can appeal for assistance from the state. The contrary view is that, whatever their circumstances, all individuals with the legal right of citizenship have a social right to a reasonable life-style. Welfare services therefore exist ideally, not to assist the needy, but to redistribute society's wealth and services in a more egalitarian fashion than a free market would allow. The concept of 'positive discrimination', for instance in enhanced funding for schools for Blacks in the USA and in Education Priority Areas in the UK, is a telling example of this frame of mind. The stigma of being recipients of such provision, so this argument runs, is erased in the appreciation of the ultimate goal. The needy are not being grudgingly offered charity because they cannot 'make the grade' as citizens. They are participating in an overall social policy of a drive to greater equality. Civic self-respect is only possible, however, if the ideal is seen to be credible. And again, the crucial feature lies in the opportunities to give – to participate in however humble a way by contributing a personal service to the community of which one is a conscious, proud and full member. It also raises, of course, the question of the willingness of the social citizen to recognise not just his right to participate but his obligation. This message can be heard alike from left and right. T. H. Marshall, while emphasising the crucial significance of the social facet of citizenship was adamant that it implied responsibilities. The social citizen has the duty to avoid irresponsible strikes and to work and work conscientiously for the welfare of the community as a whole. The need of socialist parties and trade unions to harp upon rights because they have in the past been so sadly denied must not blind us to the need for balancing responsibilities. Put at its crudest, should not the able-bodied who refuses to discharge his obligation to work or train for work still enjoy the right of unemployment benefit? Conservative writers and parties can, of course, be relied upon to reiterate such reminders. One of the most distinguished contributions to the argument is from the American Lawrence Mead, whose book *Beyond Entitlement* is forthrightly sub-titled *The Obligations of Citizenship*.

The problem of balancing the right to receive welfare support with the responsibility to give in such a manner as to preserve the quality and dignity of citizenship has been usefully exemplified in the American 'workfare' schemes. These provide benefit payments as loans, which are required to be paid off by various kinds of work. The system has often been condemned for undermining the citizen's right to welfare support and for undercutting normal wage levels. On the other hand, there have been examples of schemes operated in a sympathetic way: the needy recipients of the aid genuinely participate and benefit from the experience.

The existence of so much disagreement on the matter of social citizenship has inevitably contributed to the persistence of problems of social inequalities and deprivation, the curtailment, in short, of the status of citizenship for many citizens. Immediately one posits the idea that all citizens have an equal right to enjoy a full life in society, attention is drawn to those groups who are evidently disadvantaged in some way in this respect: the poor, women, children, the infirm, the aged, ethnic minorities. And as they become conscious of their deprived condition so they campaign for their rights as social citizens. Hence movements like Black Civil Rights, Gay Power, Rights of Children. However, the process has not been entirely a one-way extension of rights. In the words of Professor Turner,

Citizenship can be conceived as a series of expanding circles which are pushed forward by the momentum of conflict and struggle. This is not an evolutionary view of citizenship since these rights can also be undermined by economic recession, by right-wing political violence, by inflation and by the redefinition of social participation through the law. [43]

There have indeed been sufficient examples of retrogression in recent years to give credence to an ebb and flow model of social citizenship in the contemporary world. Let some figures from the USA exemplify the point. In 1987 a group of American doctors produced a report entitled *Hunger Reaches Blue Collar America*. It showed that millions of working people were suffering from malnourishment. The numbers on the official poverty line were 24.5 million in 1978, increasing to 35.3 million in 1983. Even in the wealthy state of California they noted that infant mortality was increasing for the first time in twenty years. Both the proportion of the population which is poor and the income gap between, say, the richest 10 per cent and poorest 10 per cent have been increasing. The figures provide some measure of a retreating social citizenship in the USA.

A similar phenomenon may be observed more intensely in many a Third World country. As rising populations press upon exiguous fuel, water and food resources, the rural poor and especially the women suffer increasing hardships of malnutrition and excessive work-loads. At the same time the wealth of the urban administrative, professional and commercial classes has increased conspicuously in recent decades. Perhaps the saddest example of a decline in a sense of citizenship cohesion with the attendant decline of socio-economic welfare is Tanzania. After two decades of Nyerere's programme of African Socialism, prompted by the keenest sense of egalitarian social citizenship, there was more poverty and less sense of social cohesion between rural and urban populations than at the start of the policy.

A powerful set of reasons for this slippage in the progress of social citizenship has obviously been economic. It is all very well to argue, as the British Socialist, Anthony Crosland did in his more optimistic mood, that all social equality and welfare need for their realisation are political will and economic growth. Levelling up by means of economic growth looks much more difficult from the perspective of the late 1980s than the mid-1950s. The pessimism is justified whether one focusses on the situation as a state- or as a world-citizen. In 1956 Crosland wrote that 'socialists must always remember that international now surpass inter-class injustices and inequalities.'[44] How much more true is that today when the wealth gap between the affluent north and the poverty-stricken southern hemisphere daily widens? In what sense, therefore, can we refer at all to social citizenship in a cosmopolitan context?

Global distributive justice

Powerful arguments can, in truth, be marshalled against both the desirability and practicality of the very notion. Some of these are extrapolations into the global context of the case against social citizenship in the domestic setting. First, the diversion of wealth from the affluent to the impoverished is unfair on the affluent since they should have the right to enjoy the fruits of their energetic and skilful labour. The poverty of the Third World, so it is argued, is at least partly the effect of the economic incompetence of these peoples. Why should the rich countries of the North bail them out? Furthermore, secondly, any assumption of global responsibility for the welfare of these less fortunate members of the human race will instil in them an attitude of dependency. The very concept of world social citizenship would be a disincentive to harder efforts to raise their own standards of living autonomously. Thirdly, if the egalitarian thrust of social citizenship is taken too far, the results could be deleterious even calamitous for the planet. Raising the standard of living of the poorer nations to any significant degree means more industrialisation, more intensive agriculture, more extensive agriculture or improving the terms of trade *vis-à-vis* the rich nations. Each of these options is fraught with danger. Industrialisation would accelerate the depletion of raw materials and environmental pollution. The killing and maiming of thousands in the Bhopal industrial accident in India in 1984 was a small but dramatic example of local pollution. Intensive agriculture leads to top-soil erosion and, by reliance on artificial fertiliser, nitrate pollution of water supplies. Extensive agriculture also leads to desertification and involves in addition deforestation. The felling of the Amazonian rainforest is the most notorious example. Any substantial increase in Third World commodity prices would so upset world trade that all would suffer from, for example, inflation – witness the effects of the 1973 oil price increase. A global levelling of wealth would therefore, by these arguments, mean a levelling down and/or environmental deterioration. The signs are already clear to see. An intensification of these trends would not lead to global distributive justice but to global economic and ecological catastrophe.

To these arguments, which parallel the domestic case against social citizenship, may be added the specific problem concerning the relationship between state and world social citizenships. I, as a citizen of my nation-state, may fully accept the social element of that status. In return for the educational, health and welfare services provided by the state I willingly pay taxes both for my own personal use of those facilities and for the use made of them by my fellow-citizens. The systems are organised and work at the national level insofar as there is a national commitment to them. There is a certain rough justice in paying taxes when healthy and employed and receiving benefits when not. In contradistinction, there is neither administrative linkage with nor sense of commitment to a person who falls ill or unemployed in an unknown land ten thousand miles away.

Even so, compelling as these negative arguments are, the contrary case has substantial countervailing strength. As in other aspects of cosmopolitan thinking, so the rights of welfare and of access to the earth's resources to realise these rights are viewed globally. There can be no moral justification for suggesting that the social rights of one human being should be fundamentally different from another's. This tenet of universal human social rights has been enshrined and explicated in the International Covenant on Economic, Social and Culture Rights, which asserts that

. . . the ideal of free human beings enjoying freedom from fear and want can only be achieved if conditions are created whereby everyone may enjoy his economic, social and cultural rights, as well as his civil and political rights.[45]

In other words, world social citizens have a right too expect a minimum level of welfare and conversely the obligation to ensure that this is universally enjoyed. But if the cosmopolitan considers the human race as one in social rights, he has also come to consider the planet as a common resource. This view was propounded, for instance, as early as 1940 by the four British religious leaders as an indispensable condition for world peace. They wrote:

The resources of the earth should be used as God's gifts to the whole human race, and used with due consideration for the needs of the present and future generations.[46]

If these twin beliefs are true, then their truth is perennial. However, there are several additional arguments relating to the specific conditions of the contemporary world, which reinforce the case for international distributive justice. We may identify four main elements. The first is the element of chance. Like Count Almavira's privileges due to chance of birth, so the richness of resources and the clemency of climate enjoyed by any given country are fortuitous. What opportunities have the people of Bangladesh or Mali to improve their lot when the cruel disadvantages of geography press so particularly hard in the late twentieth century? Do they not have a right to some compensation from the geographically favoured nations? The second argument relating to the contemporary world concerns the effects of imperialism. The indigenous colonial economics were often distorted in the interests of the metropolitan countries; and these distortions, in the form particularly of reliance on a limited range of primary products, have continued to the present day. The affluent former imperial powers owe the poor former colonies some tangible consideration for this lack of resilience to fluctuating market-forces. Thirdly, the whole world economic system, it can be cogently argued, is biassed against the interests and needs of the developing nations: hence the call, first voiced in 1974, for a New International Economic Order. This is conceived as a package to tilt the mechanisms for commodity prices and the international monetary and trading systems more in favour of the developing countries. The need for a fairer régime was epitomised by the drafting of a Charter of Economic Rights and Duties of States to ensure that weak nations are not cheated or bullied out of their own resources. 'In effect,' it has been said, 'the NIEO would be an international welfare state.'[47]

Perhaps the clinching argument is that the growing economic and monetary interdependence of the whole world is rendering state boundaries increasingly irrelevant. Autarky is obsolete. In that case, the argument for operating a policy of distributive justice within the strict confines of the nation-state starts to crumble. If economic mechanisms are transnational, so too should be economic justice. It follows that social citizenship cannot but take on a global connotation.

All these are moral arguments in favour of a world social citizenship. What of the practicalities? Progress towards national welfare states has in all conscience been halting enough; one must not underestimate the even graver difficulties of translating the institution to the global level. Nevertheless, three signs of progress in that direction may be noted. One is the action taken by UN agencies, national governments, voluntary bodies and individuals at the times of great human crisis. When large numbers are made refugees, rendered homeless or are stricken by famine, whether by natural disaster or human action, responsibility for the relief of suffering is now accepted as being universal. This is a relatively recent phenomenon. Despite the cosmopolitan mood of the age, no such international rallying to the needs of the unfortunate was forthcoming, for example, when two-thirds of Lisbon was devastated with horrific loss of life by earthquake on All Saints Day 1755. The contrast with the multinational relief operation for the Armenian earthquake in 1988 (when the same number – 50,000 – perished) is striking. Yet we must not be too hasty in interpreting present-day relief operations as evidence of a sense of world social citizenship: the motive could be one of charity towards the af-flicted rather than the maintenance of social justice for fellow-citizens.

Secondly, clearer evidence of activity based on an embryonic understanding of world social citizenship has lain in the work of the various League and UN specialised agencies. In 1919 the International Labour Organisation was founded on the principle that social justice in individual states is the concern of all. While the ILO is concerned with employment and trade union condi-tions, WHO has a similar universal function for health, UNESCO, for basic education, UNICEF, for the welfare of children. Furthermore, the emphasis has gradually shifted since 1919. Whereas the work of such agencies was originally justified as a means of sustaining peace by alleviating discontent, the stress since the late 1940s has increasingly been on rights. The work of the UN agencies has been consciously presented in the context of the several declarations and covenants which define universal social rights.

The third practical example of an emergent recognition of world citizenship may be found in the shift in governments' attitudes and world opinion. The strivings of the UN to establish that the sea-bed is a common resource not to be nationally exploited has gained widespread acceptance, while the USA and UK have been much criticised for their refusal to accede to the treaty. The Brandt Report has sharpened awareness of the problem of North-South relations. Even more agreement perhaps has been forthcoming for the Bruntland Report and its concept of sustainable development, which it defines as 'development that meets the needs of the present without compromising the ability of future generations to meet their own needs.' The report high-lights 'the concept of "needs", in particular the essential needs of the world's poor, to which overriding priority should be given.'[48]

These positive arguments for the concept of world social citizenship must surely carry considerable weight. The practical problems concerning a more even distribution of the planet's wealth cannot be dismissed by simplistic arguments. Subtle and complex changes in managing the earth's resources and environment may well be possible given the political will. The Brandt and Bruntland reports have provided some guidelines. The moral case against greater universal social justice can, as we have seen, be quite convincingly countered. There remains the argument that the citizen owes his prime obliga-tion to the welfare of those politically, culturally and socially closest to him − to his kith and kin. Does social justice, like its first cousin, charity, begin at home? We have referred (p. 101) to Rawls' argument that in any co-opera-tive society distributive justice requires the least advantaged to benefit from changes in social and economic conditions. The American scholar, Charles Beitz, has argued that international interdependence has reached such a level that this principle should now be judged to be applicable on the global plane.

However, if the status of world social citizen should lead the individual to expect social and economic just treatment as a right, the behaviour of in-dividual world citizens must reflect this condition. In the domestic setting, the recipient of welfare benefits must not abuse this redistribution of wealth; and the contributor must willingly assist in the relief of want and suffering.

Similar obligations must be considered to rest on the shoulders of world citizens. The recipients of transnational welfare must not divert and fritter their aid in excessive expenditure on weapons and the corruption of well-placed officials. Global distributive justice demands local distributive justice within any given community. In turn, the more fortunate have the responsibility of giving some of their time, skill and wealth for the benefit of the less fortunate. This action needs to be taken not just directly in the international arena (for example, by supporting Oxfam or working for Voluntary Service Overseas); it also requires the world citizen to exert pressure on his own national government. The failure of most developed states even to approach the UN target of a 0.7 per cent of GNP allocation to overseas aid is some indication of the non-fulfilment by the community of nations of the world social citizenship ideal. Insofar as the primary purpose of the nation-state is to protect the interests of its own citizens, perhaps this should occasion no surprise. For instance, the British commitment to global redistributive justice has been sustained in the 1980s only by the generous consciences of individuals counterbalancing the government's reduction of the overseas aid budget.

Progress towards a world of greater distributive justice depends therefore on an increase in the number of individuals thinking of themselves as world social citizens and taking opportunities to behave in this way. And that means primarily living up to the responsibilities of the status. For no matter how ably the morality and practicality of the status is demonstrated, the necessary changes to bring it more effectively into realisation will be resisted if the complementary obligations are not evidently being met. That is a matter of attitudes and therefore in the broadest sense a matter of education. Willy Brandt, in his report, expressed the hope that the younger generation

. . . are more concerned with human values than with bureaucratic regulations and technocratic constraints. And we are convinced of the great role education has to play [in alerting young people to] their own responsibilities and the opportunities of cooperation.[49]

The message was reiterated by Mrs Bruntland (p. 154). It is time therefore to turn our attention to the educational processes necessary to prepare young citizens for their social status, rights and obligations.

Education for social citizenship

Much education for citizenship has been political education of a rather constitutional kind. But once teachers and pupils start asking the question, What is politics for? they soon arrive at Harold Lasswell's famous definition of politics – who gets what, when, how? And the 'who' is often a social question; the 'what', an economic question. The education of young citizens must therefore embrace sociological and economic understanding for two reasons: because the political cannot be comprehended without the socio-economic; and because, as we have seen, citizenship has as intrinsic social content. Social citizenship education must therefore equip the young person with the knowledge, understanding and skills to participate fully in the welfare society

276

or state of which he is a member. He must also be sensitised to the problems of competing claims for scarce resources and to have had some elementary experience in struggling with self-interest and conscience in order to make a judgement and a decision. In short, he must be taught that socio-economic issues are moral as much as technical. In the words of the Russian philosopher, Berdyaev, 'Bread for myself is an economic problem. Bread for my neighbour is a spiritual problem.'[50]

The elements of an education in social citizenship at the state level are threefold. The first is Social History. The aims of this element would be to provide an understanding of how the present pattern of social welfare in the pupil's own state had developed and to contrast that with what has operated in previous periods. The assumptions about the rights and obligations of the individual under different welfare régimes may then be compared. The second element should be an understanding of the current meaning of social citizenship in terms of institutional provision and the policies of the government and other parties (where they exist) towards the system. Finally, the pupil needs social 'life skills'. These should include activity as both donor and recipient: ways of helping the less fortunate in society (p. 207); and ways of claiming welfare benefits if one becomes numbered among the less fortunate oneself. Since History has ceased to be merely past politics in the narrowest of senses, Social History has become increasingly popular in schools. For example, in England the 16+ examination boards offer options, usually for the period since c. 1750, which are extremely popular; and the issues of the Poor Law and the origins of the welfare state naturally feature in the syllabus. More contentious are the contributions which are made by Economics, Sociology and Development Studies.

The need to educate young people in economic awareness is becoming increasingly recognised. However, the selection of material will be partial insofar as the teacher's understanding of citizenship is partial — as is so often the case. The point may be illustrated with a touch of irony by reference to some of the advocacy for economic literacy in England in recent years. In 1975 Sir Keith Joseph, then an Opposition MP, addressed a meeting of the Politics Association. Commenting on the project to advance political literacy then being conducted under the aegis of the association, Sir Keith declared,

I cannot forbear to point out that the fashionable collectivist bias of our time creeps into what are admittedly only draft documents . . . . I hope that more place will be accorded to the view that, given the right framework of laws and institutions, men and women will provide for each other . . . most of the needs, be they of goods, services or amenities, that are desired.[51]

Four years later he was a minister and a close adviser to Mrs Thatcher as prime minister in implementing a stern monetarist policy. As a direct consequence, unemployment rose very substantially. In 1983 Dr Robert Stradling noted that, since one in four school leavers could not obtain a job, teachers 'find themselves in an invidious position. Should they . . . encourage appropriate attitudes to work . . . . Or, should they prepare school leavers for . . . the prospect of recurrent periods of unemployment throughout their working lives?'[52] In providing practical advice for teachers for the latter strategy he implicitly contradicted Sir Keith Joseph's message. The long-term or recurrent unemployed cannot behave as socially independent and self-reliant citizens; they are dependent on government training schemes and welfare benefits. Effective social citizenship education needed to reflect this reality.

The argument over whether the state provision of welfare should be restricted or expanded has become a central issue of controversy between left and right in a number of states. If a teacher selects and/or presents material which presupposes support for either a socially divisive or egalitarian policy, he could justifiably be accused of bias. Paradoxically, by trying to make their subject more academically respectable, teachers of Social Studies (in the USA initially and in many other countries subsequently) have attracted two major criticisms. The 'New Social Studies' have emphasised basic concepts and investigative techniques: the resultant thinness of subject-matter has led to accusations of intellectual shallowness. Use of case-study investigations of social issues, which might counter this criticism has led to accusations of pedagogical bias in their selection. Because one of the main functions of Sociology is to understand the problems of society, lessons must inevitably, implicitly if not explicitly, involve a *critical* assessment of the society in which the pupil and school are placed. Add the crucial role of Marx in developing the discipline, and one has a recipe for suspicion and complaint from parents and those in authority in capitalist states: they feel that teachers of Sociology are endangering the social status quo. Maybe accusations of slanted teaching are sometimes warranted. But the general air of distrust that can thus be bred makes a thorough and critical teaching of social citizenship difficult, even hazardous. Siegfried George, a professor of Social Studies at a West German university, has provided this telling anecdote in the context of teaching about social justice:

I am the coauthor of a textbook . . . which immediately provoked public discussion when it was published ten years ago [1971]. By some the book was labelled 'communist' and by others 'destructive of our society', but by many scholars and some *Bundesländer* it was considered progressive and educationally sound. Today, I think, it would be impossible politically for such a textbook to be admitted into our schools.[53]

But the use of Political Science, Economics or Sociology to illuminate the issue of social citizenship presents an intellectual difficulty in any case. The very fact that each of these disciplines can throw some light on the matter is merely another way of saying that it requires multi-disciplinary treatment. The area of Development Studies, properly understood, can cast the appropriately wide-angled beam. It does not simply relate to poverty in the Third World. In the words of the Irish authority, Dr H. O'Neill,

That economic growth *is* development is a myth. Development is concerned with the development of the whole man, and of all men. It must embrace considerations of equity and justice.[54]

The goal of development is social citizenship. The relevance of development is consequently universal. It is not only in so-called developing countries that social injustice may be found. Comprehensive Development Studies in schools can therefore raise very pertinent questions about social citizenship in the pupil's own country, in countries of contrasting economies and cultures, and as a cosmopolitan ideal.

In practice, Development Studies are usually interpreted as meaning pupils in affluent countries learning about poverty in countries of the Third World. Indeed, the UN definition of 'development' is 'the process of sensitisation of citizens in industrialised countries to the problems of global development [and] their particular effect on the Third World.'[55] Even this narrow attempt at creating empathy among school children of the North for the disadvantaged of the South is often resisted. A French educational researcher, for example, has reported that

development education is hardly spontaneous on the part of teachers or of the Ministry officials responsible . . . . Will development education involve a one-sided politicisation? Some parents express this fear . . . . Will development education be in contradiction with the assimilation of national community values? Some officials are concerned about this.[56]

How much more threatening would a holistic programme of Development Studies be in such circumstances? A programme of this kind would attempt to bring young people to an understanding of the need for levelling up the provision of education, health services, housing and employment opportunities for the least advantaged. These could well be identified as women or ethnic minorities in the pupil's own, relatively affluent state. He might then come to see his own society in some way as a microcosm of the whole world. And if co-operation between the socially privileged and socially disadvantaged in a mutual effort for greater social justice is the mark of conscientious social citizenship, then such co-operative endeavour is as valid on the cosmopolitan as on the state level. Development Studies, truly taught, offers the cardinal lesson that social citizenship is globally indivisible.

REFERENCES

1. *Encyclopedia Americana*, p. 742.
2. Judgment in *Perez v. Brownell*, 1958.
3. J. Rawls, *A Theory of Justice* (Clarendon Press, 1972), p. 97.
4. A. V. Dicey, *The Law of the Constitution* (Macmillan, 10th edn, 1959), p. 39.
5. Aristotle, *Politics*, p. 96.
6. *Magna Carta*, clause 39.
7. Lord Devlin, quoted in J. Harvey & L. Bather, *The British Constitution and Politics* (Macmillan, 5th edn, 1982), p. 345.
8. 1789 Declaration of Rights, Article 2.
9. Universal Declaration of Human Rights, Preamble.
10. 1793 Declaration of Rights, Preamble, reprinted in J. M. Thompson, *French Revolution Documents*, p. 238 (author's translation).

11. Marx, *On the Jewish Question*, p. 53.
12. H. Jackson, 'Crossed lines in the pursuit of liberty', *Guardian* 11 May 1985.
13. P. Wright, *Spycatcher* (Stoddart, 1987, General Paperbacks edn, 1988), pp. 438 & 439–40.
14. An Act for Declaring the Rights and Liberties of the Subject . . . ., reprinted in J. H. .W. Verzijl (ed.), *Human Rights in Historical Perspective* (Enschedé en Zonen, 1958, p. 27.
15. J. Bentham, *Anarchical Fallacies;* see Stewart, *Dictionary of Political Quotations*, p. 14.
16. Tennyson, 'You ask me, Why' (1833).
17. S. Carmichael, quoted in A. Oakley, *Subject Women* (Collins, 1982), p. 29.
18. M. Wight, 'Why Is there No International Theory?', in H. Butterfield & W. Wight (eds), *Diplomatic Investigations* (Allen & Unwin, 1966), p. 20.
19. Kant, *Perpetual Peace*, quoted in Linklater, *Men and Citizens*, p. 53.
20. Helsinki Final Act, 'Basket One', clause 7, reprinted in *Keesing's Contemporary Archives*, 1975, col. 27302 A.
21. M. Dean, 'Why Britain remains Europe's guilty party', *Guardian*, 18 March 1985.
22. Grotius, *The Law of War and Peace*, quoted in P. F. Butler, 'The Individual and International Relations' in J. Mayall (ed.), *The Community of States* (Allen & Unwin, 1982), p. 117.
23. The Law in Education Project, *'Understanding the Law' Teaching Pack*: Notes (School Curriculum Development Committee, n.d.), p. 2.
24. Reprinted in Muñoz, *La educatión politica*, p. 462 (author's translation).
25. Jarolimek, 'The Social Studies: An Overview', p. 16; C. L. Hahn, 'The Right to a Political Education' in N. B. Tarrow (ed.), *Human Rights and Education* (Pergamon, 1987), p. 183.
26. K. Joseph, 'Why Teach History in School?' *The Historian*, quoted in H. Kaye, 'The New Right and History', *The Socialist Register*, 1987, p. 351.
27. Section 18 (3).
28. J. Edwards & P. Cook, 'Law Course for Fifth Formers', *Law in Education News* (School Curriculum Development Committee, Summer 1988), p. 5.
29. *Final Document of the International Congress on the Teaching of Human Rights*, quoted in J. V. Torney-Purta, 'Human Rights', in N. J. Graves *et al.* (eds), *Teaching for International Understanding, Peace and Human Rights* (UNESCO, 1984), pp. 59–60.
30. Swann, *Education for All*, p. 377.
31. Quoted in H. Starkey, 'Human Rights: the values for world studies and multi-cultural education', *Westminister Studies in Education* vol. 9 (1986).
32. From D. Heater, *Human Rights Education in Schools* (Council of Europe, 1984), p. 13.
33. Marshall, *Citizenship and Social Class*, p. 10.
34. Burke, *Reflections on the Revolution in France* (Dent ed., 1910), p. 57.
35. M. Walzer, *Spheres of Justice* (Martin Robertson, 1983), p. 67.
36. Thompson (ed.), *French Revolution Documents*, p. 113.
37. R. H. Tawney, *Religion and the Rise of Capitalism* (1922, Penguin ed. 1938), p. 280.
38. Rousseau, *Discourse on Political Economy*, quoted in B. Jordan, *The State: Authority and Autonomy* (Blackwell, 1985), p. 110.
39. Conservative Party, *The Next Moves Forward* (Election Manifesto, part 2) (Conservative Central Office, 1987), pp. 15–16.

40. J. Moore, 'An independent approach to the welfare state', *Guardian*, 2 October 1987.
41. G. Myrdal, *Beyond the Welfare State*, quoted in W. A. Robson, *Welfare State and Welfare Society* (Allen & Unwin, 1976), p. 177.
42. Moore, 'Independent approach to the welfare state'.
43. B. S. Turner, *Citizenship and Capitalism* (Allen & Unwin 1986), p. xii.
44. C. A. R. Crosland, *The Future of Socialism* (Cape abr. edn, 1964), p. 78.
45. United Nations Organisation, *International Covenant on Economic, Social and Cultural Rights*, Preamble, reprinted from UN Monthly Chronicle, vol. iv (1967) p. 5.
46. *The Times*, 21 December 1940, quoted in W. Temple, *Christianity and Social Order* (Penguin, 1942), p. 74.
47. Myers, *Gaia Atlas*, p. 231.
48. World Commission on Environment and Development, *Our Common Future*, p. 43.
49. Independent Commission on International Development Issues, *North-South*, p. 11.
50. Quoted in P. Jones *et al.*, *Development Studies: A Handbook for Teachers* (School of Oriental & African Studies, 1977), p. 2.
51. K. Joseph, 'Education, Politics and Society', *Teaching Politics*, vol. 5 (1976).
52. R. Stradling *et al.*, *Teaching Controversial Issues* (Edward Arnold, 1984), p. 28.
53. S. George, 'Society and Social Justice as Problems of Political Education in West Germany', J. Morrissett & A. M. Williams (ed.), *Social/Political Education in Three Countries* (Social Science Education Consortium, Inc./Eric Clearinghouse, 1981), pp. 238–9.
54. Quoted in P. Jones *et al.*, *Development Studies Handbook*, p. 2.
55. UN Working Group on Development Education, quoted in C.-H. Foubert, 'Working in Partnership with the Third World' in NGLS, *Development Education: The State of the Art* (United Nations Non Governmental Liaison Service, 1986), p. 67.
56. M. Margairaz, 'In-School Development Education', ibid., pp. 101–2.

CHAPTER EIGHT

Barriers to A Holistic Concept

8.1 GENERAL DIFFICULTIES

The common good can never be actualised. There will always be a debate over the exact nature of citizenship. No final agreement can ever be reached.

Chantal Mouffe[1]

Irreconcilable ideals?

Citizenship as a useful political concept is in danger of being torn asunder; and any hope of a coherent civic education left in tatters as a consequence. By a bitter twist of historical fate, the concept, which evolved to provide a sense of identity and community, is on the verge of becoming a source of communal dissension. As more and more diverse interests identify particular elements for their doctrinal and practical needs, so the component parts of the citizenship idea are being made to do service for the whole. And under the strain of these centrifugal forces, citizenship as a total ideal may be threatened with disintegration. Maybe that the attempt we are making in the present book to bundle so much meaning into the term is unrealistically to overload its capacity. Certainly the difficulties confronting any attempt to achieve widespread agreement to a generous and holistic definition are so formidable that they must be squarely faced before the positive case can be presented.

The evidence of history provides little cause to believe that any search for an agreed, all-embracing and permanent definition of citizenship might be successful. Both its theory and practice have constantly changed in response to particular economic, social and political circumstances. The justification for the concept and institution, it can well be argued, lies precisely in its pragmatic flexibility. The nature and utility of citizenship in the Greek city-state must surely be recognised as utterly different from the ways in which the concept has become realised in the modern nation-state. The extraordinary diversity of manner in which citizenship has manifested itself is evident from the historical outline provided in Part One above. Particular disagreements over interpretations and ideals have also contributed to the analysis in chapters

5–7. Neither at any given point in time nor over any span of time has there been even a vision let alone the practice of a citizenship that was both all-embracing in its nature and acceptable as a universal principle. The Greeks came close. Some, notably Socrates, even achieved the most difficult feat of simultaneously embracing the ideas of state and cosmopolitan citizenships. But the circumstances were peculiar. There was a homogeneity of culture within and among the city-states. Large portions of the population were excluded from the status, as were all the 'barbarians' beyond the geographical limits of Greek colonisation. And citizenship of the *polis* and *cosmopolis* were compatible because the latter remained a metaphysical ideal and not a political reality.

If the Greeks barely managed a comprehensive understanding of citizenship in their confined political world, how much more difficult is it today? Virtually all inhabitants of a given state are citizens; some 170 states throughout the world need to be incorporated in any universal definition; and local, national, regional and global levels of political activity vie with each other for a portion of the citizenship blanket definition. The search for such a definition – applicable and acceptable for all times and places – would appear in principle, therefore, rather pointless. What is more, there is considerable evidence to suggest that what universality the concept might have had is being rapidly weakened by a series of tensions. Incompatible pairs of definitions are each displaying some increase in power. As they tug towards their opposite poles, so any hope of salvaging, let alone strengthening the concept as a whole, seems to fade into unreality.

Four sets of polarising trends

We may identify four main trends. The first is the division between those who focus on the individual and those who emphasise the importance of citizenship for society. In the words of Alasdair MacIntyre, 'the crucial moral opposition is between liberal individualism in some version or other and the Aristotelian tradition in some version or other.'[2] The liberal tradition defines citizenship largely in terms of individual rights. By Lockean contractual argument or the utilitarian case of a John Stuart Mill the individual *qua* citizen has certain rights to be free of interference from, or oppression by, the state. It is this freedom which distinguishes a citizen from a subject. The essential character of the citizen is consequently vigilance in defence of his rights and liberties. Morality consists in the full flowering of the individual person, and citizenship provides the necessary freedom for this to occur. The alternative, Greek tradition places priority on the positive view of liberty – citizenship provides opportunities to serve the community. Morality consists in the conscientious discharge of one's civic duties and obligations.

The modern western democratic interpretation of citizenship, whether by political philosophers or politicians or citizens themselves, has tended to accept the liberal version. Furthermore, by the 1980s more citizens were enjoying more freedoms than ever before – of thought, expression, assembly and association. Yet unease about the loss of the Greek tradition was being voiced. Already in 1928 the English political scientist, Harold Laski, wrote,

Anyone who compares the quality of citizenship in ancient Greece with that of our own day cannot help but perceive a certain loss of spiritual energy. We have believed that the mere conflict of private interests will, given liberty of contract, necessarily result in social good.[3]

Laski's co-operative solution is not one that would commend itself to all those who today seek a revival of civic virtue. For there are many on the right of the political spectrum who, while emphasising the urgent need for a rediscovery of the civic virtues of community obligations and cohesion, argue fervently the case for economic freedom. Moreover, right-wing (as opposed to moderate) advocates of a communitarian style of citizenship also hold that in some Western states the political negative freedom from state control and the positive rights of social citizenship have advanced too far and must to some extent be rolled back. Furthermore, as hundreds of millions of citizens become gradually liberated, both economically and politically in western style in the Communist states, the architects of these changes (notably Gorbachev and Deng Xiaoping) are struggling with the same fundamental problems of harmonising individualism and communitarianism. Thus have the two traditions now come to stand in increasingly stark competition with each other.

The second, closely related intensifying antithesis is between the private and the public citizen. It is a truism that the state impinges on the individual's life with so much greater pressure than at almost any other time in history. The demands and opportunities for the citizen actively to participate in this relationship have similarly never been greater – at least in states which claim some semblance of democracy. But, then, the reaction simply to 'switch off' is equally powerful. Let 'them' 'get on with it' and let me do my best to avoid involvement – by legal and moral means if possible; and if not, a shrug of the shoulders will clear the conscience. It is too, less cynically, a clash between the demands of two kinds of freedoms: the freedom from civic concerns in order to pursue a private, family life; and the need to participate democratically in order to preserve political freedom.

The third area of disagreement derives from the difficulties of trying to incorporate a complex society into a coherent relationship with a unitary polity. As we have seen in Part One, until recently in the long history of state citizenship, the status belonged to a limited group of property-owning men, bound together by social and cultural affinities. Democracy demands that there be no such exclusiveness. The fact of the matter is that, even in states with the firmest citizenship traditions, many so-called citizens are decidedly more equal than others. What to do? Should every effort be made to progress to a homogeneous citizen-body? Or should the distinctive needs and problems of the various groups of second-class citizens be treated on separate terms, ignoring any attempt at citizenship uniformity, especially of the social kind? It is difficult to find a generic term for these groups who so evidently miss out on full citizenship rights. The term 'minority' is commonly used; though, of course, it must be understood in a qualitative not quantitative sense. Women, a significant disadvantaged group, are scarcely a numerical minority! Add to them, according to circumstance, religious, cultural and racial minorities and the 'underclass' of the poor, and collectively the 'minorities' are a clear majority of any given population.

The clash within the citizenship ideal has arisen because of the rejection of the traditional goal of assimilation among and for the 'minorities' in favour of the alternative goal of integraton. Assimilation may be understood as the process of equalisation by the loss of separate identity. For the sake of an escape from discrimination the minority is willing to discard its particualr identity and become absorbed into the majority, taking on its culture and standards along with its privileges. The alternative is integration, whereby the minority is accepted as a group equal in worth and dignity to the majority, but has privileges or rights and a culture apt for itself. The terms are normally applied to cultural policies and trends in multiracial societies. Nevertheless, the concepts and the distinction they contain would seem usefully extensible to the citizenship status of minorities of all kinds. Citizenship entails total legal and political assimilation and at least a modicum of social and cultural assimilation. Citizens are equal before the law, their votes are equal and they have equal opportunities for political office. The concept of social citizenship presupposes at least a 'floor' of living standards, including health care and education, below which no one should be allowed to fall. Culturally state citizenship implies a sufficient sense of common identity to generate a loyal commitment to the land and one's fellow citizens. In the integrationist model citizenship is barely relevant to the requirements of the particular groups. The just needs of each minority will be different from each other's and from the needs of the majority. These particular needs should be treated separately and on their own merits and not according to the design of some universally applicable citizenship blueprint.

Let us take a few examples of these opposed treatments of the problem of so-called minorities. The story of the fight by women has historically been a struggle against the assumption that the sexual distinction made the human female not just different from but, in legal and political terms, inferior to their male counterparts. The struggle for the right to be considered competent and legally able to enter into contracts, own property, be individuals in their own right, not merely as wives, was originally and continues to be a fight for recognition of female worth. Women should be treated as citizens not because they are or are not capable of being the same as men, but because they undertake their own distinctive functions of equal significance to the purpose and success of the state. This is the integrative argument. The assimilationist has evolved more recently. This is the bra-burning feminist campaign to be treated as if they are men. Citizenship, so this argument runs, has historically been a male preserve. Women must renounce their unique attributes in order to gain access. The equality of citizenship can be achieved only by sameness. Men have full citizenship, therefore women must behave as men. Carole Pateman has highlighted these contrary traditions:

The suffrage, the more recent reforms such as the participation of women on juries, equal pay and anti-discrimination legislation, reform of marriage and rape law, decriminalization of prostitution, are all seen as allowing women to become citizens like men and owners of property in their persons like men. Historically this argument is unusual; until recently, most feminists demanded civil equality in the expectation that they would give their equal standing a distinctive expression as women.[4]

Similarly the policy of integrating the poor into society preceded the goal of fully assimilating them into society. Historically property (and not just of one's own person) was held to be an essential precondition of citizenship (p. 162). The poor, because of their inability to meet this criterion, could not therefore be considered full citizens. The relief of the poor was an act of charity. The poor were able to obtain support from the state not by right of citizenship but by proving to a humane state that their condition would otherwise be intolerable. T. H. Marshall cited the classic case of the effects of the 1834 Poor Law Amendment Act in England:

The Poor Law treated the claims of the poor, not as an integral part of the rights of the citizen, but as an alternative to them — as claims which could be met only if the claimants ceased to be citizens in any true sense of the word.[5]

It is an attitude that is still widely held. But it now has to compete with the social citizenship approach to the matter (pp. 265–277). This is, that certain services should be available as a right to all citizens irrespective of wealth. The financial cost of universal provision, whatever the ability to pay, is worth the saving of the poor from the uncitizenly humiliation of begging for assistance. As the ideological Left defend with passion the citizenship principle of universality against the 'targeting' of the truly needy by the Right, another source of tension in interpreting the citizenship ideal becomes increasingly plain.

A third case of variant policies relates to the problem of multi-ethnic states. The issue may concern either the citizenship status of an ethnic minority diffused geographically or one concentrated in a particular province or region. Although the detailed policies will differ between these situations, both present the same basic question of whether assimilationist or integrative goals should be pursued. A state bent on national cohesion will wish to absorb its minorities: hence the Russification policy of Alexander III in the 1890s and the Africanisation policy of Idi Amin in the 1970s, for instance. The aim is to ensure the cultural uniformity of the population in the belief that the loyalty of the citizens will be enhanced thereby. The alternative is to concede separate cultural identities, even provincial autonomy. Such a policy may be adopted either as a positive preference or because of the dangers of assimilation. For although the objective of assimilation is greater strength, it can often backfire, provoking the minorities to vigorous protest, even to attempts at secession if the geographical circumstances are propitious. One political scientist has noted that as a general rule,

Minorities subjected to persistent discrimination, particularly where this is accompanied by arbitrary misgovernment or brutality, quickly develop a desire for independence.[6]

Unless assimilation is undertaken gently, therefore, integration may be a more prudent programme. For example, the recent policy of French governments has been to decentralise as much power as possible. One of the motives has been to defuse the peril of mini-nationalist movements in Corsica, Brittany and Languedoc. Movements for provincial autonomy or secession are multiplying throughout the world, including most famously in the late 1980s in the Soviet Union as Gorbachev's reforms have encouraged honest openness of expression. Assimilation of all citizens in a greater national identity or a loosening of the ties of citizen-nationality remain the opposed options.

If a number of states are faced with the dilemma of whether to treat all citizens alike or to adopt differential policies according to the needs and demands of separate groups, how much more difficult is it to conceive of a definition of citizenship that will be internationally applicable? So much discussion about state citizenship tends to be predicated upon the West European/North American contractarian and liberal traditions of political thinking and revolutionary and parliamentary experiences. Is it realistic to expect 'tribal', Islamic, Communist and authoritarian societies to adapt to these assumptions or for the western tradition to expand to accommodate these very different doctrinal and institutional systems? The quarrels over interpreting the basic ideal of universal human rights provides a lesson germane to any attempted universal definition of citizenship. An Australian commentator has described the launching of the Universal Declaration:

The six communist bloc nations abstained because, among other things, there was a lack of adequate economic and social rights, the absence of a denunciation of Fascism and aggression and the lack of a listing of duties which each person has to the state. Saudi Arabia believed that the Declaration clashed with the philosophy of Islam. South Africa, inevitably, also abstained, since it thought that the Declaration went too far on racism.[7]

Forty years later much the same disagreements persist.

If different national traditions and conditions have produced different styles of state citizenship and different conceptions of universal human rights, how much greater difficulty will attend any attempt to develop more fully a cosmopolitan citizenship? The dichotomy between the demands of state and world citizenship is the fourth example where contrary trends are pulling with gathering strength in opposite directions. Whenever cosmopolitanism has seemed to be a realistic force it has competed with state citizenship in the individual's consciousness for his sense of identity and loyalty. The two stances have seemed incompatible. In the aphorism of John Le Carré, 'We are patriots because we are afraid to be cosmopolitan, cosmopolitan because we are afraid to be patriots.'[8] The point to be made here is that this incompatibility is becoming increasingly noticeable. The polarisation of the two ideals has become so much more evident in recent years because the multiplication of the number of sovereign nation-states has coincided with the mounting realisation that a cosmopolitan frame of mind may well be essential for human survival.

Each of some 170 states now claims virtually complete loyalty of its citizens as a means of sustaining its claim to sovereignty, in many cases only very recently acquired. This requirement of citizen-loyalty can be more easily assured than hitherto because of modern means of mass communication. Additionally, the more awesome the planet's economic and environmental problems become, the more the threatened inhabitants cleave to their own kind. The bewildered and frightened seek security in the community they know. Fear of the submergence of a comforting patriotism in an amorphous macro-global community is unnerving. National *sauve qui peut* is, of course, no novel phenomenon: but today there are so many more self-conscious and autonomous political units in the world than in the age of the great European empires. Equally, those who recognise the dangers of unrestrained nationalism are becoming increasingly articulate. The English political scientist, John Dunn, is nothing if not forthright in voicing this judgement:

Nationalism is the starkest political shame of the twentieth century, the deepest, most intractable and yet most unanticipated blot on the political history of the world since the year 1900.[9]

And so, as more and more people become aware of the hazards of continuing national sovereignty and the perils facing the planet as a whole, they fear not to think of themselves as world citizens. But not only has this growing sense of the reality of global interdependence to tussle with the persistent reality of national sovereignty and identity, it has also to cope with the continued centrality of the state in political theory. As Dr Linklater has shown in his *Men and Citizens in the Theory of International Relations*, throughout the history of political theory a sharp distinction has almost always been drawn between the individual *qua* man and the individual *qua* citizen. Moreover, the moral obligations of the one role are in tension with the moral obligations of the other. This thesis may be strengthened by the addition of two further points especially relevant to the argument being outlined here of the exacerbation of tensions in our own time. The first is that, insofar as the tradition of grand political theorising has been resumed by the writings of, *par excellence*, Rawls and Nozick, this conventional concentration on the state as the assumed sole arena for the citizen's political activity has not been effectively questioned. In past centuries when there was so little opportunity for individuals to behave as world citizens, this preoccupation of political theory was an effective reflection of reality. Now, at the end of the twentieth century this continuing concentration on the political theory of the state as a discrete entity is looking inceasingly obsolete.

A term stretched beyond its elasticity?

At bottom the problem may be this: that as the concept of citizenship is required to take on both broader and deeper meaning, it cannot take the strain of the semantic burden. When the Greeks developed the institution of citizenship it was never intended to embrace so many people claiming so many rights as today. They would certainly have found the following statement from present-day Australia about animal rights incomprehensible:

Within the diet of most families, we could say that cod and chickens have relatively low equal status and are obviously excluded from the notion of citizenship . . . . The question is: are dogs citizens in the making? The character of such legal personalities on the margins of society illustrates the contention of my argument that citizenship expands outwards creating anomalies on the periphery of society which are typically resolved by law in a universalistic manner.[10]

But the process of extending and deepening has always caused difficulties. The struggle by the citizens of the Greek city-states to prevent the broadening of the membership led to internal tensions and warfare, which contributed in large measure to the collapse of the Greek city-state system. In the Roman Empire the extension of the status led to a feeling that the privilege was being diluted and to a consequent dilution of the sense of pride and loyalty which had contributed so much to the strength of the Republic and Empire at their height. In the Middle Ages the defence of citizenship privileges led both to the economic inhibitions of the guilds' restrictive practices and to tension between the cities and their rural environment.

Today, we see disillusionment and incompatibilities among the different strands of citizenship. Political rights, so hard-won and so extensive in the western world, are unused by many. In the great land of democracy, the USA, only half the voters voted in the 1988 presidential elections, so that Bush achieved this great office with the support of a mere 26 per cent of the electorate. Seventy million had not even bothered to register. In Western Europe a French MEP has said that, '. . . in all our countries, there has been, to varying degrees a falling off in participation, a gradual erosion in the numbers turning out to vote.'[11] In his Reith Lectures, Ralf Dahrendorf perceived more complex problems. He spoke of the welfare state endangering freedoms; of bureaucracies interposing themselves between citizens and their elected leaders; of the paralysis of decision-making by excessive participation; of the exaggerated demands by, for example, trade unions and feminists for fear of the backlash of increased unemployment and reduction of women's rights. Thus, in his view, are old rigidities being replaced by new rigidities. The very success that has attended the expansion of citizen rights

. . . is thwarted by our doing the right thing in the wrong way, liberating the subject of old to become a citizen, only to lock the citizen into the case of his own perverted rights.[12]

Perhaps we should not have come to this pass if citizenship had not accumulated so many meanings. The alternative would be to recognise that on the social stage man and woman play many parts. In his relationship with the planet and mankind as a whole the individual is not 'citizen' but 'Man', identified by species and not juridico-political status. As an economic unit, the individual is earner, consumer or recipient of charitable poor relief. As a person whose life must willy-nilly be to a considerable extent shaped by government decisions over which he has no real control, even in the most democratic states, the individual remains a subject. Citizenship is then confined to very specific areas of status and activity: national identity, protection against arbitrary legal action, the right to vote and some access for a limited number of citizens to political participation.

Contending educational objectives

If citizenship in its fullest sense contains so many tensions and contradictions, there can have been little chance for educationists to construct comprehensive and coherent programmes of citizenship education. The American, Jack Nelson, has identified six views of citizenship, namely, 'nationalistic loyalty, exemplary behaviour, junior social scientist, social criticism, reconstructionism [i.e. world citizenship], social activism'. He comments:

The above views often coexist in school districts where individual teachers have differing viewpoints of the nature and purpose of citizenship education. Conflicts are inevitable among advocates of differing views of citizenship. [13]

The pedagogical problems are highlighted by the ineffectiveness of much of the teaching. A number of studies, especially in the USA, have shown how little impact formal political teaching has on attitudes necessary for the effective citizen – for example, interest in public issues, a willingness to participate, belief that involvement is worthwhile. To take one of the most frequently cited American investigations: Langton concluded in 1969, 'Our findings certainly do not support the thinking of those who look to the civics curriculum in American high schools as even a minor source of political socialisation.' [14] Clarification of objectives and a more effective marrying of teaching techniques to those objectives is necessary. True, much progress has been made; but at the very least, the best practice needs more widespread application. Yet however skilled the educationists might become in tackling this task from their purely professional point-of-view, they are still impeded by the lack of clearcut answers to three essential questions.

The first is how to resolve the basic dichotomy between democratic and élitist goals. The idea that schools for the majority should cultivate a deferent and disciplined demeanour is scarcely new. However, it has gained renewed strength in a number of countries in reaction to youthful outbursts of various kinds since the 1960s. Whether these have expressed themselves as radical political demands or nihilistic violence, the schools are urged to ensure 'more responsible' behaviour. At the same time the very contrary view is widely and firmly held. This is that a healthy democracy requires sure foundations to be laid in school by instilling in young people an understanding of their rights and responsibilities. Two conditions have strengthened the competitiveness between these two opposed philosophies in recent years. One is the recognition that school ethos, teaching style and subject-content all interact. The traditionalists stand for didactic presentation by teachers who demand respect and teach the civic virtues of honour and duty and the acceptance of social competition and hierarchy. The reformers emphasise co-operative learning among pupils and teachers as both an effective mode of education and preparation for an egalitarian society in which the exercise and preservation of rights must be crucially defended against the abuses of the privileged. Every component in each of these teaching philosophies is essential for the effectiveness of the whole. It is both hypocritical and inefficient − to caricature the argument − for the teacher to shout 'Sit still, fold your arms, don't ask questions and learn by heart this list of our country's freedoms which I am going to write on the blackboard'. The other condition is the co-existence of the two opposed views of civic education. In no previous age has the reformist model been so widely accepted and implemented by teachers. In no previous age, therefore, have the two models faced each other in such stark opposition. The intensity of mutual hostility is vividly illustrated by events in the German *Land* of Hessen when a new Social Studies programme was produced in 1972. The Dutch educationist, Langeveld, has reported:

This plan came under severe criticism from the Christian Democratic party and affiliated newspapers, like *Bild*. The accusations were that the plan was not based on the constitution of the FRG; that self-determination and participation in democratic procedures were the main goals; that conflicts were emphasized one-sidedly; that the class struggle was stimulated and particular interests fostered; and that by these goals the plan prevented the identification of the students with the state.
The whole affair ended with the retraction of the plan and the retirement from politics of the minister of education of Hessen, Ludwig von Friedeburg.[15]

These dramatic events were but a reflection of a general political and popular demand for a return to the more conservative teaching of traditional values which became common throughout North America and Western Europe in the 1970s and 1980s. How, then, can teachers be expected to undertake the task of citizenship education with any assurance when such a fundamental disagreement runs like a geological fault-line across the debate about objectives?

The second basic question concerns education for state versus education for world citizenship. One of the objections to the Hessen plan was that it 'prevents the identification of the students with the state'. This aim, with the implied need to foster a sense of loyalty, has been a common purpose of civic education throughout the ages. New nation-states are anxiously striving to consolidate their identity; even mature states are conscious of the political dangers of ethnic differences within their borders. All therefore look to the schools to instil a lasting sense of loyalty. Attempts to render young people conscious of and conscience-stricken about global issues can therefore be interpreted as a dangerous diversion of that insecure feeling of national identity. In advocating teaching for global awareness the Secretary-General of the Finnish United Nations Association has referred to the distinction that has been drawn between 'maintenance learning' and 'innovative learning':

Most of the learning in schools is more likely to be maintenance learning, which is designed to maintain the existing system and the established way of life. . . . The only innovative stimulus must come through surprise events or 'learning by shock'. But under current conditions of global uncertainty, learning by shock may prove to be a formula for disaster.[16]

Again, teachers are receiving contradictory messages: bolster and conserve the established nation-state; or adapt to preserve an endangered planet. And the dilemma has never been more acute because state/national objectives for citizenship have never before been so effectively challenged by well-planned and cogently argued programmes of World Studies.

Furthermore, World Studies advocates strenuously argue the case for inter-disciplinary study. The defenders of discrete subjects remain powerful. Thus are teachers faced with the third basic question: how to resolve this curricular disagreement. The division of opinion about whether citizenship education should be undertaken through separate treatments in various subject contexts or through an integrated programme has, in fact, two facets. The arguments for separate subjects include the need to educate young people in established modes of understanding or forms of knowledge and the difficulties for the teacher of handling integrated styles of teaching. In the words of the English educational philosopher, Paul Hirst, 'The demands of seriously, through-and-through, rationally planned curriculum work on a topic or project basis seem to me absolutely gargantuan.'[17] The opposite point-of-view is that the planning of separate citizenship inputs into History, Geography, Religious Studies and classes in the native language is equally gargantuan. And if citizenship involves an understanding of Law, Politics, Sociology and Economics, as surely it does, the time-table cannot bear the strain of so many disparate specialist disciplines. An identifiable multi-disciplinary time allocation with an integrated syllabus is, so the alternative argument has it, the only reasonable solution. In practice, however, the teacher faces pressures from many interest groups as well. This is the second facet of the subject v. interdisciplinary debate. In recent years enthusiasts for particular approaches to social education have urged teachers to accommodate their needs. Political Education, Sociology, Economics, Law-related Studies, Environmental Education, Development Studies, Peace Studies, Multicultural Education, Life Skills. All these in addition to the social and civic aspects of the more traditional school disciplines. Schools which conscientiously try to include them all have enormous problems of finding separate time allocation. And in any case, separate treatment will almost certainly deny the pupils the crucial understanding of the interrelationships and overlaps of the subject-matter. For it is precisely these interconnections, so characteristic of the modern world, that should be the core message of this teaching. Even if these subject areas are clustered, then there is a very real danger of a division between Social/Political Studies in a local/national setting and World/Global Studies in a planetary setting. The loss to a potential holistic understanding of the concept of citizenship is very evident. Without clearer thinking and guidelines from those responsible for overall curricular planning the classroom teacher can be forgiven for being utterly confused.

8.2 THE DEBATE IN BRITAIN

Something is rotten in the state of Britain, and all the parties know it . . . . The buzz-word emerging as the salve for this disease is something called citizenship . . . . Somewhere out there is an immense unsatisfied demand for it to mean something. But it needs to become much more than a word.

Hugo Young [18]

The British tradition of citizenship

Albeit haphazard, implicit and barely defined, characteristically British traditions of citizenship and citizenship education have none the less existed. In the late 1980s the citizen ideal was expounded and commended by politicians who seemed scarcely aware of these traditions. Citizenship suddenly became the simple panacea which they could easily communicate to the electorate. Here was the magic potion – though strangely mixed to different recipes by the various political pharmacists – which would palliate the moral, social and economic ills of the declining nation. However, disregard of the social, political and educational traditions of citizenship has tended to veil the true complexities of the concept. Paradoxically, while politicians have been peddling their simplicities, scholars have suggested that former historical explanations of the growth of British citizenship have been equally simplistic.

One may discern four distinctive elements in the British tradition of citizenship. First is the weakness of the state-citizen nexus. The retention of the monarchy as head of both state and a hierarchically-structured society; the principle that sovereignty resides in parliament and not the people; and the lack of a written, defining constitution and bill of rights have all been cited as reasons for the frailty of both state and citizen concepts in Britain. The conservative manipulation of the 1688 'Revolution' prevented Britain from cutting through these archaisms. The changing of all or some of these ancient principles and conventions has been canvassed as a necessary precondition for the proper flowering of the citizenship ideal. Interest in whether the Speaker of the House of Commons wears black tights or stockings and a suspender-belt epitomises for these critical observers the sheer obsolescence of the British political system.

On the other hand, England has been the proud and envied initiator of so many civic freedoms and rights: this is the second distinctive facet of British citizenship. How are these achievements to be truly interpreted? The pattern of Whig history – of the stately progress of the English parliamentary system – has long been questioned. What is now also being queried is the relationship of the bulk of the people to the freedoms and rights which did find their way into English law. How real were these freedoms and rights to the peasants, women, industrial workers, Roman Catholics, Jews and Irish, for example, over the course of centuries of English history? In particular, Marshall's quasi-Whig interpretation of the sequential achievement of civil, then political, then social citizenship (p. 100–101) has been thrown into doubt. Perhaps a truer picture is one of constant struggle by the disadvantaged, during the course of which some ancient rights have been lost as well as new ones gained. The lesson to be drawn therefore is that, in a period of attacks on the principle of social citizenship, not only must Marshall's optimism concerning its continued progress be discarded, a new phase of struggle by the poor, women and ethnic minorities is imperative. Harvey Kaye draws the following conclusion from this alternative, Marxist reading of English history:

By reversing the forward march of citizenship against the domain of class, Thatcherism has raised up the image of 'lost rights' which inspired popular movements from the fourteenth to the nineteenth century.[19]

The third tradition is the discharge of citizenly functions by amateur administrators, and voluntary helpers in a local context. The privileged gave of their time to be magistrates, mayors, local councillors; the concerned individuals of whatever status formed societies for civic purposes; and the religiously faithful undertook voluntary work through the churches. Denis Brogan drew the contrast with Britain's continental neighbours:

Alone among the great states, England kept and rejuvenated the medieval concept of the autonomous society, and those societies stepped in where the English state refused to tread . . . ..
In serving . . . church bodies, the ordinary man . . . gained the idea that there were duties that he *ought* to fulfil which were not imposed by law or sanctioned by punishment. If, as the French believe, the English are superior in 'civisme', here is one of the causes of the superiority.[20]

Some of these ways of acting the role of citizen have either been eroded or are no longer appropriate. As we shall see below, much of the Thatcherite appeal for more effective citizenship is an appeal for the reinvigoration of these traditional styles. The survival of a strong commitment to voluntary societies would seem to support the validity of the policy. On the other hand, it is quite clear that by no means all the tasks formerly undertaken by private citizens can be re-privatised; nor are the churches any longer in a position to mobilise the efforts of the bulk of the population. More seriously the initiative and pride of the local citizen has been severely undermined. The centralisation of communications, health and welfare provision over the past half-century has done much to weaken local autonomy. Ironically, the Thatcherite government, which has so lauded the Victorian municipal civic virtues, has further and very substantially undermined the authority of local government. Local control of housing, finance and education has been systematically assaulted. Civic initiative is difficult to sustain without autonomy.

The final British tradition of citizenship, though of briefer duration, was the identity with Empire. This sense of imperial citizenship may well have been an artificial veneer, though few would deny its strength at its height. For some, the mentality persists in its less attractive form of a nostalgia for 'greatness' and offensive xenophobia. The conscientious superiority of the white man's burden has become the repulsive arrogance of skinhead fascism. However, in the view of one academic analyst the social memory of empire

294

runs deeper than this. Nicholas Boyle has argued (though without using these terms) that current British notions of citizenship suffer from the shadow of the past imperial age.[21] Political citizenship suffers because of the retention of obsolete institutions adapted for and left over from the administration of the Empire. Social citizenship suffers because the welfare state, founded on the wealth of exploited colonial dependencies, can no longer be afforded. And citizenship as national identity, shorn of its imperial context, exists in a condition of amorphous confusion. To adapt Dean Acheson's quip, the British citizen has lost an Empire and not yet found a new identity.

Running as a thread through these interpretations of the past and its legacies has been an academic debate prompted by Almond and Verba's *The Civic Culture* (p. 176). They sketched a portrait of the ideal citizen as someone who combined most judiciously a mixture of active citizen and passive subject qualities. Such a model citizen, they claimed, was most likely to be found in Britain. The various elements in their proposition have all been challenged. The homogeneity which they claimed for British society took no account of the differences and resentments of the Celtic fringe, particularly the difficulties of Northern Ireland, nor of the multi-cultural nature of English society. Both of these features, it is true, have become much more prominent since their book was first published in 1963. Furthermore, the picture of a deferent, law-abiding society and gentle government is sadly disfigured if one paints on to it the history of Scotland in the early eighteenth century, England in the early nineteenth century and Ireland at almost any time. And the latent capacity for a clash between resentful citizens and harsh policing in England resurfaced in the urban riots of 1981 and the bitter miner's dispute of 1984.

Current problems

What, then, are the current problems facing Britain and which relate to the idea of citizenship? Let us list them under the five categories of the above chapters, namely, identity, civil/legal, political, social and moral. Old certainties of national and imperial citizenship identities have collapsed or are collapsing; the claims of new competing identities add to the sense of insecurity and confusion. If citizenship is a device to cultivate a sense of community and a common sense of purpose, evidence of widening divisions is an index of the weakening of the citizenship bond. And the gaps that have been stretching during the 1980s are in full display throughout the kingdom. Women struggle for equality with men. For example, in 1986 only 4.1 per cent of the English judiciary were women compared with 14 per cent in France; only 3.5 per cent of members of parliament compared with 28 per cent in Sweden. But at least women as a whole have not ceased to think of themselves as 'British'. In the division between the majority Whites and the ethnic minorities there is a danger of the minorities being neither thought of nor thinking themselves to be really British. Lord Scarman has asserted that 'Black people must think of themselves as "truly British" and heirs to the country's future if they wish to overcome racial discrimination.'[22] In pleading for an anti-racist movement, Keith Tompson has made the complementary point that 'The fight to end racism is a fight for unity in the midst of fragmentation.'[23]

The feeling of a cohesive British national identity is also being weakened by the underscoring of regional differences – partly ethnic, partly economic. Professor Ridley of Liverpool University posed the question, 'Have we still got a national government?' He continued,

The Government is London-based and shares with many southerners a peculiar view of the provinces. The north, particularly Liverpool, is not only a different world, but inhabited by a troublesome people who cost it money and irritate it politically. There is something almost racialist about this view . . . . A nation cannot survive without a national government committed . . . . to the security of all its citizens . . . . It cannot survive with a government that appears foreign to large parts of the country.[24]

Moreover, to many a nationally-conscious Welshman, Scot and Northern Ireland Catholic the very notion of an overarching British identity smacks of English political, cultural and economic imperialism. And as the rising unemployment of the 1980s hit most severely those regions of the kingdom most distant from the capital, the ethnic and cultural resentment was correspondingly inflamed.

Supporters of tighter integration in the European Community rejoice at any tendency to a heightening of regional, at the expense of national, consciousness. Brussels may be less politically oppressive and more economically just than London. 'L'Europe des régions' would then be preferable to the present 'l'Europe des patries' to the disadvantaged British provinces as much as to the Calabrians in Italy or Corsicans in France. But, of course, the implication of tighter European integration is the cultivation of a supranational European identity. The prospect of the coming into force of the Single European Act in 1992 has excited some committed Europeans, notably President of the Commission, Jacques Delors, to believe that the United States of Europe as dreamed of by the founding fathers is once again a feasible goal. No political leader has reacted to this objective in a more hostile manner than the British prime minister, Mrs Thatcher. At a speech in Bruges in 1988 she declared.

To try to suppress nationhood and concentrate power at the centre of a European conglomerate would be highly damaging . . . . It would be folly to try to fit [the nation-states] into some sort of identikit European personality.[25]

Finally, in the problem of citizenship identity which faces Britons at the end of the twentieth century we must note the issue of world citizenship. British citizens have been in the forefront of promoting the idea in recent decades – from campaigners like H. G. Wells, Bertrand Russell and James Lovelock (of the Gaia hypothesis) to humanity- and planetary-conscious pressure groups like Amnesty International, Oxfam, Greenpeace and Friends of the Earth. Yet at the same time, government policies and much of public opinion remain antipathetic to the ideal. Deep-seated racism, xenophobia and nationalism neutralise the message of world citizenship.

However, *qua* Europeans, British citizens have been able to defend their civil rights by appeal to the Strasbourg Commission. This access is important in the context of the erosion of such rights by government especially in the 1980s. In 1986 a Professor of Law went so far as to argue that the rule of law no longer exists in Britain and that the judiciary is incapable of restraining the government's abuse of power.[26] We have already seen how civil rights have been slightly chipped away in a number of different areas. (pp. 252–254). In the case of measures introduced to combat IRA terrorism, the abridgement of civil liberties has been arguably justified. What has been less easy to accept is the loss of civil rights by so many citizens who have in no way acted illegally. Fear of the threat to 'the national interest' from external assault or from 'the enemy within' reached, in the judgement of many British and foreign observers, a level of virtual paranoia. It is interesting to note that Mrs. Thatcher's designation of militant trade unionists as 'the enemy within' was echoed by Peter Wright's statement on 'domestic subversion' that 'The enemy was diffuse'.[27]

To Mrs Thatcher's mind any form of socialism is contrary to Britain's interests and must be expunged. Because a number of municipal authorities have been in the control of Labour majorities, local authority powers have generally been reduced – especially in the spheres of finance, housing and education. From the time of the Industrial Revolution and certainly for the century since the local government reorganisation of the 1880s, a significant portion of the political rights of the citizen lay in his ability to influence through his local councillors much of the quality of his day-to-day life. This tradition is now under threat. The ex-Canadian academic, Michael Ignatieff, has summed up the situation:

As a private individual I have been a beneficiary of Mrs Thatcher's revolution; as a citizen I have become poorer . . . . I can't use my tax cut money to repair the pavement outside my door . . .. I cannot get my street lights repaired . . . . I cannot spend the money on improving my son's decrepit school . . ., built in 1908 at the dawn of a century that once seemed to belong to British civic invention.[28]

Meanwhile, the rights of political citizenship at the national level seem less than hitherto. The split in the anti-Conservative vote between Labour and the smaller parties has combined with the vagaries of the electoral system to ensure continuation in office throughout the 1980s of Conservative governments with very substantial majorities returned by a minority of the electorate. In 1987 a majority of 101 seats was secured by a mere 42 per cent of votes cast. Professor Ridley suggested that if a test of democracy is the level of the popular support for a government as measured by the percentage voting for the party of government, then Britain has little claim to the title. In his 'league table' Britain came bottom of a list of seventeen European states; only seven others had governments elected by a minority of the electorate.[29] What is more, this discrepancy has been of greater significance to the anti-Conservative citizenry than it would have been in, say, the 1950s because of the conscious overthrow by the Thatcher governments of the politics of consensus. With a numerically ineffectual Opposition in both houses of parliament, the Conservative government has become, in the view of many commentators, an 'elective dictatorship' − ironically a term coined by Lord Hailsham to warn against a possible abuse of power by a Labour government.

The area of policy where the former 'Butskellite' consensus has been most conspicuously discarded is that of social citizenship. Any notional civic right to work, to shelter, to a reasonable level of subsistence has been under attack. In spite of the continuous withdrawal of various categories from the unemployment figures, they remained above 2 million from 1981. By 1988 an estimated 130,000 British citizens were homeless. From 1979 to 1988 the number living below the official poverty line almost doubled − to 9 million. Meanwhile, old-age pensions declined in real value and social security benefits became more difficult to obtain.

Against this background of decline in the rights of British citizens during the 1980s, a parallel decline in 'good citizen' behaviour has been plain to see. The growth in hooliganism, vandalism, litter and graffiti has been sad to behold. The 50 per cent increase in reported crime from 1979 to 1986 was even more worrying. This collapse of civic morality has been variously explained. However, since it has been most striking in the decayed urban areas − the centres blighted by economic decline and consequent high unemployment − the correlation between these factors is compelling. A report commissioned by the Archbishop of Canterbury pinpointed the problem:

Social disintegration has reached a point in some areas that shop windows are boarded up, cars cannot be left in the streets, residents are afraid either to get out themselves, or to ask others in, and there is a pervading sense of powerlessness and despair.[30]

Paradoxically this degeneration in domestic civic morality has occurred simultaneously with unprecedented expressions of concern for the suffering of the starving and homeless fellow human beings in African lands stricken by natural and man-made disasters. Maybe those individuals who respond as good world citizens are totally different individuals from those who so signally fail to be good local or national citizens. But then, if so, this division within British citizenry is itself a phenomenon to evoke concern.

Citizenship and the political parties

It was in melancholy recognition of the depth of Britain's social malaise and erosion of rights that all three major political parties latched on to the concept of citizenship in 1988. The Conservatives set the scene. In February of that year, Douglas Hurd, the Home Secretary, contemplating a socially degenerate nation, marked the bicentenary of the birth of Robert Peel by a speech on the theme of citizenship at the Staffordshire birthplace of his great predecessor. Since the speech attempted a reconstruction of Tory doctrine and consciously echoed Peel's essay at the same task in the same place, the address was inevitably dubbed the second Tamworth Manifesto. Harping on the Thatcherite theme of Victorian values, he recalled the social cohesion enjoyed in that age. He declared,

We have to find, as the Victorians found, techniques and instruments which reach the parts of our society which will always be beyond the scope of statutory schemes.

I believe that the inspiring and enlisting of the active citizen in all walks of life is the key.[31]

He returned to his theme of active citizenship on a number of occasions. In April he wrote:

Underpinning our social policy are those traditions – the diffusion of power, civil obligation, and voluntary service – which are central to Conservative philosophy . . . . The diffusion of power is . . . the key to active and responsible citizenship.

He continued by attacking established local bureaucracies and commending 'government bodies, tenants' co-operatives, housing associations, neighbourhood watch schemes.'[32] In other words, self-help in education, housing and policing. At the same time the prime minister added health care to the list. Commenting on the need of the National Health Service for more funds, Mrs Thatcher urged a greater role for private charity in line, again, with Victorian practice. 'When you have finished as a taxpayer,' she announced, 'you have not finished as a citizen.'[33]

Then, in September, the junior Home Office minister, John Patten, added his voice. He provided the following definitions:

The active citizen is someone making more than a solely economic contribution to his or her community; nothing more or less . . . .
 It is . . . about tapping a reservoir of talent and energy and enabling it to flourish outside both the public and the private sectors – a third force which has an enormous and vital contribution to make.[34]

It was very much a party-political message. He contrasted favourably the expansion of this kind of civic consciousness in the 1980s with the Labour-dominated scene of the 1960s when the attitude was that the high taxation extracted from the citizen should pay bureaucrats to undertake these tasks. And yet, at the same time he denied that the Conservatives were trying 'to hijack a strand of civic decency which runs through British life.'

As the new centre Social and Liberal Democrat Party came into existence in 1988, it quickly became evident that they had no intention of allowing the Conservatives a monopoly of the citizenship idea. Already, before its birth, writers from the two wings of the merged party had asserted the relevance of the concept for their purposes. In 1987, a former President of the Liberal Party, Richard Holme, published a book in which it appeared as one of his major themes. He noted the fragmented way in which the inhabitants of the British Isles identify themselves: by ethnicity, sex, age, class and economic role. And yet, he asserted, 'The firm place on which each individual should stand in society is the rock of citizenship, an idea . . . strangely neglected in British life.'[35] What worries Holme is the denial of effective civil rights to so many British citizens and of social rights to so many Blacks and women especially. His solution is institutional: to render British government and law, by means of electoral reform and a bill of rights, much more responsive to the rights which British citizens should be able to enjoy; and by more effective education to render British citizens more capable of exercising those rights.

From the former Social Democratic Party came a less partisan and more scholarly work by one of the founders of the party, Professor David Marquand. In *The Unprincipled Society*, published in early 1988, his focus was the collection of faulty policies and institutions which have caused Britain's long economic decline and the irrelevance of either neo-liberal or neo-socialist (i.e. Thatcherite or Labour) policies to arrest the slide. Citizenship appears as part of the essential institutional restructuring, both in the book and in his journalism. His argument very briefly is that Keynesian social citizenship is collapsing and a major reason for this is that it has not been underpinned by a proper sense of political citizenship – a concept alien to the British traditional system. Social citizenship involves state intervention, but this implies lively political citizenship:

An active State needs active citizens, willing to accept their share of the obligations its activities imply. It also needs a shared morality, which will rank some outcomes higher in the moral scale than others. But Britain's political culture of rulers and ruled, insiders and outsiders, monarch and subjects has no place for active citizens or a civic morality.[36]

Marquand's solution is to move towards a totally different style of polity. He imagines that

. . . a flourishing community will be a mosaic of smaller collectivities, which act as nurseries for the feelings of mutual loyalty and trust which hold the wider community together, and where the skills of self-government may be learned and practised.[37]

Clearly this vision owes much to the ideas of G. D. H. Cole (p. 98). Marquand is also indebted to J. S. Mill (p. 73). For he argues that politics should be seen as 'mutual education', a process of learning the mentality and arts of reconciling differences. The main thrust of the argument is therefore for more active citizen participation by power-sharing and decentralisation from national government. However, Marquand does not forget that he once worked for the European Commission and admits that some functions should move not downwards but upwards to the supranational level. He also concludes that his small collectivities might well be in danger of pursuing their own selfish interests. In order therefore to protect the common good, the implications of widespread power-sharing must be fully accepted: all 'organised groups [must] argue their case in the open and share public responsibility for the ultimate decisions.'[38] Secrecy and citizenship are mutually self-cancelling.

Both Marquand and other Social Democrats such as Shirley Williams popularised these ideas. Then, when the SLD came into being, its leader Paddy Ashdown, peppered his speeches with the word 'citizenship'. In Newcastle in June 1988, he mused aloud:

I believe that our party should now consider development of a new, enhanced concept of the citizen in the modern state. Indeed, I wonder whether this could be the very centrepiece of our new way of thinking.[39]

At the party conference in September he outlined policy proposals to flesh out the idea. These included reform of the electoral system, industrial democracy, parliaments for Scotland and Wales, a Freedom of Information Act, a Bill of Rights and defence of social welfare provision in the fields of education, housing and health.

In contrast to the Conservatives and SLD the Labour Party's playing of the citizenship refrain has been muted. One element in the recent struggles to redefine the nature of Socialism has been to emphasise fraternity and its relationship to equality (p. 186). Bernard Crick, whose membership of the Labour Party dates from the days of Harold Laski, wrote at length about fraternity in his little classic, *In Defence of Politics*. More recently he combined with the Labour MP, David Blunkett, to produce a draft document of aims and values. In this they wrote:

. . . we believe that if men and women were free of the constraints of a class society that there would be . . . far more spontaneous sociability and helpfulness to neighbours and strangers — fraternity.[40]

And they add a sense of community, which, together with fraternity, they believe are capable of 'unlocking, enlisting and enlarging the too often frustrated goodness, sociability, generosity and concern of each of us.' At the autumn party conference, the leader, Neil Kinnock, echoed these thoughts by contrasting Labour ideals with what he derided as the Thatcherite ethic of selfishness: 'No obligation to the community, no sense of solidarity, no sisterhood, no brotherhood, no neighbourhood, no number other than one, no person other than me . . . .'[41]

However, as is so often stated, the Labour Party is 'a broad church.' It is scarcely surprising, therefore, to discover that these priorities of the moderate centre are different from those of the Marxist left. Here we find two main preoccupations. One is a combined suspiciousness of the Liberal faith in devolution of power and support for the Liberal policy of a bill of rights. In a paper delivered to a Bennite conference in the spring of 1988 Anthony Arblaster and David Beetham worried that,

The more that a decentralised authority has the power to affect things (and thus be worth voting for), the more room there is for variation between localities, which can affront the principle of equal citizenship.

While the need for codified rights of citizenship is urged on the grounds that, 'The alternative is to surrender the initiative to an unrepresentative and unpredictable judiciary.'[42] The other concern of the Marxist thinkers is to find a flexible response to the employment conditions now evolving in a post-industrial society. Articles in the journal *Marxism Today* in 1988 addressed the challenge of the 'New Times' or 'post-Fordism'. Geoff Mulgan argued that new more flexible modes of economic production and management have not been reflected in new more flexible political systems. He borrows the ideas of diverse networks of interest-groups (p. 241), horizontally related, instead of the vertical power relationships of our present polity. What is needed, he argues, is, '. . . multiple structures of accountability that allow the citizen to exercise control simultaneously as a voter, a customer and as a participant.'[43] In essence this involves the diffusion and therefore dilution of power.

However, a systematic analysis of Citizenship, Rights and Socialism had to await the appearance of a Fabian Tract of that title, written by Professor Raymond Plant and published in October 1988. The purpose of the tract was to persuade the Labour Party to adopt the idea of democratic citizenship as 'the key idea' in the refashioning of the party's aims, values and programme. Plant is realistic. He sees citizenship as a way

. . . to attract people back to support the Party on a wider basis of interest. This is wholly unlikely to happen if the Party were to retreat into a laager of restricted class interest . . .
[However] The numbers of people for whom such communitarian visions are good and mean something at the level of their everyday experience are declining, attenuating their moral force.[44]

The body of the paper is a careful rebuilding of the case for Social Citizenship. Plant places the concept in the Socialist tradition and answers the contrary case of the New Right point by point. His central message is that Socialism must learn to live with the mood of individualism and the undoubted benefits of market forces. Nevertheless, within this context, social rights must be recognised as being as absolute as civil and political rights. The state must improve its provision within the economic and welfare sectors so that the citizen's reciprocal obligation to contribute something to society can realistically be demanded.

All the major British parties have thus been hard at work rediscovering citizenship and showing just how snugly it fits each of their basic philosophies. The fact that the concept can be so generally serviceable leads one to a number of possible conclusions. One is that there is a remarkable degree of agreement across the British political spectrum. The second is that the concept of citizenship must be very capacious. Or thirdly, the parties are using the term in rather different senses. Each of these explanations contains an element of truth. Despite the conscious destruction of the politics of consensus by Mrs Thatcher, there are many basic political agreements. For all the radical rhetoric, even the hard-line Conservatives have recognised that public opinion is too powerful to allow a dismantling of the welfare state. Social citizenship has remained more secure in Thatcherite Britain than Reaganite America. The parties of the left are soft-pedalling both the role of class and of central planning; and both these shifts make more room for the community-conscious and autonomously responsible citizen. All the parties look to an enhancement of small-scale participation. Burke expressed the attitude with particular vividness. He wrote, 'to be attached to the subdivision, to love the little platoon we belong to in society, is the first principle (the germ as it were) of public affections.'[45]

That same quotation has been used by both Marquand and Hurd.

On the other hand, given the full range of meaning contained in the term 'citizenship', all parties have been very selective. Little has been said concerning identity or the matter of world citizenship. Indeed each party has tended to emphasise the particular features which specially strengthen the main thrust of its policies. The Right is interested in the discharge of obligations by the good citizen; the Centre, in civil and political rights; the Left, in social justice.

The Conservatives have been the most vulnerable to criticism in their portrayal of what they mean by citizenship. There are three main reasons for this. One is that as the party of government they have the awkward task of trying to make their theory of citizenship work in practice. The programmes of the other two parties must remain largely hypothetical at least for the time being. Secondly, Thatcherite Conservatism has very deliberately developed policies which are utterly antipathetic to many characteristics of the citizenship ideal. And thirdly, unlike the other two parties, the Conservatives' definition of citizenship has remained largely at the level of rhetoric: they have not used the intellectual services of academics of the calibre of Marquand and Plant. As a consequence of the second condition the charge of hypocrisy has been levelled at the adoption of citizenship by the Thatcherite Conservatives. And as a consequence of the second and third conditions, academic leadership has been conceded to the centre and left to identify the common ground they occupy on the issue. A few words are needed on each of these developments.

Commenting on Mr Hurd's definition of the active citizen, the journalist Neal Ascherson noted with some acidity:

Well, that is one kind of active citizen. Government makes the policies: the active citizens take over bandaging the casualties. Parents take the blame for teenage bad behaviour in times of youth unemployment. Householders watch their streets when police resources fail. Big companies give money to inner-city schemes . . . because the budgets for local authorities have been cut . . . .[46]

The accusation of hypocrisy has, in fact, five main elements. One is that the New Right totally rejects the validity of the concept of social citizenship. Secondly, the Thatcher governments have made a number of inroads into civil liberties (p. 252–254). Thirdly, the New Right concept of society as an arena for engagements between market forces downgrades the role of politics as a mode of reconciling differences. By the same token the importance of the political citizen is also downgraded. Fourthly, this reliance on market forces is an encouragement to personal striving for wealth, a divisive ethic whose antipathy to citizenship had already been a subject of concern two centuries ago (p. 166). Finally, the clarion call to more active citizenship was considered insulting to those many individuals and organisations already participating in the long and honourable British tradition of voluntary work.

Concern at the partiality of the Conservative government's conception of citizenship led to the foundation of two broadly-based, intellectually-inspired and overlapping movements. One was *Samizdat*, a journal consciously taking its name from Russian clandestine anti-government literature. Its declared purposes are

. . . to change the political climate in a society where opinion is controlled not by fear of the gulag, but more subtly, through the persuasive powers of the deferential media. . . .

[to create] a popular front of the mind, if not of the ballot box. . . .
[*Samizdat*] is passionately biased against the government and in favour of citizens.[47]

In the same month, November 1988, was launched *Charter 88*. This also took an east European parallel (the Czechoslovak human rights movement, Charter 77). It is a pressure-group of those individuals concerned that the imprecision of British constitutional arrangements has contributed to the recent erosion of civil and political liberties. The programme involves the replacement of the faulty 1688 Revolution Settlement by a new, up-to-date constitutional settlement. This would include a written constitution 'anchored in the idea of universal citizenship.'

And so, by the end of 1988 even those Britons endowed with but the faintest political consciousness can hardly have failed to have heard of the idea of citizenship. Yet for all the expenditure of intellectual effort, politicians' breath and journalists' ink, the emerging definitions were incomplete in one way or another. A truly comprehensive view of what citizenship in its full sense might mean for the British citizen seemed to have eluded all those who spoke and wrote about the concept. But, then, they were probably not even looking for anything so embarrassing for their particular causes as an all-embracing definition and commitment. And, then again, if citizenship is seen to be little more than a slogan, it will fail in the intended popular appeal and disappear from the politicians' lexicons. It deserves a better fate.

The condition of citizenship education

The schools therefore continued to be faced with the difficult task of transmitting an appreciation of an amorphous concept. Any attempt by the teaching profession to mould it into shape must now take account of a new climate of forceful central government policy and pronouncements. We may conveniently identify three elements in the framework erected by the Conservative governments and their supporters in the 1980s. These are the adaptations to the school system as a whole; attitudes specifically expressed about citizenship education; and the relationship of such work to the National Curriculum.

Part of the characteristic style of English citizenship has been the strength of local — county and municipal — autonomy and loyalty. Since 1870, the local administration of schools has been an integral feature of this local autonomy. Also, a core component of the concept of social citizenship has been comprehensive education — an essential method, it has been thought, of eroding class differences and the barriers to equal opportunities. Both of these principles have been attacked by the New Right. Local authority control over education has been weakened in four major ways: accusations of misuse of funds and encouragement of left-wing indoctrination (to which we shall return); enforced reduction in staffing and equipment by limiting the central-government supplements to local funds ('rate-capping'); a considerable enhancement in the 1988 Education Act of the minister of education's executive powers; and, by the same legislation, the granting of opportunities to state schools to secede from their local authority and be maintained by direct, central-government funding. The justification of this last policy is the provision of more parental choice and better opportunities for the more able. Another scheme is the creation of 'privatised' City Technology Colleges. Speaking of these, the Secretary of State for Education said that he was 'trying to revive some of the traditional standards nourished in the grammar schools.'[48] The uniform and comprehensive system of education was to be dismantled. Many fears have been voiced concerning the quality of education that will be possible, especially for poorer pupils, when middle-class parents have ensured that their offspring are taught in schools in the private sector, CTCs or those in the state sector centrally funded (and, possibly, selective in intake). The principle of a socially cohesive citizenship ensured by a common educational experience, already weakened by the existence of the public schools, was under further threat.

Just as in 1979, at the time of Mrs Thatcher's accession to power, there had seemed to be a consensus concerning the place of local authorities in the English state and of the comprehensive schools in the educational system, so by that same date political education seemed accepted as a legitimate function of schools. And just as those first two features of the politics of English education have been weakened, so too has been this third. The Labour Party, it is true, has remained quietly supportive. The shadow spokesman on Education declared in 1986,

In my view, political literacy should be a basic educational right, part of the core curriculum for all pupils. Everybody, not just the few, should be educated for citizenship.[49]

However, by that time the hostility of the Right had so effectively set the tone that a leading teacher-educator in the field was driven to the despondent conclusion that 'Political education is now, more than ever, a "low status, high risk" area of the curriculum'.[50]

The Right-wing attacks were made on a broad front (pp. 219–221 and 229). We may detect four, overlapping phases. The first consisted of accusations of left-wing bias in teaching about domestic political issues, including Feminist and Multicultural Studies. The second was the charge pro-Soviet bias in Peace Studies. The third consisted of attacks on the empathetic style of learning in GCSE History, especially in English Social History. These negative criticisms of the ways in which young people were being prepared by the schools for their citizenship role was felt by many teachers to be unfair and ill-informed. The National Union of Teachers described Sir Keith Joseph's issue of guidelines on bias as 'insulting' and Mr Kenneth Baker's accusations of left-wing bias in teaching, as 'slander'.[51] On the other hand, and fourthly, Conservatives have not been merely negative; they have argued that something more acceptable should be undertaken in the schools. In terms of subject-matter, faith has been firmly placed in the teaching of British History. Some, like Mrs Thatcher, the historian Lord Thomas and Lord Rees-Mogg, former editor of *The Times*, have emphasised its importance for reinforcing feelings of identity and pride. Others, such as the Education Secretaries Joseph and Baker, have underlined the need for young citizens to have an appreciation of how British political institutions and civic rights have evolved. Furthermore, in drafting the guidelines for the National Curriculum (pp 307–308), Baker placed political education for those up to 16 squarely in the History syllabus. Left-wing critics have expressed concern. Some have warned that a Whig interpretation of English constitutional progress would be simplistic: Magna Carta was a defence of baronial privilege; the Bill of Rights consolidated the power of a tiny landed parliamentary élite; neither had much to do in origin with the principle of equality of citizenship rights. Indeed, in the eighteenth century the lower orders suffered an *ancien régime* not as different from the French as we have thought. Others, fearful of the enhanced powers placed in the hands of the Secretary of State by the 1988 Education Reform Act, have questioned the honesty of these moves. They have interpreted them as deriving more from considerations of political dogma than the pursuit of objective educational goals. The Canadian Marxist historian, Harvey Kaye, has written,

The nationalisation of the history curriculum arose not only out of an intention to arrest the decline in young Britons' historical education and knowledge, but also, arguably, Thatcher's and Joseph's desire to turn the teaching of history to Conservative purposes in the 'battle of ideas'.[52]

Keith Joseph saw History as playing a crucial role in what he considered to be an urgent task for schools, namely, 'the preservation of our society's fundamental values'.[53] Many of his government colleagues and their supporters have felt that the deterioration in the honouring of these values has expressed itself most alarmingly in anti-social and particularly violent behaviour. Parents and schools have been castigated for the decline. The loss of Victorian codes of parental and pedagogical discipline has been deplored. Child-centred education and the laxity of the 1960s, it has been asserted, have been especially culpable. And if schools are to blame, they have a clear responsibility to mend society's ways. It has even been suggested that schools should bear the stigma of public identification with their pupils who break the law out of school hours. Teachers, in turn, complain that they did not enter the profession to become society's policemen nor to shoulder the responsibility which some parents so casually ignore.

The constant harping on the need for better citizenly conduct and on the failure of the schools to provide the essential foundations led to the initiation in 1988 of a scheme for a course in Active Citizenship for the 16+ GCSE examination. The idea derived from the Community Service Volunteers, a body already facilitating the civic and social work of thousands of young people. The political tone of the project was provided by the appointment of the Speaker of the House of Commons as the patron of the Commission to draft the course. Although a privately organised and funded scheme, it seems at the time of writing to reflect quite faithfully the government's concerns and hopes. In the meantime the Farrington Trust, a charity for the promotion of Christian education, had started work on a project to develop the teaching of beliefs and values to counter the decline in behavioural standards.[54]

As well as the continual adjurations to schools to do better in the way of producing more civically moral and law-abiding citizens, the Conservative government of the late 1980s put much effort into the production of a National Curriculum. The general purpose of trying to ensure reasonably common curricula, syllabuses and standards for 5–16 year-olds throughout the country was widely supported. Indeed, proponents of citizenship education could rejoice in at least the partial words of encouragement to be found in the initial consultative document: the curriculum should 'develop the potential of all pupils and equip them for the responsibilities of citizenship'; 'help to develop their capacity to adapt and respond flexibly to a changing world'; and develop 'personal qualities and competence, such as self-reliance, self-discipline, an enterprising approach and the ability to solve practical real-world problems.'[55] On the other hand, the emphasis on responsibilities and not rights seemed to slant the document; and worries in relation to citizenship education were raised by four general features of the proposals as they developed. These were: the required subjects, the non-academic pupil, multiculturalism and testing.

The keystone to the National Curriculum is the requirement for schools to teach a list of clearly identified core and foundation subjects. The insistence on this principle has raised two worries in terms of curriculum design among teachers engaged in citizenship education of various kinds. The Social Science disciplines (Sociology, Politics, Economics, Law) do not feature in the list. If the core and foundation subjects consume the bulk of the time-table time, then there will be little opportunity, below the 16+ examination level, for these subjects to be incorporated. Secondly, although the need for 'multidisciplinary themes' is recognised, these too will be competing for the minority time with many other claims. Consequently, it is argued, established and successful multidisciplinary programmes of citizenship education may well be squeezed out: still less will the climate be favourable for devising new ones. The Centre for Global Education at York University dispatched a response to the Department of Education and Science as part of the consultative process. The document expressed concern that the National Curriculum would be

. . . both narrow and inflexible and . . . will inadequately prepare students for life in a fast-changing interdependent world. The important skills and insights to be obtained from, for instance, the fields of anthropology, ecology, economics, political science and sociology are jeopardised by the proposal as it stands. Even more disturbing is the apparent relegation of the importance of interdisciplinary approaches.[56]

The reaction of the (Conservative) chairman of the House of Commons Education Select Committee to such expressions of concern was to brush them aside with some contempt:

Can there actually be greater nonsense than to say that a curriculum which covers Maths, English, Science, History, Geography, Technology, Music, Art, Physical Education, Religious Education and for many people a language, is a narrow curriculum? It is a curriculum of the most enormous breadth that anyone can imagine.[57]

There would appear to be little common ground between these two staunchly held positions.

Government spokesmen indeed made it clear that this consolidation of, basically, conventional disciplines was a deliberate attempt to undermine 'candyfloss' courses like Media Studies and 'subversive' studies like Peace Education. A problem which this traditionalism seemed to ignore, however, is the inappropriateness of a strictly academic curricular structure for the less able and intellectually-inclined pupils. Learning citizenship through the medium of History – mainly, as ministerial preference seems to indicate, nineteenth- and twentieth-century English History – may look appropriate to the Oxbridge-educated Cabinet and civil service. Is it really fit for the children of the under-class of, say, Liverpool? Writing in 1981 from his experience as chairman of the Merseyside Job Creation Programme, Professor Ridley rejected the usefulness of any academic style of political education for this, quite large, sector of the school population. He concluded that

They are likely to take the policies of government, like the weather, as acts of God, things which they know, quite realistically, that they cannot alter . . ..
What they really want is an umbrella to protect them against the immediate thunderstorm of government policies. . ... how individually to protect their rights, for example, how, as a group, to promote their immediate interests.[58]

By 1988, when the National Curriculum was being introduced, unemployment among the black youth of the Toxteth area of Liverpool was 90 per cent; school absenteeism, reflecting the despair of this situation, was probably about 25 per cent. Was the National Curriculum likely to provide a meaningful citizenship education in conditions such as these?

Yet the schools of a multicultural society like Britain should be contributing in a vital way to enhancing the chances of minority ethnic groups feeling, acting and being treated as citizens on a par with the ethnic majority. The prejudice of the police, law-courts and the public at large keep so many Blacks in a second-class citizen status that the schools have a formidable responsibility of compensation. How far has recent government legislation helped the schools in the process of rendering the host majority more tolerant and the immigrant minority more confident of their citizenship? We have already seen how the Swann Report of 1985 underscored these messages (p. 111). The need for effective multicultural education was dramatically and tragically illuminated in that same year when a mentally-disturbed white boy killed a fellow Asian pupil. The attack took place in a Manchester school, which was most ineptly pursuing an overt anti-racist policy.

Three years later, when the Great Education Reform Bill (GERBIL) was being debated, the issue of multicultural education arose in the context of the provisions which should be made for Religious Education. The issue had been controversial enough in the arguments over the 1902 and 1944 Education Acts. But at least in those earlier decades Britain was a very much more evidently Christian country, albeit divided by denominational squabbles, than in 1988. In that year it was estimated that Britain contained some 2 million adherents to non-Christian religions (Muslims, Jews, Hindus and Sikhs), while attendances at Christian church religious services were still declining. The prime minister could none the less assert the need to instruct children in 'the truths [sic] of the Judeo-Christian tradition'. Furthermore, legislative force was given to this asserted need by the House of Lords amendments to the Education Bill. These required that schools should conduct daily assemblies, which would normally be 'wholly or mainly of a broadly Christian character' and teach Religious Education lessons of similar style. The argument was that Britain has been and still is a predominantly Christian country and all young people should understand the basics of Christian belief. Pupils of other faiths were, it is true, allowed the possibility of their own assemblies.

Although it is too early at the time of writing to assess whether initially expressed worries will prove well-founded, they were certainly widely voiced. Humanists accused the government of enforcing blatant indoctrination. Supporters of multicultural school provision warned of the establishment of separate, almost ghetto schools, particularly by Muslims, in order to escape the imposition of Christianity upon their children. And those who prize the objective of tolerant young citizens regretted the incipient divisiveness of the law in multi-ethnic schools. The Islamic Society for the Promotion of Religious Tolerance foretold

. . . a situation whereby non-Christian students will have to leave the class and their classmates during that lesson, and that will emphasise their feeling of being 'different'. Those who remain in the class will be seen as privileged by virtue of being Christian, and those who are out will learn from an early age that to identify as British one must be Christian.[59]

If that indeed proves to be the outcome, two quite distinct concepts of a crucial feature of citizenship, namely the nature of British identity, will be contending for acceptance — the unitary Christian and the pluralist multi-ethnic.

The final controversial feature of the Education Act relevant to citizenship education was the requirement that all pupils be tested at specified ages throughout their school careers. The problem here is that assessment of cognitive learning is so much easier than measuring progress in affective learning. The suspicion therefore arises that teachers will concentrate on the testable to ensure the highest possible scores for their pupils. Now although the teacher of citizenship would never be perverse enough to disclaim the need for knowledge and understanding, he is just as concerned to promote appropriate attitudes. Identity, loyalty, efficacy, empathy and tolerance, for example, demand so much more than a grasp of facts. Yet they are the core attributes of the true citizen, whether of the state or of the world. Moreover, the teaching styles which have been shown as the most effective for nurturing these qualities are not those most apposite for the accumulation of facts. Informal class discussion, simulation and gaming and practical projects are the most likely to stimulate the required citizenly properties. Their effectiveness is not, however, easily assessed by an examination paper.

Nowhere in the United Kingdom is the affective domain of learning in schools more crucial than in Northern Ireland. And before leaving the survey of the recent debate in Britain a few separate words are required on this un-happy province. Tension between the Protestant and Catholic communities and the contrary pulls of identity, towards mainland Britain for the Unionists and the Irish Republic for the Nationalists, were, of course, not new phenomena in the late 1980s. However, two developments at that time did throw the issue of citizenship there into a sharp relief – one political; the other, educational.

In the balance which must, sadly, be struck today between measures to combat terrorism and the preservation of citizens' rights, Mrs Thatcher made it quite clear that the latter had in some measure to be sacrificed. Thus the government showed irritation, perhaps impeded, investigations concerning the possible illegality of actions by the security forces; weakened the rights of those arrested on suspicion of terrorism, for instance, by removing the right of silence during interrogation; and forbade broadcast interviews with mem-bers of Sinn Fein, an otherwise legal political party. Irish citizens of the United Kingdom lost a range of civil rights generally available in democratic states and all citizens had their access to information restricted. Should loyal citizens regret these infringements or applaud the vigilance of the government?

In the meantime some Ulster teachers have been wrestling with the prob-lem of showing the younger generation how they might think of themselves in civic rather than sectarian terms. Although most schools are segregated in reflection of the religious divide, a few integrated schools have been organised (8 out of the total of 1,374 in 1988). These are conscious attempts to forge the citizenly virtue of tolerance in the young as a weapon against the ingrained prejudice and bigotry of the adults. In an effort to strengthen the integrative influence of the curriculum, the Northern Ireland Minister of Education in-troduced a White Paper in 1988 proposing a new element, namely 'Education for Mutual Understanding'. The aim was to teach Protestants about Catholic traditions and vice versa in all the relevant subjects – a conscious government initiative to promote civic harmony.

The minds of professional politicians and pedagogues and the lay public alert to political and educational matters were alike concentrated in a quite remarkable way on the issue of citizenship in Britain during the course of the year 1988. The experience seemed, nevertheless, merely to exemplify the problem so general throughout the world: disagreement is rife about what citizenship means and consequently about the educational processes most ap-propriate to support the citizenly status, role and qualities. This cannot surely be a satisfactory condition. At best it leads politicians and educationists into semantic confusion; at worst, adult and young citizens are being fobbed off with only a portion of that whole citizenship which should in fact lay at the very heart of their life as social beings. If, then, 'citizenship' is indeed a 'Humpty-Dumpty' word, as suggested in the Preface, it is worthwhile to make the effort to put him together again and then to convert him from his lexical licence.

REFERENCES

1. C. Mouffe, 'The Civics Lesson', *New Statesman and Society*, 7 October 1988.
2. A. MacIntyre, *After Virtue* (Duckworth, 2nd edn, 1985), p. 241.
3. Laski, *Recovery of Citizenship*, p. 6.
4. C. Pateman, *The Sexual Contract* (Polity, 1988), p. 227.
5. Marshall, *Citizenship and Social Class*, p. 24.
6. P. Calvert, 'On Attaining Sovereignty' in A. D. Smith (ed.), *Nationalist Movements* (Macmillan, 1976), p. 140.
7. K. Suter, *Reshaping the Global Agenda* (UNA of Australia, 1986), p. 49.
8. J. Le Carré, *The Perfect Spy* (Hodder & Stoughton, Coronet edn, 1987), p. 161.
9. J. Dunn, *Western Political Theory in the Face of the Future* (Cambridge University Press, 1979), p. 55.
10. Turner, *Citizenship and Capitalism*, p. 100.
11. M.-C. Vayssade, quoted in Council of Europe, *Forum*, February 1988, p. 30.
12. R. Dahrendorf, *The New Liberty* (Routledge & Kegan Paul, 1975), p. 41.
13. J. L. Nelson & J. V. Michaelis, *Secondary Social Studies* (Prentice-Hall, 1980), pp. 9–10.
14. K. P. Langton, *Political Socialization* (Oxford University Press, 1969), p. 115.
15. Langeveld, 'Political Education: Pros and Cons', p. 42. See also, for general trends, J. Torney-Purta & C. Hahn, 'Values Education in the Western European Tradition' in W. K. Cummings, S. Gopinathan & Y. Tomoda, *The Revival of Values, Education in Asia and the West* (Pergamon, 1988).
16. Hilkka Pietila, 'International Co-operation' in N. Graves *et al.* (eds.), *Teaching for International Understanding, Peace and Human Rights* (UNESCO, 1984), pp. 158–9. The distinction was originally made in E. & M. Botkin, *No Limits to Learning* (Pergamon, 1974).
17. P. Hirst, 'The Contribution of Philosophy to the Study of the Curriculum' in J. F. Kerr (ed.), *Changing the Curriculum* (University of London Press, 1968), p. 59.
18. H. Young, 'Citizens! The cure-all rallying cry', *Guardian*, 1 September 1988.
19. H. Kaye 'Our island story retold', *Guardian*, 3 August 1987.
20. Brogan, *Citizenship Today*, pp. 15 & 29–30.
21. N. Boyle, 'Thatcher's Dead Souls', *New Statesman and Society*, 14 October 1988.
22. Quoted in E. MacDonald, 'Racial hatred poisoning us', *Observer*, 20 November 1988.
23. K. Tompson, *Under Siege* (Penguin, 1988), p. 153.
24. F. F. Ridley, 'The government of divide and rule', *Guardian*, 22 November 1985.
25. M. Thatcher, 'Heirs to Europe' (ed. extract), *Guardian*, 21 September 1988.
26. G. Zellick, 'Government Beyond Law', *Public Law*, January 1986.
27. See Chapter 7 note 13.
28. M. Ignatieff, 'The tide will turn', *Guardian*, 4 April 1988.
29. F. F. Ridley, 'At the bottom of the democracy league', *Guardian*, 10 August 1987.
30. Commission on Urban Priority Areas, *Faith in the City*, quoted in D. Blunkett & K. Jackson, Democracy in Crisis (Hogarth Press, 1987), p. 20.
31. Quoted in J. Carvel, 'Restrain greed, Tories urged by Hurd', *Guardian*, 6 February 1988.
32. D. Hurd, 'Citizenship in the Tory Democracy', *New Statesman*, 29 April 1988.

33. Quoted, *Guardian*, 14 October 1988.
34. J. Patten, 'Launching the Active Citizen', *Guardian*, 18 September 1988.
35. R. Holme, *The People's Kingdom* (Bodley Head, 1987), pp. 30–1.
36. D. Marquand, 'The old politics is over', *Observer*, 31 January 1988.
37. Marquand, *The Unprincipled Society*, p. 239.
38. Ibid., p. 240.
39. P. Ashdown, quoted in J. Carvel, 'Leading questions', *Guardian*, 29 July 1988.
40. D. Blunkett & B Crick, 'The Labour Party's aims and values' in *Guardian*, 1 February 1988.
41. Quoted in M. Linton & D. Bowcott, 'Kinnock sets out "price of victory"', *Guardian*, 5 October 1988.
42. A. Arblaster & D. Beetham, *Democracy versus Authoritarianism* (mimeo, 6 April 1988).
43. G. Mulgan, 'Collapse of the pyramid of power', *Guardian*, 28 November 1988.
44. R. Plant, *Citizenship, Rights and Socialism* (Fabian Society Tract no. 531, 1988), p. 2.
45. Burke, *Reflections on the Revolution in France*, quoted in Marquand, *The Unprincipled Society*, p. 211 and Hurd, 'Citizenship in the Tory Democracy'.
46. N. Ascherson, 'Citizens put on the active list', *Observer*, 16 October 1988.
47. *Samizdat*, no. 1, November 1988.
48. Speech to Young Conservatives Conference, reported in *Guardian*, 9 February 1987.
49. G. Radice, 'The Role of Political Education – Labour's View', talk, press release, n.d., 1986?
50. A. Porter, 'The Training of Teachers in Political Education' in C. Harber (ed.), *Political Education in Britain* (Falmer, 1987), p. 176.
51. Quoted in *Guardian*, 6 May 1986 & 10 February 1987.
52. Kaye, 'The New Right and History', pp. 351–2.
53. K. Joseph, 'Statement of Principles on treatment of politically controversial issues in schools and colleges', February, 1986.
54. See J. Richards, 'Throwing off the yoke of the yobbo', *Daily Telegraph*, 4 July 1988.
55. DES, National Curriculum 5–16 Consultation Document (HMSO, 1987), paras. 4, 8i, 68.
56. Centre for Global Education, *A response to the National Curriculum 5–16 Consultation Document* (mimeo, 17 September 1987).
57. T. Raison in 'Understanding the World through the National Curriculum: Report of a Discussion' (mimeo, CEWC, 1988).
58. F. F. Ridley, 'Schools, Youth Programmes, Employment and Political Skills', *International Journal of Political Education* (vol. 4, 1981).
59. Quoted in M. Phillips & D. Gow, 'Onward Christian Soldiers', *Guardian*, 28 June 1988.

PART THREE

Synthesis

CHAPTER NINE

Multiple Citizenship

9.1 THE CUBE OF CITIZENSHIP

In all the professions — lawyer, doctor, minister, teacher, citizen — we have in mind a standard of excellence that forms an essential part of our definition of them . . . politics is a kind of profession, a profession engaged in by citizens. Like some carpenters, they may be poorly prepared, jackleg citizens. . . . But . . . this doesn't mean that nothing higher is practicable.

Harvey Wheeler (1968)[1]

Need for a comprehensive definition

The great violinist Heifitz was once advised to play a wrong note now and again lest the gods be angry with his perfection. Ordinary mortals — and there are billions of us — can live serenely in the comfortable knowledge that we shall never attract divine wrath, at least, in that particular way. The vision of the ideal is nevertheless a very real human need, voiced ever since Plato and which finds both sacred and profane means of expressing itself: saints and Miss World competitors each hope to be able to approximate to their different models. The case for defining an ideal of perfect citizenship for the world is even more cogent: the whole social and political tone of the life of mankind depends on the construction of such an ideal and the will of states and in-dividuals to strive towards its realisation. To put the matter starkly and negatively, if the concept and institution of citizenship were suddenly erased from all human consciousness and behaviour, morality and justice would be acutely impaired. Citizenship is so ingrained now that social morality depends heavily upon the idea of civic duties, and social justice, on civic rights. Since citizenship is so evidently part of our social and political environment, we would do well to try and ensure that it is lived and operated with the greatest possible virtue and efficiency.

One may, in fact, identify four particular reasons for attempting a holistic ideal definition: the pessimistic, the optimistic, the pragmatic and the educa-tional. First, the case of the pessimist. Dark visions of the collapse of the ideal of citizen virtue attend on many a *fin de millénium* observer. Crime and corruption, drug-addiction and delinquency, apathy and alienation spell moral collapse. The pursuit of the individual good has overwhelmed the care of the public good. With Cassandra eloquence Alasdair MacIntyre has argued that the decay has eaten into the very hearts of our western polities as it had in the declining years of the Roman Empire. He concludes that,

What matters at this stage is the construction of local forms of community within which civility and the intellectual and moral life can be sustained through the new dark ages which are already upon us. . . . This time however the barbarians are not waiting beyond the frontiers; they have already been governing us for quite some time.[2]

This solution appears to involve the surrender of a great deal that citizenship has come to mean. Is such a great strategic retreat either necessary or prudent? Should not citizenship adopt rather a Dantonist strategy of audacious attacks on all fronts? To drop the metaphor, the response to this school of pessimism may better be a clearer understanding of what the totality of the citizen ideal can positively offer.

One may detect this more aggressive frame of mind in the pessimists who concentrate their analysis on evidence of the denial of citizenship rights. Organisations such as Amnesty International, which monitor the violation of civil rights and lesser-known bodies like the censorship watchdog *Index* regularly compile a sombre catalogue of the violation and withholding of basic rights of citizenship throughout the world. Similarly, UN and voluntary organisations concerned with fundamental social rights are never short of the most melancholy tales of human wretchedness. Even in affluent countries Marshall's comfortable interpretation, using the case of Britain, of the steady progress from civil through political to social citizenship is being criticised for its naive assumption of inevitability. But in all these instances, the analysis is used as a condemnation of complacency and a call to action. Moreover, each of these categories of campaigners has some notional standard against which judgements are made about the failure of certain states to uphold the status and dignity of citizenship. These standards, however, relate to the particular problem in hand or particular criteria, not to any holistic conception. For example, when in the 1970s and early 1980s US and Soviet spokesmen exchanged insults about each other's record on citizenship rights, they appeared not just to be making propaganda, but to be genuinely dismissive of the other's argument. This is what the leading Soviet ideologue and briefly Party Secretary, Yuri Andropov, had to say in response to western condemnation of Soviet violations of civil rights:

Surely one cannot speak of real civil rights for the broad popular masses in the capitalist countries, where people live in constant fear of losing their jobs and consequently their wages. . . . Really, these millions of unfortunates [i.e. unemployed] and their families do not feel better because they are allowed to go up to the gates of the White House or Hyde Park's Speakers Corner and express themselves on particular questions there.[3]

A universally applicable standard of citizens' rights would have highlighted the partiality of these exchanges and indeed the greater hypocrisy of the Soviet propaganda. Even in the current period of *détente* and liberalisation inaugurated by Andropov's protégé, Gorbachev, the process of *rapprochement* could be facilitated by an agreed conception of citizenship.

Overt optimism is less easy to exemplify than the pessimist schools. It exists rather in the implications of those who note an expansion of mass communications for improved civic awareness or register the virtually universal lip-service accorded to the idea of human rights. And whatever its value in real-life terms, the title of citizen is now for all intents and purposes ubiquitous. Political and some elements of social and legal discourse would now be inconceivable without the idea. And in its progress to this position, so the optimist would argue, citizenship has reached a platform of acceptance from which it can assuredly make further inroads into authoritarianism, hierarchy, injustice and ignorance. The going may be hard, as the pessimists warn; but consciousness of the values of citizenship and the means of disseminating an understanding of them are so widespread that further consolidation and advance are assured. If that is so, then the ultimate goal needs to be clear.

The pragmatist, our third category, needs a full and agreed definition of citizenship too. Reserving judgement about the current and likely future situation, the pragmatist argues that all that is meant by citizenship must, for the sake of mankind, be more universally honoured. The Soviet Union in the age of *glasnost* and *perestroika* has been the source of much of this thinking. With the ideals of social citizenship and citizenship as civic duty both accepted by the régime's ideological foundation, commentators have started to embrace the liberal principles of civic and political rights. Furthermore, the appeal to strengthen these elements of citizenship has been couched in global terms, as we shall see below.

Finally, the teacher cannot possibly be expected to prepare young people for adult life as citizens without a complete and agreed understanding about what the status entails. Teaching for citizenship can be a hazardous undertaking. If the state demands a biassed exposition, then the teacher who is neither utterly self-interested nor ideologically committed to the regime is faced with a dreadful decision: to compromise his professional standards or job. The choice was posed in stark form in totalitarian régimes; but even where there is the faintest tinge of authoritarianism, the dilemma exists, albeit in a less polarised manner. Take the case of the nationalistic regulations to be introduced in Japan in the early 1990s. Singing the Imperial national anthem and raising the flag will be obligatory: teachers who refuse to participate in these ceremonies will be punished. The existence of a universally accepted and balanced meaning of the term citizenship would afford the teacher some professional protection. Less dramatically, it could provide an invaluable framework for syllabuses. We have already cited the confusion which exists in the USA because of the lack of an agreed definition (p. 290). Thomas Englund has written of 'three currently competing conceptions of political and citizenship education' in Sweden.[4] The examples could be multiplied. Without political agreement concerning the meaning and nature of citizenship, teachers are forced to teach a partial view or flounder in confusion depending on the circumstances prevailing in their state.

Since the status of citizenship is now so widespread, any definition or yardstick for judgment must have a truly world-wide application. No two states will show the same approximation to any ideal; nor will any given state reveal the same citizenship characteristics over a period of time. The forces shaping the interpretation of the citizenship ideal are so diverse and the results of so many complex historical forces. Nevertheless, political philosophers have written about the concept as if their principles have general meaning; and politicians often speak in the same vein. The fact of a variety of practices reinforces rather than undermines the need for a globally relevant definition. All may then be tested by the same criteria and the effects of particular conditions weighed and assessed. Each state could understand the quality of its citizenship practices as set against a universal standard or its parading of the term 'citizenship' could be exposed as hypocritical or an abuse of language if conditions warrant such a judgement. This is precisely what the UN has tried to do in the particular field of human rights.

The case for a universally agreed standard is further supported by the concept of the world citizen. If it is impossible to achieve an international definition of state citizenship, clearly a supranational definition of world citizenship is out of the question. Unless the status of world citizenship is totally to supplant that of state citizenship – a development that is certainly, within the foreseeable future, impractical and probably undesirable (p. 287–288) – then the state and world citizenship ideals must be compatible. This involves a two-fold process: a universal interest in the quality of citizenship in the several nation-states and a concern to enhance the individual's identity as a world citizen. The first process has been recommended recently by the Soviet *Literary Gazette* in the following extract concerning civil rights:

The task of guaranteeing basic rights, of equal treatment before the law, of freedom of conscience, speech and association, the right to the franchise and, most of all, the right to life, is a task for the whole of human society. This is not an issue which can any longer be regarded as the sole prerogative of individual states, or of any one ideology.[5]

The second process is one which has been canvassed among a small coterie of enthusiasts: the converted preaching to the converted. However, when a highly popular and powerful world figure, namely Mikhail Gorbachev, has been converted by these arguments (in this case it seems by his fellow-countryman Andrei Sakharov), then the need to give his thoughts greater substance becomes both more urgent and more possible. In his famous speech to the UN General Assembly in December 1988 the Soviet President declared,

We have concluded that we should jointly seek the way leading to the supremacy of the universal human idea over the endless multitude of centrifugal forces, the way to preserve the vitality of this civilisation. . . .[6]

This objective has little chance of success without marshalling the commitment of millions of human beings. And this can only be achieved by a sense of world citizenship. We need to understand what this could and should mean. If, as in the fourth century BC, cosmopolitanism is an idea whose time has again come, the need to incorporate the world dimension fully into any definition of the citizenship concept has become compelling.

A suggested pattern

What, then, are the considerations which should be borne in mind when attempting to shape a definition of citizenship? In the first place, the historical legacies of two and a half millenia cannot possibly be ignored. They persist in our collective memories as both present inheritance and, in some cases, prudential warnings. The various historical themes must be considered and, by adaptation or conscious rejection, be welded into a new coherent concept suited to our own age. Six fairly distinct traditions need to be handled in this way. The *republican*, with its emphasis on civic virtue and military service may need to be revived in adapted form. The *cosmopolitan* ideal perhaps needs strengthening vis-à-vis the *nationalist* tradition of patriotic cohesion and pride. The *liberal* tradition has yet to become firmly rooted in some authoritarian states, where resistance to the temptation to *totalitarian* mobilisation should be encouraged. At the same time the liberal tradition of legal and political rights needs to be related to and balanced with the *socialist* emphasis on socio-economic rights.

The first point of reconstructing these legacies is not just to clarify our civic ideals for the present. For the present is a meaningless point in time. Such a reconstruction must therefore be composed from an analysis of current trends which one can confidently extrapolate into the immediate future. The development of education and the news media may well increase the numbers conscious of public affairs and of the rights they feel they should enjoy. Ethnic and religious differences and consciousness will clearly persist. The need for the handling of environmental degradation on a global scale will become increasingly imperative. The wealth-gap between the northern and southern hemispheres will continue to cause strain. And where poverty-induced discontent leads to pressures on governments for improved standards of living, many governments will no doubt continue to use repressive measures against their own citizens, whatever their constitutions and laws proclaim.

Any attempt at producing a universal expression of citizenship must therefore search for the highest common factor possible in these circumstances. This must be capable of incorporating the diverse traditions and situations just outlined, while yet embracing the civic needs which the condition of citizenship has been designed over the centuries to meet. The design, to change from an arithmetical to a geometrical analogy, must be three-dimensional. Hence we may talk of the cube of citizenship. We have already suggested in Part Two that citizenship needs to be conceived as having five elements, namely, identity, virtue and the legal, political and social aspects of the status. However, each of these elements must be experienced in a geographical context. In drawing upon examples from recent times we have referred almost exclusively to the nation-state and world levels. In fact, it is becoming increasingly evident that the function of citizen can be discharged at a multitude of levels, from local government and functional interest groups through to the cosmopolis. The third dimension is education. It is part of the thesis of the book that education for citizenship is not an optional extra, but an integral part of the concept. One may be born a little citizen in status, but one must learn about the rights and duties, the attitudes and skills this status entails. Citizenship is meaningless if that learning does not take place; defective if the educational process is not thorough.

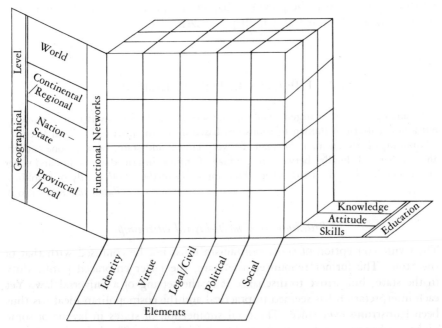

Fig. 9.1 The Cube of citizenship.

The diagramatic presentation of this multidimensional pattern of citizenship produces a cube sub-divided into numerous cells. But these must not be thought of as self-contained. The components of each dimension must be interconnected. The five elements along the horizontal dimension must be related and balanced with each other. And so too with the geographical levels and the educational objectives. Furthermore, the three dimensions themselves must be linked in harmony. The five elements must be applicable at every geographical level and the educational preparation of the young citizen must include both the other dimensions in full. A definition of citizenship which fulfils all these requirements may seem to make unrealistic demands on both citizen and teacher. One must not, however, exaggerate the preferred size of the cube. It must be placed firmly in a person's life, even centrally perhaps, but with plenty of surrounding space for the pursuit of private affairs. A society which inflates citizenship so that it expands to occupy the total area of an individual's life is indeed in danger of becoming totalitarian. The consequence of totalitarianism is that vital components of the citizenship cube are distorted or squeezed out altogether. The public citizen and the private individual cannot afford to dispense with each other. At the same time, however, the public area must be accessible to all. In particular, the traditional belief that while men can operate in both the public and private domains, women are confined to the private, is unacceptable. With these important provisos concerning the private space of life, it should be possible so to define the three dimensions of this cuboid form of citizenship as to overcome the difficulties outlined in the previous chapter and provide a mental construct of the human social animal as a multiple citizen.

9.2   THE GEOGRAPHICAL DIMENSION

. . . amongst the most urgent issues facing serious thinkers today is that of working out a new pattern of human relationships based on truth, justice, love and freedom: relationships between man and man, between citizen and state, between one country and another and, finally, between individuals, families, intermediate bodies and states on the one hand, and on the other, the community of the whole family of mankind.

Pacem in Terris (1963)[7]

Precedents for a multi-layered citizenship

The Cynic conception of cosmopolitanism must not be confused with that of the Stoic. The former renounced the state; the latter embraced public duty in the state, but strove to discharge it in the setting of a universal law. Yet each interpretation has seemed impractical and the cosmopolitan ideal has thus been hamstrung ever since. The total submersion of states in favour of some global authority is either inconceivable or frightening. The balancing of state and cosmopolitan authority is too delicate a trick to effect. Or is it? The attendant difficulties are basically three-fold. One is the problem of the division of the citizen's loyalty between state and cosmopolis. The second is the problem of apportioning and balancing the power exercised by the two levels. And the third is the propensity of states to cling to the authority they have rather than cede a portion of it to an overarching body. There may well be, however, a dual way of escaping from this triple bind. First it is necessary to accept as perfectly feasible the notion that an individual can have multiple civic identities and feel multiple civic loyalties. Secondly, the conceived confrontation of state and cosmopolis in antagonistic competition for power and authority might be dissolved by the recognition that the diffusion of power and authority through many levels can be positively beneficial.

The belief that political power and authority can co-exist in several layers and that the individual can identify simultaneously with them all is by no means a novel idea. We have already had occasion to emphasise the inventiveness of the Romans in devising the principle of dual citizenship (p. 16). Medieval Europe provides even richer exemplification of the basic notion of multiple loyalty, even if rarely expressed in terms of citizenship. Feudal society and monarchical authority required of the individual two different forms of loyalty, the one as man to lord, the other as subject to king. Each form was recognised as legally distinct in England, for example, from the Conquest until the constitutional reforms of Edward I. Oaths of homage usually required the man to support his lord, *salva debita fide Domini Regis*, except for the loyalty owed to the lord king. By the twelfth century intensification of religious devotion and commercial activity had spawned innumerable corporate bodies throughout the continent. Whether ecclesiastical, like universities and monasteries, or secular, like guilds and communes, each was a legally distinct entity commanding the loyalty of its members, who were at the same time subjects of princes of varying degrees. There were even attempts to conceive of the Holy Roman Emperor as a universal monarch atop them all. In the thirteenth century Engelbert of Admont argued that the proper ordering of the authority in Europe should be pyramidal – from city through kingdom to the revived universal Roman Empire.

In the early seventeenth century the Dutchman Althusius combined, in his theory of federalism, these medieval ideas of corporate and pyramidal structures with a secular, Stoic belief in the naturalness of human social cohesion. By 1603, when Althusius published his major work, the Holy Roman Empire had declined to a shadowy existence. His theory therefore related to a hierarchy of governments in large sovereign states below that level – from city through province to state. Moreover, at each level government must be based upon the consent of the people, he declared, emphasising the contractual theory of politics then coming into vogue.

Two hundred years later the massive power of the doctrines of nationalism and national sovereignty almost overwhelmed the medieval traditions of diffused power and manifold loyalties. Almost, but not quite. Italy remained keeper of the memory of the universal Roman Empire and home of the almost equally venerable papal tradition that the state must never be allowed total sovereignty over human beings. Perhaps only in Italy therefore could a foremost theorist and practitioner of the creed of nationalism insist on its compatability with, more, its indispensability to, a hierarchical pattern of man's duties. This was Mazzini. He believed that the quieting of nationality disputes by the provision of independence for all ethnic groups was an essential precondition for a harmonious world. Mazzini inspired others by the fire of his passion, kindled by the triple flame of his Christian devotion, his conviction in the beneficent destiny of Italy and his faith in the potential, through 'angelification', of mankind's virtuous assumption of its duties. He addressed the readers of *The Duties of Man* thus:

You are citizens, you have a country, in order that in a limited sphere. . . you may labour for the benefit of all *men* whatever they are and may be in the future. . . . Those who teach morality, limiting its obligations to duties towards family or country, teach you a more or less narrow *egoism* and lead you to what is evil for others

321

and for yourselves. Country and family are like two circles drawn within a greater circle which contains them both.[8]

But multiple citizenship must involve not just diverse sets of duties and loyalties. It raises also the difficult issue of power and authority. Upon what principle should these attributes of political organisation be disbursed? It is to this question that papal political thinking provides a simple but useful solution. Clearly the Roman Catholic church has a deep interest in preserving the familial and ecclesiastical realms of life from excessive state interference (p. 98). Leo XIII wrote vigorously on this matter in his Encyclical *Rerum Novarum*. His successor, Pius XI, proclaimed the basic principle of allocation by asserting that

. . . it is an injustice, a grave evil and a disturbance of right order, for a larger and higher association to arrogate to itself functions which can be performed efficiently by smaller and lower societies. This is a fundamental principle of social philosophy, unshaken and unchangeable.[9]

He described this as the 'principle of subsidiary function'. What concerned Pius XI was the threat to the freedom of 'smaller and lower societies' by the totalitarian tendencies of the age, especially Italian Fascism. A generation later, John XXIII extended the principle to argue the case for some form of world government as a means of achieving global peace. In *Pacem in Terris* he wrote that

. . . the relationships between the world government and the governments of individual nations must be regulated according to the principle of subsidiarity, in exactly the same way as the relationships within any country between the state government on the one hand and the citizens, families and intermediate bodies on the other.[10]

Multiple identity and loyalty

How, then do these precedents relate to the desirability and possibility of multiple citizenship in the world at the turn of the millenium? Can one and should one diversify the relationship between citizen and state, which has come to be accepted as virtually the only true expression of citizenship in the age of the nation-state? If multiple citizenship is to be a reality, two sets of assumptions and experiences of the citizen of the state must be adapted. The one relates to identity, loyalty and the acceptance of obligations; the other, to the institutional framework for discharging obligations, exercising rights, participating in public affairs and having a recognised status.

The issue of multi-layered identity and related feelings may be analysed into three facets. The first is the psychological. To sustain the argument for multiple citizenship it is necessary to show that individuals are not meanly endowed with the capacity for loyalty — a capacity reserved for their kith and kin. Although the devout patriot and nationalist assumes the naturalness and necessity of such a concentration of feeling, one American educational psychologist has reminded us that

322

. . . many psychologists would argue that an individual's potential for loyalty and identity can be enhanced in an almost limitless fashion by participation in different groups rather than being 'used up' by relationship to one.[11]

A famous student of the psychology of politics from an utterly different background was Frantz Fanon. Now although he was primarily concerned with the psychic damage he considered to be perpetrated by colonialism, he none the less recognised the widespread acceptance of the dual identities it encouraged. He reported that,

It will be . . . quite normal to hear certain natives declare 'I speak as a Senegalese and as a Frenchman . . .' The intellectual who is Arab and French, or Nigerian and English, when he comes up against the need to take on two nationalities, chooses . . . the negation of one of these determinations. But most often, since they cannot or will not make a choice, such intellectuals . . . take up a fundamentally 'universalist standpoint'.[12]

The individual who genuinely feels a multiple identity does not, of course, need to experience this richly coloured persona every moment of his conscious life. The different identities and loyalties come into play on different occasions. It is a matter of context. Just as a duck will fly, swim or waddle depending on circumstances, so the citizen will identify with his locality, state or the world depending on circumstances. True, the state citizen, mentally conditioned to think of himself in solely national terms, may take to that identity like a duck to water and could no more think of himself as a world citizen than fly. But it *is* a matter of conditioning. Awareness of context and emotional flexibility are psychologically perfectly feasible. Education and experience and an understanding that, while crucially important, the nation-state is not the be-all and end-all of political life can enhance that awareness and flexibility. Tom Paine distinguished between one's fellows recognised as neighbours, townsmen and countrymen, depending on the circumstances of the contact. He commented:

It is pleasant to observe by what regular gradations we surmount the force of local prejudice, as we enlarge our acquaintance with the world.[13]

Paine's reference to 'local prejudice' and 'neighbour' is a salutary reminder that the most natural focus of loyalty and one that retains very considerable power is the local. A concentration of identity and loyalty on the nation-state is psychologically artificial. Liberated from that obsession, citizenship as multiple identity could well flourish. Social and demographic mobility made local loyalty seem obsolete and the emergence of nationalism possible: nationalism was an inconceivable idea in a society where denizens of one village or town continued to think of those living twenty or thirty miles away as 'foreigners'. By the same token, the twentieth century has seen, and no doubt the twenty-first will increasingly see, so much more mobility, communication and education as to render identity entirely determined by the nation-state similarly obsolete.

Apart from the psychological possibility of this burgeoning of a multi-layered identity, there are, secondly, powerful pragmatic reasons for believing that human beings will come increasingly to accept the notion. For although the state is still very obviously essential for the well-being of its citizens, it is becoming ever clearer that total identification with the state is not always in the citizen's best interests. The good of the locality is not always necessarily synonymous with the good of the state as a whole. It may therefore be prudent for the citizen to sustain his allegiance to his locality, be it city, county or province. At the other end of the citizenship spectrum loyalty to the human species and the planet as a whole has the very practical purpose of sheer survival. Identity and loyalty are essential ingredients of a sense of common civic purpose. These feelings are not unnaturally experienced most intensely when the object of one's loyalty is under threat. Patriotic citizens rally to the defence of their own state in time of war; the case for identifying oneself as a world citizen strengthens as the threat of ecological collapse looms ever more realistically.

The issues of loyalty and obligation are at root moral questions. And so, thirdly, we must ask what are the moral arguments in favour of multiple citizenship? The fundamental proposition to be advanced is the negative one, namely, that a person incapable of a variety of identities and loyalties is morally immature. Durkheim was quite adamant about this. He wrote,

Family, nation, and humanity represent different phases of our social and moral evolution, stages that prepare for, and build upon one another. Consequently, these groups may be superimposed without excluding one another . . . . Man is morally complete only when governed by the threefold force they exercise on him.[14]

The path to a single, simplistic loyalty is the one which leads to fanaticism, the antithesis of balanced moral behaviour.

Since, however, citizenship has evolved as a relationship between the individual and the state, assertions such as Durkheim's about moral completeness cannot be left untested against the widely accepted primacy of the citizen's loyalty to the state. Arguments relating to the organic incorporation of citizen with state and to contractual obligations support the powerful contrary case. A number of counter-arguments can nevertheless be marshalled. In the first place, the state can have no moral right to expunge private life altogether. This may happen in totalitarian dystopias; but the advantages of a cultural and familial identity untouched by the state are quite evident. Individual identity *qua* citizen is therefore not the individual's total identity. As a moral, autonomous being the individual has both a need and a right to shape his own good life. And since it is unreasonable to expect the state to be able to satisfy all facets of this life, exclusive identity with and loyalty to the state is unjustified. Furthermore, if the state is conceived not as a political entity *sui generis*, but merely as an amalgam of communities, then allegiance to those communities as well as to the state cannot be denied. Has not the great Braudel depicted France as a conglomeration of local *pays* with local patriotisms rather than a tightly-knit nation-state? And of how many other states is that not very evidently true? Then, looking beyond the state, one may view it, with Mazzini, as a necessary stage towards and component of a

consciously integrated humanity. All these arguments relate to the diversification of the senses of identity, loyalty and obligation away from their sole
concentration on the state, irrespective of the particular style or policies of
any given polity.

How, then, does one choose between the several levels of loyalties? Are
there no tensions between them? One could be forgiven for drawing this conclusion from some authorities. T. H. Green and Emile Durkheim both
distinguished between the male individual as father, citizen and man. The
one concluded that, insofar as he performed these roles well, 'there is no such
thing really as a conflict of duties'[15]; while the other asserted that, 'Despite
certain simplistic statements that have been made, there is no necessary an-
tagonism between these three loyalties . . .'[16] But this is surely not good
enough. In real life the individual is faced with choices: he has to make
decisions in the context of particular issues and policies. For instance, if I am
a Glaswegian, do I think of myself as primarily a Scot or a Briton? This may
depend on the level of sympathy for Scottish problems forthcoming from the
national government in London. And given the presence of US nuclear sub-
marines at Holy Loch, my loyalty to Britain as a member of NATO may be
strained by my conviction as a world citizen that they are a threat to mankind.
How are these real conflicting demands on the multiple citizen's feelings of
identity and loyalty to be resolved?

A number of suggestions can be advanced. First, we may appeal to the
papal principle of subsidiarity. Now although both Pius XI and John XXIII
used the verb 'to arrogate' and were clearly primarily concerned with the exercise of power, the argument may also be used *pari passu* in connection with
identity and loyalty. Local, national and world issues should draw upon the
civic sense as appropriate. And the distinctions between the different levels
are often very clear. My identification with my state is more pertinent in time
of war. My identification with town properly comes into play when plans for
redevelopment will affect its character. My identification with the planet is
most relevant in the face of natural disaster. Circumstances can, however,
change the level at which this personal identification should properly operate.
To take a simple, barely contentious example. The era of particular urban
pride in Britain from the late nineteenth century produced carefully tended
parks encircled by iron railings. The erection and retention of these railings
was a matter of local pride for the protection of the park periphery until the
outbreak of war in 1939, when their uprooting for conversion to war material
became a national obligation.

But loyalties cannot always be so easily compartmentalised or harmonised.
The Nazi régime and the subsequent Nuremberg Tribunal, as we have seen
(pp 144–145), posed the problem most starkly in the context of national loyalty clashing with obligations to the natural law of humane conduct. It is
precisely in circumstances where the citizen is forced to make a choice between
opposing demands on his loyalty that the difficulty occurs. It is then not a
matter of expanding his quantum of loyalty to meet increasing demands. It
is a matter of allocating that loyalty to one of two (or more) incongruent

objects. For by its very nature, loyalty cannot be made to serve utterly in-compatible ends. The choice then concerns the conscience. In extreme cases, it becomes a test of courage. The dilemma as between national and cos-mopolitan identities is likely in forthcoming decades to mount in urgency. The pursuit of narrow national self-interest multiplied scores of times over is threatening the planet and mankind with intolerable hazards and strains. The loyalty required of the patriot and cosmopolite might seem therefore irreconcilable. This is, nevertheless, not necessarily the case if the state, in Kant's formulation, adheres to the cosmopolitan law (pp 54–55); or if the patriot can find pride in helping his country serve the overall global interest. Durkheim understood this form of resolution:

To eliminate all such contradictions, it suffices that the state commit itself . . . to the goal of realizing among its own people the general interests of humanity – that is committing itself in such a way that there is always a closer correspondence between the merit of its citizens and their condition of life with the end of reducing or preventing individual suffering. . . .
. . . when the group ideal is only a particular manifestation of the human ideal – when the citizen-ideal merges in large measure with the generic ideal of mankind – then it is to man *qua* man that we are bound, at the same time feeling more strongly linked with those in whom we find most clearly our society's particular concept of humanity.

Does this not encapsulate the citizen ideal of the immediate future? The truly good citizen, then, is he who perceives this sense of multiple identity most lucidly and who strives most ardently in his public life to achieve the closest concordance possible between the policies and goals of the several civic levels of which he is a member.

Practical considerations

When the citizen has come to accept this multi-layered identity, how can he live it in practice? Can he have a multiple status, participate in the several strata of institutions and exercise rights and perform obligations at the different levels? After all, a feeling of multiple citizenship will be barely more than hypothetical if it cannot be expressed in some tangible ways. Conversely, if tangible means of expression are not available, then the nascent feelings could well atrophy. What evidence is there, therefore, that multiple citizenship does exist, in however embryonic a way? And what further practical measures might be introduced for its promotion?

At the sub-national level there are many states which provide ample opportunity for the feeling of local identity to realise itself in practical forms of quasi-autonomy and participation. It is the very essence, of course, of federal systems of government. Devolution of responsibility for services like education, health and police can enhance the sense of citizenship because the relationship between citizen and official can be that much closer. Some twenty states, accounting for half the world's land surface, categorise themselves as federal in structure. At the same time, it is important to distinguish between devolution and balkanisation. Multiple citizenship could not, naturally, be achieved if present nation-states disintegrated into their smaller component parts. Supporters of multiple citizenship in the European Community notably foresee the alternative, more desirable development. This involves a reduction in the powers of the national governments, some of that power being devolved downwards to provincial administrations and some transferred upwards to the supranational Community. The process of integration is being accelerated by the timetable for a single market by 1992 and plans specifically related to citizenship status such as a European passport and a Social Charter. Simultaneously, 1992 could well strengthen provincial allegiances, both by the positive thrust of regional economic development policies and also by the negative effect of lowering national boundaries. The need for a common sense of identity to tackle common local problems could be facilitated, for instance, among French and Germans in the Rhineland and French and Spanish in the Pyrenees. Moreover, the possibilities for flexible multiple citizenship will expand geographically in Europe if pressures for further membership (from Malta, Cyprus, Turkey, Norway and Austria) are responded to positively by the current twelve. There have even been suggestions that other regions in the world might, at some much more distant date, follow the envied European example: the Association of South-East Asian Nations, perhaps, or the members of the Gulf Co-operation Council in the Middle East or the Latin American Cartagena Consensus?

Meanwhile, an increasing number of citizens are participating in functional networks which have a civic purpose and which operate at local, national and global levels (see also p. 241). The expansion of the numbers of bodies which have some kind of international coverage has been quite extraordinary. Designated in current acronymic vocabulary, INGOs (International Non-Governmental Organisations), they numbered 176 in 1909 and some 20,000 three-quarters of a century later. True, the great majority are continental rather than totally global in their international membership. Nevertheless, millions of citizens are already members of organisations which operate at more than one geographical level. Moreover, in the West particularly the number of INGOs with civic objectives is increasing. Although writing specifically of the USA, Professor Elise Boulding's comments about newly-founded bodies are widely applicable:

What is of special interest about these groups is that they are linking disarmament, development, environmental conservation, high levels of local community participation, and world peace. . . .
Much of the new organizational energy for peace and environmental work comes from women.[18]

Of particular significance from the point of view of citizenship is the great fund of expertise which these organisations are gathering together. The age-old case against active citizenship – that the government expert knows best – is compellingly challenged by these developments. The collective knowledge, understanding and wisdom of politicians and civil servants is by no means necessarily greater than the corresponding collective expertise of non-governmental organisations. Moreover, where central governments formulate policies according to perceived national interest or received party doctrine, citizens' groups are often much more able to judge these policies against what might be rather different local and transnational concerns. For instance, the Sellafield nuclear power station may make an important contribution to the National Grid for the supply of electricity in Britain. On the other hand, Greenpeace have publicised the abnormally high incidence of cancers in the Cumbria locality and the pollution of Ireland's territorial waters by the discharge of radioactive waste.

Evidence of the evolution of multiple citizenship in practice must include two important tests. First, it must be shown that the citizen is working through and on behalf of more than one institutional level; and second, that this style of political activity is becoming acceptable. Leaving aside the regional, sub-continental level for the sake of simplicity, the active multiple citizen has the options of acting on global issues either directly, or via his state, or by means of changing the nature of his state. All three strategies are being adopted, though given the difficulties of institutional access of the first and the entrenched patterns of behaviour common in the second, it is the third that is causing most interest. This approach involves attempts to implement imaginative new relationships between citizen groups, the state and world issues. The objective is to change the state from being the political unit *par excellence* to one of a range of institutions sharing loyalties and activities appropriately. An example of a group using the state system in an unusual way on a foreign issue and their action being upheld as acceptable has been cited by the distinguished American Professor of International Law, Richard Falk:

A case in Vermont not long ago involved a group of protesters disturbed by US policies in Central America. They had been charged with criminal trespass against the office of their Senator and defended their actions, in part, as *necessary* to induce their representative to take steps to end a course of foreign policy they believed to be illegal. Invoking the Nuremberg Obligation as a justification, the judge charged the jury that if they believed the defendants acted out of a sincere conviction . . ., then they could be acquitted. They were acquitted, and the outcome celebrated even by the state as a kind of victory by Vermont over Washington.[19]

Needless to say, only a tiny minority of the world's population think of themselves or act or deploy their skills as citizens in a multiple sense. What more needs to be undertaken to strengthen this trend? In the first place, since the sovereign state tends to lay claim to a monopoly of the citizen's loyalty and political activity, the weakening of that monopoly, already detected by a number of observers, needs to be encouraged. The solid, unitary state must allow some fragmentation into effective federalism: for a number of populous and complex states lack effective provincial institutions, even some which have federal constitutions on paper. Similarly, the hermetic sovereign state must open up gateways of opportunity for their citizens to identify with and participate in the global community.

However, and secondly, these developments must not take place solely within the context of European political thought. True, as we have seen (p. 2), citizenship evolved almost uniquely within that context and has been super-imposed on other, totally different political cultures. Even so, some eastern traditions not only survive as powerful alternative influences, but have positive characteristic contributions to make to the concept of multiple citizenship. Confucianism, Hinduism and Islam have all had a vision of unity in diversity, of local differences held together by the bond of a common humanity. Where, in western thought, the family is the sphere of private in contrast to public life, in Chinese tradition responsible family behaviour is linked to loyalty to the clan; and from the clan there extends the obligation for co-operative inter-clan relations. The whole pattern provides a social morality based upon an ever-widening understanding of multiple identity – in Confucian thought, ul-timately to the universal state. In India the significant cause of diversity has been seen not as kinship but culture. *Dharma*, the natural moral law, provides the unity, but it lays no claim to the coalescence of local diversity, richly displayed in the myriad cultural and linguistic entities in the sub-continent. This ready acceptance of multiculturalism contrasts sharply with the modern western concern for national uniformity. The Hindu tradition could conse-quently fit more comfortably than the western into a pattern of multiple citizenship. Islam too has an important contribution to make. Local cohesion is ensured by the mosque's provision of a focus for both private and public life, a distinction which is blurred in any case. Secondly, the stress placed by the teachings of Mohammed on the duty of acting on the principles of social justice for all believers, extensible to non-believers too, provides an interesting basis for the concept of a world social citizenship.

If all relevant traditions are to be harnessed to a conscious drive for an effective multiple citizenship, then certain problems concerning identity, par-ticipation and equality require attention. The western tradition, transmitted to other continents, has emphasised the crucial importance of the political unit being a cultural unit. The citizen is required both to embrace the declared national culture and be loyal to the state, each commitment inseparably de-pendent upon the other. Those who could not or would not be of the dominant culture would not be fully accepted. The discrimination has operated with varying intensity. In the post-bellum South the freed slaves were not 'proper' Americans; in Europe for centuries Jews could not be citizens in any real sense of the term; even in nineteenth-century France, Breton children had clogs hung round their necks to shame them into speak-ing the 'proper' national language. If multiple citizenship is to be an increasing reality, then this reinforcement of state political identity by an in-sistence on cultural conformity must be considerably loosened. At the same time the rituals and symbols of nation-state identity must be complemented by a resuscitation of local equivalents and the popularisation of the potential of regional and global styles of identity. In Europe no Common Market sym-bol exists to command the emotional appeal of the Union Jack or Tricolore. And how many citizens who revere their national flag would even recognise the wreathed planet on a light blue field of the UN flag (though a picture of the globe itself has greater emotional appeal (p. 187)?

Allegiances, however, require opportunities for practical expression in civic activity. Two examples of proposals for enhancing citizenship participation at different levels may be mentioned. One is the simple institutional suggestion that the UN should be restructured in order to incorporate a 'Second Assembly' or 'House of Citizens' so that the peoples and not just the states of the world might be represented. The other is the concern, expressed by Professor Alger of Ohio State University, for a closer correspondence between what he calls 'the international relations of cities' and the foreign policies of states. He has noticed that citizens' groups organised in numerous localities often have interests much more sympathetic to other peoples and global problems than the policies pursued at national level. He has declared,

. . . I strongly believe that the prevailing division of labor between local people in voluntary organizations and national officials is preventing local people from doing all they might toward the end of building the kind of world they would like to live in. . . .
Presently most people are prevented from participating by their *periphery mentality* and by a *myth of incompetence*.[20]

His remedy is better education for citizen self-confidence in pressing their vision of the good life.

And yet, it may be objected, official foreign policies are largely determined by economics and that even an approximate harmony of interests is impossible while standards of living are so desperately incomparable. If the principle of citizenship equality requires the concept of social citizenship at the state level, it is just as necessary at all others. Gross socio-economic inequalities as between provinces, states and regions must therefore undermine the very concept of local, national and world citizenship respectively. The multiple citizen, if he be true and good, must therefore be committed to the erosion of these injustices at whatever levels he can most effectively bring his influence to bear.

9.3 THE FIVE ELEMENTS

. . . if we wish to maximise our own individual liberty, we must cease to put our trust in princes, and instead take charge of the public arena ourselves.
. . . unless we place our duties before our rights, we must expect to find our rights themselves undermined.

Quentin Skinner [21]

Reconciling differences

Citizens are omnipresent; citizenship is rare. Apart from stateless persons, mainly refugees not yet resettled, every human being has an international legal status as a citizen of a state. But although billions are classified as citizens, only a small proportion of that number can be truly said to enjoy citizenship as a status of social dignity and a source of effective rights. And only a small proportion can be said to exercise citizenship as a mode of moral behaviour. This failure of the quality of citizenship to match the quantity of citizens can be explained by the incomplete or unbalanced acceptance for historical, social, ideological and psychological reasons of the five elements of citizenship (p. 319).

The nature of citizenship as identity and civic virtue; the nature of the legal, political and social facets of citizenship; and the relationships between these five elements all differed in various historical periods and continue to differ today. The diversity of interpretations has been the result of the varied philosophical assumptions concerning the nature of man and the good life and the assumed priorities which the institution of citizenship should emphasise. This lack of theoretical uniformity has been supplemented by the variety of practical needs which citizenship has been summoned to meet. The desirability of achieving some conformity of definition and understanding of the five elements and their relationships therefore derives not just from the importance of resolving theoretical arguments. It is also crucial to prevent its abuse by propagandists; by selecting only those facets which suit his purpose, the propagandist can use the all-embracing term 'citizenship' to camouflage his denial of the full ideal. Citizenship cannot be said properly to prevail unless all five elements exist, the extremist tendencies within are held in check and the elements themselves are kept in balance. Thus a citizenship which incorporates all the elements except the opportunity for political participation is no true citizenship; a version which insists on political rights without duties or vice versa is similarly counterfeit. A properly balanced citizenship benefits society as a whole; a partial citizenship has the very purpose of excluding or diminishing some ideal or group of individuals, and the potential benefits become alloyed. Citizenship must be multiple in its qualitative characteristics as well as its geographical expression.

The purpose here is to probe the possibility of reconciling the competing, even conflicting traditions in order to provide a comprehensive portrayal of citizenship which captures and preserves its essence. This essence may be understood to comprise rights as contributed by the state to the citizen; public spirit and judgement as contributed by the citizen to the state; and equality of dignity as contributed by citizens to each other – the amalgam designed to minimise injustice and tyranny. (And for 'state' read the several strata of the geographical dimension.)

Guidelines for synthesis

Considerable academic interest has been aroused since the 1970s by a renewed consciousness of the republican tradition of citizenship.[22] Can the classical concept of civic virtue, revived in the Renaissance and in the French, Scottish and American Enlightenment supply a valuable corrective to the distortions of the citizenship ideal as perpetrated by the individualism, liberalism, capitalism and socialism of the last three centuries? Such debates reveal a number of variant interpretations gleaned from all the traditions and which we must try to reconcile. We may cluster the problems into three main questions: What are good and bad citizens? What is meant by citizen equality? How

331

may ideological differences be resolved?

A good citizen is one who so orders his life that at least a part of it is consciously directed to the benefit of the society in which he lives (however defined). For much of the history of political theory the matter could be simply stated. In the very opening paragraph of the *Politics* Aristotle asserted that 'all associations aim at some good: and [the polis] will pursue this aim most, and will thus be directed to the most sovereign of all goods.'[23] It followed that the civic duty of the good citizen was to comprehend and advance the public good, that is, those policies which would be of shared, communal benefit. However, from the seventeenth century an alternative view emerged, namely a denial of

. . . any conception of society as a community united in a shared vision of the good for man (as prior to and independent of any summing of individual interests) and a *consequent* shared practice of the virtues.[24]

The reconciliation of these two opposing conceptions about the good life is at one and the same time one of the most basic and most difficult problems in the task of constructing an ideal definition of citizenship.

We may, however, be helped by recalling the plurality of society. So-called individual interests are rarely pursued in total isolation. In both framing the goals he wishes to achieve and in acting to accomplish them, the individual operates in association with others – most simply as part of a family or business. And compromises have to be made. The whole of social life is a compromise. The state itself, as the contract theorists have reminded us, is a compromise between the ideals of total human freedom and the requirements of security. The responsibility of the citizen is to act when circumstances demand in an altruistic fashion to advance the good of the state or the good of some subsidiary or supranational association. For if the citizen must be recognised as owing multi-layered loyalties, his virtue must lie in pursuing different goods. Furthermore, it must not be forgotten that the citizen's moral obligations operate horizontally to his fellow citizens as well as vertically to the institutions which form the framework of his social and political life. In a sense, therefore, the philosophical problem of whether the public good is merely the sum of or more than the sum of individual goods is a minor consideration for the citizen weighing the relative merits of the practical issues commanding his attention.

Having judged what is the most appropriate good to suppport in a given circumstance, the citizen must decide what action if any to take. We are then faced with the contrary arguments relating to the active and passive modes of citizenship. Here again a compromise is the mark of civic virtue. Constant political involvement by the whole body of citizenry is neither practicable nor desirable. What is required is that the conscientious citizen keep himself well informed so that when his intervention *is* timely he will act in a judicious manner. In this way surely a happy mean may be contrived between the destabilising agitator and slothful egoist. In the words of Bernard Crick,

The irritable matrimonial alienation between rulers and ruled does not lie in the system of representation so much as in the system of communication. And it does not lie in the scale, size or complexity of government as such but in its comprehensibility – in its lack of publicity and popularisation.[25]

Citizenship is the enemy of extremism. It requires balance and judgement. The concept of balance means that identification of the civic spirit with only one pole of opposed interpretations must be faulty. And if an amalgamation of so many diverse capacities renders citizenship a difficult role to play, then that is but a recognition of the truth. Similarly, the attribute of sound judgement is at the same time crucial and hard to cultivate.

The faculty of political judgement, as Ronald Beiner has demonstrated[26], involves the capacity to identify and discriminate in the framework of a dispassionate understanding of the historical context of the issue to hand and on the basis of a humane moral awareness. This faculty is vital for the citizen in an age in which his role is undermined by the authority of the so-called expert and degraded by the portrayal of politics as media spectacle. Even if the citizen has limited opportunity to exercise his judgement as an active participant, the faculty must not be allowed to atrophy. For,

. . . attending to the faculty of judgment may be a way of recouping one's status as a citizen, in a world that systematically frustrates any real sense of citizenship. (Judging then becomes a kind of vicarious political action!). . . .
When deprived of the possibility of meaningfully affecting, and therefore meaningfully deliberating about, the basic conditions governing the shape of the world we share with others. . ., we can at least continue to judge – and in this hope finds a refuge.[27]

A pessimistic minimalist position, but one which nevertheless emphasises that political judgement lies at the very core and heart of citizenship; and is therefore a vital catalyst for blending a sensible amalgam of other civic qualities.

What, then, of the bad citizen – he who lacks judgement and a moral social conscience or the will to bring them into play? Once again we are faced with a dichotomy of interpretations. There are those who hold that absence of citizenly virtue is explicable in terms of the individual's nature – his psychological and moral make-up. Others believe the explanation lies in the corrupting influence of an unjust social environment. In addition, some seek reformation by means of threats and violence – the imposition of virtue; others place their trust in persuasion and opportunity – the encouragement of virtue. An acceptable embracing of these disagreements must feature the common-sense observation that human beings are shaped by both nature and nurture and the insistence that citizenly virtue must be gently encouraged, not violently imposed. The technique of force must be rejected on two grounds. The one is the empirical evidence that it is destructive of human dignity and indeed life. Civic virtue imposed is Robespierrist terror. The other argument is the logical one that the virtue of citizenship must by very definition derive from inner motivation; to implant virtue by fear is a contradiction in terms.

Let us now turn to the second main question, namely that relating to the idea of citizen equality. It is obvious that both within any given state and as between states, citizenship is enjoyed with wide variations of assurance. Some citizens are more equal than others in terms of identity and legal, political and/or social rights. However, this observed disparity does not necessarily have to be interpreted as an unfortunate failure to achieve the citizenship ideal. The phenomenon can instead be used as a reminder that élite and graded conceptions of citizenship vie with an egalitarian conception for acceptance.

Can these tensions be resolved? It is surely self-evident that some individuals will have a greater propensity to lead and others, to follow. In army parlance there are some with OQs. (officer qualities), others, without; some who would accept commissions, others, who prefer to remain in the ranks with their mates. So too with citizenship. Nevertheless, the fact that a minority are always more active and visible than the rest does not necessarily negate the principle of citizenship – always providing that individuals who so wish have opportunities to exercise the functions of the élite citizen. What *is* a negation of citizenship is the denial of rights to any given individuals or groups as a matter of principle, either by means of social prejudice or by legal enactment. What citizenship requires therefore is an equality of dignity and opportunity incorporating a diversity of appetites for civic activity and needs for civic rights. Michael Walzer has indicated a way of achieving a broadly acceptable conception of citizenship equality by propounding the notion of 'complex equality'. This, he explains,

. . . establishes a set of relationships such that domination is impossible. In formal terms, complex equality means that no citizen's standing in one sphere or with regard to one social good can be undercut by his standing in some other sphere, with regard to some other good. Thus, citizen X may be chosen over citizen Y for political office, and then the two will be unequal in the sphere of politics. But they will not be unequal generally so long as X's office gives him no advantage over Y in any other sphere – superior medical care, access to better schools for his children, entrepreneurial opportunities, and so on.[28]

Mention of élitism and social services raises the issue of overt ideological disagreements concerning the nature of citizenship. The simplest form of the quarrel is that between the insistence on rights by the Left and on obligations by the Right. The current rhetoricians of the Left, using their jargon vocabulary, echo the incantatory words 'entitlement' and 'empowerment'. The Right meanwhile preach civic responsibility. The academically sophisticated have identified the same kind of polarisation of ideals in more subtle and complex form in the separate republican and liberal traditions of citizenship. Where the republican style emphasises duties, stern virtue and the positive freedom to participate, the liberal adopts the more casual approach of minimal involvement and therefore negative freedom from interference in the citizen's private life.

A synthesis can, however, be achieved by recalling the basic proposition that citizenship must incorporate both rights and duties and that in the citizen's behaviour they must be kept in equilibrium. And on the matters of virtue and freedom citizenship entails a judicious middle path, eschewing both fanaticism and complacency. Professor Skinner has even suggested that the bifurcation between rights and duties is false and unnecessary. The libertarian tradition of self-interest and individual rights on the one hand and the republican belief in the need for active involvement in social life as a means to true human fulfilment on the other should properly be fused. Or rather, that the republican tradition must be revived as a means of preserving the benefits of liberalism. As is clear from the quotation at the head of this section, he has suggested that, far from rights and duties competing, rights *depend* upon the effective discharge of duties.

The other main ideological tension exists between the view that social welfare provision by the state is an act of philanthropy and the alternative view that it is a civic 'entitlement'. Again, true citizenship must seek a middle course. Without a certain minimum of education, standard of living and leisure time neither the aptitude for civic awareness nor the dignity of the egalitarian principle is possible. In a world of economic inequalities market forces alone cannot achieve these desiderata for all. Since citizenship is a right of the individual *vis-à-vis* the public realm, then that public realm, whether state or cosmopolis, must accept the responsibility for ensuring these minimal conditions for its exercise. What is more, the grounds must be clearly accepted as deriving not from charity and compassion, but from the rights and justice which accrue to the status of citizen. On the other hand, citizenship respects the right of the citizen to individual autonomy and a private life. As a consequence, state interference is not justifiable once the minimum conditions of social citizenship have been established.

In this identification of the holistic nature of citizenship as properly conceived we have made no overt mention of the five elements, though they have been implicit throughout. But if the idea of multiple citizenship is to be fully applicable along the horizontal dimension of our cube, then it must also be demonstrated that the five elements are themselves interdependent.

In the first place, social and political identity means a recognition of mutual commitments. As a British citizen I share with other British citizens a certain, albeit imperfect, style of citizenship with legal, political and social elements. Without that recognisable style I might have an ethnic or cultural identity but not a proper citizen identity. A sense of identity is of course essential for feeling and displaying the virtue of loyalty. It has furthermore been argued that citizenly loyalty is dependent upon the provision of welfare or social citizenship by the state (or whatever the focus of loyalty might be). 'How shall men love their country,' Rousseau asked, 'if it is nothing more for them than for strangers, and bestows on them only that which it can refuse to none?'[29] The civil and political elements are also symbiotically related. The suffrage is barren of meaning without the rule of law; the rule of law is precarious if undefended by a politically alert citizenry. And finally political citizenship and social citizenship are intertwined, not just for the reasons already outlined, but also because of the dangers of alienation. Quasi-citizens who lack the security and justice of a minimum of welfare provision will, if sufficiently incensed, use their political citizenship in a destabilising way to achieve their social rights.

Citizenship is not a pick-and-mix collection of attributes arbitrarily selected. If individuals and governments, states and the world community want and need the institution, they must accept it whole. And they must accept that the whole is neither a simple nor an easy concept to practise. But then the very complexity and difficulty of multiple citizenship can only reinforce the case that education for citizenship is a fully integral feature of citizenship itself.

9.4 EDUCATION

It is of first importance to you that your sons should be taught what are the ruling principles and beliefs which guide the lives of their fellow-men in their own times and in their own country; . . . what the spirit of the legislation by which their deeds will have to be judged . . . . And it is important to you that they should feel themselves from their earliest years united in the spirit of equality and of love for a common aim, with the millions of brothers that God has given them.

Mazzini[30]

The educational task

A citizen is a person furnished with knowledge of public affairs, instilled with attitudes of civic virtue and equipped with skills to participate in the political arena. The acquisition and enhancement of these attributes is in truth a life-long undertaking; even so, a firm foundation must be laid down in schools to ensure both their early and systematic learning. In the words of Professor Janowitz,

It is widely recognised that effective citizenship rests on a rigorous and viable system of civic education which informs the individual of his civic rights and obligations.[31]

In fact, any attempt to define the knowledge, attitudes and skills required and to translate them into learning objectives will reveal that the teacher's task is considerably more complicated than that. It is convenient to start with a bare outline of the learning objectives for the young multiple citizen. This may be presented in the following tabular form[32]:

knowledge	attitudes	skills
facts	self-understanding	intellect & judgement
interpretation	respect for others	communication
personal role	respect for values	action

Although tabulation is convenient, it must be remembered that here again, as with the cube diagram, the categories need to be understood as highly permeable. Knowledge about citizenship is only partially useful if it does not lead on to the formulation of attitudes and the acquisition of skills; attitudes are but prejudices unless grounded in a firm and clear understanding; and action is wanting direction without attitudes and is irresponsible and/or inefficient if born in ignorance.

Learning objectives

Let us now sketch in some suggestions for each of these categories of objectives. First, knowledge. A young citizen should absorb some basic facts. He needs to understand how the status and role of citizen have evolved in history, particularly in his own state. He needs also to be informed how citizenship is articulated through institutions and laws in the present day. But since citizenship operates in relation to practical issues, he must be introduced to the major problems and controversies with which, as an adult citizen, he is likely to be confronted – at local, national, regional and global levels. However, information in itself provides only the elementary components of understanding. The pupil should be introduced at the appropriate level to the primary concepts of which the all-embracing concept of citizenship is composed. These include: identity, loyalty, freedom, rights, duties, justice, social justice, representation. Related to this process is the ability to distinguish between the different geographical levels and the five elements of citizenship as already identified.

Not that this material should be presented in an analytical, theoretical way for the majority of pupils. Interest may be stimulated and relevance highlighted by bringing the young citizens to an understanding of their potential personal roles. They must be equipped with information concerning the repertoire of participative activities that will be open to them on attaining the age of majority. They should also be brought to an understanding of how they are likely to be affected individually by certain laws and issues; how their own locality is placed in national and global contexts. And this teaching may be even more personalised by the teacher inviting each pupil to identify those civic matters in which he takes a particular interest and whose cause he would most wish to protect and advance.

The first task of any teacher, it hardly needs repeating, is to stimulate interest in the subject-matter he is purveying. Therefore the basic attitude which the teacher of citizenship must instil is a predisposition to be interested in public affairs. The teacher has, too, a responsibility, shared it is true with other agencies, to clarify the pupil's feelings of identity and loyalty. Closely related to this objective of self-understanding and of cardinal importance is the task of leading the young person to an appreciation of his own prejudices. In a society which is culturally divided by intense ethnic or religious allegiances, this is an exceedingly delicate matter. Acceptance across cultural divides of common citizenship is crucial for civic harmony and equality; yet the teacher must be sensitive to the power of competing identities. Indeed, the more complex the pupil's social identity, the greater the responsibility of the teacher to bring him to an understanding of the wisdom of the Delphic Oracle's admonition 'Know thyself'.

Having established these foundations of self-understanding the teacher needs to encourage rational and flexible thought. The citizen needs to have been educated to an attitude of mind which embraces a willingness to be critical and a capacity to question information, policies and views, while at the same time being ready to advance reasons for his own views and to change them in the light of weighty contrary evidence or argument. Finally, the teacher must cultivate in his pupils a realistic confidence in their own abilities to participate in public affairs.

The mirror-image of awareness of one's own prejudices is toleration. The citizenship principle of equality of dignity requires a positive respect for fellow citizens. Young people need to learn therefore to be tolerant of views divergent from their own. They must also be sympathetic to those who do not enjoy the status and rights of citizenship to the full.

Embodied in citizenly behaviour is, of course, a respect for values. The young citizen should therefore be taught in a comprehensible way respect for evidence, freedom, justice, fairness and altruism. Even more basic and a matter of lively concern is the responsibility of the teacher to emphasise the reciprocal nature of rights and duties.

Thirdly, since citizenship is an art to be practised, a range of skills needs to be added to knowledge and attitudes. Some of these are fairly basic intellectual skills such as collecting information, organising and evaluating data and the ability to reason and argue. More difficult but vital for the development of effective citizenship is education in judgement. In the view of Beiner,

Judgment is . . . irreducible to algorithm. What is required is not a 'decision procedure', but an education in hermeneutic insight, taste, and understanding.[33]

In pedagogical terms judgement may be analysed into four component objectives. First, the young citizen needs to understand the values he prizes and against which he will judge issues, policies and decisions. He must also have a sensitive critical faculty for the detection of bias and special pleading. At the same time he must appreciate the likely consequences of citizen action or inaction. This, of course, includes effects on other people, so that the attribute of judgement must include empathy – the ability to put oneself in someone else's situation.

Because citizenship involves debate and the exchange of views, skills of communication are crucial to the educational programme. These involve the ability to express one's own views lucidly, both orally and in writing; to understand others' views similarly communicated; and to exchange views in discussion. These particular skills obviously involve interpersonal and group conduct. This leads naturally to proficiency in organising and participating in a group for the achievement of a clear purpose. Additional action skills are those required for effective petitioning and lobbying.

Problems facing the teacher

In pursuing these learning objectives the teacher must have regard to the subject-content and relationships presented in the body of the present work.

However, since we are here searching for a reconciliation or synthesis of competing interpretations of the concept of citizenship, some of these difficulties as they particularly face the teacher need separate consideration. We may identify three clusters of problems. One concerns the general political delicacy of teaching in this difficult area. The second is the realistic recognition that different social and political conditions will need or indeed enforce particular emphases. And thirdly there are the problems relating to curriculum organisation.

The fullness and style of citizenship enjoyed and displayed by citizens are powerful contributions to social and political culture. Education for citizenship cannot therefore be conducted in the purity of academic isolation. In this it differs from Political Education, to which it is evidently closely related. Although many would argue that a totally value-free programme of Political Education is undesirable, it might at least be hypothetically possible if constructed from objective Political Science (though see p. 204). Citizenship education, however, has as a major goal the development of certain values and attitudes integral to the very concept of citizenship. As a consequence, politicians and parents as well as teachers have a legitimate interest in the ways schools interpret their task.

Educationists have vital functions to perform. They must preserve a vision of the ideal of citizenship; and they must judge the most appropriate pedagogical methods for leading their pupils to the best approximation to that ideal they are likely to achieve in the prevailing circumstances. In discharging these functions, it must be faced, they may find themselves at odds with other interested parties. For, as we shall see below, there may well be compelling reasons for particular facets of citizenship to be emphasised at the expense of others. In these conditions, it is unreasonable for the teacher utterly to resist the general climate of opinion. Only if those pressures threaten to undermine the very essentials of citizenship should the teacher recognise it as his duty to defend the ideal. In conditions where the principles of citizenship are not imperilled the teacher's responsibility is clear: to keep in balance the precepts of the ideal and the demands of society.

Within these prudential guidelines the teacher must use his professional judgement with regard to four particular problems where opposing aims need to be reconciled. The first is the balance which needs to be struck between support for and criticism of the nation, the national system of government and the government in office. The basic principle is that a citizen must display loyalty and concern for political stability on the one hand and a critical awareness of faults on the other. The teacher should prepare his pupils for this role of political Janus. Yet, obviously, the very societies where the citizen as critic is in greatest need of cultivation are precisely where the teacher's opportunity to undertake this work is least likely and most hazardous. But this harsh reality does not undermine the professional principle.

The second problem concerns the need to teach the values of citizenship. Both the ideal of citizenship and the ethics of the teaching profession shun indoctrination. In the former case it is contrary to the exercise of autonomous judgement, which is one of its basic tenets. In the latter, it is an abuse of the discipline and authority which the teacher wields over those in his charge. But if the teacher has the intention of persuading his pupils that the intrinsic values like tolerance and freedom, listed on p. 202, are good, is his intention not indoctrinatory? 'Indoctrinating someone,' the educational philosopher John White has written, 'is trying to get him to believe that a proposition 'p' is true, in such a way that nothing will shake that belief'.[34]

If the teacher is educating according to the true principles of citizenship, it can, however, be argued on two grounds that he is both responsibly inculcating civic values while at the same time blameless of the charge of indoctrination. The first argument requires us to distinguish between two kinds of propositions. One is the kind which in normal parlance we associate with the term indoctrination, namely those concerned with political and religious ideologies. There are some features of citizenship education which, it is true, fall into this category. To implant an unshakeable belief in the unquestioning duty of patriotic loyalty or constant political participation would be as objectionable as implanting an unshakeable belief in Marxist or monetarist economics. But if the principle of multiple citizenship informs the teaching, such biases would not be present in the classroom in any case. Furthermore, the other propositions of citizenship are of a different order: justice, fairness, freedom and so forth are values inseparable from the good human life. They are universal truths, not subjective propositions.

The second ground on which the teaching of citizenship values may be defended against any charge of indoctrination is that the very concept of citizenship involves the individual being a rational autonomous being endowed with the capacity for independent judgement. 'Indoctrination,' in the words of the philosopher Richard Hare, 'only begins when we are trying to stop the growth in our children of the capacity to think for themselves about moral questions.'[35] The very heart of citizenship education is to provide young citizens with precisely that 'capacity to think for themselves'. Citizenship education is thus the very reverse of indoctrination.

The two other general problems which require some form of reconciliation may be dealt with more briefly. A balance must be struck between the encouragement of a sense of civic efficacy on the one hand and by that process inviting the dangers of future alienation when the realities of citizen impotence are experienced. Similarly, the aims of patriotism and world-mindedness must be harmonised. Both of these difficulties may be handled by the common-sense application of the principle of multiple citizenship.

The second cluster of problems arises from the felt need for different emphases in teaching depending on particular circumstances. The fostering of an historical consciousness is naturally given priority over some other facets of citizenship in states with a fragile sense of unity. Tolerance needs to be accorded particular salience in societies threatened with religious or ethnic arrogance and prejudice. Where authoritarian forms of government exist, citizenship education should, if possible, stress the importance of legal and political rights. Similarly, where social and economic rights are barely recognised or are under threat, their legitimacy should be emphasised. And where narrow national loyalty is a barrier to a supranational identity, then citizenship education should underplay the element of patriotism.

It is clear from this list that there are numerous circumstances in which a balanced sense of citizenship requires an unbalanced programme of teaching. For education must be brought into play to counteract the social and political forces of disequilibrium. It will also be clear that in some instances the teacher will be acting in concert with official policy and in others, against. In the case of a new state like Nigeria or Sri Lanka, for instance, with only a fragile political unity or a mature state like the USA with incipient cultural disharmony, the educational emphasis on historical consciousness and toleration respectively will accord with official policy. On the other hand, where civil rights are denied, as in Chile, for example, or social rights are under attack, as in Britain, then any attempts by teachers to counterbalance these policies will involve confrontation with the government. And there is a mid-way situation where official policy is fluid or hesitant – in Hungary or Poland, for example, on the issues of civil and political rights and in the Community countries with regard to European citizenship. The responsible teacher must be alert to these needs and circumstances, judge his duty by reference to the ideal of citizenship, and proceed with discretion to bring the vision of that ideal as close as possible to his pupils.

The social and political hazards of this task are sufficiently awesome; hence the teacher should not have to face the additional complication of confused curricular arrangements. The problem as experienced in the USA has been described by R. Freeman Butts in the following way:

Three major drives are competing to reshape the social studies in American schools. Despite their common interest in social studies, those efforts to redirect the curriculum are often carried out independently of one another. There has been too little effort to interweave the three and too little recognition of their natural affinity. Indeed, they are often disparate, and sometimes even antagonistic, in their impacts or pressures upon the schools.[36]

He identified the three drives as: international or global education; multicultural studies; and citizenship education for social and civic cohesion.

In some other countries, notably England, the confusion is even worse confounded. Since c.1960 the demands for the incorporation of new courses or subject-matter in the general social studies field have become overwhelming: Political Education, Education for Economic Awareness, Sociology, Law-related Studies, Environmental/Ecological Studies, Third World/Development Studies, Multicultural Studies, Peace Studies, Human Rights Education, Moral Education, World Studies. Although some advocates of World Studies would argue that their programmes comprehensively embrace the rest, the proponents of the more specific studies would not necessarily agree. And although there are obvious overlaps of subject-matter across the whole length of the list, that observation by itself does not advance us very far in the task of curriculum design. The potential quantity of material is too great and the interconnections are too confusing for school pupils to handle.

Two examples of methods used to teach about the different geographical levels of public life may be used to indicate the limitations of previous attempts to tackle this problem. In the 1950s some Social Studies syllabuses in England adopted a concentric approach. But teaching sequentially about the locality, the state and the world rarely revealed the interconnections between them. More recently, the Resources International programme in Columbus, Ohio, has received considerable acclaim. The basic idea is that

The program is designed to help elementary and secondary teachers bring a global dimension to their instruction through the use of the local community as an international learning laboratory.[37]

RI has been based on the work of Chadwick Alger, already cited (p. 330). However, it is a technique rather than a principle of curriculum design.

The pertinence of multiple citizenship

What is needed is a basic and important organising principle, which can embrace the essential concepts and subject-matter of all the disciplines and fields of study listed above. The idea of multiple citizenship fits this requirement perfectly. In the first place, the list of learning objectives outlined above would bear a remarkable similarity to lists compiled for each of these eleven different areas of study. And most of their core concerns are the concerns of multiple citizenship. Since citizenship is a political status and role, there is an easy correspondence between Political Education and citizenship education. So much of public affairs in our own age relates to economic management and priorities that basic economic literacy and the element of social citizenship would be the contributions by Education for Economic Awareness. Sociology would also provide the element of social citizenship as well as an understanding of the nature of identity. For the issues of legal status and civil rights citizenship education needs to draw upon Law-related Studies. Environmental/Ecological management must, of course, be a prime concern of the good world citizen. Development Studies also provide this aspect and also the element of social citizenship at the global level. Multicultural Studies must be concerned with the issues of civic identity and the virtue of tolerance. The idea of the good world citizen must necessarily draw upon the insights of Peace Studies. Human Rights Education coincides at all geographical levels with the principle that citizenship involves civil, political and social rights. Moral Education, although concerned with spiritual as well as secular matters, nevertheless in its second facet provides an understanding of the nature of civic virtue. Finally, World Studies presupposes a cosmopolitan interpretation of citizenship.

Harold Laski categorically stated that 'The education of the citizen . . . is the heart of the modern State.'[38] Can we not add that, accepting the basic needs of literacy and numeracy, that the education of the citizen should be the heart of modern education?

342

9.5 CONCLUSION

> . . . the dominion of citizenship, unlike the dominion of grace (or money, or office, or education, or birth or blood), is not tyrannical; it is the end of tyranny.
>
> Michael Walzer.[39]

The modern citizen is the legatee of two and a half thousand year of fluctuating and episodic political thinking, popular pressure and educational preparation. Fifth-century Athens and Republican and Imperial Rome, Renaissance Florence and Revolutionary Paris provided the most powerful energising forces for the development and consolidation of the citizenship idea. At the turn of the twentieth century we are perhaps in another period of comparable political creativity. The directions in which citizenship will evolve in the coming generation will depend on the extent to which the troika of political thinking, popular pressure and educational preparation can be harnessed in its support in some half-dozen critical areas.

In underdeveloped states citizenship means little to large portions of their populations. To the peasants of scattered villages or the huddled masses of megalopolitan slums national, let alone cosmopolitan, identity is meaningless. Political consciousness, where it exists at all, is a resigned acceptance of manipulation by local leaders or of sheer and utter impotence. Indeed, paradoxically, attempts to assemble a modern political structure often reinforce local, communal identity to the exclusion of national or multiple identities. In an American study of south-east Asia, the author noted that

> . . . most patrons have followings that are almost exclusively drawn from their own communities. Intercommunal integration tends to take place near the apex of the political structure with the base of each communal pyramid remaining largely separate.[40]

Effective citizenship will depend on the rate at which education to a secondary level, the diffusion of the mass media and the creation of a civil society infrastructure of interest-groups and associations can be accelerated.

Despite the need for a real sense and institutionalisation of multiple citizenship, national cohesion is still an absolutely essential ingredient. Not only is that inhibited by the continuing magnetism of local, communal or tribal loyalties in newly constructed states; the citizenship ideal is threatened in mature states by particularist zealotry. Some fundamentalist Jews find it difficult to accept Muslim Palestinians as equal Israeli citizens. Some fundamentalist Muslims find it difficult fully to identify with what they believe are the prevailing lax mores of fellow Britons.

Migration has always placed a strain on citizenship. Yet there are plenty of examples where groups have benefited. In the nineteenth century, the Jews of the Pale of Settlement, denied legal citizenship in Russia, found it in Britain; the Irish from beyond the Dublin Pale, denied any effective rights of citizenship, found them in the USA. However, in recent decades the strength of migratory movements has loosened the cultural homogeneity which some states had relied upon for their style of citizenship: Latin Americans in the

USA, Turks in Germany, Algerians in France, British citizens of West Indian or Pakistani origins.

If the citizenship ideal is to remain strong, then multicultural education for both the host and minority populations is imperative. Multicultural education may well, indeed, be the key to achieving further progress in consolidating citizenship in both its cosmopolitan and national democratic senses. It can strengthen world citizenship by showing that, if people of diverse ethnic and religious backgrounds can live in harmony in a state, then the division of the world into separate states on those same ethnic and religious criteria is not immutable. The relationship between multicultural education and democracy has been demonstrated by a British authority on the subject:

> . . . Western societies have no alternative but fruitless recourse to coercive and authoritarian . . . means, if they do not respond positively and creatively to the opportunity presented by the ethnic revivals and cultural dilemmas with which they are now convulsed. For this task, they need to recognise new ways of forging creative coalitions across issues and groups in society and . . . reinterpret . . . commitments inherent within a democratic way of life . . . the new ethnicity is a pathfinder to a new democracy, and multicultural education remains a potentially efficacious means of achieving that new democracy.[41]

Cultural tension is not the only excuse (on both sides of a cultural divides) for coercion and authoritarianism. Many governments are very active in curtailing the civil rights which the status of citizenship requires. Military regimes, which have been so common in Third World countries, are, of course, incompatible with effective citizenship. However, in the late 1980s two large states, Argentina and Pakistan, restored civilian government — evidence that the urge to sustain civil and political rights need not be permanently frustrated. At the same time the political thaw in the Communist world has opened up further possibilities for bolstering the spirit of citizenship. The main spokesman for the Polish trade union, Solidarity, said of developments in his country in early 1989: 'For the first time in history the ruling Communist Party is accepting the principle of democratisation.'[42] This is not to suggest that the infringement of human rights has ceased to be a widespread phenomenon, but rather that there are signs of hopefulness for further progress.

The matter of social, as opposed to civil and political, citizenship is an area for greater pessimism. In many states social equality has by no means been approximately achieved; or it is denied as a valid test of citizenship; or both. At the global level social citizenship is even further from achievement in both theory and practice. But all the while the basic idea of citizenship is still accorded universal lip-service, at least its principle of social mobility, if not of social rights, can be preserved.

Greater security of social rights can often be achieved by social mobility being translated into geographical mobility. Dick Whittington walked from Gloucestershire, so legend has it, and became Lord Mayor, the first citizen of London. Migration, both internal and international, may be a way of seizing social rights which are not available by automatic entitlement. Locke, admittedly in a weak argument, asserted that in certain circumstances the citizen has no obligation to his state and 'is at liberty to go and incorporate himself into any other commonwealth.'[43] It has recently been suggested that,

If international migration were freed from its present constraints, or if it were greatly expanded within agreed international limits, it could become an important factor in alleviating North-South differences.[44]

There is already considerable fluidity of populations, and no doubt even more would do a power of good for the principle of social citizenship at both state and world levels. In Europe much hope for an evolving Community citizenship is indeed pinned on such geographical mobility. The costs in communal tensions, however, are likely to increase with any increase in migration, and to increase proportionately with the breadth of cultural differences. In Britain a Yorkshireman meets much less prejudice in London than a Dutchman, who meets less prejudice than a Pakistani. Social citizenship provided as a right is not only closer to the basic ideal of citizenship than its acquisition by migration, it is less perilous.

But is the concept of citizenship beyond the nation-state likely to become more widely accepted, even in the most generalised terms, in the foreseeable future than it has been in the past? Despite the theoretical and practical obstacles, two significant developments suggest that a more positive attitude could well be emerging. One is the growing acceptance of the European Community as a quasi-supranational entity. Even in a poll conducted in xenophobic Britain in 1989, 38 per cent replied that they already saw themselves as European citizens. Seven years earlier two distinguished American international lawyers had reported

. . . a willingness on the part of hard-headed international lawyers to entertain the prospect and even to affirm the need for *systemic* changes in the international legal order.[45]

What, finally, are the prospects for citizenly virtue? Classically, it can plausibly be argued, the commitment of the citizen was founded on property ownership, military enrolment and patriotic identity. In today's world, however, huge proportions of the world's population of so-called citizens, both urban and rural, own precious few possessions; military service is either confined to volunteers at best or destructive of civilian rule at worst; and the nation-state, let alone the city, can no longer be the sole focus of loyalty. Temptations to anti-social behaviour are rife. Yet human nature has not changed. The potential for responsible and altruistic behaviour remains. More than ever the ideal of civic virtue needs to be recaptured, reinterpreted and retaught in contemporary terms.

Citizenship is the foundation of human dignity and secular morality. Bereft of these values, mankind will decline into tyranny and fanaticism. It is essential that the light of citizenship, shining through its multi-faceted prisms, ward off the darkness of these evils.

REFERENCES

1. H. Wheeler, *Democracy in a Revolutionary Era* (1968, Penguin ed., 1971), pp. 10–11.
2. MacIntyre, *After Virtue*, p. 263.
3. Y. V. Andropov 'So-called "Pure" Democracy' (speech), reprinted in M. Ebon, *The Andropov File* (Sidgwick & Jackson, 1983), p. 191.
4. Englund, *Curriculum as a Political Problem*, pp. 325 *et seq.*
5. *Literary Gazette* (English language version, vol. 1, 1988), reprinted in *Guardian*, 25 July 1988.
6. Quoted in M. Walker, 'Dosvidanya to all that, comrades', *Guardian*, 9 December 1988.
7. John XXIII, *Pacem in Terris*, para. 163.
8. Mazzini, *The Duties of Man* (Dent edn, 1907), p. 41.
9. Pius XI, *Quadragesimo Anno*, p. 58.
10. John XXIII, *Pacem in Terris*, para. 140.
11. J. Torney-Purta, 'Three Models of International Education', p. 258.
12. F. Fanon, *The Wretched of the Earth* (1961, Penguin edn 1967), pp. 175–6.
13. T. Paine, *Common Sense*, p. 85.
14. E. Durkheim, *Moral Education* (1925, Free Press of Glencoe edn, 1961), p. 74.
15. Quoted in Richter, *Politics of Conscience*, p. 217.
16. Durkheim, *Moral Education*, p. 74.
17. Ibid., pp. 77 & 82–3.
18. E. Boulding, *Building a Global Civic Culture* (Teachers College Press, 1988), p. 45.
19. Falk, 'State System and Social Movements', p. 41.
20. Quoted in J. W. Burton, *Global Conflict: The Domestic Sources of International Crisis* (Harvester, 1984), pp. 78 & 82.
21. Q. Skinner, 'The Paradoxes of Political Liberty' in S. M. McMurrin (ed.), *The Tanner Lectures on Human Values*, vol. VII (University of Utah Press & Cambridge University Press, 1986), pp. 249 & 250.
22. See, for example, J. G. A. Pocock, *The Machiavellian Moment* (Princeton University Press, 1975); M. Ignatieff, *The Needs of Strangers* (Chatto & Windus, 1984); Skinner, 'Paradoxes of Political Liberty'. See esp. p. 166 above.
23. Aristotle, *Politics*, p. 1.
24. MacIntyre, *After Virtue*, p. 236.
25. B. Crick, 'Them and Us' reprinted in *Political Theory and Practice* (Allen Lane, n.d. but 1972?), p. 151.
26. R. Beiner, *Political Judgment* (Methuen, 1983).
27. Ibid., p. 167.
28. Walzer, *Spheres of Justice* p. 19.
29. Rousseau, *Discourse on Political Economy*, quoted in ibid., p. 64.
30. Mazzini, *Duties of Man*, p. 86.
31. M. Janowitz, 'The Good Citizen – A Threatened Species?' in W. K. Cummings *et al.*, *Revival of Values Education*, p. 59.

32. The following works have useful lists of learning objectives in cognate fields: Pike & Selby, *Global Teacher, Global Learner*, pp. 63–9; A. Porter (ed.), *Principles of Political Literacy* (University of London Institute of Education, n.d., but 1985?), p. 106.

33. Beiner, *Political Judgment*, p. 163.

34. J. P. White, 'Indoctrination' in R. S. Peters (ed.), *The Concept of Education* (Routledge & Kegan Paul, 1967), p. 181.

35. R. M. Hare, 'Adolescents into Adults' in T. H. B. Hollins (ed.), *Aims in Education* (Manchester University Press, 1964), p. 52.

36. R. Freeman Butts, 'International Human Rights and Civic Education' in M. S. Branson & J. Torney-Purta (eds), *International Human Rights, Society and the Schools* (NCSS Bulletin No. 68, 1982), p. 23.

37. M. E. Gilliom, R. C. Remy, R. Woyach, 'Using the Local Community as a Resource for Global Education', *Teaching Political Science*, April 1980.

38. H. J. Laski, *A Grammar of Politics* (Allen & Unwin, 4th edn, 1937), p. 78.

39. Walzer, *Spheres of Justice*, p. 311.

40. J. C. Scott, 'Patron-Client Politics and Political Change in Southeast Asia', quoted in G. A. Heeger, *The Politics of Underdevelopment* (Macmillan, 1974), p. 92.

41. J. Lynch, 'Multicultural Education: Agenda for Change' in J. A. Banks & J. Lynch (eds), *Multicultural Education in Western Societies* (Holt, Rinehart & Winston, 1986), p. 193.

42. B. Geremek, quoted in M. Simmons, 'Polish reform "holds key to Gorbachev's future" ', *Guardian*, 21 February 1989.

43. Locke, *Second Treatise on Civil Government*, s. 121 (ed. E. Barker, Oxford University Press, 1947), p. 103.

44. C. E. Black & R. A. Falk, *The Future of the International Legal Order: Retrospect and Prospect* (World Order Studies Program Occasional Paper no. 11, Center of International Studies, Princeton University, 1982), p. 55.

45. Ibid., p. 19.

Index